Faith
of a
(Woman)
Writer

Recent Titles in
Contributions in Women's Studies

Charity, Challenge, and Change: Religious Dimensions of the Mid-Nineteenth Century
Women's Movement in Germany
Catherine M. Prelinger

Woman as Mediatrix: Essays on Nineteenth-Century European Women Writers
Avriel H. Goldberger, editor

Women and American Foreign Policy: Lobbyists, Critics, and Insiders
Edward P. Crapol, editor

From Ladies to Women: The Organized Struggle for Woman's Rights in the
Reconstruction Era
Israel Kugler

Unlikely Heroines: Nineteenth-Century American Woman Writers and the Woman
Question
Ann R. Shapiro

Beyond the Public/Domestic Dichotomy: Contemporary Perspectives on Women's
Public Lives
Janet Sharistanian, editor

Speaking of Friendship: Middle-Class Women and Their Friends
Helen Gouldner and Mary Symons Strong

Sex and Pay in the Federal Government: Using Job Evaluation Systems to Implement
Comparable Worth
Doris M. Werwie

New Dimensions of Spirituality: A Biracial and Bicultural Reading of the Novels of
Toni Morrison
Karla F. C. Holloway and Stephanie Demetrakopoulos

Women and Music in Cross-Cultural Perspective
Ellen Koskoff, editor

Venomous Woman: Fear of the Female in Literature
Margaret Hallissy

Hard News: Women in Broadcast Journalism
David H. Hosley and Gayle K. Yamada

Faith
of a
(Woman) Writer

Edited by
Alice Kessler-Harris
and
William McBrien

Prepared under the auspices of Hofstra University

Contributions in Women's Studies, Number 86

Greenwood Press
New York • Westport, Connecticut • London

Library of Congress Cataloging-in-Publication Data

Faith of a (woman) writer.

(Contributions in women's studies, ISSN 0147–104X ;
no. 86)
    Includes index.
    1. Literature—Women authors—History and criticism—
Congresses. 2. Literature, Modern—20th century—
History and criticism—Congresses. 3. Women authors—
20th century—Biography—Congresses. I. Kessler-Harris,
Alice. II. McBrien, William. III. Series.
PN471.F35   1987   809'.89287   87–11976
ISBN 0–313–25956–9 (lib bdg. : alk. paper)

British Library Cataloguing in Publication Data is available.

Library of Congress Catalog Card Number: 87–11976
ISBN: 0–313–25956–9
ISSN: 0147–104X

First published in 1988

Greenwood Press, Inc.
88 Post Road West, Westport, Connecticut 06881

Printed in the United States of America

The paper used in this book complies with the
Permanent Paper Standard issued by the National
Information Standards Organization (Z39.48–1984).

10   9   8   7   6   5   4   3   2   1

Contents

1. Introduction   1

2. The (Woman) Writer
   Joyce Carol Oates   5

3. Joyce Carol Oates's *The Dead* and Feminist Criticism
   Elaine Showalter   13

4. Acts of Self-Creation: Female Identity in the Novels of
   Margaret Drabble
   Anne Golomb Hoffman   21

5. "Grave Endearing Traditions": Edith Wharton and the
   Domestic Novel
   Jeanne Boydston   31

6. Margaret Atwood, Margaret Laurence, and Their
   Nineteenth-Century Forerunners
   Ann Edwards Boutelle   41

7. THE Poetic World of Snezhina Slavova
   Yuri V. Karageorge   49

8. Kay Boyle: In a Woman's Voice
   Sandra Whipple Spanier   59

9. Two Women: The Transformations
   Alison Rieke   71

10. Effects of Urbanization in the Novels of Christiane
    Rochefort
       Anne D. Cordero   83

11. Irmgard Keun: A German Deviation
       Livia Z. Wittmann   95

12. Charlotte Bronte, Emily Bronte and Jean Rhys: What
    Rhys's Letters Show about that Relationship
       Joan Givner   105

13. Literary Criticism
       Catharine R. Stimpson   115

14. Miles Franklin: Chronicler of the Australian Bush and
    Early Feminist
       Paulette Rose   119

15. Edna St. Vincent Millay—Saint of the Modern Sonnet
       Jean Gould   129

16. Domestic Comedy, Black Comedy, and Real Life: Shirley
    Jackson, A Woman Writer
       Lynette Carpenter   143

17. Records of Survival: The Autobiographical Writings of
    Marieluise Fleisser and Marie Luise Kaschnitz
       Ruth-Ellen B. Joeres   149

18. Jhabvala's Fiction: The Passage From India
       Charmazel Dudt   159

19. Luise Rinser's Autobiographical Prose: Political
    Engagement and Feminist Awareness
       Elke Frederiksen   165

20. Women and Choice—A New Look at Simone de Beauvoir
    and *The Second Sex*
       Carol Ascher   173

21. Virginia, Virginius, Virginity
       Louise A. DeSalvo   179

22. Sexual Politics and Female Heroism in the Novels of
    Christina Stead
       Louise Yelin   191

23. Agnes Smedley's "Cell Mates": A Writer's Discovery of
    Voice, Form, and Subject in Prison
       Judith A. Scheffler   199

24. The Transformation of Privilege in the Work of Elena
    Poniatowska
      Bell Gale Chevigny   209

25. Marguerite Yourcenar's Sexual Politics in Fiction, 1939
      Judith L. Johnston   221

26. A Way of Ordering Experience: A Study of Toni
    Morrison's *The Bluest Eye* and *Sula*
      Robert Sargent   229

27. A Voice of Authority
      Jane Marcus   237

28. Charlotte Delbo, A Woman/Book
      Rosette C. Lamont   247

29. The Case of the Dangling Signifier: Phallic Imagery in
    Eudora Welty's "Moon Lake"
      Patricia S. Yaeger   253

30. An End to Torment: H.D.'s Metonymic Course
      Paul Smith   273

31. Leslie Stephen Revisited: A New Fragment of Virginia
    Woolf's "A Sketch of the Past"
      Katherine C. Hill-Miller   279

32. Defeating the False God: Janie's
    Self-Determination in Zora Neale Hurston's *Their Eyes
    Were Watching God*
      Gay Wilentz   285

33. *The Woman Warrior:* Claiming Narrative Power,
    Recreating Female Selfhood
      Joanne S. Frye   293

34. In Search of "Ordinary Human Happiness": Rebellion and
    Affirmation in Mary Gordon's Novels
      Susan Ward   303

    Program of Conference   309

    Index   337

    About the Editors and Contributors   345

Faith
of a
(Woman)
Writer

1

Introduction

The papers contained in this volume were selected from those presented at a four-day conference on twentieth-century women writers held at Hofstra in the fall of 1982. Although not concerned to say anything theoretical about feminist criticism, they do reflect salient undercurrents of contemporary opinion about women writers.

When we sat down to shape the conference we agreed to seek papers with two kinds of directions. We would look for criticism that honored the work of acknowledged writers of stature, and, in the light of the vast changes in consciousness and in social roles around gender in the past ten years, we would look as well at how a new generation of critics had come to terms with the work of distinguished women. In short, this would be a conference in which literary critics appraised the work of the writer as woman. It would explore how women generated their art, developed and presented it. The conference would ask not whether women were as great in their achievement as men, but about what was unique to gender.

Accordingly, we sent out a call for papers, requesting submissions that stressed either "the aesthetic attainments" of women writers, or centered "around the general theme of women's self-realization." We indicated that we would by no means confine ourselves to the boundaries of the United States. Gender crosses national boundaries, as it transcends lines of color and race, and we hoped to find its shared elements.

The response encouraged us to believe we had proposed a theme that resonated in the academic community. Without financial incentive of any sort, without even the offer of transportation, nearly 300 people volunteered papers. A committee of faculty at Hofstra and neighboring universities ultimately chose about

80 from among the papers submitted and we extended invitations to these authors to appear and read their work at the conference.

Delighted as we were by the response, we were nevertheless chagrined to discover that the final selection reflected less diversity of subject than we had hoped. Papers about U.S. writers were in the majority; those submitted by and about women of color were fewer than we would have liked. Canadian writers were minimally represented; Central and South American writers nearly entirely neglected. Western European writers showed up well; Eastern Europeans poorly. African writers appeared not at all, and Asians appeared largely in evaluations of writers from the Middle East. We speculated that this reflected the mechanisms of advertising, the interests of U.S. academics, the accidents of critics holding jobs in universities that would or would not pay transportation, or the ill-luck of others holding no job at all. So, we compensated. Eager to expand the discussion, and to include writers as well as critics, we sought out some thirty practitioners in their fields and invited them to participate in panel discussions. Writers came from Tokyo, from Senegal, from the U.S. Black community, from Germany, from France, and from Puerto Rico.

When the conference concluded, we faced the task of developing a single volume out of all the diversity. How now to cut once again? We eliminated from consideration most of the invited guests, many of whom had spoken from notes, and others, like Paule Marshall, who had committed their papers elsewhere. For the rest, quality could clearly not be a criterion, as most of these papers had been widely and sometimes highly praised. So we chose to select papers that touched on what had inspired the most enthusiasm among the participants—the issue of the ''woman'' writer.

This volume presents critics' perceptions about how women writers have dealt with the complexity of changing female life styles in the twentieth century. Each of the 34 essays in this book speaks to the work of a particular twentieth-century woman writer. Separately each essay constitutes a contribution to the scholarly debate; together they reflect the range of recent critical thought about women writers in the twentieth century. They do not pretend to represent the diversity of material offered in the meetings. Much less do they speak to the wide subject matter of women's creativity, of which the conference itself was not even a microcosm. Because this is, in the end, primarily a volume of criticism, we abandoned any attempt to include every well-known writer, or to cover every genre. Instead, working with the material at hand, we sought essays that spoke to emerging critical perspectives. Some readers will look in vain for their favorite writers. Others will protest the neglect of particular groups. Writers of color are, for example, discussed only in two essays. The contemporary generation, which has made an enormous impact on recent literature, is invisible. We assume that ten years from now, criticism and analysis of their work will occupy the space that their present importance suggests. But if these papers do not reflect the scope of today's women writers, they do capture the mood of contemporary criticism. We hope they will bring something of the vitality and urgency of the field to life and that they will offer a hint of where today's students and critics of women's literature are heading.

That direction is not yet charted. As critic Myra Jehlen suggests, confusion derives from questions about the appropriate posture a critic should adopt. Should a critic of women's writing deal with the work as the product of a woman's hand, dwelling on the sensibilities of the female consciousness, and representations of female reality? Or should the critic assume that the proper point of departure remains the artistic and aesthetic norms that have emerged from generations of male-defined practice? Especially for the feminist critic of the female writer, the desire to create a canon—to develop standards of criticism that reflect a culture that is at once part of and not part of the male tradition is often a political issue as well as an aesthetic consideration. The literary critic, who, as Jehlen puts it, "is also a critic of her society and its culture" has difficulty being neutrally aware when all of her perceptions reflect her stance in the world in which she lives. Yet to urge a divorce of the aesthetic from the political, calling on the example of an earlier mode, is to fail to see the politics prevalent in question-framing and thus to deny the curtain that feminist critics seek to lift.

The difficult issue of what constitutes a feminist criticism is perhaps the subtext of this volume, whose central themes lie in the larger stories or pictures that emerge when women's writings are considered both as part of the genre to which they belong and as the products of their own realities. The essays reproduced here reveal a rejection of the New Criticism, and reflect instead a search for a more human and sensitive stance—one that connects the daily existence of the writer with the substance of her plots. So Lynette Carpenter tells us that Shirley Jackson expresses in the violence of her fiction the repressed anger of her conventional life. And Rosette Lamont suggests that Charlotte Delbo's literary spirit remained tied to the concentration camp long after her body had left it. But while the scope of critical inquiry is extended by the search for the wellspring of inspiration, none of these critics succumbs to the lures of psychoanalysis. Perhaps as a reflection of the influence of contemporary politics, they choose instead to see in the social construction of the writer the source of her particular aesthetic. It is no accident then that the biographer wonders about her stance towards her subject (Ascher), that the critic asks about her response to audience (Stimpson) and the writer puzzles over her relationship to her craft (Oates).

The areas that give the critic pause seem, too, to be directly related to the struggles of everyday life. These critics explore representations of female reality, including female bonding (Rieke, Scheffler, Boutelle), and women's attempts to cope with domesticity in its various guises (Boydston, Cordero, Keun). In Cordero, for example, we find that focus on the details of everyday life creates a surrealistic portrait of women as well as of their communities.

And, finally, today's critics of women writers find it necessary to come to terms with the androgynous possibilities of author, character and plot. Carol Ascher's discussion of De Beauvoir poses directly the issue of how, given an analysis of patriarchy that holds woman's oppression constant, women can ever achieve freedom. The aggressive and the gentle emerge side by side in Scheffler's analysis of Smedley, and in Wilentz' discussion of Hurston. The adventurous and the nurturing appear in the dual selves (and therefore divergent possibilities) of Christina Stead, as interpreted by Louise Yelin, and of Miles Franklin, as described by Paulette Rose.

In a recent article Carolyn Heilbrun notes that "the study of literature cannot survive if it cannot . . . illuminate human experience; and human experience cannot today be illuminated without attention to the place of women in literature, in the textuality of our lives, both in history and in the present." We think this volume illustrates her point.

2

The (Woman) Writer

Joyce Carol Oates

What is the ontological status of the writer *who is also a woman*?

She experiences herself, from within, as a writer primarily: she does not inevitably view herself as an object, a category, an essence—in short, as "representative." In the practice of her craft she may very well become bodiless and invisible, defined to herself fundamentally as what she thinks, dreams, plots, constructs: in contrast, that is, to what other persons see her as *doing*. Life consists, to adroitly paraphrase Emerson, of what a person is thinking day by day.

Perhaps it follows, then, that when the writer is alone, when she is alone with language, with the challenging discipline of creating an art *by the way of language alone*, she is not defined to herself as "she"—? Does the writer require the specification of gender? Is memory itself gender-bound? Are impressions filtered through the prism of gender? Is there a distinctly female voice?—or even a feminine voice? Or is "gender" in this sense an ontological category imposed upon us from without, for the convenience of others?—a category which dissolves the uniquely individual in the Abstract, in what Melville called, in quite another context, "hideous, intolerable Allegory."

All artists are idealists and romantics; even cynicism, as you may frequently have noticed, is artful. It has been said that the artist requires a special and even secret world to which he alone has the key: and it is also true that an incalculable faith, innocent and unwilled as the color of our hair or eyes, and prior, certainly, to both reason and experience, underlies all motives for sustained creativity. "Faith" is notorious for attaching itself to virtually any object, visionary or hallucinatory or "real": but the possibility of being deluded—one might almost say, the *hope* of being deluded—is one we must accept, if we are going to continue to write. If the ideal reader experiences the classic "enlargement of sympathies" by way of serious fiction, it is to be assumed, perhaps to be taken on faith, that the writer immersed in these sympathies experiences a similar enlargement of vision.

Here is a genderless meditation upon the secret motive for art, by a twentieth-century writer, in English, who was absolutely obsessed—which is to say, fascinated, intoxicated, redeemed—by language in its infinite variations, coaxed and threaded into the most formidable of structures: coldly mandarin and nearly unreadable to some, cherished as one of the literary geniuses of our time by others—

Whenever I start thinking of my love for a person, I am in the habit of immediately drawing radii from my love—from my heart, from the tender nucleus of a personal matter—to monstrously remote points of the universe. Something impels me to measure the consciousness of my love against such unimaginable and incalculable things as the behavior of nebulae (whose very remoteness seems a form of insanity), the dreadful pitfalls of eternity, the unknowledgeable beyond the unknown, the helplessness, the cold, the sickening involutions and interpenetrations of space and time. . . . When that slow-motion silent explosion of love takes place in me, unfolding its melting fringes and overwhelming me with the sense of something much vaster . . . then my mind cannot help but pinch itself to see if it is really awake. I have to make a rapid inventory of the universe, just as a man in a dream tries to condone the absurdity of his position by making sure he is dreaming. I have to have all space and all time participate in my emotion, in my mortal love, so that the edge of its mortality is taken off, thus helping me to fight the fact of having developed an infinity of sensation and thought within a finite existence.[1]

This eloquent statement attests not only to the little-understood connection between private emotion and the impulse for art, the mysterious motive for fiction and metaphor, but speaks frankly of the "edge of mortality" that underlies it: our sense, which increases with the passage of years, that the present moment, undeniably and perhaps wonderfully real as it feels, is not, in its swift retreat into the past, so "real" as we might wish; and arguably less real than the experience would be, for instance, of slipping quietly away, and opening a novel written many decades ago, in a "present" now otherwise lost. Time is in love with the productions of Eternity: or with those creations one hopes will at least seem eternal, within the span of our culture's life. Writing is not antithetical to "experience," and it is certainly not an escape from such: it *is* experience: but one which looks, however hazily, into the future. The effort that is *now* will endure *then*.

So the days pass and I ask myself sometimes whether one is not hypnotised, as a child by a silver globe, by life; and whether this is living. It is very quick, bright, exciting. But superficial perhaps. I should like to take the globe in my hands and feel it quietly, round, smooth, heavy, and so hold it, day after day.[2]

This insatiable desire to write something before I die, this ravaging sense of the shortness and feverishness of life, make me cling, like a man on a rock, to my one anchor.[3]

There are writers, born women, who do not think of themselves—at least by their testimony—as women, when they write: and there are other writers, born women, who believe their writing to be conditioned at all times by their gender. Much is made of the elusive Female Voice without regard for the fact that Voice always means voices, if we are being at all attentive to subtleties of pitch and nuance. As for content—hasn't it been a heady consequence of Modernist aesthetics, that one is free to write about anything?—that even the most ignoble and despicable of subjects is soluble in art?

What is the ontological status of "Virginia Woolf," who died more than forty years ago? The woman does not exist; the woman-writer does not exist; we have only a number of books—novels, essays, sketches, letters, a diary. The "Virginia Woolf" of the public writings is a fastidious craftsman, even when it is her intention to simulate the spontaneity of life (so "fluent and fluid," one observer worried her by saying, "it runs through the mind like water"); the "Virginia Woolf" of the diaries and letters impresses us as being less postured, less willed, less *self*-conscious. But how can we judge? Where does personality reside—in a resolutely artful (and artificial) utterance, or in a presumably unpremeditated speech? Diaries and letters are after all art forms, their energy in the present tense, but their gravitational centers in the future. And there are biographies. An immense sea of biographies. There are anecdotes, thumbnail portraits, curious allusions that would altogether astonish those to whom they allude. (As in the title of Edward Albee's "Who's Afraid of Virginia Woolf?") Thus, not one "Virginia Woolf" exists, now that the woman herself is dead, but a vertiginous multitude. They are all assemblages of words; a considerable number are works of supreme art; but where can personality reside in such a phenomenon as— words? Yet more crucially, where can gender reside? If not even handwriting communicates sexual characteristics, can the printed word?—can typeface?

One can become deluded into thinking that one "knows" Virginia Woolf in some fundamental way, but in fact one knows only diverse texts by diverse hands. The writer "Virginia Woolf" exists, now, not only primarily but exclusively as an assemblage of words; and it might be argued that the language of Virginia Woolf, however, capably translated into another language, is not hers: cannot be *her*. (How curious they are, these books of ours, translated into foreign languages!—we may sense the oblique kinship but know, perhaps with a sense of poignancy and loss, that the language is not our own: the book is therefore by another author.)

Our immediate response to a book, to what must be called an artful assemblage of words, is therefore wholly a response to language, not unlike a response to music heard for the first time: are we fascinated by it?—at least interested in it?—disturbed by it?—provoked?—amused?—irritated?—confused?—bored?— angry?—indifferent? Along a similar spectrum the student of any art form finds himself vis-à-vis a certain work of art at various stages in his life. A genuine response is incalculable—unpredictable—unwilled. Should we be predisposed to "like" a work of art because its creator (distant, legendary, perhaps long dead) was identified, during his or her lifetime, as *male* or *female*? And what, considering the evidence of mouldering bones in remote graves, does *male* or *female* now mean?

Most artists, and certainly the writer, aspire to invisibility by way of art, however, blatantly, and often vulgarly, they exhibit their visibility in a consumer-oriented culture. Most novelists—though not of course all—really do attempt to refine themselves out of existence by way of an immersion, a systematic and disciplined immersion, in language. (If this were not the case, the writer would be something else: a politician, a preacher, a dancer, an actor: one, that is, who performs in public, in person, in the personalized flesh. But to be a writer is to abrogate that public identity or persona for the time one is in fact writing. The craft is often said to be a lonely one, and we should be astonished if it were not.)

My faith in the craft of writing, in the writer's role, most succinctly put, is that it is—as others have noted—a form of sympathy. And, being mimetic, being bodiless, consisting solely of words, it necessitates no displacement or intrusion in the world; it exults in its own being.

Luxury of Being Despised

> In revenge and in love, women
> are more barbaric than men
> —Nietzsche

The sneering shout in the street, the anatomical female stretched wide
   across the billboard: St. Paul's contempt.

Montaigne instructs us that poetry belongs to
   women—
a wanton and subtle art, ornate and verbose,
all pleasure
and all show: like themselves.
And Freud, that women have little sense of
   justice.
And De Kooning, in these angry swaths of paint:
how crude, how magnificent, such monster women!

The fiery sightless eye which is your own.
The booming breasts, the maniac wink.
All is heat, fecundity, secret seeping blood.
Flesh is here: nor are we out of it.

   What bliss, to be so despised:
the closed thighs all muscle,
the Church Fathers' contempt,
the Protestant chill, what freedom
since we have no souls!—
what delight.

The angry swaths of flesh which are your own.
The blank stare,
the cartoon heart.
Virginity a mallet.
Mad grin worn like a bonnet.[4]

Though it is true that the writer is bodiless, and transformed by craft into invisibility, what of the (woman) writer? Does she occupy a significantly different space? What is the *objective*, as opposed to the *subjective*, state of her ontological existence?

A woman who writes is a writer by her own definition; but she is a woman writer by others' definitions. The books she writes are indeed artful assemblages of words—she does have immense, and at times naive, faith in their worth—but her sexual identity is not thereby dissolved or transcended. Books are neuter objects, *its*: writers are *he* or *she*: for this is the ontological fact of flesh, nor are we out of it. Of course one can speak casually of "Virginia Woolf" when, strictly speaking, one means a book ("I have been reading Virginia Woolf"). One can make elaborate critical judgments, or reduce all complexity to a blunt statement (by saying, for instance, "Are we not somewhat over-saturated with Virginia Woolf?"). Here there is some confusion of *it* and *her*, but none that violates a convention of usage. As one moves farther and farther away from the actual, existential, minute-by-minute immersion in specific passages in specific works by Virginia Woolf, one may readily confuse her prose with that of prose written about her, by biographers, memoirists, critics, reviewers. Our sensibilities become blurred; dulled; lazy. Soon everything that pertains to "Virginia Woolf" is saturated with the biographical fact (perhaps significant, perhaps not) of her femaleness.

Since I am a woman who writes, I see that, in the eyes of most observers, I must be a "woman writer," though there are, so far as I can determine, no "men writers." Sometimes the extraordinary praise is thrown at me, like a bouquet of roses that lands in one's face instead of in one's arms, that *I write like a man*. (One wants to inquire—Which man?) It was once a central issue in a fairly vicious negative review of a novel by a contemporary writer that he was a "male Joyce Carol Oates"—an insult of the most sombre dimensions, quite apart from the fact that, in some quarters, it is seen to be a despicable thing to be a female Joyce Carol Oates.

As a (woman) writer, consequently, I find myself (which is to say, *I am found*: I do not will, or wish, or invent myself) in an impersonal category that is my birthright for better or worse. Not all women are despised by all men, at least not all of the time, but it is a fairly commonplace dilemma—whether it is consciously articulated or not—that a man's quarrel with the feminine in his own nature will be a quarrel with women: the impulse may be abstract and psychological, but its fruition is always concrete. One need not consider the misogyny of the ages—for one thing, it is too familiar, and too depressing—for there are examples close at hand, in even the most well-intentioned of literary forums: too many, indeed, to contemplate. (For instance, in the *Harvard Guide to Contemporary American Writing* of 1979, clearly a standard reference text, one finds chapters titled "Intellectual Background," "Literary Criticism," "Experimental Fiction," "Drama," etc., and "Women's Literature"—a potpourri of virtually everyone whose name might come to mind under this rubric, with an inevitable emphasis, the heart sinks to see, upon those books by those writers who write about "female" subjects. Being thus ghettoized feels like an insult until one stops to realize—the (woman) writer stops to realize—that a ghetto, after all, is a place to exist: dissolve it, and one may find oneself with no place in which to live at all.

In the general adulation of John Berryman there seems rarely to have been space for an examination of the tacit prejudices of (male) poets regarding their respected peers:

> Them lady poets must not marry, pal.
> Miss Dickinson—fancy in Amherst bedding her.
> Fancy a lark with Sappho,
> a tumble in the bushes with Miss Moore,
> a spoon with Emily, while Charlotte glares.
> Miss Bishop's too noble-O.
>
> That was the lot. And two of them are here
> as yet, and—and: Sylvia Plath is not.
> She—she her credentials
> has handed in, leaving alone two tots
> and widower to what he makes of it—
> surviving guy. . . . [5]

That was the lot, Berryman casually informs us: the grotesquerie of the situation being the ease with which, in a drunk's babyish prattle, centuries of women poets are dismissed; and those who are deemed worthy of attention are nonetheless "lady poets"—a despicable or quaint category, depending upon the degree of one's charity.

And there is Robert Graves's famous declaration: "A woman is a Muse or she is nothing."

And—I open a book at random, this very instant, to feel my eye at once snagged by the remarkable observation, "What is mere confession in a female writer [Doris Lessing] amounts to intuitive genius in Knut Hamsun."[6]

Clearly, the (woman) writer who imagines herself "assimilated" into the mainstream of literature, the literature of men, is mistaken, or deluded, or simply hopeful: or is her faith based upon a stubborn resistance to what is, set beside what *may one day be*? To pretend that one is not what one is, in the flesh, in the historical flesh, is naive; to brush lightly aside the evidence of being despised is symptomatic of that interesting variation of hysteria called denial.

Yet—must one insist upon it?—must one focus upon injustice, and loss, and insult, and pain? The luxury of being despised is an embittered and satirical one, yet it allows for a certain energizing of forces, away from the self, perhaps, and into the work: away from the distractions and the immediate gratifications of visibility, and toward the semi-permanence of art.

So it is, the (woman) writer has faith in the nobility of the craft to which she has dedicated herself; but she is, we might say, no fool, in gauging her relative position in it. One moves between the poles of idealism and pessimism, well within the limits of euphoria and despair, steering a middle course, as the handy cliché would have it, and trying to maintain a sense of humor. A writer may be beleaguered by any number of chimeras, but only the (woman) writer is beleaguered by her own essential identity. How can the paradox be accommodated, one asks, and an answer might be, *With difficulty*.

NOTES

1. Vladimir Nabokov, *Speak, Memory: An Autobiography Revisited* (New York: Pyramid Books, 1968), p. 219.

2. Virginia Woolf, in *A Writer's Diary*, edited by Leonard Woolf (New York: Harcourt Brace Jovanovich, 1954), p. 135.

3. *Ibid.*, p. 117. (An amusing counterpoint to Modernist preoccupations with the redeeming nature of the "permanent" word can be found in a novella by an early contemporary of Woolf's, H. G. Wells. This is that sobering parable *The Time Machine*, in which, in the year Eight Hundred and Two Thousand Seven Hundred and One, A.D. the Time Traveller happens upon a library in the vicinity of what had once been London. He discovers brown and charred "rags" that appear to be the decaying vestiges of books. "They had long since dropped to pieces, and every semblance of print had left them. But here and there were warped boards and cracked metallic clasps that told the tale well enough. Had I been a literary man I might, perhaps, have moralised upon the futility of all ambition. But as it was, the thing that struck me with keenest force was the enormous waste of labor to which this sombre wilderness of rotting paper testified.")

4. "Luxury of Being Despised" originally appeared, in a slightly different version, in *The Bennington Review*, June 1982. Copyright Joyce Carol Oates.

5. John Berryman, *The Dream Songs* (New York: Farrar, Straus & Giroux, 1969), p. 206.

6. From John Updike's *Picked-Up Pieces*, (New York: Knopf, 1975), p. 151.

3

Joyce Carol Oates's *The Dead* and Feminist Criticism

Elaine Showalter

My remarks are in some respects a postscript to what Joyce Carol Oates so eloquently tells us in her introduction. In other respects they constitute a dialog with her from the perspective of feminist criticism, which of course takes as one of its assumptions the existence of women's writing and the reality of a female voice. And I thought perhaps I should rename my comments "The Faith of a Feminist Critic." Obviously the jobs of a feminist critic and the woman writer are very different. I've always thought that the first responsibility feminist criticism had toward women's writing was to buy it. But in any case I don't think feminist criticism or any criticism ever has the right to dictate to artists how they create or what they create or to try to interfere in that essentially private act of the imagination that Joyce Carol Oates described to us. The activity of feminist criticism, of criticism in general, is the objective aspect of writing, not the subjective, and it's to that context that I want to address myself.

Let me begin by sharing with you a letter that I received last year from a woman editor at a well-known magazine. The letter opens, "Dear Friend," (always an ominous note):

I cordially invite you to join Pearl Buck, Shana Alexander, Edna St. Vincent Millay, Gloria Steinem, Erma Bombeck, Joyce Carol Oates, and thousands of other women who have commanded the attention and respect of the world as writers. Today's great demand for writers [this letter goes on] is being met by people from all walks of life. If any single group has a competitive edge, it would be women. We are generally more perceptive of details, sensitive to undercurrents, and attentive to character than men.

I can imagine that, in the context of advertising, this letter would be a success, with its flattering appeal to the reader to become a member of the cozy sorority of women writers in which Shana, Edna, Gloria, Erma, and Joyce seem to be the officers, and one supposes Edna and Pearl are the patron saints. And it's charming to think of womanhood as a walk rather than as a fact of life; and pleasant, too, to hear of one's perception, sensitivity, and attentiveness so richly praised. But in the context of a feminist criticism that's trying to work out a theory of female creativity and women's writing, such a letter is a profound embarrassment, because despite its commercial cynicism it is recognizably a kind of parody of an extreme feminist criticism that makes gender the most important category in the careers of women writers with drastically different interests and traditions.

Reacting recently to a much more serious critical work, the *Harvard Guide to Contemporary American Writing* Joyce Carol Oates wrote ruefully about her representation in that volume and wrote particularly about "the great lump of women writers" to which her novels had been consigned. "How am I to feel," she asked, "when the only works of mine analyzed are those that deal explicitly with women's problems, the rest of my books, in fact the great majority of my books ignored as if they had never been written? What should a serious woman writer feel? Attempting to rise out of categories—and there are many besides that of women—the writer is thrown back by critics frequently as well-intentioned as not. Of course, the serious artistic voice is one of individual style, and it is sexless. But perhaps to have a sex-determined voice or to be believed to have one is after all better than to have no voice at all."[1]

Oates's comments not only raise questions for a serious woman writer but also provide a challenge to a serious feminist criticism. Is it appropriate for feminist criticism to address itself to women's writing when some of its most serious practitioners resist assimilation to such a category?

Is there a sex-determined voice in art, or is the serious artistic voice indeed sexless? What do feminist critics mean when we describe a female voice, and is it necessarily the voice of feminist ideology? Is the woman's text about women's problems, and characterized by the sensitivity to undercurrents that *The Writer's Digest* finds in Erma Bombeck and Edna St. Vincent Millay? Or can the woman's text reflect as much individuality, power and diversity of style as the man's text and yet reveal a female voice and a female tradition.

Before trying to answer some of these questions by looking at Oates's fiction, I ought to acknowledge first of all that her questions have been echoed by many other major women writers of our time. Anne Sexton writes in *Consorting with Angels*, "I was tired of being a woman,/ tired of the spoons and the pots,/ tired of my mouth and my breasts,/ tired of the cosmetics and the silks,/ I was tired of the gender of things." In a recent interview in the *New York Times*, Susan Sontag insisted that the awareness of being female had never entered into her writing. She said, "I never thought 'There are women writers. So this is something I can be.' No. I thought 'There are writers, so this is something I want to be.' I never felt consciously or unconsciously that there was any conflict between my vocation and being a woman.''[2]

Both the comment and the idea, of course, are historically specific to the mid-twentieth century. Only in the past few decades have women writers had the freedom that Virginia Woolf prophesied would come with economic independence and a room of one's own, the freedom to be tired of the gender of things and to think about writing as a creative act that transcends the determinations of sex. When the great nineteenth-century women novelists chose pseudonyms, it was not to lay claim to a sexless artistic voice but to a masculine one. Responding to a sexist review of her novel *Shirley*, Charlotte Bronte wrote an angry letter to the critic, who was George Henry Lewes. ''I wish you did not think me a woman. I wish all reviewers believed Currer Bell to be a man. They would be more just to him.''[3] Bronte was a writer who knew not the luxury but the desperation of being despised. And despite the contemporary vision of writing as an activity of language, imagination and craft that transcends gender, it still seems to me that the dualities of Western thought and the realities of historical experience determine our conception of the writer and the work. Since masculinity is identified with universality, the male writer may never have to be aware that his texts are also sex-determined. But when the serious woman writer tries to move away from the subjects and themes that have been traditionally and stereotypically associated with the feminine, she will be seen, not as sexless or universal, not as a writer only, but as male.

Joyce Carol Oates herself, of course, knows this very well, and has acknowledged, too, that the inevitable pressures of such judgments come, not so much from feminist critics, but from masculinist reviewers. In an essay in the *New York Times Book Review* in 1981, Oates bitingly satirized the sexist bias, which expects women's writing to be charming, amusing, and delightful, certainly not violent or serious. She writes:

If the lot of womankind has not yet widely diverged from that romantically envisioned by our Moral Majority and by the late Adolf Hitler, the lot of the woman writer has been just as severely circumscribed. War, rape, murder, and the more colorful minor crimes evidently fall within the exclusive province of the male writer, just as, generally, they fall within the exclusive province of male action. Occasionally, however, a woman writer is told gravely, ''You write like a man,'' and since this is the highest accolade presented as a judgment from above and closed to any further discussion, it would be impolite to ask, ''Which man? Any man? You?''[4]

No matter how weary she may be of the gender of things, the serious woman writer's hopeful belief that she creates as a writer only is no more a cultural possibility than it was a century ago. As Nancy Miller points out, were a woman writer to forget her double bind, the phallic critics would remind her that she's dreaming.[5] And beyond the external pressures of criticism, there are all the interrelations of experience, history, and culture that make every invidual talent or style inescapably part of, and in a sense determined by, a larger tradition. The tradition of the twentieth-century American woman writer, however, cannot be reduced to the context of women's problems or limited to the domestic and the sensitive. And feminist criticism can, I hope, place its subjects within a significant context of women's writing without violating the writer's just insistence upon her own intentions and her own voice. To try to demonstrate this utopian intention, I want to look from a feminist perspective at Joyce Carol Oates's remarkable story "The Dead," first published in 1972, and then very briefly at her new novel, *The Bloodsmoor Romance*. I am linking these two very different fictional works because they share a few significant characteristics: both are about women's writing. The heroine of "The Dead," Ilena Williams, is a young novelist who has written a bestseller called *Death Dance* about suicide among American adolescents. The narrator of *A Bloodsmoor Romance* is a wickedly observant nineteenth-century female sentimentalist writer steeped in religious and romantic popular slush. Yet both of these female storytellers, the dark and despairing contemporary heroine and the mischievously ironic nineteenth-century songbird, function in texts which are bold alliances of male and female literary tradition—texts which if anything are over-determined by sex and which yet have a remarkable freedom and power that I as a feminist critic see as their possession of the female voice.

"The Dead" is an absorbing and haunting story about a woman writer whose sickness, depression, and anxiety come from her guilt about literary creativity, or so I read it. Repeatedly described as "virginal," "delicate," "childlike," and "chaste," Ilena Williams seems almost like an Emily Dickinson figure, a deliberate incarnation of the woman writer for whom the adult female role means aesthetic death, and who constructs her own myth of whiteness, madness, and absence in order to have the freedom to create. Ilena finds her celebrity and success both a burden and a threat. She's increasingly depressed, anxious, insomniac, and numb, and yet the doctor she consults tells her that she is normal, that her symptoms have no organic basis; so she drinks a lot, indiscriminately swallows pills, thinks about suicide. Returning in the fall of 1970 to read and be lionized at the Catholic university where she had taught during her marriage in the sixties, Ilena hears that her favorite former student has died after an antiwar demonstration, not from police brutality, but from hepatitis and heroin addiction. Drugged, despairing, and exhausted, she goes back to her hotel with a professor who had been her lover, lets him make love to her again, and at the end of the story, falls into unconsciousness, perhaps breakdown, as the snow outside falls shapelessly upon them all.

In some respects "The Dead" seems to fit the disease model of anxiety in women's writing outlined by Sandra Gilbert and Susan Gubar in *The Mad Woman in the Attic*. Ilena's sicknesses can be seen in Gilbert and Gubar's terms as projections of her conflicts about femininity and authority. In one traditional sense, her sickness, her delicacy, her fragility is the badge of her womanhood. In another traditional sense, it is the dis-ease of her troubled relation to the male institutions of the university, marriage, and literature. The story also comments explicitly and ironically on the social and economic contexts of women's writing, on the double bind of the serious woman novelist. Ilena has been both exploited and trivialized by the public interest in the achievement of women in male-dominated fields, of which fiction is apparently one. When her picture appears on the cover of a national magazine, the caption reads, "Are American women avenging centuries of oppression?" Her psychiatrist tells Ilena that even her modest success as a novelist is unmanning to her husband, who would like to be a writer himself. In order to save that marriage, he advises, she should fail at something. But instead she writes a bestseller and feels ashamed because it makes so much money. Nominated for a national award, it loses, someone tells her, because a woman on the committee is jealous of her; her mother has warned her that the world is full of jealous people. She feels an obligation to be feminine and gracious to everyone, and thus no one takes her seriously as a writer.

Yet Ilena thinks she has also failed at being a woman, and there are many indications of this failure in the text. Her marriage has failed, her menstrual periods have stopped. Despite her perpetual feminine smile and her carefully maintained prettiness, she cannot feel her body. Her lovers become interchangeable phantoms who possess her without knowing or understanding her, who make her unpersonalized, unhistoric. She's addicted to pills, insomniac, suicidal. In short, Ilena's sterility is her self-enacted punishment for writing well.

But if we read the story only at the level of women's problems, which is essentially what I have just done, we'll miss most of its specialness and art. In order to supply the other half of the story, we need to look at the dialog that "The Dead" carries on with the male literary tradition. First of all, "The Dead" is one of a group of stories Oates collected under the title *Marriages and Infidelities*—stories which experiment with or allude to classical fictional texts. Among the other stories in the collection are some called "The Metamorphosis," "The Lady with the Pet Dog," "The Turn of the Screw," "The Spiral," and "Where I Lived and What I Lived For"—titles which audaciously summon up the ghosts of Kafka, Chekov, James, Flaubert, and Thoreau. James Joyce is thus one of the dead Oates meditates upon in her story, which takes its title and many of its themes, images, and details from his masterful story in *Dubliners*. Describing the texts of *Marriages and Infidelities*, Oates has explained in an interview that "These stories are meant to be autonomous, yet they are also testaments of my love and extreme devotion to these other writers—I imagine a kind of spiritual marriage between myself and them."[6] Ilena Williams in "The Dead" has also written such a book, a series of short stories in honor of certain dead writers with whom she feels a kinship: " 'I don't exist as an individual but only as a completion of tradition, the end of something, not the best part of it, but only the end,' she explained, wondering if she was telling the truth or if this was all nonsense. 'And I want to honor the dead by re-imagining their works, by re-imagining their obsessions—in a way marrying them, joining them as a woman joins a man, spiritually and erotically.' ''

If we follow this metaphor of literary marriage, the author of "The Dead" thus becomes Joyce Carol Joyce, who in re-imagining the male literary tradition becomes doubly herself. Yet, as the book's title declares, Oates's relation to her literary precursors is not simply one of love, honor, and devotion. The re-imagined stores are also betrayals: infidelities, transgressions of form and theme. "The Dead" re-imagines the obsessions of James Joyce's story but from an American contemporary and female perspective which is totally transforming and which expresses Joyce Carol Oates's own literary obsessions. For the woman writer to enter literary history, I would argue, is never simply a marriage, a spiritual, esthetic, and intellectual bonding. It is inevitably also an infidelity because of the irreducible difference that comes from the historical experience, the historical perspective of growing up female and encountering literary history as the other, as the despised.

For Ilena Williams in "The Dead," the erotic side of marriage itself, ironically and revealingly, symbolizes the loss of self. In her relationships with men, she is reduced to protoplasm. She becomes a vessel for male energy. She is warned against the exploitative patterns of an admirer with a habit of marrying young artistic women and then ruining them. Ilena's transgression is simply the integrity of her own artistic imagination. In "The Dead," however, Ilena's infidelity, her betrayal of the male tradition is an isolated cultural act. Significantly, in the story she has no women friends, no female precursors, no women's community of love and ritual from which to gain nurturance. Her lovers, her internist, her psychiatrist, her editor—even the few articulate boys who occasionally show up in her classes—bombard her with the guilt of her difference, with what her favorite student calls her female trick. The story must end in sterility and death, because Ilena cannot bring to her literary marriage the fertilizing stream of a female history and a female tradition.

The pattern is very different, however, in *The Bloodsmoor Romance*. In this feminist novel we have the story of five American sisters, the Zinn sisters, each of whom breaks out of the bonds of womanhood to become in the novel's words "the personage God meant me to be." For one, this means to be an actress, for another a spiritualist, for another an inventor, for a fourth, comically and wonderfully, a man. As Joyce follows the complicated plot in which the sisters find their serio-comic destinies, she also weaves a remarkable tapestry of literary marriages and infidelities. As its title indicates, *The Bloodsmoor Romance* merges the female and the male literary tradition, the female Gothic romance with *The Blithedale Romance* of Hawthorne. Mark Twain appears as a character in the novel, indeed, as the lover of one of the sisters, but the novel is also populated by the lively ghosts of Emerson, James, Longfellow, and Thoreau in a rich and entertaining dialog with Emily Dickinson, the Brontes, Louisa May Alcott, the *Ladies' Annuals*, the nineteenth-century female sentimentalists, and the best-selling authors of novels such as Susan Warner's *The Wide, Wide World*. Bloods-

moor Romance ends on a triumphant note of feminist vision as the other of the Zinn sisters joins the suffragists in their campaign. Oates's juxtaposition of the nineteenth-century ideologies of transcendentalism and feminism is managed in this novel through a female voice—the voice of the narrator, herself a writer who ironically pretends to be timid, incompetent, and conventionally feminine but who is in fact resourceful, eloquent, and brilliant. For Diane Johnson, who reviewed *Bloodsmoor Romance* in *The New York Times*, the narrator is one of the triumphs of the book, and she adds, "It is tempting to hear under this narrator's Victorian disguise the voice of Joyce Carol Oates herself, a voice that is female, clever, and mischievous."[7] Joyce Carol Oates has reminded us, and would remind us, that the artist has many voices and perhaps no ontological existence beyond the sum of the texts, the sum of the words. But my faith as a feminist critic is for a future in which the female voice is understood to encompass all the power, the range, the fullness of language, the freedom of subject that has always been available to the male voice—a future in which we will have gone beyond the dubious luxury of being despised and in which a serious woman writer will be able to acknowledge one or many female voices and be no longer tired but exhilarated by the gender of things.

NOTES

1. "Is There a Female Voice?" in *Gender and Literary Voice*, ed. Janet Todd (New York: Holmes and Meier, 1982), pp. 10–11.

2. Charles Russ, "Susan Sontag: Past, Present, and Future," *New York Times Book Review*, October 24, 1982, p. 11.

3. See Winifred Gerin, *Charlotte Bronte: The Evolution of Genius* (London: Oxford University Press, 1967), p. 400.

4. Joyce Carol Oates, "Why Is Your Writing So Violent?," *New York Times Book Review*, March 25, 1981, p. 35.

5. Nancy K. Miller, "Emphasis Added: Plots and Plausibilities in Women's Fiction," PMLA 96 (January 1981): 46.

6. Joe David Bellamy, "The Dark Lady of American Letters," an interview with Joyce Carol Oates, *Atlantic Monthly* (February 1972), p. 65.

7. Diane Johnson, "Joyce Carol Oates," *New York Times Book Review*, September 5, 1982, p. 16.

4

Acts of Self-Creation: Female Identity in the Novels of Margaret Drabble

Anne Golomb Hoffman

At the start of Margaret Drabble's most recent novel, *The Middle Ground*, we see Kate, the protagonist, sifting through her morning mail, an array of marketing materials, each abusing and exploiting women in its own particular way. Kate's comic despair questions the notion of progress in the face of such flagrant instances of degradation and may well cause us to wonder if the situation of women in the late 1970s is to be the focus of the novel. As Kate herself asks, is she "a special case," and as such "of little general relevance," or is she "on the contrary an almost abnormally normal woman, a typical woman of our time, and as such of little particular interest."[1] The question is playful and perhaps more than a little misleading. For while Drabble will provide a small gallery of women making their way, the "new women," Kate calls them, she makes no polemical or sociological efforts to categorize or typify; indeed the achievement of this most recent novel rests just in its acceptance of its characters, their actions and conflicts, small resolutions, in their most ordinary and individual sense.

Kate is a journalist, whose articles originate in her situation as divorced mother of three (we hear the resemblance between author and character); Kate has made herself who she is through the act of writing which both expresses her kinship with women, and gives her the additional role of observer. At the time of the novel's opening, however, she is at the point of weariness with herself and her writing. As she remarks to a friend, "I'm as bloody sick of bloody women as you are, I'm sick to death of them, I wish I'd never invented them, but they won't just go away because I've got tired of them. Will they?" (p. 4). Kate chafes in the constraints of her subject matter and indeed her discontent may well serve Drabble as the opportunity to comment on the limitations of some women's writing, which remains mired, obsessively, in the delineation of women's problems, women's work.

Kate's comments capsule some of the dissatisfaction Drabble expressed a number of years before writing *The Middle Ground* and echo the author's conviction that while one may start out by writing out of one's own situation, this is something of a limitation to be outgrown. For example, after publication of *The Ice Age*: "I'm on better terms with my own interior life. I don't feel the need to write about it. I'm very interested in the way society works."[2] Has Drabble indeed shed the more private concerns of femaleness for larger public issues? In what sense is she to be considered (or does she consider herself to be) a women's writer? In *The Middle Ground*, Drabble explores the life of a woman whose work—writing—is fashioned out of her life, yet Kate does not offer Drabble's self-portrait. Rather, the novel itself constitutes for Drabble the opportunity to bring together the public and private, the political and the maternal.

Susan Gubar has described the closeness of the female artist to her art, the lack of distance that originates in the concept of the female body as artwork. Traditionally, the female body has functioned as the material that is fashioned into art by the male creator (for example, Pygmalion), but one can find the subversion of the traditional notion of art as masculine activity by paying attention to the unnoticed or overlooked areas of female creativity. Indeed Gubar comments on the kind of "revisionary theology" by which late nineteenth- and early twentieth-century women writers were able to "reappropriate and valorize metaphors of uniquely female creativity and primacy."[3] Drabble is one of that company of writers who restore to the novel the examination of an area of experience that had been disregarded. With a kind of controlled closeness, she incorporates much of herself into her creations, sustaining a semi-ironic awareness of her own maternity as well as that of her characters.

As a writer and as a person, Kate of *The Middle Ground* is deeply rooted in femaleness, and so cannot dismiss it with witty comment or detached observation. Writing is directly connected to maternity for Kate. Nevertheless, having created herself out of her situation, and having fashioned for herself a role, the question of what is to be next confronts her. A recent abortion expresses her dilemma: she is not to be a mother again, not this time; indeed, Kate is blocked in her life, haunted in her dreams by the image of the child that might have been. Thus at the outset, Kate is moved to consider all the things she is not, but the question remains of what she is to do, how she is to focus her considerable energies.

By the end of the novel this question remains more or less to be answered. On the outside nothing much has changed. The novel ends as a party is about to begin; it is a party that draws together, perhaps only in a physical sense, the persons who have walked through the novel, the various strands of Kate's life, the important relationships and casual encounters of her urban existence. And so it concludes with Kate poised on the threshold, about to descend the stair: "A child calls her from downstairs. The doorbell rings. The telephone also rings. She hears her house living. She rises" (p. 277). It is surely not too remote an association to invoke the presence here of another literary lady and her party:

as her novel ends, Clarissa Dalloway too stands ready to descend the stair and draws into herself the fragile strands of the moment.

In a 1973 tribute to Virginia Woolf, Drabble acknowledges her initial aversion to the writer who was to become for her something of a literary progenitor. Put off by Woolf's reputation as a difficult, even an elitist writer, Drabble could not, she avers, place herself in relation to Woolf. Via the feminist stance she discovered in *A Room of One's Own*, however, Drabble describes a journey that for her culminated in an act of identification: "And here I sit, in my own room in Bloomsbury, feeling myself uncannily a product of her imagination." It is with a significant leap of her own sympathetic imagination that Drabble appropriates Woolf for her literary family; in Woolf's novels, she notes, she finds no pictures of businesswomen with freezers and washing machines, nor any of "women novelists with many children, rushing from typewriter to school to butcher. . . . but they were about to be born and she welcomed them."[4] We have here the recording of a kinship, perhaps more accurately the act of creating a progenitor who, from the distance of time, casts her approving gaze upon one who has come after. Here we find the establishment of the kind of continuum women writers are so often said to have lacked; in the course of acknowledging their differences, Drabble is able to feel also a necessary closeness and support for her own acts of self-creation.

Indeed, in describing what she finds to be Woolf's lasting contribution to the novel, Drabble underlines those qualities which she has grown to achieve in her own prose: "her perceptions of the slightest connections, her lack of interest in a heavy conventional narrative, her passion for the inconsequential psychological detail" (*Virginia Woolf*, p. 7). These Woolfian qualities are most to be found in Drabble's more recent work from *Realms of Gold* to *The Middle Ground*. She has grown to this point, I think, leaving behind her the propensity to melodrama that structures such novels as *The Waterfall* and *Jerusalem the Golden*. Now she offers the kind of glancing, panoramic view of the urban scene that Woolf carried out in *Mrs. Dalloway*. Kate, at one point in *The Middle Ground*, looks at the urban landscape from her friend's hospital room and achieves, for the breadth of the moment, the "aerial view of human love, where all connections are made known, where all roads connect" (p. 243). Such wholeness is something the eye gives to a scene and achieves for the duration of a moment. The perception may well arise from the absorption in all the details of the everyday, so that as Drabble notes of Woolf, daily life takes on "such absorbing interest, so rich in terror and joy, that she needed no other stimulants" (*Virginia Woolf*, p. 7).

Is this perhaps a particularly feminine capacity to perceive, indeed, to create the moment? Drabble on Woolf's achievement: "To seize the moments of calm in the very midst of smoke and music and noise and flux—Mrs. Dalloway poised on her staircase to greet her guests; Mrs. Ramsay ladling out soup, endlessly concerned about her family, feeling suddenly the 'still space that lies at the heart of things,' alone in the midst of company—this is triumph indeed" (*Virginia*

Woolf, p. 10). Such moments imply not grand resolutions, but acknowledgments and acceptance of the values of kinship, of the values of community, the fragile unities that arise amid the disorder of daily life.[5]

The Middle Ground considers the forms that women's lives take. As a novel, it may well constitute for its author the kind of opportunity that Judith Kegan Gardiner describes—to "define herself through the text while creating her female hero." Even further, it may offer the woman reader access to an analogous process of empathic identification.[6] In an effort to articulate the spectrum of women's roles here, we can perhaps define polar opposites: at one extreme, the offering of the body as art or ornamental object and, at the other, the function of nurturing. In her investigation of her own past, Kate comes upon the sister of an old school chum who has gone from a flair for the dramatic to become a second-rate film star in cheap movies and who now sits, reified and decaying, amid the emblems of her brief period of success.

Perhaps at a polar opposite is Evelyn, the social worker who moves amid urban chaos, trying to administer some order and warmth, to heal broken families. Possessed of a large measure of insight and professional competence, Evelyn wonders at the kind of necessity that has compelled her to care for the lives of strangers and thinks back, by way of pondering her role, to her early years when each girl at school had to contribute sixpence of her pocket money to something called the Self-Denial Fund. Such precedents, in one form or another, structure early female experience, help to instill the habit of self-sacrifice and may show themselves to be at the root of the vocation of so sophisticated and self-aware a character as Evelyn.

The film star suggests use of the body as emblem, or object to be adorned expensively; Evelyn's role as social worker points to the opposite side of the coin, offering of the body in an act of service. Both hark back to the notion of the female body as ground to be worked. Bouncing somewhere between the two is a young woman, in the novel, who offers a bizarre repudiation of the female body and the nurturing role. This is Irene, who lives with a man and produces a child, but rejects each of these elements of her femininity in her periodic flights to her lesbian friends and in physical abuse of her child. The novel enacts something of a mythic play around these varieties of female experience, a drama that culminates, with ironic appropriateness, in an accident in which Evelyn is seriously injured and for which Irene is responsible.

It is Irene's very repudiation of femaleness that strikes out at Evelyn's kindly nurturance and benevolent interventionism, the novel seems to suggest. Indeed this significance is not lost on Kate and Evelyn, who laugh ruefully at the entanglements into which the instincts of mothering have led them. The human capacity to recoup and even redeem the moment receives its due, however, for it is Evelyn's recovery from the accident that provides the occasion for the party with which the novel concludes. The party as human creation counters the force of the accidental and offers its own tentative assertion of meaning.

The novel traces such a spectrum of women, but concentrates its gaze more

on the mothers, "the new matriarchy," as Kate designates them, with an awareness of the difficulties of single parenting. Here, Drabble wants to say, it is
going on, all around us, people making do, women raising children, struggling
to make ends meet, not to mention to create themselves. That struggle, that work
is what she adds to the novel; her novels are about women in the process of
becoming, a process, one would think, that has brought her to where she is.
Claiming a development of her own, Drabble says in an interview: "It's true
that in my earlier novels I wrote about the situation of being a woman—being
stuck with a baby, or having an illegitimate baby, or being stuck with a marriage
where you couldn't have a job. But I'm less and less interested in that now:
one's life becomes wider as one grows older and books reflect one's life. Inevitably."[7] While her books reflect a growing breadth of concern, this expansion
has been achieved within the realm of the ordinary and, in significant ways,
through the ongoing concern with the realm of feminine, even maternal, experience. Drabble is, I think, no less concerned with women's situations now, but
her concern has altered to produce novels that are less reflective of the obsessions
of a single mind.

Drabble's early novels such as *The Millstone* tend to be monothematic, each
with a theme that reflects the mind of the protagonist; one might term these
novels of female development. There is a marked contrast between the early and
the more recent novels, a contrast having to do in part with the larger sphere of
activity and fulfillment that seems to open up for the female protagonists. The
early protagonists chafe in a world defined in terms of masculine prerogatives,
masculine action. Bright and talented, they either entrap themselves in relationships where their potential for autonomous action is limited or else they try to
escape such traps in ways that isolate them from the rewards of human relationship.

One might be reminded here of Patricia Meyer Spacks' discussion in *The
Female Imagination* of power and passivity in nineteenth-century novels by
women. Spacks notes that female dependency on a man is a basic fact in these
novels, regardless of the attitude that writer or character takes to it.[8] It has been
noted, incidentally, that Drabble is flattered by comparisons of her work to
George Eliot's, less so by references to Charlotte Bronte; it is perhaps Bronte's
preoccupation with obsession, emotion thwarted and intense, that Drabble rejects
in herself, has tried to move beyond in her fiction.[9] The pleasure Drabble takes
in relationship to Eliot reflects an identification with Eliot's more comprehensive,
social portrayal of English life; it is no accident that *Middlemarch* is subtitled
A *Study of Provincial Life*. In *The Ice Age*, Drabble attempts a more encompassing sweep; the novel is her state of England book, the national health explored
via the rises and falls, the financial ups and downs, the passing political concerns
of its characters.

Drabble's early novels have something to say about the problem of passion—
problem because the protagonists, women, chafe within the bonds of attachment
to one man, living through a man; they reject too the rejection of passion. Passion

can create a claustrophobic setting, in which the characters are compressed by the intensity of their feelings. In *The Waterfall*, for example, we find a tale of obsession, here presented with some significant experimentation with narrative form: the protagonist presents herself in both first and third person. In the third person, Jane takes extraordinary pleasure in endless descriptions of her obsession with James who seems to exist to give form and outlet to her sexuality. Jane and James, her sometimes twin, live out an obsessive fairy tale in which she is the imprisoned maiden; indeed, the narrative locates itself within the constrained world of the fairytale, acknowledging only occasionally the existence of the larger social world. Although an automobile accident falls, like grace, to release Jane from the confinement of her affair with James, it is only with the possibility of this emergence that the novel ends.

While in *The Waterfall* we are on the inside, only rarely looking out, *The Middle Ground*, as its title suggests, moves outward to a larger perspective without losing the preoccupation with inner experience. The protagonists of both novels are writers, but Jane suggests the writer at an early stage, hesitant about the place of her work beyond private experience. Kate's writing is of a different order—articles, rather than poems—a more public form, quite in keeping with her outwardly directed nature.

Towards the end of her novel, Kate visits a museum where her attention is caught by a painting titled "Psyche Locked Out of the Palace of Cupid," which pictures Psyche sitting, large-limbed and abandoned, in "an attitude of despondency" (p. 222). Why does she not look around her, Kate wonders. "She should look up, and move, and go. The castle of love was a prison, a fortress, a tomb, how could she not appreciate her luck in being locked out, in being safe here in the open air? Let her rise and go" (p. 223). Kate sees in the picture an emblem of a situation she has left behind. Psyche remains trapped, in Kate's eyes, by her failure of vision; she remains trapped in masculine definition of her universe, so that she can only sit on the beach and mourn, unaware of the life around her. It is as if Kate had looked back into the world of the early novels and seen Jane trapped in her erotic relationship with James, Rosamund of *The Millstone* trapped in her strenuous evasions of her own erotic nature, Emma of *The Garrick Year* trapped both in relationship to men and to children. The painting serves emblematically too to suggest the kind of novel Drabble has left behind her—the novel of a female in a male-structured universe, alive only in her passion for the male and in the energy of her repression. "Psyche Locked Out of the Palace of Cupid" describes the problematic of passion without the possibility of release.

It is, of course, in *Realms of Gold* that Drabble brings together work and questions of personal relationship through her protagonist, Frances Wingate. The novel moves with Frances, from conference on archaeology to London kitchen, encompassing the variety of women's work and allowing in Frances for both scholarly breadth and maternal concern. The novel has been criticized by Elizabeth Fox-Genovese for its failure to explore female identity. Fox-Genovese sees in Drabble's female protagonists generally a repudiation of feminine being, one which culminates perhaps in Frances Wingate and the man she loves, Karel, whose sexually ambiguous names suggest that Drabble is groping for a model of androgyny.[10] One might see here rather a probing from the opposite end of the spectrum of the need for relationship in a woman who has established herself eminently in her profession.

A particular strength of Drabble's in these most recent novels is to raise the issue of relationship (particularly of parent and child) for consideration. We move closer to Frances through her responses to her own mother's professional eminence and cool disregard of her offspring, her brother's alcoholism, her nephew's pain and inability to sustain the defenses necessary for survival in the world, her cousin Janet's narrow and restricted existence. It is the fact of relationship that comes before our consideration, an abstraction that exists only through the various instances that give rise to it, an abstraction that can never be detached from those varieties of human connection.

In a discussion of narrative strategies in *Realms of Gold*, Cynthia Davis notes that "we must view the narrator as reporting and shaping the tale but not fully controlling it." She sees the narrator "struggling to give [the story] shape but also to respond to its inherent shape. The story is not just an artifact, but a part of living reality."[11] Similarly, *The Middle Ground* acknowledges the arbitrariness of narrative choices, suggesting that the narrator is not simply the ruler of the fictional universe, but rather a somewhat privileged observer, an interested neighbor, caught up in the flow of events. It is important for Drabble to remove omniscience from the catalogue of narrative characteristics: no one can know; one can record, perceive a bit of meaning here or there and call attention to it, but we are all subject to accident. Thus meaning is not, as Fox-Genovese suggests, denied "in favor of the multifarious variety of human life,"[12] but is rather generated out of acknowledgment of that variety, variety which admits of the momentary emergence of a pattern while continuing to assert the primacy and inscrutability of experience.

This ongoing life of the fiction is suggested also in Drabble's use of tenses in *The Middle Ground*. Kate's crisis, her period of coming to terms with herself, is presented to us in the present tense; Drabble alternates her tenses, filling in the past and moving forward, suggesting thereby that she too is engaged in the act of observing Kate Brewster as she goes through an interlude of self-assessment. In *The Middle Ground* we have a narrator and, beyond, an author, in extraordinary sympathy with the protagonist.

In this concern with the totality of a woman's experience, Drabble finds important literary kin in Doris Lessing, particularly the Lessing of *The Golden Notebook* or the early Martha Quest novels. Kate shares with Anna Wulf of *The Golden Notebook* the acts of self-creation that their authors perceive as central to a woman's experience. Drabble and Lessing both use female friendship as a mode of exploration and both suggest the awareness that women are "living the kinds of lives that women have never lived before," as Anna puts it in *The Golden Notebook*; Drabble picks up the phrase and uses it in a 1978 review of

Lessing's collected stories, a review which becomes the occasion for her of recording an indebtedness or, put another way, of establishing a literary kinship. Lessing has been, she observes, "both mother and seer.... A difficult role, inviting—as mothers do—as much blame as praise." Lessing has charted new territory in the novel, has reported, as Drabble puts it, on "an area of experience not yet made available to the general literate consciousness."[13] As with Woolf, Drabble finds her ancestors; in the act of recording an indebtedness, she defines and confirms her sense of her own territory. Of course it is in the exploration of ordinary experience that Drabble feels close to Lessing and thus she feels quite comfortable reviewing stories that fall into that mode. (When she must acknowledge the apocalyptic side of Lessing's more recent writing, Drabble is less at ease, a discomfort I sense in her explicit refusal to assume a critical stance.)

It is in this area of shared feminine experience that Drabble has worked most effectively, although this kind of concentration has caused her discomfort. Indeed, *The Middle Ground* achieves significant breadth of concern, but does so by bringing the larger into the smaller, that is, by working through the immediacy of its characters' lives. Issues of urban violence and even international politics are raised through the relationship of people to one another, within the dynamics of friendship and family life.

Drabble is perhaps all the more able to have Kate express her exasperation with "women, bloody women" because she herself has worked through the problem of limitation that "women's writing" poses. In interviews, she stresses the expansion of her own concerns, suggesting that she is less compelled to write of herself, to write out and so resolve herself. But while such growth is indeed apparent in her work, it has not led to impersonality of subject or of viewpoint. Keeping in mind her response to Virginia Woolf as well as to those aspects of Doris Lessing's writing with which she identifies herself, we can see that she has made her way with her literary progenitors as guides, towards a breadth and depth of concern that may begin but does not end with women, and that includes a feeling for the particulars of human relationship as well as for the larger concerns of society.

NOTES

1. *The Middle Ground* (New York: Knopf, 1980), p. 12. Subsequent references appear in the text.

2. Mel Gussow, "Margaret Drabble: A Double Life," *New York Times Book Review*, October 9, 1977.

3. Susan Gubar, " 'The Blank Page' and the Issues of Female Creativity," *Critical Inquiry* 8, ii (Winter, 1981): 243–63, p. 261.

4. *Virginia Woolf: A Personal Debt* (New York: Aloe, 1973), pp. 4, 8. Subsequent references appear in the text.

5. These are the kinds of epiphanies or transformations of the ordinary that Jane

Lillienfeld discusses in "Margaret Drabble and Modernism," unpublished paper delivered at the Modern Language Association, December, 1981.

6. Judith Kegan Gardiner, "On Female Identity and Writing by Women," *Critical Inquiry* 8, ii (Winter, 1981): 347–361, p. 357.

7. Nancy Poland, "Margaret Drabble: 'There Must be a Lot of People Like Me,' " *Midwest Quarterly* 16: 3 (April, 1975): 155–67, pp. 162–63.

8. Patricia Meyer Spacks, *The Female Imagination* (New York: Knopf, 1975; Avon, 1976) p. 82.

9. Poland, p. 255.

10. Elizabeth Fox-Genovese, "The Ambiguities of Female Identity: A Reading of the Novels of Margaret Drabble," *Partisan Review* 46, ii (1979): 234–48, p. 247.

11. Cynthia Davis, "Unfolding Form: Narrative Approach and Theme in *Realms of Gold*," *Modern Language Quarterly* 40, iv (1979): 390–402, pp. 391–392.

12. Fox-Genovese, p. 243.

13. *Saturday Review*, May 27, 1978, pp. 54–57.

5

"Grave Endearing Traditions": Edith Wharton and the Domestic Novel

Jeanne Boydston

Certainly, Edith Wharton admitted no debt to the women who preceded her in the development of the United States novel. She recalled that even as a child she had been "exasperated by the laxities of the great Louisa''; as an adult, she was openly contemptuous of the "rose-and-lavender" productions of the local colorists.[1]

In terms of Wharton's early fiction, the antagonism appears justified. Ann Douglas has pointed to the passivity of nineteenth-century domestic literature—its celebration of a female ideal characterized by Christian "nurture, generosity and acceptance" and identified with wife and motherhood in the home.[2] Wharton, too, had much to say about homes, but homes which the benevolence of a Stowe or a Sedgwick seems never to have touched. Under Wharton's withering glance, home appears the embodiment of all that is wrong in society: the place where aspirations die, in *Ethan Frome* (1911); the setting merely of a mother's greed, by the conclusion of *The Custom of the Country* (1913); and in *The Age of Innocence* (1920); but a habit to be settled into when the effort at redemption becomes too hard.

Nevertheless, at the end of her career Edith Wharton was writing fiction which, if more secular than the novels of her nineteenth-century predecessors, seemed, in theme and rendering, almost closer to their work than to her own sharp critiques of several decades before. As Elizabeth Ammons has querulously observed,

The overall change in Edith Wharton's argument, which begins with *The Glimpses of the Moon* in 1922 and runs through *The Gods Arrive* ten years later, could scarcely be more drastic. Conventionally speaking, she moves from a liberal to a conservative position on the woman question. She argues that woman's duty as a mother must take precedence over her desire for personal freedom.[3]

In a dizzying reversal, the homes which had before seemed to condemn society became its only salvation. In *The Glimpses of the Moon* (1922), Wharton began to explore marriage as a vehicle of self-understanding. *The Mother's Recompense* (1925) is a 300-page paean to maternal self-sacrifice. In *The Children* (1928), she posed only the instinct of motherhood between the future generations and chaos. Indeed, in its implications for the function of the home and for the power of the family to provide sanctuary in a brutal world, Wharton's post-World War I perspective could not have come more into line with the visions of the domestic tradition.

The apparent transformation of Wharton's themes has been variously attributed to old age, nostalgia, and the impact of the war.[4] While some or all of these may have been influences upon her later work, we are on safer ground in seeking the origins of the change in Wharton's own earlier writing. An analysis of three of her major novels—*The House of Mirth* (1905), *The Custom of the Country* (1913), and *The Age of Innocence* (1920)[5]—reveals that Wharton's worldview had always contained within it an angle of vision close to the domestic tradition.

In order to evaluate both the presence and the problems of "domesticity" in Edith Wharton's fiction, it is useful to situate the domestic genre as a whole in its historical context in the United States.[6] Particularly in the Northeast, the domestic novel emerged from and in response to the welter of conflicting values and social goals that characterized the early nineteenth-century transition to industrialization. Like many of their contemporaries, the domestic novelists expressed a marked ambivalence toward what they saw. On the one hand, they shared with much of their society a belief in progress and admired, as Catharine Sedgwick put it, "all the insignia of an advancing, busy population."[7] On the other hand, they were in temperament latter-day Puritans—women socialized to accept a deep personal responsibility for the moral and ethical organization of daily life; they deplored the poverty, ignorance, greed and rootlessness that appeared to be the direct social consequence of economic development.

Perhaps precisely because they were women (and so the designated guardians of feeling in Victorian culture), the domestic novelists as a group shared a preoccupation with the psychological aspects of industrial culture. They worried that industrial capitalism both spawned and required a pervasively instrumental mode of self-understanding and social relations, in which love, compassion, and loyalty were necessarily rendered subordinate to the exigencies of profit and loss. In historical works, the domestic novelists searched their culture's past for a time when self-interest was secondary to the common good.[8] In novels set in the present, they detailed the impact of a marketplace mentality in creating marriages without love, in blinding parents to the needs of children, and in destroying the satisfactions of labor, and they devised patterns of familial and social experience through which their characters and their readers alike might be educated anew to charity and self-abnegation.[9]

As the title of the most famous of these novels, *Uncle Tom's Cabin*, suggests, the domestic writers looked to the home for an alternative model of human relations. They were not naive about the reverberations of industrialization in family life: ruined homes were the stock-in-trade of the domestic genre. Rather, the domestic novelists turned to the home out of a conviction that (whatever its present trials) the household was not an intrinsic factor of industrialization and that it had consequently preserved in ideal form a habit of nurturance, a directness of contact, and a tangibility of allegiances which offered a model for a radical restructuring of society. As the characteristic inhabitants of the domestic sphere, women and children became the exemplars of a new social psychology based on nurturance and altruism.

Although the elevation of household life was intended, in the domestic novel, to underscore the bankruptcy of industrial culture, in practice it implicated the genre all the more deeply in the ideologies of that culture and contributed to the eventual failure of the domestic vision itself. For the paradigm of society as a terrain naturally divided into public and private spheres took root in nineteenth-century United States culture as an accommodation to the ethos of the market-place—a way of asserting, as Ann Douglas has convincingly argued, that "the values a society's activity denies are precisely the ones it cherishes."[10] In fact, the home was not a realm distinct from the economy. Very probably, the gender and class stratification of industrial society found its prototypes in the family. Certainly, the household functioned to ease the dislocations of capital accumulation and to socialize individuals to industrial values, and it replicated within itself many of the patterns of ownership, appropriation and dependency that characterized the relations of industrial work.[11] An analysis whose program of social change assumed an intrinsic difference between "public" and "private" life—as did "domesticity"—was based on a contradiction of nineteenth-century ideology and experience. It was a contradiction that would recur in the early twentieth-century writings of Edith Wharton.

However caustically she disparaged their skills, Edith Wharton shared the domestic novelists' apprehensions about industrial society. Indeed, in her, ambivalence became a settled dislike: "All that I thought American in a true sense is gone," she declared in 1919, as if to confirm the worst fears of her predecessors, "and I see nothing but vain-glory, crassness, and total ignorance."[12] For Wharton as for the domestic novelists, moreover, the great danger of capitalism was less its formal existence in the marketplace than its power to permeate social relations and to establish itself as the wellspring of individual identity. She observed that "Every Wall Street term had its equivalent in the language of Fifth Avenue," and grieved for the loss of human bonds based on "strength . . . and tenderness for others. . . . "[13] As early as 1905, Wharton began to search for those bonds in an image of the home.

The House of Mirth recounts the last year-and-a-half in the life of the beautiful but moneyless Lily Bart, whose survival among the elite of late nineteenth-century New York depends upon her skill at selling herself in a lucrative marriage. As Elizabeth Ammons emphasizes, Lily Bart is the Veblenesque victim of an industrial society that values women only as objects of conspicuous consumption.[14] At the same time, Bart's slow descent into social oblivion and death is not so much imposed from without as it is nurtured from within. Lily has been raised to be a "highly specialized" commodity, "fashioned to adorn and delight." (*Mirth*, p. 311). Although she comes finally to perceive a moral dimension in life, she is too fully a product of her world to realize an identity separate from it.

Wharton locates Bart's tragedy in the failure of the home. Mirroring the social relations of the society in which they exist, the households of *The House of Mirth* are but stages for the ongoing spectacle of wealth, mere "improvisation[s]" (*Mirth*, p. 139) of relationships, created and dissolved according to their success in providing the props and trappings of fashion. Lily's own childhood home is described simply as a "turbulent element"— "a house in which no one ever dined at home unless there was 'company.' " Her father (a "neutral-tinted" man) became "extinct" when he could no longer bankroll a lavish social life. From her mother, Lily learned only an abhorrence of domestic dinginess and a fatal habit of self-objectification (*Mirth*, pp. 32–39). It is the lesson that shapes her existence: on the morning of the last day of her life, Lily Bart

. . . lay late in bed, refusing the coffee and fried eggs which the friendly Irish servant thrust through her door and hating the intimate domestic noises of the house. . . . [S]he yearned for that other, luxurious, world, whose machinery is so carefully concealed that one scene flows into another without perceptible agency (*Mirth*, p. 312).

She remains a creature of the stage.

This perspective locates Lily Bart in the tradition of the heroines of the domestic novel. Like Lucretia Fitzherbert of Child's *The Rebels*, Ellen Montgomery of Warner's *The Wide, Wide World*, and Christie Devon of Alcott's *Work*,[15] Bart is above all an orphan in search of a home. Born in the house of mirth, she must pass through a process of repeated "re-orphanings" before she can, at last, enter the harsher but more enduring realm of the house of mourning.[16] To this end, Wharton traces Lily's break with her Aunt Peniston, her virtual abandonment by her cousin Jack Stepney, her official disinheritance, and her final expulsion from society—at the hands, appropriately, of the friend who offered to guide her through the Gryce affair with a "mother's unerring vigilance," Judy Trenor (*Mirth*, p. 96).

The alternative vision toward which Lily moves is not Lawrence Selden's "republic of the spirit": Selden is far too comfortable in his own role of spectator to venture into the unscripted world of passions and trust required for Lily's salvation.[17] Rather, the home Lily finds at the end of the novel is the "grim," "meager" household of Nettie Struther, an abandoned unwed mother from the working classes who "gather[s] up the fragments of her life" and starts over (*Mirth*, p. 332). Against the "studied luxury" of a Bellomont, this home has but "the frail, audacious permanence of a bird's nest. . . ." (*Mirth*, pp. 43, 332). It is a permanence Wharton affirms, and its essence, seen now by Lily as "the central truth of existence," (*Mirth*, p. 332) resides precisely in the courage of its members to confront what is hard and unpleasant in life. At the moment of her death, Lily becomes, symbolically, both mother and child in Nettie Struther's daughter—and in that union her homelessness ends.

In strictly formal terms, the Struther episode works. Nettie Struther's home can provide Lily sanctuary because it is the opposite of the home that produced her, and because Struther herself both parallels and reverses Bart's decline. Nonetheless, this conclusion seems false. We have, by the end of *The House of Mirth*, seen all too vividly the power of the "public" world to manifest itself in the "private." That the Struther household is so poor only underscores its vulnerability—particularly when we recall that it was poverty that initiated the chain of theft and potential blackmail that put Bertha Dorset's letters in Lily's hands in the first place. The conclusion of *The House of Mirth* is credible, finally, only if we accept it on terms which exist outside of the world of the novel and in our own beliefs: that there is redemption and truth in the bond of mother and child.

The eight years that intervened between publication of *The House of Mirth* and the completion of Wharton's next major New York novel, *The Custom of the Country*, seem to have determined Wharton to purge everything romantic from her view. Certainly, when she turned to Undine Spragg, the anti-heroine of *The Custom of the Country*, Wharton chose a character as different from Lily Bart as can be imagined, and she approached her, not with the detached irony that had shaped the earlier novel, but from the more derisive angle of parody.

At the same time, both Wharton's themes and the motifs through which she developed those themes remained unchanged. The relations of fashionable New York society are still compared to an elaborately staged illusion,

. . . a phantom "society," with all the rules, smirks, gestures of its model . . . [enacted by] a new class of world-compellers [who] bind themselves to slavish imitation of the superceded [while maintaining a] prompt and reverent faith in the reality of the sham. . . . (*Custom*, p. 273).

If the main character of this drama now unabashedly embodies the materialism of turn-of-the-century society, the tumultuous impact of her spirit is still most dangerous in the realm of the home. If Undine is successful in her marrying, where Lily fails, it is because she never wants to be anything but a beautiful object. If she creates household after household, while Lily dies alone, the families through which she moves are characterized by rootlessness and sharply inverted roles;[18] they are described by Wharton merely as "appropriate setting[s]" for the re-enactment of Undine's favorite childhood game, "to 'dress up' . . . and 'play lady' . . . ." (*Custom*, pp. 548, 22). The career of Undine Spragg is but another expression of Wharton's perception that the chief tragedy of industrial wealth was its capacity to invade the ordered values of the home.

The dominance of parodic structures renders the essentially "domestic" nature of Wharton's analysis particularly visible in *The Custom of the Country*. Parody works on a principle of inversion; by showing us the comic distortion, the author causes us to think about the original and to assess it with a new clarity. Thus, the grotesque marriages of Undine Spragg, each of them undertaken with an eye to financing a more and more elaborate background for her performances as a woman of fashion, serve most forcefully to keep before us their opposite: a model of family life *not* shaped by money, manipulation, and fraud—a family, indeed, apart from the material world.

In *The Custom of the Country*, that ideal is most fully realized in the traditions and allegiances of Saint Desert, the ancestral home of Undine's third husband. Wharton wished here, not so much to celebrate the European model, as to present a household as far as possible from its Wall Street parodies:[19] the two are separated by an ocean, a culture, and, symbolically, an impenetrable barrier of time. Saint Desert stands as a monument to pre-capitalist life—a time when families lived on their own land, made their own goods, and recognized birth, death, and marriage as the deepest demarcations of human life. Significantly, Saint Desert is the only household in which Undine is expected (initially, at least) to fulfill her commitments as mother and wife.

Saint Desert represents the values extolled in the domestic tradition: the sanctity of family, the joy of sacrifice, the redeeming love of mother and child, and the transforming power of truth. For Raymond and his family, no bonds supersede those of the home. They assume as a matter of course that Undine will want her son Paul with her, and Raymond is appalled beyond explaining that Undine would wish to sell the tapestries that have been handed down as a symbol of family continuity. If he himself is eventually forced to accept Moffat's price, it is only that the household may go on, much as Mrs. March in *Little Women* gladly accepts the modesty of her home. Indeed, Raymond is the mother-figure of this novel—the adult who takes pleasure in Paul's company and inspires the boy's trust. Most telling of all, at the end of *The Custom of the Country*, Paul's future disenchantment with Undine is foretold, not in his loneliness or in his indifference to the sumptuousness of her suites, but in his amazement "that she had said things that weren't true of his French father." (*Custom*, p. 586).

Like Nettie Struther's home, however, Saint Desert is an unconvincing ideal. Distant from New York though it may be, Raymond's estate seems more deeply shaped by American values than its owner would like to admit. Raymond, of course, is a man of integrity, but he is also a snob whose strong sense of personal superiority has the effect of converting kinship itself into little more than a backdrop for social exclusivity. He seems, moreover, merely to "acquire" Undine, and to prize her as but the newest of his cherished possessions. Undine's repugnant materialism notwithstanding, she is a woman of awesome and attractive energy—energy which finds no chord of response in Saint Desert. One comes away from *The Custom of the Country* more convinced than ever that, whatever the antidote for the social relations of capitalism may be, it is not to be found in the family.

Published only two years before *The Glimpses of the Moon, The Age of Innocence* represents Wharton's attempt to move back through the history of her own culture to discover an alternative model of social life. The "new people" loom distinctly on the horizon of Newland Archer's world, to be sure, ready at a moment either to buy up or simply to rebuild old New York's most cherished symbols of community. But the novel is not about the invaders *per se*. It is, instead, about the people whose lives they would later invade—an extended meditation (through the vehicle of Newland Archer's life) on the nature of human relations *before* Fifth Avenue became a mere social equivalent for industrial wealth.

Perhaps because of its more singular focus, *The Age of Innocence* has a beguiling sense of unity; from Archer's first introduction to the Countess Olenska to his final farewell, the novel develops with a flawlessness of tone that characterizes neither *The House of Mirth* nor *The Custom of the Country*. Nonetheless, *The Age of Innocence* is an unsettled work which finally achieves reconciliation only in an affecting but telling recourse to the mysticism of an idealized vision of the home.

The lessons Newland Archer learns by the end of this novel are, like those of *Little Women* and *The Wide, Wide World*, the lessons of the home: to renounce personal well-being for the good of others, to nurture familial bonds, to value the refuge of the family above the pleasures of the world, and, at all costs, to protect the home from the corruption of "public" life. This is what Ellen Olenska, who has experienced life without a home, knows; as much as May's pregnancy, it is why she leaves: ". . . happiness bought by disloyalty and cruelty and indifference"[20] is always got at too dear a price. Over the course of his engagement and marriage, Archer slowly comes to agree. At the end of the novel, he has not only given Ellen up, but, in a type of "innocent family hypocrisy," (*Innocence*, p. 276) he has never even spoken of her. Rather, through the years he has devoted himself to the world of his family: to parenting, to work in the civic arena, and to the preservation of his home. Indeed, after May's death, Archer himself becomes an emblem of motherhood, combining affectionate single-parenting and a public career of benevolent reform with a civilizing role reminiscent of the eternal "feminine": if, as he recognizes, he has in some respects missed "the flower of life," he concludes that "it did not so much matter if marriage was dull duty, as long as it kept the dignity of a duty: lapsing from that, it became a mere battle of ugly appetites." (*Innocence*, p. 275).

A dull duty, however, is hardly an engaging alternative to the ugly appetites of industrial wealth. Indeed, the domestic life to which Archer submits himself is both arid and silent. Communications are constantly flawed; whatever he may think, Archer never accurately assesses May's thoughts—even less those of Ellen Olenska. Family allegiance, moreover, is in fact little more than habit and a respect for social forms. Archer's sudden insight that his wedding is virtually indistinguishable from "a first night at the opera" (*Innocence*, p. 147) echoes throughout the novel and raises unanswered questions about how the protocol of his world is finally to be differentiated from the shallow spectacle of Lily Bart's or Undine Spragg's. Wanting to discover homes bound together by "grave endearing traditions," (*Innocence*, p. 331), Wharton found only the deep malaise of a dilletante's way of life.

Nonetheless, Newland Archer is, by the end of the novel, a clearly sympathetic and victorious character. Few scenes in Wharton's fiction are more gently rendered than Archer's final leave-taking as he sits alone on a bench, five floors below Ellen's home. A decade and a half after the publication of *The Age of Innocence*, Wharton would remember Archer's as a "mild and leisurely" world which, whatever its other failings, held always to "scrupulous probity in business and private affairs." They were values she thought worth preserving.[21] It was for herself as well as for the character Newland Archer that Wharton wrote, at the end of *The Age of Innocence*, "he honored his own past, and he mourned for it." (*Innocence*, p. 275).

Undoubtedly, Wharton's nostalgia resulted, in part, from the personal and public losses of her middle and later years. But the origins of this tone lie as well in the polarities that had always characterized her analysis of industrial society. Perhaps precisely because in her lifetime the ravages of capitalism grew so glaring, Wharton clung to the belief that industrialism was a phenomenon of the "public" world, and that its opposite still existed in the home. Early in her career she began to formulate the home, not simply as a symbol, but as an objectively different set of conditions. From there, the plunge into a fully romanticized celebration of motherhood, such as characterized her later works, was but a matter of degree.

The problems of credibility which marked Wharton's invocation of the powers of the home had been growing throughout the nineteenth century. From Sedgwick's vision of the home as mediator of cultures through Stowe's argument for domesticity as an alternative organization within a culture to Alcott's plea for the single household as a last repository of love, the claims for the home grew narrower.[22] Whatever Wharton's final views, the vivid travesties of *The House of Mirth*, *The Custom of the Country*, and *The Age of Innocence* diminished those claims even more.

NOTES

1. Edith Wharton, *A Backward Glance* (New York: Appleton Century 1934), pp. 51, 294.

2. Ann Douglas, *The Feminization of American Culture* (New York: Alfred Knopf, 1977), pp. 8–12.

3. Elizabeth Ammons, *Edith Wharton's Argument with America* (Athens, Georgia: The University of Georgia Press, 1980), p. 160.

4. For discussions of the possible origins of this change, see: Ammons, *Edith Wharton's Argument*, pp. 160–171; R.W.B. Lewis, *Edith Wharton: A Biography* (New York: Harper Colophon Books, 1975), pp. 442–532; Cynthia Griffin Wolff, *A Feast of Words: The Triumph of Edith Wharton* (New York: Oxford University Press, 1977), pp. 341–

406; and Louis Auchincloss, *Edith Wharton* (Minneapolis: The University of Minnesota Press, 1961), pp. 32–43.

5. I have found the following to include especially useful discussions of these novels: Wolff, *Feast of Words*; Blake Nevius, *Edith Wharton: A Study of Her Fiction* (Berkeley: The University of California Press, 1953); and Gary H. Lindberg, *Edith Wharton and the Novel of Manners* (Charlottesville: University Press of Virginia, 1975).

6. I have found the following general studies of the domestic novel to be especially useful: Helen Waite Papashvily, *All the Happy Endings* (New York: Harper, 1956) and Nina Baym, *Woman's Fiction: A Guide to Novels by and about Women in America, 1820–1870* (Ithaca, New York: Cornell University Press, 1978). Ann Douglas' *Feminization of American Culture* offers a provocative analysis of the impact of domestic writing on nineteenth- and twentieth-century culture in the United States. For discussions of "domesticity" as a cluster of social conventions about Womanhood see: Nancy F. Cott, *The Bonds of Womanhood: "Woman's Sphere" in New England, 1780–1835* (New Haven: Yale University Press, 1977) and Barbara Welter, "The Cult of True Womanhood: 1820–1960," *American Quarterly* 18 (summer, 1964).

7. Catharine Sedgwick, *Clarence: A Tale of Our Own Times* (London: Henry Colburn and Richard Bentley 1830), I, 215.

8. See, for example, Lydia Maria Child, *The Rebels, or Boston before the Revolution* (1825) and Harriet Beecher Stowe, *Oldtown Folks* (1869).

9. See, for example, Sedgwick, *Clarence* and Susan Warner, *The Wide, Wide World* (1851).

10. Douglas, *Feminization of American Culture*, p. 12.

11. For discussions of the role of the family in industrialization, see: Hans Medick, "The Proto-Industrial Family Economy: The Structural Function of Household and Family during the Transition from Peasant Society to Industrial Capitalism," *Social History*, 3 (October, 1976), 291–315; Christopher Clark, "The Household Economy, Market Exchange and the Rise of Capitalism in the Connecticut Valley, 1800–1860," *Journal of Social History*, 13 (Winter, 1979), 169–190; and my own study-in-progress, tentatively titled "Home and Work: The Industrialization of Housework in the United States." A valuable critique of the two-sphere model from an anthropological perspective is: Michele Rosaldo, "The Use and Abuse of Anthropology: Reflections on Feminism and Cross-Cultural Understanding," *Signs*, 5 (Spring, 1980), 389–417.

12. Quoted in Lewis, *Edith Wharton*, p. 424.

13. Edith Wharton, *The Custom of the Country* (New York: Charles Scribner's Sons, 1956), p. 537; Edith Wharton, *The House of Mirth* (New York: Signet Classics, 1964), p. 331. Subsequent references appear in the text.

14. Ammons, *Edith Wharton's Argument*, pp. 31–36.

15. Louisa May Alcott, *Work: A Story of Experience* (1873).

16. The title of the novel is from Ecclesiastes 7.4: "The heart of the wise is in the house of mourning; but the heart of fools is in the house of mirth."

17. For a discussion of Selden's role as spectator, see: Michael Wayne Vella, "Technique and Theme in *The House of Mirth*," *Markham Review*, II (May, 1970), 19.

18. As the novel opens, the Spraggs have given up housekeeping to live in an expensive New York hotel. In this decision, Undine acts the part of "parent"; hers is the determining voice. Additional illustrations of Wharton's use of role inversion include Ralph's view of himself as parents to Undine and Paul's perception of Undine as a newspaper celebrity rather than as his mother.

19. Saint Desert is balanced by Ellen Olenska's European marriage in *The Age of Innocence*.

20. Edith Wharton, *The Age of Innocence* (New York: Signet Classics, 1962), p. 142. Further references are given in the text.

21. Wharton, *Backward Glance*, pp. 61, 21.

22. Catharine Sedgwick, *Hope Leslie* (1827); Harriet Beecher Stowe, *Uncle Tom's Cabin* (1851); Louisa May Alcott, *Little Women* (1868–1869).

6

Margaret Atwood, Margaret Laurence, and Their Nineteenth-Century Forerunners

Ann Edwards Boutelle

Of the many distinguished literary figures in nineteenth-century Canada, there can be few more fascinating than Catharine Parr Traill and Susanna Moodie, sisters and survivors. Emigrating with their respective husbands to Canada in 1832, they lived close to each other in the Ontario wilderness, each writing of her experience there (to very different effect), each defining the self as much through the role of writer as through the role of woman.

In the 1970s a second literary immortality has been granted to each of them; and, a full century after the creation of their individual (and contradictory) myths, each sister has succeeded in becoming legendary. Susanna Moodie is the first to rise victorious from her grave, thanks to Margaret Atwood's poetic sequence *The Journals of Susanna Moodie* (1970); and Catherine Parr Traill is elevated as a Canadian saint in Margaret Laurence's novel *The Diviners* (1974), the last volume in the Manawaka series. The reincarnation of these sisters, the incorporation of their spirits and energies and words into twentieth-century works, reveals much about the contemporary writers' relationship to the inherited tradition.

That a woman writer should look to the past for predecessors and forerunners should not surprise us. One thinks of Woolf's description of masterpieces as "not single and solitary births; they are the outcome of many years of thinking in common, of thinking by the body of the people so that the experience of the mass is behind the single voice."[1] More recently, Ellen Moers's *Literary Women* and Sandra Gilbert and Susan Gubar's *Madwoman in the Attic* have presented elegantly compelling evidence of the extent to which a female tradition exists, a tradition reinforced at every step by the conscious (and unconscious) turning of the woman writer towards her forerunners. And a work such as Jean Rhys's *Wide Sargasso Sea*, erected on the foundation that Charlotte Bronte supplied in

Jane Eyre, provides explicit evidence. Atwood's sequence and Laurence's novel, meanwhile, belong in the company of Rhys's work, acknowledging explicitly the work of the woman writer who went before, but with the addition of a particular Canadian perspective.

By choosing to incorporate the nineteenth-century Canadian woman writer in her work, each of the contemporary writers defines herself clearly as a Canadian woman writer and places herself consciously in the tradition, both as it has existed, and as it will exist.

Each twentieth-century writer, moreover, chooses the sister who best fits her contemporary purpose. Susanna Moodie was the more gothic of the two sisters, hence the more appealing to Atwood whose forte is the gothic ("Speeches for Dr. Frankenstein," *Surfacing, Lady Oracle*). In her 1852 *Roughing It in the Bush*, Moodie had attempted to scare off would-be emigrants by emphasizing the dangers, toils, and difficulties of her first few years in the bush. Hence she presents herself as never in control, always terrified: at any moment the vulnerable human family, beset by heat, cold, fire, ice, murderous neighbors and beasts, may perish; survival alone is something of a miracle.

While this nerve-racking account, together with Moodie's 1853 *Life in the Clearings*, forms the base on which Atwood builds her sequence, Atwood takes pains to emphasize the non-rational and partly uncontrollable genesis of the work—more fuel to the gothic fire—in a manner similar to Mary Shelley's account of the genesis of *Frankenstein*. The starting-point is a dream: "I dreamt I was watching an opera I had written about Susanna Moodie. I was alone in the theatre; on the empty white stage, a single figure was singing."[2] This dream leads to Atwood's reading of Moodie's work (which she had not read previously), her subsequent "forgetting" of the books, and—at a later date—the writing of the sequence: "The poems occurred later, over a period of a year and a half" (*Moodie*, p. 63)—almost, it would appear, writing themselves. Atwood chooses to emphasize that it was not Moodie's "conscious voice but the other voice running like a counterpoint through her work that made the most impression on me." (*Moodie*, p. 63).

All of this serves to establish a mysterious and almost mystic connection between Atwood and Moodie: an atmosphere of ghosts and possessions, of art created against the conscious will of the woman writer. (One thinks here of Charlotte Bronte's description of the passive role of the writer, in defense of Emily Bronte's creation of Heathcliff. Or of Atwood's own description of the possessed writer in *Lady Oracle*: "When I would emerge from the trance. . . there would usually be a word, sometimes several words, occasionally even a sentence, on the notepad in front of me.")[3]

The poems themselves, accompanied by Atwood's collages, increase the sense of ghostly presences:

> My brain gropes nervous
> tentacles in the night, sends out

> fears hairy as bears,
> demands lamps; or waiting
>
> for my shadowy husband, hears
> malice in the trees' whispers.
>
> I need wolf's eyes to see
> the truth.
>
> I refuse to look in a mirror. (*Moodie,* p. 13)

As the speaker describes the arrival in the strange land, her awakening to the illusion in which the men place faith, she is invaded by darkness, the surface of her being shatters, and the buried shapes emerge:

> I was frightened
> by their eyes (green or
> amber) glowing out from inside me. (*Moodie,* p. 27)

Waking nightmares and sleeping nightmares interweave, occasionally echoing Moodie's work, occasionally departing from it, plunging us farther into terror:

> Around my feet
> the strawberries were surging, huge
> and shining
>
> When I bent
> to pick, my hands
> came away red and wet
>
> In the dream I said
> I should have known
> anything planted here
> would come up blood. (*Moodie*, p. 34)

Meanwhile, the identity of the speaker cannot be pinned down, adding to the reader's sense of disorientation and terror, and placing the reader in a similar position to that of the speaker:

> What is this
>
> (you find only
> the shape you already are
> but what
> if you have forgotten that
> or discover you
> have never known) (*Moodie*, p. 25)

And while the speaker does not know who she is, we do not know it either. Is Atwood adopting Moodie's voice? Is Moodie using Atwood's voice? Is either real? Is neither?

Whoever the speaker is, she is clearly more disturbed than the nineteenth-century Moodie ever gave evidence of being. In her own writings on the Canadian experience, Moodie had—it is true—presented herself as something of a hysteric, frightened that wolves might descend the chimney, scared even of the cows. This adds to the humor and to the interest of the account—but neither terrifies nor disturbs, as the reader quickly assumes some exaggeration, realizing that Moodie herself is far more in control than the protagonist of her work.

But the ''Susanna Moodie'' revealed in Atwood's poems is both terrified and terrifying; and the paranoia of her vision compels. For example, in ''The Planters,'' the speaker watches the men planting, realizes the hopelessness of their dream; and we, seeing with her clear eyes, identify with her position:

> I see them; I know
> none of them believe they are here.
> They deny the ground they stand on,
>
> pretend this dirt is their future.

Yet, this in no way prepares us for the opening into terror, the invasion of the self, predicated on clear sight:

> And they are right. If they let go
> of that illusion solid to them as a shovel,
>
> open their eyes even for a moment
> to these trees, to this particular sun
> they would be surrounded, stormed, broken
>
> in upon by branches, roots, tendrils, the dark
> side of light
> as I am. (*Moodie*, pp. 16–17)

The separate ''journals,'' ordering the material chronologically in three sections, control the flow of experience—or try to—while the collages and the poems move in defiance of time, breaking free from any decorous and imprisoning container.

The climactic journal (1871–1969) brings ''Susanna Moodie'' to death, and—through death—to the present moment: ''I am the old woman / sitting across from you on the bus, / her shoulders drawn up like a shawl.'' As the speaker rises victorious and destructive from the grave, serenely heading towards the future on her Toronto bus, it is the reader's turn to become the ghost:

> out of her eyes come secret
> hatpins, destroying
> the walls, the ceiling

Turn, look down:
there is no city;
this is the centre of a forest

your place is empty (*Moodie*, p. 61)

Emotional forces have been joined, between Atwood and the "other voice" heard in Moodie's work, to demonstrate not only the closeness of the twentieth-century writer to her nineteenth-century forerunner, but also the power released in acceptance of this closeness. The reader, meanwhile, with an overriding sense of her own transience and powerlessness, is overwhelmed by the combined force of the two visions.

There are some initial similarities between Laurence's *The Diviners* and Atwood's *Moodie*. Both works consider the relationship between art and time; and both protagonists, like the original Traill and the original Moodie, are women writers living in Canada. However, the bulk of Atwood's work was set in the nineteenth century, with a speaker close to the original Moodie, whereas in Laurence's work the setting is contemporary Canada and the protagonist is far removed from the original Catharine Parr Traill. Becalmed in her writing career, Morag Gunn circles her way towards acceptance of her past and present, acceptance of her daughter's separate being, waiting impatiently but with the necessary passivity for the moment of the final paragraph, a moment which returns the reader to the beginning of the novel: "Morag returned to the house, to write the remaining private and fictional words, and to set down her title."[4]

To Morag, the figure of Catharine Parr Traill is a foil—impossibly efficient, as Traill had indeed presented herself in *Backwoods of Canada* (1836) and her *Canadian Settler's Guide* (1855). Mother, breadmaker, gardener, writer, botanist, Traill impresses the reader—and Morag—with her seemingly inexhaustible energy. Her life of action and self-confident accomplishment (very different from Moodie's tales of disaster) is used by Laurence as a contrast to Morag's situation, a figure half-envied, half-mocked: "Catharine Parr Traill, one could be quite certain, would not have been found of an early morning sitting over a fourth cup of coffee, mulling, approaching the day in gingerly fashion, trying to size it up. No. No such sloth for Catharine P. T." (*Diviners*, p. 96).

Traill appears three times, a summoned presence, a granted vision; and each time she appears with diminished force, as if the saint is losing her halo before our eyes.

In her first appearance, her commonsense sturdiness ("In cases of emergency, it is folly to fold one's hands and sit down to bewail in abject terror. It is better to be up and doing.") (*Diviners*, p. 171) is undercut by our sympathy for Morag's anxiety about her daughter.

In Traill's second appearance, the twentieth century and its sweeping destruction of the planet make Traill's faith antiquated, irrelevant:

The evidence of your eyes showed you
Jerusalem the Golden with Milk and Honey
Blest, at least if a person was willing to
expend enough elbow grease. No plastic
milk jugs bobbing in the river. No
excessive algae, fish-strangling. The
silver shiver of the carp crescenting. My
grandchildren will say *What means Fish*?
Peering through the goggle-eyes of their
gasmasks. Who will tell old tales to
children then? Pique used to say *What is a
Buffalo*? How many words and lives will be
gone when they say *What means Leaf*? Saint
Catharine! Where are you now that we need
you?
C.P.T.: I am waiting. (*Diviners*, p. 171)

In her third and final appearance, Traill is rejected as a model; Morag is winning her way towards slow acceptance of herself:

I'll never till those blasted fields, but this place is some kind of a garden, nonetheless, even though it may only be a wildflower garden. It's needed, and not only by me. I'm about to quit worrying about not being an old or a new pioneer. So farewell, sweet saint—henceforth, I summon you not. . . .
C. P. Traill: (voice distant now and fading rapidly) "In cases of emergency, it is folly to fold one's hands and sit down to bewail in abject terror: it is better to be up and doing."
M. Gunn: I'll remember. (*Diviners*, p. 406)

Through rejection of what Traill represents, Laurence has used C.P.T. as a means of defining the role of the twentieth-century Canadian woman writer. Unlike Atwood, she finds in the earlier writer a necessary enemy, not an ally. The C.P.T. figure is closer to Woolf's "Angel in the House" than she is to Moodie. She is the phantom who must be destroyed before the woman writer can write without interruption, self-censorship, guilt. She fades from view, while the ghost of Moodie rides triumphantly onward.

Just as Moodie and Traill had, in their day, found separate paths in the wilderness, so today Atwood and Laurence find their separate ways towards the creation of their art. For each, that way involves confrontation with the ghosts of the past, those forerunners who broke the silence, making it possible for the single voices now to be heard.

NOTES

1. Virginia Woolf, *A Room of One's Own* (New York: Harcourt Brace, 1957), pp. 68–69.

2. Margaret Atwood, *The Journals of Susanna Moodie* (Toronto: Oxford University Press, 1970), p. 62. Further references are given in the text.

3. Margaret Atwood, *Lady Oracle* (New York: Avon, 1976), p. 24.

4. Margaret Laurence, *The Diviners* (New York: Bantam, 1975), p. 453. Further references are given in the text.

7

THE Poetic World of Snezhina Slavova

Yuri V. Karageorge

Snezhina Slavova's work is analyzed here on the basis of a very impressive, albeit small, volume of poems: *Dujdovete moite priateli.*[1] It contains twenty-nine pieces, (all translations from the Bulgarian used in this text are mine), the majority of which are rather short. However, in this brief body of poetry, Slavova, has succeeded in projecting a powerful and distinctly personal poetic vision.

Slavova expresses herself through complex metaphors and archetypal figures and experiences which often bear many meanings, few of them specific or precise. The themes of Slavova come at times through flashes, sometimes too blinding; at other times, through the play of numerous shadows. The best poems of Slavova escape the narrower world of confessional poetry, allowing her to capture human experience in a greater reference of universal transmutation, of permanent forces of order and disorder.

Slavova was born in Plovdiv, Bulgaria, in 1942. Her early education was in Batak (the subject of the first poem of the book), a town in southwest Bulgaria, and the scene of one of the most brutal Turkish atrocities of the nineteenth century. For her secondary education, she returned to her native Plovdiv. This city, with its roots in remote history, is a central point of reference for her creative imagination and is the subject of one of her most moving and impressive poems. Subsequently, she studied business at the University of Varna, an old city on the Black Sea. It is important to note these details because Slavova's work draws so much on the landscapes and history of her country. The first and immediate impression of Slavova's poetry is that of great strength, of personal sincerity, of a woman revealing herself profoundly, both as human being and as a creator. Here poetic materials are the phenomena of nature in their many permutations. These she sees and understands in direct relation to herself as living organism (a kind of micro-universe) or as a Sybilline observer, a "knower of the names of mysteries.'' Thus, the rain, the soil, the mountains, and the seas constitute the language elements of her poems. Through these, she perceives and expresses the working of nature in and around her. In the rhythms and seasons of the earth she grows wonderingly aware of life: its colors, smells, shapes, and mysterious changes.

For the purposes of analysis and discussion, Slavova's poetry most profitably lends itself to a twofold consideration: (1) *Themes* which seem clearly to fall into two distinct groups—the closely personal (expressing her attitudes and feelings as lover, mother, sister, daughter, and citizen) and the ultra-personal (visionary, celebrational, vatic); and (2) *Language*, including characteristic diction, imagery, and metaphors.

In her book, Slavova has arranged the poems into three sections: "Shores," "The Rain My Friend," and "Crossroads." It is difficult, however, to make out the rationale of this ordering. *Shores* features poems as essentially different as "Strandja Mountain" and "Burgas." The former is surrealistic, somewhat obscure; the latter, directly confessional and accessible. And in her second grouping, which contains principally poems addressed to her family, there appears as well "The Rain My Friend" which is completely different in tone and intention. Perhaps the book's order is simply a chronological one. In examining the themes of this work as they take shape in pieces which can all be divided into either the personal or the ultra-personal, we are brought more immediately and dramatically to the heart of Slavova's poetic world.

"Cosmos," "Milk," "The Rain My Friend," "Standja Mountain," and "Plovdiv" offer different ways of participation in the mysteries which, in Slavova's view, penetrate everyday life. Slavova appears to have found access to an archaic level of powers and forces. In "Cosmos," Slavova gives a glimpse of what poetic creation is for her, an "unsayable, untameable act." The substance of the poem is the "wringling rainbow body," "luminous," "cool," paradoxically both strong and defenseless, forever anonymous. The stages of her search "upstream" are rendered like ritual steps. The capture and the exposure of the "trout" reveal a kind of beautiful power—instantly "slipping from her hand/ falling back/into the water of the brook."[2]

"Milk" is similarly a poem which works as ritual. Here again, the poet enacts an initiation. The subject would appear to be most mundane—a visit to Slavova's farm to procure milk. The poem opens at the moment of the evening "when the sky loses itself"; that is, when the day and night touch briefly creating a moment for an encounter with the unknown. Here the ritualistic approach is more explicit: a steep descent; three highly charged presences—a torrential brook, a lowing cow, a white horse; and, at the bottom of the descent, the whitewashed house of Slava. She has arrived at the moment which is sacred, removed from the ordinary. She meets the beneficent, reassuring, and radiant milkmaid: "The beads swing between her breasts/the milk flows quietly towards my hand." For the duration of the sacramental outpouring, the poet knows the "name of any mystery." Slava awakens in her that intuitive knowledge which nourishes and also heals confusion and fear: "I am bewildered that at times I have cried." But like all such moments of lucidity and communion, this too comes to an end. And the poet returns to the "steep ascent" of the hills, back to life and her human lot.

"The Rain My Friend" gives the book its title. The themes of harmony and chaos, two facets of the same nature, are central to the majority of poems in this collection. "The Rain My Friend" relates the poet's tremendously intense and contradictory perception of the male principle. He is a duality of reassuring presence and threatening otherness: "You were with me? With me always/True friend how good to be with you." Yet, at the same time he has threatened to "crumble" her, "as the sea wears away its shore."

The "friend" then is an enthralling, joyful complementary entity:

> There is a song in your voice
> In your languor wild strength
> In your laughter stunning gentleness
> It is beautiful to be with you.

But this is also a force that may destroy her. At the moment of actual encounter, when she first knows him, the "rain," now clearly male and personal, brings her only confusion and suffering: "I am in pain now/I did not know/You were red fruit/Blood wine." The poet appears unable to accept the physical essence of the complementary being. Her knowledge of him becomes the precursor of her annihilation. A rather long last part of the poem is but a succession of impulsive statements, each revealing another flash of the contradictory experience. The "friend" at the end has become that "certain rain" that may "burn" her to "ashes," her "body blackened" her "hair buried in the earth." Slavova fears that the realization of completion between man and woman is not salutary and may indeed imply woman's demise. On a broader level, however, through usage of such elemental forces as the fertilizing and fulfilling principle the "rain" and the purifying "fire," along with the repeated references to "blood," "wine," "red fruit," Slavova creates also the impression of the sacrificial mysteries of union.

"Stradja Mountain" develops as a poem on the theme of exploration of the female being. Here the poet, by using the pronoun "I" establishes herself as the main object of the poem, with an elemental presence—the mountain—once again subjected to the action of the same "other." Here that force is violent from the outset:

> Wind
>
> wayfarer with a thousand feet
> a thousand hands

a thousand mouths
tumultuous one
jealous one

To this "other" she was "vowed—offered in sacrifice." The juxtaposition of
the two forces is traditional in character. The wind, unrestrained, unpredictable,
is seen as the male, the impregnator, the possessor. And her desire is that it
should be so: she wants only for him to find her when the time is right. "When
the soil is being turned," at the hours of old mysteries when "the magic mountain
girls dance in a ring," then:

. . . I will come to you
under the drowsing leaves, the leaves
hissing like embers.

The coupling becomes sacramental because each mutually will discover the
other's deepest nature. So she (the mountain) will bestow the full, versatile
bounty of her nature:·

If you are a man, you will discover
in my hands men cry. . . .
If you are newborn you will first know speech—
in my breast there is milk to suck.
If you are mother you will sing—
in my heart there is a child falling asleep.
If you are an old man, you will lament—
for my forehead is a wound.

In these last lines there is a cumulative ability to fulfill all essential human needs.
In this respect, "Stradja Mountain" is not only a figure of archetypal woman,
but one of universal beneficence.
    "Plovdiv" is another poem bearing the name of a Bulgarian city. The history,
physicality and enigma that old cities share, provoke in Slavova an intense
emotion and response. Plovdiv is Slavova's birthplace, and has a long history
dating back to 100 B.C.
    "Plovdiv" introduces us at once to the city's assault upon the senses:

pouring heat of the noon-sun—
rank richness of your living loam—
My heart slows down and
I am ravished to oblivion
    embraced
in your fatal sweetness Plovdiv.

Then she opens herself to the wider geographical context of the surrounding
countryside, and to the vital forces of nature.

> white peaks of the north
>
> deep breaths of coriander
> and the first greening of the woods
> glide down toward me
> like female eagles.
> Torrential rains and waterfalls
> batter me with eagle wings.

As she experiences these forces with intensity, the poet falls into a trance:

> Painfully my fingers unbraid with me
> unbelievable movements of hissing wings
>   of hands sowing seed
>   of thundering discoplanes.

The tumultuousness of this happening is conveyed with strong, dramatic, surrealistic devices:

> I tear out from the huge sun-clock face
> a tiny shadow,
> I throw it like a knife
> into your leaden silence Plovdiv.

In this shattered silence is revealed the vision of the city. The present city becomes one with its past—a past rekindled into the city's "windows" and revived by:

> the ritual dance of Pulpudeva
> the torch feast of Trimontium
> the wild burning of Philippolis
> the Paschal candles of Philibe.[3]

The cumulative weight of the vision makes of her trance an experience of shaman: "The pounding of my heart grows/grows so heavy—all memory is lost." She sees herself to be launched into the stratospheric infinity. Before her, a "yawning" and "enormous moon strip" displays itself. Suddenly "shut into the clouds," she unites herself with the larger perspective of the universe. The poet becomes one with "silent nebulae," with "wombs" of new worlds, which too, we are brought to understand, like the city's past and present, are created and exist in the eternal "swaying flame." In turn, the vastness of the universe is contained in "the earthy smell/of the sheaves of wheat," gathered and fixed by humans.

Confessional in character, Slavova's personal poems are as intense in feeling, mood, and images as are the ultra-personal poems. In these, Slavova draws the curtain to unveil her intimate thoughts, beliefs, and emotions about herself, family, marriage, relationships, places, and her fatherland.

The poems reflecting Slavova as a person present her as passionate, gentle, "immovable," sensuous, strong and vulnerable. To achieve fuller expressions of woman's emotional and physical life, Slavova has recourse to elemental entities in nature. In "Interior," she speaks for both her lover and herself:

> we are thirsty for the sky.
> We have the craving of a bough
> or wings

In "You Pass Through Me," her vulnerability is conveyed through the metaphor of a snowflake melting in "warm hands." She wants the "effulgence" of the "ghost" of her lover to become part of her after her death, when she will become mist or rain, enjoying the taste of his lips and the "spring smell" of his body. Yet, in everyday life, she cannot bear the exclusiveness of a relationship: "At times I want to run away, with the wind smelling resin." She wants absolute freedom, freedom from her lover and from her own passion for him:

> Like the yogi convincing himself
> with such great difficulty
> I tell myself:
> you were part of my life. . .

An eloquent and emotionally charged moment is chosen to mark the end of a relationship:

> that blue cool night
> that enormous and mighty night
> in which
> you will be
> a memory.

Yet, she cannot live without commitment, without "belonging," as she puts it in "It Is Frightening":

> It is frightening
> not to belong
> only the earth waiting for you
> and to kiss the dust at the cross-roads.

Her agony increases as she realizes that a relationship is not a vehicle potent enough to carry her from anxiety to the "place" of oblivion. The poet feels threatened even when the man she loves and lives with is at her side: "Even with you I am alone/Even with you the worst stands by me." Her existential anxiety is identified both as alienation typical of the modern human and of the poet isolated by and in her unique sensibility.

She wants to be loved and be in love, hoping that in the ecstasy of love, it will be possible to:

> . . . crush my fright
> like a dry leaf in my hand
> and in the clear bright breath, at dawn
> to whisper
> my moon, my star,
> my sun-like-one.

When no human solution is at her grasp, she wants to cease being, to escape awareness of self. In several poems, she envisages herself as a "tree," "dew," or "misty drops/among the leaves of milk white beech."

Two poems emerge as particularly indicative of her personality. "Motherland" appears as an authentic statement of her attitude towards her country. Bulgaria is, above all, a stretch of land with fauna, flora, and other physical characteristics familiar to her, forming the whole that she calls motherland. She feels it—the "smell of the rotting foliage" and of the "mud" on which she walks. She knows "the country paths" flowing dazzlingly through the meadows and woods "like pure springs." What she feels about her country is not nourished by ephemeral social and political concepts. Her motherland is the space in which she lives, a "motherly" living organism of which she is an extension.

"Burgas" is a sober, self-controlled statement about the moral norms she establishes for herself. The poem implies a painful disappointment that had just defined itself to her. She has been vulnerable, somewhat mistreated, misunderstood. But she is not plunged into despair. She conveys firmly her determination to be implacable and stoic before the destructiveness of society. She wants to model her attitude on the configuration of the citadel, Burgas, an ancient city on the Black Sea. The poem begins with the admonition that integrity is not appreciated in her society:

> There is no mercy for honesty.
> You are hurt
> in your vulnerable tenderness.
> You are hurt
> in the defenselessness of your outburst.

The rejection, suffering and frustration to which she has been subjected are expressed intensely:

> The petals of your youth falling.
> You burn in your abused confidence
> You burn in your never-caressed beauty.

But the abuse against her and the waste of her youth have not turned her into a cynical person. Such is her sense of dignity that she responds with nobility to defeat. She is resolved to be "clear as the sea-gull's flight/the air liquid palp-able." The majestic "statuesqueness" of Burgas and its closeness to the sea represent for Slavova the purity, strength, and dignity which she desires for herself. She exhorts herself to become like the city's projected grandeur and undisturbed lucidity:

> Ask nothing more from the dawn.
> Stand up soundless like this citadel—
> Burgas
>   invincible, immovable.
> Let its dawn find refuge in you.
> And you—
> discover yourself in the dawn.

A general characteristic of Slavova's language is that it is sensuous as it estab-lishes a direct contact with the physical world. Thus, in relation to nature she constantly evokes the smell and taste of the earth in its many forms: soil, loam, dust, ashes, mud, mulch, and vegetation. Slavova goes even further in her specification of the smell of things; in "Plovdiv," there is a reference to the scent of the spring, unique to this city—an aroma which is an aggregation of all the elements and phenomena of spring. In "Father," early autumn is pow-erfully characterized as the "haying time" when "tall ripe wheat smells." Touch is expressed in several differentiations: the contact with and sensation of rain, wind, dew, snow, air, the warmth of the sun, flames, grass, branches, and wings. Slavova feels all these either when subjected to them by other forces or by her own choice. In poems such as "Plovdiv," "The Rain My Friend," "Strandja Mountain," and "Interior," the contact with things is so intense that it becomes a possibility of personal transmutation, an anticipation of becoming "blossom" or "fruit."

Imagery is another striking quality of Slavova's language. Her method of achieving imagery is reminiscent of the surrealist techniques of making metaphors through unusual comparisons of objects and ideas taken out of context, of bring-ing together the real and unreal (the concrete and the abstract), and of endowing natural phenomena with strange powers; for example, "that certain rain will burn me to ashes" or "torrential rains and waterfalls/batter me with eagle wings." "Plovdiv" has a number of such surrealistic but very personal meta-phors: "I throw a knife" (concrete) "into your . . . silence" (abstract); "window panes in houses and church-towers sink into themselves, deep as the eyes of saints of icons." Or, when in "Burgas," she says: "you burn in never caressed beauty; let the beginning of the day always be with you, clear as the sea-gull's flight." "The Rain My Friend" voices "so I begin to color you with the color of my wanting hands"—a phrase very much like St. John-Perse's "couleur d'homme."

In conclusion, the language of Slavova is like the body of a miniature universe where the basic material of her poetry dwells and from which she tears parts of "flesh" to create new versions of it. Or, as Jean-Paul Sartre wrote in *Situation II*:

. . . se retournant [the poet] vers cette autre espèce de choses que sont pour lui les mots, les touchants, les tatants, les palpants, il decouvre en eux une petite luminosité propre à des affinités particulières avec la terre, le ciel, et l'eau et toute les choses crées.[4]

(. . . the poet reaching for those different kinds of things which for him are words, touching them, feeling them, stroking them. He discovers in them a small luminosity related to the particular affinities of the earth, the sky, water and every created thing in the universe.)

NOTES

1. *The Rain Is My Friend*, or *The Rains My Friends*, to use the plural as it reads in the original Bulgarian. (Sofia, Bulgaria: Narodna Mladej, 1968).

2. The image comparing the process of writing poetry is frequently found in women's poetry. It may be an archetypal image in women's psyche. For example, Katheleen Raine, in an attempt to explicate the actual act of shaping a poem, wrote: "My private image is that of landing a fish—one marks the pool—goes home for line and fly—fishes, and with luck, lands the poem." (Richard Gilberston, *A Question of Poetry*, Bow Nr. Credition, Devonshire, England, 1969, p. 7.) Another Bulgarian poet, Nevena Stefanova, in a poem entitled "Wind," writes, "I hung up the phone and—like an old fisherman—/I sat down again to catch images for poetry." (*Otkrovenia*, Sofia, Bulgaria: Bulgarski pisatel, 1973.)

3. An ancient city in central Bulgaria, and one of the capitals of Philip the Great; at different periods of its history it was also known as Philipopolis, Pulpudeva, Trimontium and Philibe.

4. Jean-Paul Sartre, *Situation II* (Paris: Gallimard, 1948), p. 65.

8

Kay Boyle: In a Woman's Voice

Sandra Whipple Spanier

Kay Boyle was very much a part of the group of writers living in Paris in the 1920s that has since come to be known as the "lost generation." Her work appeared in the *avant-garde* magazines alongside that of James Joyce, Gertrude Stein, Hart Crane, Archibald MacLeish, William Carlos Williams, and Ernest Hemingway. Her circle of friends included Joyce, Crane, and Williams as well as Black Sun publishers Harry and Caresse Crosby, *transition* editor Eugene Jolas, *This Quarter* editor Ernest Walsh (he was the father of her first child), and Robert McAlmon, who published Hemingway's first book and whose own enormous influence on the Paris literary scene has not been widely remembered. In a 1931 *New Republic* review of Kay Boyle's first two books, Katherine Anne Porter wrote: "Gertrude Stein and James Joyce were and are the glories of their time and some very portentous talents have emerged from their shadows. Miss Boyle, one of the newest, I believe to be among the strongest."[1]

Kay Boyle's career has stretched far beyond that decade, however, and has touched on many of the major events of the twentieth century. Her subjects range from her personal experiences as an expatriate in Europe in the twenties and thirties to the causes and effects of World War II to social injustice in present-day America. She has written over thirty books, including fourteen novels, ten collections of short fiction, five volumes of poetry, three children's books, two essay collections, and several pseudonymous, edited, and translated volumes. Her current projects include a book about Irish women and "a very long poem for Samuel Beckett."[2] Hundreds of her stories, poems and articles have appeared in periodicals ranging from the "little magazines" published in

Certain passages in this chapter previously appeared in Sandra Whipple Spanier, *Kay Boyle: Artist and Activist* (Carbondale and Edwardsville: Southern Illinois University Press, 1986).

Paris in the twenties to the *Saturday Evening Post* and *Ladies' Home Journal*, and she was a correspondent for *The New Yorker* from 1946 to 1953. She has been awarded two Guggenheim fellowships, won two O. Henry awards for best story of the year (in 1935 and 1941), and is a member of the American Academy of Arts and Letters. In 1980 she received a Senior Fellowship for Literature from the National Endowment for the Arts, one of eight grants given to "individuals who have made an extraordinary contribution to contemporary American literature over a lifetime of creative work."

With the publication of *Fifty Stories* in 1980, the republication of *Three Short Novels* in 1982 and *Being Geniuses Together* in 1984, and the appearance of three new books in 1985—a translation of René Crevel's *Babylon*, *Words That Must Somehow Be Said: Selected Essays of Kay Boyle 1927–1984*, and *This Is Not a Letter and Other Poems*—Kay Boyle's work is becoming increasingly accessible. For some reason, however, she has not received the wide recognition that her contemporaries of the twenties and early thirties assumed would be her due. Today, while her name is mentioned in many of the myriad memoirs and studies of the expatriates, it most often appears without elaboration as one of the "other" writers in Paris in the twenties. The oblivion is undeserved. In the face of growing interest in women's studies and the widening awareness that women's contributions to literature have too long been underrated or ignored, Kay Boyle is a prime candidate for "rediscovery."

From her earliest short stories to her latest novel, *The Underground Woman* (1975), she has written of the power of women. Often a strong, spirited woman will play opposite a man made weak by egotism, narrowmindedness, and petty possessiveness. Most of these men are nearly as pathetic for their limitations as they are despicable for their attempts at domestic tyranny. This is the theme of "Episode in the Life of an Ancestor," the opening piece of both her first widely-circulated short story collection, *Wedding Day* (1930), and her most recent collection, *Fifty Stories* (1980). It appears that in this early work, the author bases her heroine on her own grandmother, a Kansas schoolteacher who at sixteen had married the superintendent of schools and later went off to work in Washington, D.C.

"Episode in the Life of an Ancestor" explores an incident in the girlhood of the narrator's grandmother, one of the best horsewomen in Kansas. Her father was proud of "the feminine ways there were in her, and especially of the choir voice she used in church," but "It was no pride to him to hear it turned hard and thin in her mouth" to quiet a frightened horse (FS, 17).[3] Yet the local people "were used to seeing her riding with a sunbonnet on her head—not in pants, but with wide skirts hullabalooing out behind her in the wind" (FS, 18). Kay Boyle will not reduce her heroine to the stereotype of tomboy. She contrasts the girl's competence in a wide range of skills with her father's narrow and selfish expectations of her. Although in truth he has little control over this bold spirit, he clings to the illusion that he can mold his daughter into the kind of woman who will serve his needs: "To her father it was a real sorrow that a needle and thread were rarely seen in her fingers. His wife was dead and it seemed to him that he must set flowing in his daughter the streams of gentleness and love that cooled the blood of true women. The idea was that she be sweetened by the honey of the ambitions he had for her'' (FS, 18). We see by his restlessness when he is alone that he is a weak man, far more dependent upon this girl than she upon him.

After she rides off one evening, the father roams the house in his loneliness, musing on her future, wondering if she will marry the schoolmaster, the only gentleman in the countryside. Wandering into her room, he discovers peeping out from under her quilt a poetry book ''with pictures engraved through it of a kind that brought the blood flying to his face,'' opened to a passage that begins: ''To the Nuptial Bowre/ I led her blushing like the Morn'' (FS, 21). (He does not recognize it—nor does the author identify it—as *Paradise Lost*.) Inside he finds the schoolmaster's signature. ''You fine example to the young, screamed the father's mind. You creeping out into the night to do what harm you can, creeping out and doing God knows what harm, God knows'' (FS, 21). And in his mind the schoolmaster's image balloons to monstrous proportions, the pores on the wings of his nose and the black hairs that grow between his eyes clearly visible.

The scene shifts to the young woman riding alone in the quiet night. We are not told whether she has encountered the schoolmaster, whom her father had seen earlier walking onto the prairie. But, suddenly impatient with the tameness of the ride, she kicks her horse into fury in a passage that is unmistakably sexual, with the female in the role of mastery:

Suddenly he felt this anger in the grandmother's knees and it caught and swung him about in the wind. Without any regard for him at all, so that he was in a quiver of admiration and love for her, she jerked him up and back, rearing his wild head high, his front hoofs left clawing at the space that yapped under them. To such a frenzy of kicking she urged him that he was ready to faint with delight. Even had she wished to now she could never have calmed him, and she started putting him over bushes and barriers, setting his head to them and stretching him thin as a string to save the smooth nut of his belly from scraping, reeling him so close to the few pine trunks that streamed up like torrents that he leaped sideways to save his fair coat from ripping open on their spikes. It was a long way to travel back, but he never stopped until his hoofs thundered into the barn that had shrunk too small for him. There he stood in the darkness, wet and throbbing like a heart cut out of the body. (FS, 23)

When she strides into the room where her self-pitying father is wondering how he will know what had ever become of her, he wants to ask where she had been, to say ''that he had seen the schoolmaster walking out early in the evening up on the road that led nowhere except out onto the prairie'' (FS, 24). But the ''grandmother'' stalks over to the table and reclaims her book in silent anger (and in this time warp, Kay Boyle gives her power and stature by conferring on her a more venerable title than her father). He is powerless to speak. His thoughts turn again to the schoolmaster, but now his mental image of the man he had suspected of defiling his daughter shrivels and actually caves in before our eyes:

With this woman in the room with him he was beginning to see the poor little schoolmaster, the poor squat little periwinkle with his long nose always thrust away in a book. He began to remember that the horse his daughter had been out riding all night had once backed up on just such a little whippersnapper as was the schoolmaster and kicked his skull into a cocked hat. (FS, 24)

The father must turn his eyes away from the sight of this woman who stands "with her eyes staring like a hawk's eyes straight into the oil lamp's blaze," and the story ends with the father wanting to say to her, "What have you done to the schoolmaster?" (FS, 24).

"Episode in the Life of an Ancestor" illustrates Kay Boyle's skill in rendering the psychological states of her characters, as she simply presents clearly and without comment the protean images that fill their consciousness. The story also makes a statement that many would call feminist, exploring the relationship between a patriarchal father and a daughter of independent spirit, and revealing the brittle frailty of a rigid male psyche when confronted by a woman's uncharted strength.[4]

In much of her fiction, Kay Boyle endows women with extraordinary power. It is a power that many men fear, and in order to preserve their own delicate concepts of themselves, they often attempt in her stories to reduce woman through a simplistic definition of her nature. "They're mothers or *putains*," claims a young soldier in her 1949 novel, *His Human Majesty*. "There's nothing in between."[5] In *The Underground Woman*, the 1975 novel based on the author's own arrest and imprisonment for demonstrating at the Oakland Induction Center in 1967, a nun comes to a stunning realization while in prison for protesting the Vietnam War. She tells her companion: "I knew that for centuries bishops and priests and abbots and popes were so afraid of the energy of women that they closed them all away. But I never wanted to say to myself, 'yes, this is true,' and now I can." She knows now that women were "taken away from life and cloistered in silence" because the men in the church hierarchy "were afraid that we might bring Christianity back on earth."[6]

In fact, Kay Boyle seems to see a relationship between war itself and a culture's domination by such patriarchal values and hierarchies. A number of her works depict militarism as the large-scale projection of a particularly masculine brand of egotism—the need to possess and control in order to validate one's own worth. The protagonist of *Generation Without Farewell*, her 1960 novel set in occupied Germany, traces the entire disaster of Nazism back to the paternal authoritarianism traditional in the German family. He says of his father: "He beat us, and all our teachers beat us. Every German of his generation beat whoever was weaker than himself, I suppose—every German, that is except the Jews." He adds, "My mother stood between my father and us, between us and the whole

of Germany, taking the blows. But she couldn't go to war for us'' (GWF, 77).[7]
As she was writing a modern history of Germany, a massive project that she
began in the early 1960s, Kay Boyle discovered that the "only good chapters
in that book" were about the women of Germany. "They were the first women
to have a peace movement in the world. They were against every war their men
foisted upon them," she says.[8] She decided to scrap much of the original manuscript and turn her work into a book about German women, to be called *The
Noblest Witnesses*.[9]

The author believes that women are especially powerful in the role of mother.
Again in *Generation Without Farewell*, the protagonist's lover tells him:

You know, it is only mothers who matter. . . They can give everything, or they can take
it all away. Sometimes I'm afraid to live, knowing that. Knowing, I mean, that fathers
don't matter, and simply can't matter. It's only the desperate, desperate mothers, piecing
their children together out of their own hopes and fears. (GWF, 117).[10]

Of the importance of motherhood, Kay Boyle herself has said, "I believe very
strongly that if more mothers had political power, government positions, we
would have a more rational world."[11]

She also explores in her fiction the need of women for each other. The
protagonist of her short novel "The Bridegroom's Body" is a tough-seeming
woman who grows into a painful new awareness of her loneliness in a world
where women have no place. Now that her two children have gone off to school,
she lives alone with her husband on their country estate, where all of life takes
the shape of shooting and fishing, looking after the swannery, and worrying
about foot-rot among the sheep. She is tired of this masculine world: "The sound
of men, all day, all year without a break, the sound of men: a man serving at
the table, a man in the kitchen, as if it were not only the wild cold countryside
that drew men to it but as if all life itself and right to life were man's" (TSN,
149).[12] Yet, isolated in this environment, she has absorbed its values and become
estranged from femininity. Lady Glourie has cropped hair and "a big pair of
shoulders strong as a wood yoke set across her freckled neck" (TSN, 144); she
smokes Gold Flakes and wears "heavy brogues a man might have worn" (TSN,
148). She is proud that her daughter "had never liked dolls for a minute, mind
you, never once, never at any time" (TSN, 155). And when the swanherd's
wife approaches confinement, she sends reluctantly to London for a trained nurse,
"a woman-sort-of-thing," afraid they are "probably more trouble than they are
worth" (TSN, 147).

But as she awaits the nurse's arrival, her deep need for female companionship
becomes apparent. She walks the grounds engaged in imaginary conversations
with the woman she has never met, looking forward to the time when she might
speak to someone of the son and daughter who are gone, saying: "I never thought
I'd be able to have them off to school like this and live, but then it happens,
you can bear anything, anything, and there you are. . . . " (TSN, 154). She

imagines looking for the poems she had written as a schoolgirl and reading them to the other woman, or, she thinks, "if you were not too old we might be able to laugh out loud, uproariously, senselessly, stand shouting with laughter at something the way men scream with laughter together" (TSN, 157).

Miss Cafferty is a bitter disappointment—a delicate Irish girl in a green silk dress and high-heeled shoes. Lady Glourie gruffly warns her (as though the poor nurse had anything to do with it) that the swanherd's baby must be a boy, for the swannery is passed from father to son, and she snaps that Miss Cafferty ought to get better shoes for the country. But soon she recognizes the nurse's own isolation, alone in that universe of "locked, welded mates"—an outcast among the married couples and "the violently mated swans" (TSN, 173). In a "sudden and unforeseen vortex of compassion," she sees her as "A poor little Irishwoman with nowhere to go but to other people's houses in other people's countries, a living to make with other people's clothes on her back, a green dress somebody had handed down to her and pointed shoes too narrow for her feet with heels too high for the country she was in." Lady Glourie "saw her for an instant gentle as a young lamb to be nursed in the heart" (TSN, 173). Her tenderness for the young woman grows as Miss Cafferty's spirit, sensitivity, and intelligence emerge in her conversations with the Glouries. At the same time, Lord Glourie, seeing that his attentions to the young nurse are unreturned, grows bitter and suspicious. When Miss Cafferty tries to explain to them that sometimes in the night she feels a "desperation of the heart as well as of the flesh," that she then must get outdoors and walk no matter what the weather is, Lord Glourie becomes testy (TSN, 185). His small mind, with its narrow concept of women, can grasp only one explanation: she must be seeing the local farmer.

In the climactic scene, Lady Glourie battles the vicious old patriarch of the swans to retrieve the body of the young cob he had killed in a territorial battle, while Miss Cafferty looks on, paralyzed with terror. Then, overwhelmed with admiration for the other woman's strength and courage, she bursts out in a sudden confession of passion that startles Lady Glourie: "Let me say it! I came out to think about you here alone where there might be something left of you somebody hadn't touched—some place you were in the daytime—some mark of you on the ground. . . . I couldn't sleep in the room, I couldn't bear closing the door after I'd left you, just one more door closed between what you are and what I am" (TSN, 203). She had seen Lady Glourie's loneliness and her entrapment in an existence purged of women's tenderness and cries: "Don't you think I see you living in this place alone, alone the way you're alone in your bed at night, with butchers, murderers—men stalking every corner of the grounds by day and night? . . . Don't you think I fought them all off because of you, because I knew that fighting them was taking your side against them?" (TSN, 204).

When the swanherd and Lord Glourie discover them on the path, the two women are staring at each other in the moonlight, transfixed. Then "Lady Glourie looked down at the nightdress clinging to her own strange flesh and suddenly she began shaking with the cold'' (TSN, 205). The story ends there. Lady Glourie is shaken by the other woman's declaration of love and by this confrontation with the barrenness of her own existence. Yet, in that charged moment, we sense that the newly recognized possibility of connection between these women is their only hope of finding comfort and fulfillment in a cold, masculine world.[13]

The achievements of many women writers have been grossly underrated or ignored in both the popular mind and in literary curricula. In *Silences*, Tillie Olsen has noted and deplored the fact that "as gauged by what supposedly designates [achievement]: appearance in twentieth-century literature courses, required reading lists, textbooks, quality anthologies, the year's best, the decade's best, the fifty years' best, consideration by critics or in current review," only one out of every twelve writers represented is a woman.[14] Kay Boyle has been a classic victim of this silent treatment.

Harry T. Moore attributes the neglect to bad timing. Her first novel, *Plagued by the Nightingale*, appeared in 1931, financially a bad year, and that book, along with her other early novels—three out of four centering on the inner conflicts of a young American woman in Europe— "were hardly calculated to bewitch the liberal left," whose social biases dominated literary criticism in the thirties. Moore explains that although "her novels were implicitly critical of bourgeoise society," they did not belong to the "marching-marching, make-my-bread, in-dubious-battle hammer-and-anvil school that was establishing itself as the mood of the decade."[15]

Yet there may be another explanation as to why Kay Boyle's fiction was undervalued by those early critics and is not as widely known today as it ought to be. It appears as though her subject matter—often the trials of a woman groping for an identity—simply did not interest readers concerned with more "substantial" issues. The complaint that echoes in reviews of her work in the 1930s is that she "continues to spend herself on trivial material," in the words of one *New York Times* reviewer.[16] This critic (interestingly, a woman), was referring specifically to *My Next Bride* (1934), a heavily autobiographical novel in which the author explores the plight of a woman alone, trapped by poverty into a kind of serfhood in an art colony, who finally is rescued from a disastrous pregnancy, physical and emotional collapse, and thoughts of suicide through her friendship with another woman. Perhaps even more offensive is the assessment of the *Forum* reviewer who found the book "slight, charming, and pleasantly mad."[17]

It seems noteworthy, too, that while generally slighting the importance of her subject matter, critics consistently have praised Kay Boyle's "exquisite" and "delicate" style. By the end of the 1930s it appears that she had been pigeonholed as a "virtuoso." (A 1972 study revealed that in freshman composition textbooks, only a tiny percentage of the essays provided as models of logical argument or persuasive content was written by women. Yet female authors were more "generously" represented [at a proportion of twelve to seventeen percent] in essays illustrating stylistic techniques.)[18]

But it is surprising that Kay Boyle has not received more attention from those specifically committed to recognizing women's overlooked contributions to literature. Besides the fact that hers is the classic case of a woman writer whose reputation has been stunted by critical neglect or myopia, an adequate appreciation of her work is of prime significance to women's studies for a number of reasons.

One is that she deals so extensively and so acutely with female experiences. While her central thematic concern—the individual's search for meaning in a hostile, chaotic world—is hardly peculiar to women, her protagonists most often are women alone who find they must carve their own niches without help from fathers or husbands or lovers. Some of her works depict overt showdowns between the sexes, contrasting a woman's strength, flexibility, and expansiveness with a man's narrow and brittle egotism. Also, the relationships between female friends and enemies and lovers, between mothers and daughters and sisters, are accorded at least as much importance in her fiction as are male-female relationships.

Kay Boyle embraces what traditionally has been considered feminine, and treats woman seriously in her role of "the angel who must assume the physical responsibilities for daily living, for the maintenance of life" (as Tillie Olsen puts it in *Silences*)—the "essential angel" who has been doomed to invisibility in most of the literature written by men.[19] In an article entitled "Woman and the Literary Curriculum," Elaine Showalter has noted:

Women are estranged from their own experience and unable to perceive its shape and authenticity, in part because they do not see it mirrored and given resonance by literature. Instead they are expected to identify as readers with a masculine experience and perspective, which is presented as the human one.[20]

Kay Boyle does not devalue women's traditional activities and responsibilities by ignoring them. She employs her brilliant style to describe a character "slicing fresh petals of butter" and "onions' crystal hearts" into a smoking frying pan as well as to evoke stunning landscapes and to suggest complexities of character.[21] The skilled horsewoman in "Episode in the Life of an Ancestor" can stuff a trout with dexterity, and in such stories as "Fife's House" and "One Sunny Morning" the author depicts the habits of children with a liveliness and accuracy that reflect her experience as a mother of six. In an essay she wrote in 1951, having become a grandmother, she confesses that she personally enjoys housekeeping: "I can admit at last that I like polishing things, silverware, or the copper on stoves, or the metal of doorhandles."[22]

Kay Boyle recognizes no boundaries between the private and public spheres. She respects the significance of personal relationships and of the domestic responsibilites that have fallen to the majority of women, yet her vision is not confined to the drawing room or kitchen. It extends from there to encompass the entire social world, and she writes not only of individual loves, joys, struggles, and pains, but also of the rise of Nazism, the French Resistance, the Allied occupation of postwar Europe, and the Black Panther Party.

Finally, a reevaluation of Kay Boyle and her work is important because of her personal example. In her life as in her art, she has placed great value on relationships between women. Her many deep, enduring friendships with women—Caresse Crosby, Lola Ridge, Nancy Cunard, Janet Flanner, Ruby Cohn, Muriel Rukeyser, Jessica Mitford, and Joan Baez, Sr. among them—have played a central role in her life. She herself comes from a strong line of independent women. She is proud that her grandmother became one of the first women to work in Washington for the Federal government when she took a job in the land-grant office of the Department of the Interior in 1874. Her aunt, Nina Evans Allender, was a political cartoonist whose art produced during the suffrage campaign is now in the collection of the Library of Congress. Her drawing of Susan B. Anthony appeared on a 1936 postage stamp, and today the newsletter of the National Woman's Party often features her work. And her mother, Katherine Evans Boyle, had horrified Kay Boyle's conservative father and grandfather with her political activism and interest in *avant-garde* art. Mrs. Boyle had run for office on the Cincinnati school board on the Farmer-Labor ticket in 1919 (often reading passages by Gertrude Stein and James Joyce at workers' rallies), and she encouraged her teenaged daughter's early literary efforts—works with titles like "Arise, Ye Women" and "The Working Girl's Prayer." Years later, Katherine Evans Boyle and Nina Evans Allender were "honorary co-chairmen" of the World Woman's Party, founded in 1939 by Alice Paul to "raise the status of women throughout the world." In the 1960s Kay Boyle wrote: "Because of my mother, who gave me definitions, I knew what I was committed to in life; because of my father and grandfather, who offered statements instead of revelations, I knew what I was against" (BGT, 18).[23] Of her mother, she has said, "She prevailed, while the men of the family were effaced, line by line a little more every year" (BGT, 20).

In *Silences* Tillie Olsen notes that nearly all distinguished achievement in literature by women has come from the unmarried or at least childless, and she quotes a letter in which Sylvia Plath had complained that "a woman has to sacrifice all claims to femininity and family to be a writer."[24] Kay Boyle, for one, certainly would reject that claim. She has sacrificed neither. She is a striking, "feminine" woman by the most conventional standards (her trademark is wearing large white earrings), and she has had three husbands and raised eight children—six of her own and two from the marriage of her second husband, Laurence Vail, to Peggy Guggenheim. Her family life has been very important to her. In fact, she says today that she is saddened that her whole domestic life appears to have escaped the notice of most critics and explains: "I tell my students that they should follow the example of Bill Williams, who was 'a full-time poet, a full-time doctor, and a full-time father.' In a sense I believe my life as a woman was as a full-time writer, a full-time mother, and a full-time stepmother."[25] She believes that much of her writing reflects this uniquely feminine perspective:

I think that I have that kind of mother-complex—that protective thing which has really been the motivation of my writing. I wanted other people to know what was going on in life; at least, how this person could be helped, or this person would be understood, or how awful the English are, how we must do something about enlightening and illuminating their spirit, you see. The crusading spirit, I'd say.[26]

It is indicative of her profound respect for womanhood that she defines this motivating spirit as maternal. That "mother-complex" did not go unnoticed by others, either. In 1952, when Boyle's third husband, a diplomat, had come under fire for his wife's liberal leanings, fellow *New Yorker* writer Janet Flanner was called to testify for the defense at the McCarthy-style loyalty hearing. She explained a contribution Kay Boyle had made to a suspect organization by saying, "She is extremely maternal. Tell her a hard luck story and she digs into her pocket."[27] But however soft-hearted she may be, Kay Boyle is equally tough-minded. She has taken uncompromising stands in her writing, describing with unflinching clarity the basest, most violent scenes—and in her personal convictions, publicly demonstrating and even going to jail for her beliefs.

In an article entitled "The New Feminist Criticism," Annis Pratt calls on feminist critics to seek in literature a new norm that recognizes the "androgeneity" of both men and women—"that delightful interchange of the aggressive and the gentle, the adventurous and the nurturing faculties residing in each personality."[28] Both as a woman and as a woman writer, Kay Boyle has realized this fullness, complexity, and richness in human nature. In 1951 she wrote: "Now I would like to be a poet as well as a grandmother. But this is impossible. It has never been done."[29] She has done it.

NOTES

1. Katherine Anne Porter, "Example to the Young," *The New Republic*, 22 April 1931, p. 279.

2. Kay Boyle to Sandra Spanier, letter of 4 June 1981 and in conversation, New York, 16 May 1983. Portions of the poem for Beckett appear in Kay Boyle, *This is Not a Letter and Other Poems* (Los Angeles: Sun and Moon Press, 1985).

3. Kay Boyle, "Episode in the Life of an Ancestor," in *Fifty Stories* (Garden City, New York: Doubleday and Company, Inc., 1980). All subsequent page references designated *FS* are to this edition.

4. It should be noted that while Kay Boyle's work often advocates a woman's point of view, she objects to the term "feminist" when used to describe her life or work or the lives of the other very independent women in her family. In response to another discussion in which I used the term in reference to this particular story and to the lives of her mother, grandmother, aunt and herself, she wrote, "Why must we be labeled? You do not say we were Democrats or Republicans, or capitalists or socialists, so why feminists? I know you will understand my dislike of labels, so I urge you to allow us to be four women who were trying to work out their lives in at times difficult circumstances. ...We were unknowingly possibly forerunners of the feminist movement, but only because we wanted to live out in action our beliefs" (unpublished letter, Kay Boyle to

Sandra Spanier, 19 November 1984). In a letter of 26 November 1984 she wrote, "I truly believe it is the label that distresses me."

5. Kay Boyle, *His Human Majesty* (New York: Whittlesey House, McGraw-Hill, 1975), p. 119.

6. Kay Boyle, *The Underground Woman* (Garden City, New York: Doubleday, 1975), pp. 120–21.

7. Kay Boyle, *Generation Without Farewell* (New York: Alfred A. Knopf, 1960). Subsequent page references designated *GWF* are to this edition. In an essay written in 1940 for an American symposium on current matters concerning women, Virginia Woolf makes much the same point. She, too, sees war as the product of a society structured upon "the desire for aggression; the desire to dominate and enslave," a society in which women hold no positions of public influence but are objects of possession, confined to the private sphere. "If we could free ourselves from slavery we should free men from tyranny. Hitlers are bred by slaves," she writes. See Virginia Woolf, "Thoughts on Peace in an Air Raid," in *The Death of the Moth and Other Essays* (New York: Harcourt, Brace, Jovanovich, Inc., 1970), p. 245.

8. Dan Tooker and Roger Hofheins, eds., "Kay Boyle," in *Fiction! Interviews With Northern California Novelists* (New York and Los Altos: Harcourt Brace Jovanovich/ William Kaufman, 1976), p. 28.

9. Although she has not worked actively on the book in some time, she still considers it a work in progress. "I'm saving it for my *very* old age," she said in a telephone conversation with Sandra Spanier, 16 July 1982.

10. In light of recent studies arguing that the influences and responsibilities of fathers and mothers ought to be more balanced and that "maternal thinking" and the nurturing role should be assumed by men as well as by women and incorporated more generally in our culture, this position would be controversial among feminists. See Dorothy Dinnerstein, *The Mermaid and the Minotaur: Sexual Arrangements and Human Malaise* (New York: Harper & Row, 1976); Nancy Chodorow, *The Reproduction of Mothering* (Berkeley: University of California Press, 1978); and Sara Ruddick, "Maternal Thinking," *Feminist Studies*, 6 (Summer 1980), 342–67.

11. Barbaralee Diamonstein, ed., "Kay Boyle," in *Open Secrets: Ninety-four Women in Touch With Our Time* (New York: The Viking Press, 1972), p. 26.

12. Kay Boyle, "The Bridegroom's Body," in *Three Short Novels* (New York: Penguin Books, 1982). All subsequent page references designated TSN refer to this edition.

13. While in a letter of 20 June 1981 to Sandra Spanier the author concurs with this reading, she wishes to make clear that "there were no lesbian under-tones or over-tones" to the scene. It was "never for a moment" her intention to suggest that the story "offered a lesbian affair as a solution to the problems of the loneliness of the women involved," and, speaking also of the protagonist of her 1934 novel, *My Next Bride*, she adds, "I wanted to make a statement about the comfort and the solace that being understood brought to both Lady Glourie and Victoria—two instances in which love did not fail." Yet she is not optimistic that the "connection" that the two women experience at the end of "The Bridegroom's Body" will be more than transitory. In a letter of 27 July 1981, she writes:

Like Beckett, I do not like stories of success, but only stories of failure. I don't know what happened either to Lady Glourie or Miss Cafferty, but I'm pretty sure they didn't find salvation in each other. Miss Cafferty was probably shipped back to where she came from because of delinquency in performing her duty toward the swanherd's wife, and Lady Glourie probably went back to knitting the sweater for her son.

14. Tillie Olsen, *Silences* (New York: Dell Publishing Company, Inc., 1979), p. 24.

15. Harry T. Moore, in his introduction to Kay Boyle, *Plagued by the Nightingale* (1931; rpt. Carbondale and Edwardsville: Southern Illinois University Press, 1966), p. viii.

16. Edith H. Walton, review of *My Next Bride*, *The New York Times Book Review*, 11 November 1934, p. 6.

17. Review of *My Next Bride, Forum*, 92 (December 1934), ix.

18. See Jean S. Mullen, "Women Writers in Freshman Textbooks," *College English*, 34 (October 1972), 79–84.

19. Olsen, p. 34.

20. Elaine Showalter, "Women and the Literary Curriculum," *College English*, 32 (May 1971), 856.

21. Kay Boyle, *Year Before Last* (1932; rpt. Carbondale and Edwardsville: Southern Illinois University Press, 1969), p. 144.

22. "Kay Boyle," *New York Herald Tribune Book Review*, 7 October 1951, p. 28.

23. Kay Boyle and Robert McAlmon, *Being Geniuses Together 1920–1930*, rev. ed. (Garden City, New York: Doubleday, 1968; rpt. San Francisco: North Point Press, 1984). Subsequent page references designated *BGT* are to the 1984 edition.

24. Olsen, p. 30.

25. Kay Boyle to Sandra Spanier, letter of 28 April 1983. Her comment should not be mistaken as testimony for the viability of the Superwoman myth, however. She does not claim that one can juggle these roles without paying a price. She has described her career as a writer as being characterized by constant interruptions, and she believes that she could have written "much better books" had she not been so committed to her family life. But she is glad to have had the full family life, she says. (Kay Boyle in conversation with Sandra Spanier, New York, 17 May 1983.)

26. Charles F. Madden, ed., "Kay Boyle," in *Talks With Authors* (Carbondale and Edwardsville: Southern Illinois University Press, 1968), p. 231.

27. The transcript of Janet Flanner's testimony at the hearing is among the Kay Boyle Papers at the Morris Library, Southern Illinois University, Carbondale.

28. Annis Pratt, "The New Feminist Criticism," *College English*, 32 (May 1971), 878.

29. "Kay Boyle," *New York Herald Tribune Book Review*, 7 October 1951, p. 28.

9

Two Women: The Transformations

Alison Rieke

Djuna Barnes's 1936 novel *Nightwood* is marked by eccentricities which have tended to alienate readers: a revolutionary treatment of sexuality, a dense and difficult prose style, and a strongly pessimistic view of the human condition. Thus it has been all too easy for critics to dismiss *Nightwood* as a literary oddity or a brilliant piece of cult fiction.[1] Its startling content and style do make *Nightwood* difficult to place in one literary tradition, but, more importantly, they have obscured its direct line of descent from mainstream American fiction. In fact, *Nightwood* shares aspects of theme, plot and characterization with major nineteenth-century novels, and especially striking is Barnes's continuation of the tradition of light and dark heroines. Transformed versions of New England women, often as paired heroines, appear with regularity in the writings of Hawthorne, Stowe, Howells and James.[2] Nathaniel Hawthorne's *The Blithedale Romance* (1852) and Henry James's *The Bostonians* (1886) both depict paired heroines who belong to the sisterhood of American women known as New England types and who represent a recurring conflict caused by opposing traits in women. Critics have long been aware of the specific connections between these two novels,[3] but they have not yet seen in Barnes's *Nightwood* a subtly transformed modern version of the female characters in *The Blithedale Romance* and *The Bostonians*. Here, I will place these three novels beside each other, focusing on problems between the women and their differentiation as types.

The action of *Nightwood* occurs mainly from 1920–1927, a period when the famous night life of Paris drew expatriates and vagabonds to the Latin quarter of the city. *Nightwood* explores several kinds of sexual relationships, giving special attention to a neurotic and possessive union of two lesbians, both American women, Nora Flood and Robin Vote.[4] Robin becomes Nora's lover after a brief marriage to Felix Volkbein in which one son, Guido, was born. Stumbling upon Robin at the circus in New York, Nora takes her in after her disastrous marriage and attempts a complete possession of her. However, a rival, Jenny Petherbridge, eventually "steals" Robin from Nora. Everyone in the novel seems caught up in the struggle to possess or to understand Robin. She is the focus of Dr. Matthew O'Connor's conversations with both Felix Volkbein and Nora Flood. Neither character can understand why Robin left them, and they are now obsessed with her departure. Robin is a kind of "unmoved mover" who controls others through passive consent: "Felix, Nora, Jenny come to her, and for them she serves as object of a quest each has been waiting to complete."[5]

Robin's passive, but central position in *Nightwood* remains ambiguous. Nora tries to define Robin's weak, malleable character with her stronger, more willful personality, but she ultimately fails in her quest. What seems clear at the close of the novel, when Robin returns to Nora's home in upstate New York, is that both women have been unable to dissolve the painful relation. Nora fixedly relies on the memory of Robin's love, her emotional commitments continually reverting to the girl, and Robin's incessant wanderings from America to Europe and back again keep bringing her within the circle of Nora's destructive possessiveness.

As this brief plot summary should indicate, *Nightwood* duplicates the basic structure of relationships in *The Blithedale Romance* and *The Bostonians*. A pliant, passive woman becomes the object of desire for the central characters, both male and female, who revolve around her and try to win control of her. A tangle of interactions develops from this recurring element of plot—among them, a problematic and unresolved relation between two opposing types of American women, a dominating female whose original may be the Transcendentalist Margaret Fuller and a passive, mediumistic New England girl. Their contrasting personalities result in the weaker woman's temporary submission to the stronger and the possibility for unnatural possessiveness in the relation. The stronger woman exploits or mishandles the affections of a girl who is vulnerable to her, but she loses out in the end; the dominant woman finds herself powerless to bind and keep her "victim" because the more pliant girl allows for all kinds of domination. Hawthorne hints at these conflicts in the passionate and independent Zenobia and the mediumistic Priscilla; James develops them fully in the union of Olive Chancellor and Verena Tarrant; Barnes takes the conflict to its extreme by binding Nora Flood and Robin Vote to each other in a relation so troubled that it frightens even them. Both James and Barnes stress the psychological complexities of their encounter and the progressive degeneration of both women as types.

Hawthorne, James and Barnes connect their passive girls with the tradition of mesmerism, sleepwalking or mediumship.[6] They are "magnetized" by the words, thoughts and values of others, acting as receptors and reflectors of stronger personalities. While each novelist includes a character who may be literally identified as the mesmerist—Westervelt in *The Blithedale Romance*, Selah Tarrant in *The Bostonians*, and Dr. Matthew O'Connor in *Nightwood*— all the people who try to possess the passive maidens are metaphorically the mesmerist.[7]

Corrupted spiritualism is Hawthorne's emblem for the unnatural manipulation of his passive maiden. The Veiled Lady (Priscilla) "was a phenomenon in the mesmeric line; one of the earliest that had indicated the birth of a new science, or the revival of an old humbug" (BR, 5).[8] That Priscilla could be drawn into "the epoch of rapping spirits, and all the wonders that have followed in their train" makes Coverdale shudder with horror and disgust. He sees that the wizard Westervelt has the power to annihilate "the individual soul": "Human character was but soft wax in his hands" (BR, 198–199).

A downward spiral of moral value continues in James's portrayal of Verena Tarrant. She is used to transmit the debased, socialized spiritualism of the Boston reformers. The same eccentric spiritualism which creates an interest in mediumship and mesmerism draws a variety of odd types to the salons. James echoes Hawthorne when he describes the "humbug" of Boston reform: " 'they are all witches and wizards, mediums, and spirit-rappers, and roaring radicals' " (B, 6).[9]

James's portrait of the mesmerist's daughter builds upon the prototype in *The Blithedale Romance*, and her role as medium also results in her absorption by others. James has given her the gifts to rise to Olive Chancellor's projection of the "new woman," but through the course of the novel she is only passed from hand to hand, her blank personality written upon by each successive keeper. One naturally questions whether Verena is "a parrot or a genius" (B, 66): "The girl was now completely under [Olive's] influence . . . the touch of Olive's tone worked a spell . . . " (B, 141). Verena yields to authority which is a kind of magic, first her father's, then Olive's, then Basil Ransom's.[10]

The odd conglomeration of "mediums, communists, and vegetarians" that surrounds Verena Tarrant undercuts the girl's spirituality; James's medium has stepped down from the high plane occupied by Priscilla, who at times seems so spiritually insubstantial as to be utterly transparent (BR, 186–188). Priscilla's spiritualism, which is her moral purity, is convincingly spiritual. But in *The Bostonians* is sufficient evidence that Verena's "gift" of prophecy is only a trade ingrained in her from sitting "on the knees of somnambulists" and "trance-speakers" in childhood (B, 85).

The ease with which Verena yields confuses her role as a positive or redemptive force in the novel, despite her obvious attractiveness. Her over-flexible personality perplexes Olive when Basil Ransom begins to exert an influence. Olive has chosen Verena to redeem the world for women and has every desire to imagine Verena as perfect, but she suspects that something is lacking in the pliant girl. The influence of Selah Tarrant, "a moralist without moral sense" (B, 111), has, in fact, molded Verena, and "the blood of the lecture-going, night-walking Tarrants did distinctly flow in her veins . . . "(B, 301).

Djuna Barnes also places her characters in the milieu of social radicalism and thus recalls both Hawthorne and James. In *Nightwood* is a direct echo of the odd world of the salon: Nora Flood keeps "the strangest 'salon' in America" (N, 50), and "of all that ranting, roaring crew, she alone stood out" (N, 50).[11]

Nora Flood is the "presiding genius" of a " 'paupers' salon for poets, radicals, beggars, artists, and people in love; for Catholics, Protestants, Brahmins, dabblers in black magic and medicine" (N, 50). Barnes reinforces *Nightwood*'s connections with the earlier novels: "At these incredible meetings one felt that early American history was being re-enacted. . . . Puritan feet, long upright in the grave, striking the earth again, walking up and out of their custom; the calk of prayers thrust in the heart" (N, 51).

When Barnes introduces her passive heroine, Robin Vote, the shabby transvestite Matthew O'Connor enters the scene to play the role of the arch-magician or mesmerist. O'Connor is not a "licensed practitioner," rather he performs a crude and false "medical" awakening of the "born somnambule" (N, 35). He makes "the movements common to the 'dumbfounder,' or man of magic; the gestures of one who, in preparing the audience for a miracle, must pretend that there is nothing to hide . . . while in reality the most flagrant part of the hoax is being prepared" (N, 35–36). The self-professed charlatan is as decadent as Hawthorne's Westervelt whose "delusive show of spirituality" (BR, 200) repulses Coverdale. He attempts to disguise his sleazy appearance with the cosmetics on Robin's dressing table; but the "sudden embellishment" cannot hide that he represents the "whole fabric of magic" beginning to "decompose" (N, 36). Neither can James's magician convince his audience: Selah Tarrant has not the "magnetism" to conceal the impression he belongs to a "company of mountebanks" (B, 55).

Barnes's meticulously wrought description of Robin Vote in her room invites comparisons with the stages, music and lecture halls, and promoters of *The Blithedale Romance* and *The Bostonians*:

Like a painting by the *douanier* Rousseau, she seemed to lie in a jungle trapped in a drawing room . . . thrown in among the carnivorous flowers as their ration; the set, the property of an unseen *dompteur*, half lord, half promoter, over which one expects to hear the strains of an orchestra of wood-winds render a serenade which will popularize the wilderness. (N, 35)

In this setting, Matthew O'Connor awakens Robin from her faint, and thus she begins her trance-like wanderings through the novel.

Physically, Robin fits the prototype of the fair-haired New England girl. She is fair, tall and unhealthy in appearance, just as Hawthorne's Priscilla "is one of those delicate nervous young creatures" (BR, 95) and as James's Verena looks "anemic . . . certainly very pale, white as women are who have that shade of red hair; they look as if their blood had gone into it" (BR, 59). These seemingly underfed girls are beautiful in a rare way. As Verena's rarity is her genius, Robin Vote's strange beauty initially draws people to her. She appears to possess the qualities of innocence and formlessness; Matthew O'Connor describes her: " 'Yes, oh, God, Robin was beautiful . . . sort of fluid blue under her skin, as if the hide of time had been stripped from her, and with it, all transactions with

knowledge . . . a face that will age only under the blows of perpetual childhood' ''
(N, 134).

Priscilla, Verena and Robin are all captured at a point in life somewhere
between childhood and maturity. Their retention of childlike innocence encour-
ages others to vindicate them of moral responsibility, but their contact with
something depraved taints them. Robin, in fact, has lost her innocence entirely,
and she tries to relocate it by shedding the conscious power of choice. As she
walks about in a daze, she conveys '' 'a fearful sort of primitive innocence' ''
(N, 117). Like the passive Verena, Robin has little capacity for moral distinctions
or taste. Felix Volkbein ''was surprised that often [Robin's] taste, turning from
an appreciation of the excellent, would also include the cheaper and debased
. . . ''(N, 42). Nora Flood forms a similar impression when Robin sings the
strange, incomprehensible songs which are ''debased and haunting,'' songs in
which Robin ''gave back an echo of her unknown life more nearly tuned to its
origin'' (N, 57). Robin also comes out of the tradition of the *improvisatrice*,
another ''American version of the type, a New England Corinna'' (B, 270).[12]
She utters incoherent sounds, not exactly the Sibylline speech of Verena who
''began incoherently, almost inaudible, as if she were talking in a dream'' (B,
60) the ''strange, sweet, crude, absurd, enchanting improvisation'' (B, 61).
Robin Vote's ''snatches of harmony as tell-tale as the possessions of a traveler
from a foreign land; songs like a practiced whore who turns away from no one
but the one who loves her'' (N, 57) distress Nora, tugging on her emotions and
evoking her fears about Robin's unknown past. Nora is ''sometimes unable to
endure the melody'' (N, 57). The effect these improvisations have on Nora
recalls *The Bostonians*: ''. . . if you were to see Miss Chancellor when Verena
rises to eloquence. It's as if the chords were strung across her own heart; she
seems to vibrate, to echo with every word'' (B, 223).

Like Verena and Priscilla, Robin attracts people who try to possess and shape
her ''vacuous'' consciousness.[13] The most significant test of her fidelity is forced
upon her by a stronger woman, and as in *The Bostonians*, a rival separates her
from this demanding ''owner.'' But first, Felix Volkbein, a Jew of Italian descent,
chooses Robin to be his wife: ''When he asked her to marry him . . . he was
taken aback to find himself accepted, as if Robin's life held no volition for
refusal'' (N, 42–43). Robin becomes the tool of a ''destiny for which he had
chosen her . . . '' (N, 45). But after the marriage ends, Felix spends countless
hours trying to understand Robin's ''acquiescence''; he had imposed his life
upon her as ''a condition of being that she had not, at that time, even chosen,
but a fluid sort of possession . . . '' (N, 112). Similarly, it is Robin's ''fluidity''
which allows Nora Flood to possess her temporarily, for ''in Robin there was
this tragic longing to be kept, knowing herself astray'' (N, 58). Matthew O'Connor openly refers to Nora's ''ownership'' of Robin. The struggle for Robin's
vague attention is similar to the struggle over the ''submissive'' Verena Tarrant
who likes to be ''overborne'' (B, 337). These women's worth is defined by the
intensity of the others' desire to possess them.

Important here are the spiritual and moral demands Nora imposes on the girl she supposedly loves. In their troubled encounter, the aspirations of Nora Flood pressure Robin in the same way that Olive stifled Verena. Nora has been "hunting" an "uninhabited angel" (N, 148), and Robin's pliant mind, she thinks, can contain it. Robin retaliates against Nora's moral fixation by becoming promiscuous, and Matthew O'Connor understands and explains why a "good woman" drives away, by too rigorous possession, the girl she wants to "save": Robin "Saw in [Nora] that fearful eye that would make her a target forever." (N, 148).

In *Nightwood*, we glimpse the tortured mind of a woman who cannot determine why she has no identity other than that imposed on her by other people. The successive shadows of personalities, particularly Nora Flood's blackened conscience, are the ghosts who haunt the empty, choiceless, vacuous space that is Robin's mind. Her wandering represents not only her drive to find her innocence, but also to find "herself." This need is frustrated by the others' quests to possess her. Nora knows Robin is seeking a personality, for she sees Robin's growing resentment of possessiveness: " 'She would kill the world to get at herself if the world were in the way, and it *is* in the way. A shadow was falling on her— mine—and it was driving her out of her wits' " (N, 155).

Hawthorne, James and Barnes question whether their passive maidens can recover themselves after so many have used them, and each author comes to a different conclusion. Only Hawthorne allows us to believe completely in Priscilla's assaulted, but undamaged purity: ". . . she had kept . . . her virgin reserve and sanctity of soul, throughout it all" (BR, 203). Verena Tarrant has been bought, sold, used, seduced, and manipulated, but James's satire diminishes the power of her exploiters. Barnes's passive heroine is also used, but she falls into irrevocable degradation at the close of *Nightwood*. Barnes's continuous play upon the word "down" shows that Robin is indeed a "fallen woman"—she has had too much of " 'sensuous communion with unclean spirits' " (N, 168). The hope that Nora might save her is absurd when, in an abandoned church on Nora's property, Robin becomes an animal by mimicry, mediumship or "animal magnetism." She absorbs the consciousness of a beast, and descends to the lowest point yet reached in the novel, crawling, scratching and barking with hysterical laughter at Nora's dog. Appropriately titled "The Possessed," this final chapter of *Nightwood* predicts no hope for release from the series of haunting possessions.

The compliant women in all three novels offer themselves up as victims because they lack will power or moral strength, and they have no particular impulse for active resistance. Priscilla's curious submission disturbs Coverdale (BR, 171); she is "the gentle parasite, the soft reflection of a more powerful existence" (BR, 123). Verena Tarrant repeatedly asserts that her trance-speech is guided by other, more powerful forces: " 'Oh, it isn't me, you know; it's something outside!' " (B, 80). Likewise, Robin Vote's life "held no volition for refusal" (N, 43). Because domination shapes their lives, these women rise and fall according to personal interactions. This is their flaw and the source of their failures, impotence and precarious innocence.

In taking the stronger women back to their origins, it is useful to examine the impact of Emersonian self-culture on New England women, particularly through Margaret Fuller's cult of friendship. In *The New England Girl*, John Paul Eakin argues that the heroines of Hawthorne and James owe much "to Fuller as an Emersonian seeker after self-culture . . . Hers was a drama of the inner life, of thwarted self-development . . . ."[14] Barnes's reforming woman also inherits the demanding task of measuring up to an ideal of self-culture, a striving for selfhood that is doomed to failure.

The ideal of self-culture in women is linked to a belief in their redemptive powers and their ability to cultivate their natural gifts. Margaret Fuller's life, of course, became a paradigm of this quest when, during her famous Conversations, she established herself as a peerless teacher, friend and role model for women. Using her superior learning and firm will power, she helped to draw out the gifts—the "genius"—of other women.[15] But Fuller may have slipped into the role of the too much adored priestess despite her own wariness of master-disciple relationships.[16] Fuller believed her romantic cult of friendship was based upon "a profound conviction of her mind in the individuality of every human being" (*Mem*. I, 65).[17] And James Freeman Clarke also observed of her:

Margaret possessed, in a greater degree than any person I ever knew, the power of so magnetizing others, when she wished, by the power of her mind, that they would lay open to her all the secrets of their nature. (*Mem. I,65*)

Fuller's acceptance of Emerson's code, "the mind is its own place" (*Mem*. I, 195) in some way contradicted the passionate "overstrained affections" in her circle. These friendships were tinged with "a force more distinctly personal in nature than the disinterested moral suasion which was her declared intention."[18] Something like this contradiction recurs in *The Blithedale Romance*, *The Bostonians* and *Nightwood* when the assertive women use their strength to manipulate the weaker friend rather than encourage her growth and individuality. While Fuller's female friendships may not be a direct source for these portraits, they are exemplary. In the relation, a strong woman attempts to save a weaker girl from personal inconsistences and the tendency to submit. The stronger woman wants to absorb the compliant female precisely because of the brilliancy of her gifts and her failure to cultivate them. When the friendships are misused, they have debilitating effects on both women.

Fuller's reforming spirit, then, is fictionally reinterpreted as a negative force when it seeks to alter the character of another individual. Ironically, Hawthorne, James and Barnes construct reforming, strong characters for whom true reform is impossible, either in themselves or the people they try to influence. Looking for the reasons behind this failure, all three novelists point an indicting finger at the overbearing Puritanism looming in the background of the various nine-

teenth-century reform movements, including the women's movement. The dog-
matism and rigidity of the earlier Puritans reasserts itself in the impassioned
crusaders for change and undercuts any hope for Emersonian self-culture. In
The Blithedale Romance, Hollingsworth, more than Zenobia, confuses his aims
for reform with his oppressive insistence that he get his way: in Hollingsworth
was "all that an artist could desire for the grim portrait of a Puritan magistrate
. . . " (BR, 214). However, James and Barnes relocate and develop this trait in
their strong heroines who are stiflingly rigid and moralistic and who dictate the
lives of others. Though Olive Chancellor and Nora Flood assume the rhetoric
or reform, they too revert to earlier Puritan values running counter to self-culture.

In *The Bostonians*, James concentrates the problem in a female friendship
where one woman needs to "own" another, demand complete devotion from
her and keep her isolated from other influences. Olive Chancellor's noble aims
for friendship degenerate into neuroticism, and her relation with Verena becomes
perversely possessive. Allusions to "ownership" of Verena run throughout the
novel; in fact, Olive initially buys the girl from her father. Olive "admitted that
she was jealous, that she didn't wish to think of the girl's belonging to any one
but herself" (B, 111), and she "wants to keep her in the single sisterhood; to
keep her, above all, for herself" (B, 265).

Olive convinces Verena to adore her for a time, demanding that Verena
corroborate her projection of the "new ideal woman." Olive's ability to "make-
over" Verena's personality in her own image stands as the test of a self-created
standard. "Magnetizing" Verena into an example of her affirmed identity, Olive
stakes the strength and truth of this projection upon the passive girl's success at
"staging" it, both by living it and by making the public recognize it in performance and speeches. Olive sees in Verena's gift of speech the possibility of
fulfilling a role that a reclusive Puritan, who is frequently on the verge of hysteria,
can never totally enact.

Like James, Djuna Barnes brings Puritanism to the surface of her characterization of a dominant woman with the passion for reform. Nora Flood "was the
only woman of the last century who could go up a hill with the Seventh Day
Adventists and confound the seventh day—with a muscle in her heart so passionate that she made the seventh day immediate" (N, 52). Nora, like Zenobia
and Olive, is "one of those deviations by which man thinks to reconstruct
himself" (N, 53). She talks incessantly of the end of the world, the resurrection
and the new day. That Nora represents a millennial sect cannot be accidental;
her quest duplicates the social revisionism of the earlier women who use the
language of renewal to describe the supersession of severe Calvinist law with
"gospel of woman's redemptive love."[19] For the deluded Olive Chancellor of
The Bostonians, Verena's enactment of the role of the "new woman" embodies
the beginning of a reformed age: "Olive thinks she's born to regenerate the
world" (B, 204). But the language of catastrophe controls *Nightwood*, for it is
now 1920 and the great social or religious apocalypse has not yet occurred.
Hence, Robin Vote represents "a catastrophe that had yet no beginning" (N,
48).

In Nora Flood we see a further degeneration of self-culture. Like Olive Chancellor, she struggles to absorb a girl's formless personality into her own. The language of possession, as we might expect, governs Nora's conception of the relationship. Robin accepts Nora's design "as if she were aware, without conscious knowledge, that she belonged to Nora, and that if Nora did not make it permanent by her own strength, she would forget" (N, 55). Barnes, like Hawthorne and James, uses the metaphor of mesmerism to describe Nora's magnetism of Robin: Nora's "mind became so transfixed that by the agency of her fear, Robin seemed enormous and polarized, all catastrophes ran toward her, the magnetized predicament" (N, 56). Nora projects her own internal dilemma onto Robin: first, Robin represents "a sensation of evil, complete and dismembering . . . " (N, 64) because she repeatedly debases herself; second, Nora projects onto the girl an image of the "saved" identity exactly as Olive had done with Verena, exaggerating the girl's importance until she clings to her with frantic assertion. Matthew O'Connor observes, "You've made her a legend and set before her head the Eternal Light, and you'll keep to it . . . " (N, 125). Nora admits that Robin "turned bitter because I made her fate colossal" (N, 156).

When Robin begins to wander away, Nora gradually realizes that this "love" has been the product of self-definition and self-assertion: " 'She is myself. What am I to do?' " (N, 127); and " 'I thought I loved her for her sake, and I found it was for my own' " (N, 151); and " 'Matthew,' she said, 'have you ever loved someone and it became yourself?' " (N, 152). When this possession of Robin fails, Nora inevitably feels "as an amputated hand [that] cannot be disowned because it is experiencing a futurity, of which the victim is its forbear, so Robin was an amputation that Nora could not renounce" (N, 59). Barnes allows Nora to glimpse the nature of her problem, but this does not alleviate the agony of her lover's departure. James's version of the strained gradual separation of Olive and Verena finds its duplication in *Nightwood*, and Nora is as dispossessed of "herself" with the loss of Robin as Olive was with the loss of Verena.

In *Nightwood*, Djuna Barnes constructs a fascinating web of imagery around these two women that connects them to their literary past and the original problem of the female self. This problem may only be a result of the radical splitting of traits —strong/weak, dominant/passive—which has now become traditional. But Djuna Barnes's paired heroines, separately or together, have come no closer to reconstructing the female self than their predecessors, and they carry the burden of that goal right out of nineteenth-century American fiction. Instead, the women have degenerated as types. Martyrdom and misery are the fate of Nora Flood. The fate of her weaker counterpart is a crippling passivity which renders her unable to function effectively in the world.

NOTES

1. For example, Alan Williamson's remark that "Djuna Barnes, as a lesser member of the cluster of Lost Generation writers, has suffered from becoming the idol of an avant-garde cult while remaining unknown to the general public and deprecated by critics"

summarizes *Nightwood's* reception. See "The Divided Image: The Quest for Identity in the Works of Djuna Barnes," *Critique: Studies in Modern Fiction*, 7 (1964), p. 58.

2. John Paul Eakin, in *The New England Girl: Cultural Ideals in Hawthorne, Stowe, Howells and James* (Athens: The University of Georgia Press, 1976), explores in depth the fascination with female characters during the period: what emerged as "the religion of womanhood . . . is one of the most characteristic phenomena of nineteenth-century American novels. The drive toward a literature of this kind, spurred by the demand for women's rights, seems to have sprung from the religious stirrings of the period, the outbreak of millenarian fever in the years before the Civil war, and the wave of mind-science and spiritualism that followed later on" (p. 5). For further discussion of women in American fiction, see Nina Auerbach's chapter on *The Bostonians* in *Communities of Women: An Idea in Fiction* (Cambridge, Mass.: Harvard University Press, 1978); and Ernest Earnest, *The American Eve in Fact and Fiction, 1775–1914* (Urbana: University of Illinois Press, 1974).

3. See Marius Bewley, "James's Debt to Hawthorne (I): *The Blithedale Romance* and *The Bostonians*," *Scrutiny*, 16 (1949), 178–195, reprinted in *The Complex Fate* (New York: Grove Press), pp. 11–30; Robert Emmet Long, "Transformations: *The Blithedale Romance* to Howells and James," *American Literature*, 47 (January 1976), 552–571; Robert Emmet Long, "The Society and the Masks: *The Blithedale Romance* and *The Bostonians*," *Nineteenth-Century Fiction*, 19 (1964), 105–122; Martha Banta, *Henry James and the Occult: The Great Extension* (Bloomington: Indiana University Press, 1972), pp. 90–100; and Maria M. Tatar, *Spellbound: Studies on Mesmerism and Literature* (Princeton, New Jersey: Princeton University Press, 1978), pp. 233–243.

4. James's portrayal of neurotic friendship aligns easily with Barnes's characterizations for the reason bluntly stated by Irving Howe in his introduction to *The Bostonians* (New York: Random House, 1956), xxii–xxiii: Olive is a lesbian. Charles R. Anderson in "James's Portrait of the Southerner," *American Literature*, 27 (1955), 310, also identifies Olive as an "incipient Lesbian." Other critics are not completely convinced that Olive's motivation is a "private sexual captivation of Verena" (Auerbach, *Communities of Women*, p. 140).

5. Dell Hymes, "Journey to the End of Night," *Folio*, 18 (February 1953), 44.

6. For excellent studies of mesmerism and the literary tradition, see Tatar, *Spellbound: Studies on Mesmerism and Literature*, and Howard Kerr, *Mediums, and Spirit-Rappers, and Roaring Radicals: Spiritualism in American Literature, 1850–1900* (Urbana: University of Illinois Press, 1972).

7. Tatar discusses the "masters and slaves" in Hawthorne's fiction, pp. 200–229.

8. Nathaniel Hawthorne, *The Blithedale Romance*, Vol. III, *The Centenary Edition of the Works of Nathaniel Hawthorne* (Columbus: Ohio State University Press, 1964). All parenthetical references with the abbreviation BR are from this edition.

9. Henry James, *The Bostonians* (New York: Random House, 1956). All parenthetical references with the abbreviation B are from this edition.

10. For an interesting analysis of Verena's various possessors' "spells," see Susan Wolstenholme, "Possession and Personality: Spiritualism in *The Bostonians*," *American Literature*, 49 (January 1978), 580–591.

11. Djuna Barnes, *Nightwood* (New York: New Directions, 1961). All parenthetical references with the abbreviation N are from this edition.

12. Perry Miller in *Margaret Fuller: American Romantic*, ed. Perry Miller (Ithaca,

N.Y.: Cornell University Press, 1963), pp. xix-xxviii, discusses the origin of the New England Corinna. See also Eakin, pp. 49–51.

13. Wolstenholme's opinion that "the human mind, as represented by Verena's in the novel, is utterly vacuous . . . '' (p. 589) should also apply to Priscilla and Robin in their respective novels.

14. Eakin, p. 50.

15. See essentially the chapter on Fuller's Conversations in Mason Wade, *Margaret Fuller: Whetstone of Genius* (New York: The Viking Press, 1940), pp. 68–81.

16. Eakin, pp. 54–57, remarks on this aspect of Fuller.

17. Margaret Fuller Ossoli, *Memoirs*, 2 vols., (Boston: Phillips, Sampson and Company, 1852). All parenthetical references with the abbreviation *Mem.* are from this edition.

18. Eakin, p. 55.

19. Eakin, p. 72.

10

Effects of Urbanization in the Novels of Christiane Rochefort

Anne D. Cordero

Future sociologists with an interest in the French society of the second half of the twentieth century will find a wealth of material in Christiane Rochefort's novels, especially in *Les Petits Enfants du siècle (Josyane and the Welfare), Printemps au parking*, and *Les Stances à Sophie (Cats Don't Care for Money)*.

It is not an entire society that forms the subject of Rochefort's rather satirical, yet humorous novels, but the lower bourgeois and the blue-collar working classes that live for the most part in the narrowly confined world of the *grands ensembles*, the French equivalent of public housing projects, big apartment blocks of steel and concrete, forming new cities all over France. Leftist intellectuals and anarchists also find a place in several of her novels. Historical events are absent, as are attempts to place the institutions that the author takes as the target of her implied social criticism into a political or economic context that would allow the apparent absurdities of the system to be viewed in a more subjective perspective.

In an interview the author once remarked: "I sadly realize the oppressive power of modern urbanism."[1] Christiane Rochefort is one of the first French writers to have captured the atmosphere of the new cities that have sprung up on the periphery of Paris and all other big cities in France. The French housing authorities decided to build these huge structures to alleviate the critical housing shortage that had been plaguing France since World War II. Slum dwellers would finally be able to find the airy and spacious apartment, the modern conveniences in a green, park-like setting that they had so long been dreaming of. But their dreams most often turned into nightmares. The new cities that have emerged are inhabited by families uprooted from their homes in the old cities. Even though they may have been slums, they were nevertheless home to them, with neighbors and local traditions. In *Printemps au parking* the author makes a case for the

13th Paris district, formerly a blue-collar workers' section, now populated with rich people who pay taxes. The 13th district no longer represents a scandal to Paris real estate, but brings in money for the city, instead of proletarian revolutions.[2]

Urban renewal has thus political implications for Christiane Rochefort who was born in a Paris working-class district herself. The specific renovation projects she refers to in her novels are in her view politically motivated. By destroying old city neighborhoods and replacing them with expensive modern office and apartment buildings that only the affluent class can afford, the then governing conservative parties effectively changed the voting patterns in some Paris districts which traditionally had been leftist oriented. Rochefort's political views clashed with the then dominant conservative policies of the French government and of the city of Paris known to favor the privileged classes. She argues that the working classes in being displaced have lost a place which is rightfully theirs. Relocation, in the author's opinion is thus linked to exile and even "deportation."[3] Christophe, the young hero of *Printemps au parking*, who towards the conclusion of the novel finds his vocation as an anarchist, intends to "release the deported from the camps" and to "put them back in their rightful place: in the heart of the inner city, around the Halles, the marketplace, and among the bistros."[4]

Efforts to provide housing for the working classes with a view to improving their lives have failed dismally. The experience has shown that architecture, and more specifically our urban environment, imposes a certain lifestyle and a way of thinking and feeling. This study intends to examine how Christiane Rochefort presents the problems of urbanization in her novels, and how she focuses her concerns on the effects that modern society in general and large housing projects in particular have on the lives of families, especially as they affect women and children.

The author proceeds by portraying salient features of contemporary French society through the experiences of adolescents and women. Her criticism bears mostly on the social institutions and technological inventions that rob modern people of dignity and soul. Gigantic steel and concrete housing projects of the new cities with their dehumanizing effect on the inhabitants arouse Rochefort's anger and often biting, yet humorous, and at times even lyrical satire. In *Les Petits Enfants du siècle* and *Printemps au parking* children and adolescents are the author's protagonists. They are also her favorite characters, not because they are model children, but because they are the exemplary victims of an oppressive society. They often suffer most in a world where human beings are reduced to the size of insects, overpowered by high-rise structures and where human qualities have been replaced by the efficiency of modern machines.

Through the experiences of her characters Christiane Rochefort shows that the inhabitants of the big housing projects, in addition to all their other problems, are faced with isolation, uniformity, boredom and an ensuing neurosis. At the heart of the matter lies the fact that their living quarters are anonymous, each

building being exactly like the next one. The new structures are no longer built
on a human scale. Rather the human being feels dwarfed by their dimensions.
Josyane, adolescent heroine and narrator in *Les Petits Enfants du siècle* describes
the high-rise buildings across from her apartment in the following words: "They
were big, beautiful and terrible. When I went past them, real close, I thought
they would fall on top of me. Everyone looked minuscule . . . People swarmed
like insects beneath the street lights."[5] A cold wind seems to blow constantly
through the corridors between the buildings. Rochefort compares it to the wind
sweeping Colorado's canyons, but instead of coyotes howling one hears loud-
speakers telling us how to have white teeth, shiny hair, how to be beautiful,
happy and healthy.

The few green areas and freshly planted tender trees are mistreated by children.
When Josyane makes the observation that the boys in the yard are destroying
the trees, her mother replies that this way they will keep out of trouble (*Les
Petits*, p. 30). Rochefort, with much irony, knows how to make us see that
adults often do not face reality.

The immediate reality of Josyane's life is a large, growing family, and walls
of concrete in a big housing project. The irony of the narrative only seems to
hide the tears. On the other hand, the carefully studied monotony of the narrator's
tone conveys perfectly the all-pervasive boredom and monotony that constitutes
the decor of the young girl's existence.

As the oldest child of the family Josyane has to assume ever greater responsibilities with the birth of each sibling. If domestic tasks can be performed within
a loving family relationship, some emotional satisfaction may be gained from
them. But Josyane's parents, alienated by materialistic aspirations characteristic
of the consumer society, are never shown expressing feelings of love, tenderness
or joy. Their waking hours are absorbed by the tasks of providing the necessities
for an ever-growing family. They spend their days blaming each other for life's
drudgery while being surrounded by children who detest each other. Constant
bickering fills the evenings spent in front of the television set. The parents' lack
of love and concern for each other is noticeable also in the relationship with
their children. Rochefort comments on the vacant stare, the expressionless faces
of children playing in the courtyard. In school Josyane is evaluated as "indifferent
to praise as well as to punishment" (*Les Petits*, p. 25). In fact, she is so starved
for affection that she is moved to tears when her friend Guido takes her hand.

Mothers often figure among the negative characters in Rochefort's novels. (*Le
Repos du guerrier, Les Stances à Sophie, Les Petits Enfants du siècle*). In general
the author depicts them as incapable of making decisions on their own, of thinking
only in terms that society dictates to them. Josyane's mother, like most other
mothers in the new *cité*, fits this general frame. She is made of pure matter:
nothing spiritual or intellectual could touch her. If she once was curious, sharp
and eager to learn, she no longer exhibits a trace of these qualities. They have
been buried under a mountain of domesticity. In addition Josyane's mother is
characterized by fatigue and indifference. Like a mother cat she cares only for

the child she is carrying at the moment or still nursing. As soon as her children are capable of fending for themselves, she no longer shows any interest in them. Josyane's scholastic achievements go unnoticed as do her precocious sexual activities. When the oldest son Patrick leaves for a correctional institution, the mother is happy to have his bed for the next baby. She admires the feats of modern psychology when the doctor commits her mentally retarded daughter Catherine to the asylum. The child is sent off for life after a thirty minute medical examination. Another child, Nicolas, thought to be mute because he could not talk at two and a half years of age, barely escapes the asylum. "At least," the mother comments, "he won't bother us with his blabber." (*Les Petits*, p. 35). The indifference shown to children breeds indifference in turn. Josyane seems to carry out her routine tasks with the same attitude of indifference towards her siblings as her mother. With the exception of Nicolas, her youngest brother who displays some inquisitiveness, she finds them "mean and ugly." On rare occasions indifference gives way to resentment, pent-up anger and scorn. She describes her family in the following terms: "Grass no longer grows where they've passed, as we were told in school about Attila, king of the Huns." (*Les Petits*, p. 48).

One may wonder whether the young narrator will eventually know the same fate as her mother. One scene in the novel seems to foreshadow Josyane's future: Looking at a photo of her mother as a young bride with long hair and a smile, so much like the girls Josyane sees in the housing projects on the scooters of their boyfriends, Josyane cannot imagine that the lovely person on the photo is her mother whom she knows only as worn-out and fatigued from childbirth. At the end of the novel Josyane is a reflection of the girl on the photo. She is about to marry a man whom she believes she loves; already pregnant with his child she is looking for housing in another large project, Sarcelles. Although Josyane is bright, aware of her situation, and possessing acute insight, conditions in her narrow dehumanized world will not allow her to break away. For as she herself states in a conversation with her friend Ethel who had commented on the failure of the parents in the *cité* to educate their children, ". . . how could they they don't have any [education] themselves they know nothing and they don't care." (*Les Petits*, p. 114). The circle is closed. Rochefort could not have chosen a more effective conclusion. Despite its humorous style the novel is a cry of despair, especially over the treatment of the young in our society. In both novels, *Les Petits Enfants du siècle* and *Printemps au parking* she shows that to "civilize" children means to take away their original creativity, their uniqueness in order to make them fit the mold of accepted behavior. For those who do not conform to the norm, oppression takes subtle forms, such as misguided parental authority and vocational counseling, or more brutal forms, such as medication (Céline in *Les Stances à Sophie*), and repressive institutions. The very morning the doctor sent Catherine to a life of neglect and oblivion in an asylum, he had already dispatched four other children to the "dump" as Josyane calls it. Rehabilitation would be too costly the doctor claims. After all, human life does not rank very high. It can easily be replaced. Patrick, Josyane's oldest brother who had been warned repeatedly by his parents that he would be sent to a correctional institution is arrested for auto theft towards the end of the novel.

A special target of Rochefort's criticism is the so-called vocational counseling. Christophe in *Printemps au parking* clearly refuses life in a housing project. Finding himself in the paradoxical situation of having to choose a career while being completely uninformed about the choices open to him, he runs away from home. According to him, vocational counseling means to choose among "poux, puces ou punaises." (lice, flees or bedbugs) (*Printemps*, p. 36). In other words, the positions that are offered to the children of the poor are so depressing that it is easier for them to become dropouts of society. The system operates in such a way as to reinforce the segregation of social classes in the big housing projects. "How does one become intelligent?" Christophe asks. The not surprising answer is: "by associating with intelligent people." (*Printemps*, p. 60). Rochefort seems to make the point that most adolescents in the housing projects associate only with friends of the same background. They therefore do not have the chance to break out of their social class. They are never introduced to all the possibilities for personal or professional growth. Vocational guidance counseling does not sufficiently enlighten them; on the contrary, it tries to steer them into menial, non-skilled professions. Josyane thinks that there was something she would never have "because I did not know what it was." (*Les Petits*, p. 142). Not having access to information that would allow her a deliberate choice commensurate with her aptitudes, she resigns herself to a mediocre destiny. Thus, in the new cities without a past, the future also seems blocked for Josyane. While waiting for marriage which seems the only way out, her lively and lucid mind will perhaps slowly deteriorate for lack of spiritual nourishment and hope. The paths that run between the concrete blocks lead nowhere.

Christophe echoes Josyane's feelings when he says: "I must look for things whose very existence I am unaware of. But it is absolutely vital that I find them." (*Printemps*, p. 63). Yet, Christophe does not accept the limitations imposed on him by vocational guidance counseling. Since he is refused knowledge, he leaves to search for it. His actions are entirely contemporary and reflect the doubts of many young people in the western world about the traditional ways of our existence. Idleness, even if temporary, is asocial, suspicious in our society. Christophe and his peers only claim the right to think a little before they commit themselves to action. Society, Rochefort seems to say, functions in such a way that a child's education results not in enriching but in stunting him. The author calls on children to refuse to become unfeeling adults, to leave the schools where they are indoctrinated, and the homes where they die of boredom with parents interested only in children as a source of social security allowances that will contribute to the family's ability to enrich itself modestly.[6]

A deciding factor in the gradual neutralization of the human soul is our willingness to let institutions and machines control our lives and turn us into robots. In Rochefort's novels, television and the automobile rank highest among the negative forces of our technological age that have invaded our personal lives. It is hard to imagine what most family relationships would be like, if television did not exist. In the leisure time activities of the families of Josyane and Christophe it takes on an enormous importance. How do they spend the evening? Josyane gives us a detailed account: "Papa would come home and turn on the television, we would eat, then papa and the boys would watch more television, mama and I would do the dishes, and then they would go to bed. As for me, I used to stay in the kitchen, doing my homework." (*Les Petits*, p. 10). Later on, thinking of her family, Josyane cannot imagine them other than in front of the television set or a filled plate. The repossession of the television set for failure to pay the monthly installments shocks the parents into taking stock of their lives as one would after a major catastrophe.

In *Printemps au parking* television is also an oppressive presence, a parasite, the enemy of human relationships. Christophe's father is to such a degree addicted that he cannot bear having the television screen obstructed even when the set is turned off. Christophe, realizing that his father prefers television over his son's presence, leaves home in disgust. He goes to visit his girlfriend. Without being seen or heard, he is able to enter her bedroom and spend the night with her, because her parents are immobilized in front of the television. Christophe neatly sums up the situation when he pronounces the supreme commandment of the new religion: "Thou shalt not block thy parents' television screen." (*Printemps*, p. 12).

Another target of Rochefort's biting satire is man's passion for the automobile. In *Les Petits Enfants du siècle* the author illustrates in a comic vein the mania that befalls man when he becomes the proud owner of a car, or rather when the car becomes man's owner, for the family's leisure time activities and money are sacrificed to the cult of the automobile. If in this novel Rochefort shows satirical indulgence for human vanity, in *Les Stances à Sophie* her satire changes to a bitter indictment. Both Philippe and his friend Jean are obsessed by this homicidal passion. The author claims that people lose all sense of reality behind the wheel of a powerful machine. A peaceful citizen turns into a dangerous maniac, obsessed by the demon speed. A person who behaved this way in other matters, would be committed to an asylum. Rochefort calls this attitude "a delirium of power . . . , masturbation with the sole of one's foot."[7] Celine's best friend Julia dies in a crash caused by her husband Jean who was racing his new car against Philippe's sports car. Without wanting to overdramatize, the author cites irrefutable statistics in order to illustrate concretely the disastrous consequences of the modern cult for machines.

When human beings are to such a point controlled by machines, is it any wonder that they eventually identify with them? Here Rochefort's criticism is directed against women, not women in general, but against those who fail in their duties as human beings by allowing their destiny to be identical with their biology. Rochefort calls them "les bonnes femmes. Josyane sees the women of the *cité* always pregnant, surrounded by a swarm of little children. Within their ballooning bellies they gather at the supermarket where Josyane carefully gets out of their way for fear of being flattened between them. They seem to her to be breeding machines with their down-to-earth coarseness which admits no importance for spiritual disquiet, their lack of logic, their penchant for having their children do their work for them. However, Rochefort is not entirely without sympathy for them, because it becomes clear to the reader that their lives have been profoundly affected by the new impersonal and sterile environment. The high-rise apartment blocks are now their whole universe. With their old neighborhoods they have not only lost their friends, but also their daily routine which consisted in large part of making the rounds of the small shops to buy whatever was necessary for the noon meal. They knew each shopkeeper who would keep them informed with news concerning the neighborhood. The daily errands also offered an opportunity to meet and chat with neighbors and friends. In the housing projects they have a supermarket instead where modern efficiency has replaced personalized service. Because of the isolated location of the new *cités* husbands can no longer take their noon meal at home. When they return to the *cité* in the evening, the family shuts itself off from all other activities to spend the evening in front of the television set. By ten o'clock the *cité* has become a desert. "Here people do not talk to each other; they are imprisoned in their own skin and don't look at anything else," Josyane comments. (*Les Petits*, p. 41). The civilization of concrete destroys nature and has a leveling effect on all living creatures. "People quickly lose their soul here," Guido, an Italian construction worker, says (*Les Petits*, p. 41).

Even in Sarcelles, a new sparkling community of over ten thousand apartments, a true city of the future, and so much more elegant than the one where her family lives, Josyane does not feel at ease. There are orderly rows and rows of buildings and green areas. But Josyane has the impression of being exposed like a fish in a glass bowl because of the many open spaces. The intimacy of the traditional town is lacking. True life, such as Rimbaud, who Rochefort quotes incidentally, described it is absent from those marvels of modern architecture. While walking through Sarcelles Josyane describes what life on the inside must be like. She imagines only happy families behind the lighted windows, and as in a commercial she repeats "happy" at least four times. Behind the large windows she sees in her mind all these "happinesses" lined up, one exactly like the other. (I must use the non-existing plural here to render faithfully the author's intentions for the lack of a more appropriate term.) "The 'happinesses' of the western facade could see the ones on the eastern facade as if they had looked at themselves in a mirror." (*Les Petits*, p. 81). Josyane imagines happiness all piled up and thinks—since she has a sense for mathematics—that she could calculate it in cubic feet, tons, bushels and barrels. Nothing could describe the monotony of the housing projects and how it must affect man's soul and sensitivity better than Josyane's cynical mathematical calculations.

And yet, modern conveniences and light have replaced the cold and darkness of the old slums. Strangely enough, the flaw of these modern cities seems to be

this very openness and depersonalized brightness which quickly becomes unbearable for man who, like an animal, needs shade when he suffers. "I felt
naked as a worm," says Josyane about her walk through the transparent fish
bowl. She clamors in vain for "disorder and darkness," perhaps equivalents of
her state of mind. She admits her nostalgia for "a tool shed, a storage shed, a
broom closet, a dog house, a cavern." (*Les Petits*, p. 128).

The echo of this uneasiness can be found in *Printemps au parking*. When
Christophe walks through Paris one night after he had run away from home, he
finds one oasis of life in the city: the Halles, the wholesale fresh produce market.
Thinking it too would be demolished shortly, he remarks: "If you ban from a
city everything that may disturb, what will remain?" (*Printemps*, p. 74). In the
new housing projects, Christophe thinks, it is true, nothing disturbs the residents,
no noise, no trucks, but how boring, and above all, how sad! He wants the street
lights to shine on something: fruit vendors with oranges and melons that really
smell and strawberries that are really red (*Printemps*, p. 74). Like Josyane, he
lives in exile, in a modern city on the outskirts, comfortable, but boring and far
removed from real life activities. The problem Christiane Rochefort seems to
be raising here indirectly is a question of human happiness.

Happiness and unhappiness are found in the most unforeseeable and often
paradoxical circumstances. The experience of the housing projects has shown
that human needs cannot be fulfilled by merely assuring man of material well-
being. It seems difficult to satisfy at one and the same time a community and
the individuals who make up the community.

Ironically, the institution which, according to Rochefort, seems to contribute
to a large extent to the devaluation of human life, was intended as a mechanism
to protect French citizens from the vicissitudes of life: the Social Security system
accompanies people from birth to grave and in many ways controls their lives.
At the birth of a child the parents receive a cash bonus. Originally intended as
an education fund for the newborn, the birth bonus will often be used for buying
household appliances coveted by the family. Evil tongues may insinuate that a
certain child owes his existence to his parents' dream of a refrigerator or a
washing machine. The lure of the cash bonus came into existence after World
War II to remedy a declining birthrate in France. Over the years it has given
rise to certain abuses. Rochefort skillfully exploits this phenomenon and its
consequences. Josyane thinks that she owes her life to trivial circumstances,
which inspires her with a strong sense of humility: "I was born because of family
welfare payments and a legal holiday," she says. (*Les Petits*, p. 19).

Critics of the Social Security system have denounced the practice of the birth
bonus, reasoning that families who can afford household appliances do not need
financial aid. According to them the money should be used exclusively for the
child's education. But, after all, when a family increases its daily material
comfort, all members of the family benefit from it equally.

The author must not be counted among the critics who envy poor people a
level of comfort which they themselves have always enjoyed. She does not

approach these problems from a political point of view, but as a writer endowed with a sensitivity sharp enough to perceive the scandal that money represents when it serves to measure the value of human lives. For carried to the extreme, the child bonus as a reward, a prize to be coveted, goes against human dignity. Procreation becomes an economic matter and woman's womb the receptacle for a new machine and only incidentally the place in which a child is nurtured. "My refrigerator is right here," says Mme. Mauvin, tapping her stomach in front of the other women in the supermarket. (*Les Petits*, p. 84). Josyane's mother thinks she needs triplets to be able to afford a refrigerator. Women in Josyane's *cité* have become industrial breeding machines. Failures, such as miscarriages, or still-born babies, are looked at in terms of productivity and as obstacles on the road to the Grand Prize, the "Prix Cognac," the ultimate reward for big families. Emotions here do not run deeply. Josyane's resentment of the women in her *cité* stems to a large degree from her observation that one baby easily replaces another and that maternity is considered a profitable career.

Boys are furthermore cannon fodder. Rochefort does not actually use this well-known *cliché*, but she gives a concrete illustration of the idea by making Josyane imagine the fate of the Mauvin boys in case of war: ". . . and bang, there they lie, all killed on the battlefield, and on their graves, crosses are placed: Here fell Mauvin T.V., Mauvin wheels, Mauvin fridge . . . ," each human being fusing with the machine or appliance that his birth had made it possible to acquire. As for the parents, they remain the owners of the material goods and in addition are the beneficiaries of a pension. (*Les Petits*, p. 86).

While in *Les Petits Enfants du siècle* and *Printemps au parking* the couple, seen as parents by their adolescent children, finds itself on the sidelines, it is drawn into the center of our attention in *Les Stances à Sophie* by the narrator Celine. She makes us aware of how woman is treated in a male-oriented society. Woman remains the frivolous, silly creature who can't be taken seriously, because she is not supposed to think. Man will never tolerate her as an associate, but prefers her as "une enfant infirme," a sick little child (*Les Stances*, p. 95) who depends totally on him and thus flatters his ego. Therefore, she is expected to be polite, sweet and pleasant. Philippe, Celine's husband, is fond of showing off his wife to friends and business associates, as a prize, perhaps a prized pet would be a more appropriate term. "Mon pauvre chat," my poor little kitten, is one of the more endearing names he has for his wife. With good will and almost religious zeal Celine undertakes to conform to society's image of the perfect wife. She takes charge of the household, keeps the accounts and even busies herself with decorating the home. In the process she makes surprising discoveries. She learns that work gives order to life, but that we do not work to live or live better. Work and production are goals in themselves that need not be justified. "You must understand that production obeys certain norms," declares Philippe. Celine lucidly replies: "And so we are told that we must obey in order to accommodate them." (*Les Stances*, p. 61).

Christiane Rochefort's society accepts docilely the double burden of economic imperatives that are substituted for a genuine love of life, and of a logic that favors objects to the detriment of people. "It is not supply which answers demand, but demand which must obey supply." (*Les Stances*, p. 57). What happens in a consumer society could not be better summarized. Celine rebels in vain against the dictatorship of manufacturers of kitchen appliances and decorator materials. She is obliged to buy, not what she needs and wants, but what is manufactured and sold at the time of her purchases. Man has been reduced to the status of a consumer who is anonymous and depersonalized. "Did you ever ask yourself what the world would come to, if one had to take into account each and everyone's wishes?" her father-in-law tries to explain (*Les Stances*, p. 61). Any notion of individuality has disappeared. Talking about a product that she is unable to find on the market, Celine comments with clairvoyance, tainted with bitterness: "It isn't asked for, so I, who am asking for it, do not exist. I am being negated. They only have to wait till I go away. It's a subtle mechanism to produce sheep." (*Les Stances*, pp. 57–58).

Rochefort hints that society possesses yet another mechanism to achieve this effect. Celine's doctor discovers that she is suffering from chronic agapaxia, "a sickness characterized by sadness (that the patient feels) over unhappy events, and by joy over happy events, even . . . if they do not concern the patient himself." (*Les Stances*, p. 66). The doctor hopes to cure Celine of her agapaxia by a "progressive neutralization of her sensitivity" with the help of medication which Celine promptly disposes of. Even though she feels crushed by the leveling effect of our consumer society, Celine carries on her efforts to become an acceptable wife for her bourgeois husband. However, as the new Celine emerges, the original vanishes, until only a shadow of herself remains. In the end Celine feels so alienated that she conceives of her world as an aquarium into which she looks from the outside. She finally leaves her husband and with him the trappings of bourgeois society.

In this account of the "rise and fall" of the young wife of an ambitious corporate executive, Rochefort with her customary teasing sarcasm portrays perfectly woman's position in a dehumanized society by demonstrating her loss of dignity and identity as a human being through her complete emotional, social, and financial dependence on man.

Here Christiane Rochefort's feminist sympathies become evident as the character of Philippe allows her to examine woman treated as a minor and subjected to the patronizing authority of the adult male.[8]

In all her novels Rochefort underscores the dehumanizing aspect of our contemporary society. The large urban concentrations are shown to be a fitting frame and at the same time a reflection of our depersonalized society which has a stranglehold on its members. We have seen that it dictates man's outlook on all facets of life and affects human relationships: relationships between husband and wife, parents and children, and finally between the residents of the urban centers as members of a community. All of Rochefort's concerns are intimately linked to the questions of freedom and happiness, and because of her concerns expressed in a very contemporary style, Christiane Rochefort is a writer who deeply moves her readers.

NOTES

1. Interview with Maurice Chevardes in *Ma Vie revue et corrigée par l'auteur* (Paris: Stock, 1978), p. 277.

2. Christiane Rochefort, *Printemps au parking* (Paris: Grasset, 1969, Le livre de poche), p. 99. Future references to this edition will be indicated in the text by *Printemps*, plus page number.

3. "Qu'il y ait des riches et des pauvres dans une société, cela ne relève pas de l'urbanisme. Mais lorsque tous les riches se retrouvent dans certains quartiers et les pauvres dans certains autres, le problème prend une dimension urbaine. La segregation sociale appelle l'affrontement . . . Les habitants des grands ensembles subissent leur exil comme une injustice." *L'Express*, Oct. 20, 1979, p. 12, transl.: The fact that a society counts among its members rich as well as poor people has nothing to do with the city planning. However, it does take on this [political] dimension when all the rich people end up living in certain sections of town and the poor in certain others. Social segregation invites confrontation . . . The residents of the housing projects suffer their exile as an injustice.

4. *Printemps*, p. 175. Christiane Rochefort states in the foreword to her essay *Les Enfants d'abord*, that of all the oppressed who are endowed with speech, children are most silent. Her main concern therefore focuses on children as a class of defenseless victims. (*Les Petits Enfants du siècle*, Paris,: Grasset, 1961; *Printemps au parking*, Paris, Grasset, 1969; *Encore Heureux qu'on va vers l'été*, Paris, Grasset, 1975; *Les Enfants d'abord*, Paris, Grasset, 1976). While women and minorities have been granted the status of "oppressed," society has not yet done the same for children since they cannot voice their complaints about abuse and injustice.

5. Christiane Rochefort, *Les Petits Enfants du siècle* (Paris: Grasset, 1961, Le livre de poche), p. 19. Further references will be indicated in the text by *Les Petits*, plus page number.

6. *Encore Heureux qu'on va vers l'été* (Grasset, 1975).

7. Christiane Rochefort, *Les Stances à Sophie*, (Paris: Grasset, 1963, Le livre de poche), p. 122. Further references to this edition will be by *Les Stances* plus page number in the text.

8. Christiane Rochefort anticipates by several years the French feminist movement. She admits that American feminist literature has influenced her way of thinking, and, that ideologically she considers herself a feminist. *Magazine Littéraire*, 180 (January 1982), p. 41.

11

Irmgard Keun: A German Deviation

Livia Z. Wittmann

In 1932 Fallada's novel "Kleiner Mann—was nun? (LITTLE MAN—WHAT NOW?) appeared and has since been regarded as the Neue Sachlichkeit authority on the fate of a specific social group—that of the Angestellten.* From the perspective of his hero Pinneberg, a shop assistant, Fallada describes the political and social climate of Germany in the early 1930s. But one year earlier, in 1931, a novel which also dealt with the fate of the Angestellten had appeared in Germany. Although the popularity of this earlier novel led to its being adapted for cinema and the appearance of a third edition in 1932, it was absent from literary lexica and histories of German Literature until the late 1970s. This successful novel, which was the first to deal with the problems of the Anges-tellten, is Irmgard Keun's *Gilgi—eine von uns* (GILGI—ONE OF US). Through the eyes of her heroine Gilgi, a typist with diverse skills, the almost unknown Keun offers a view of Germany in the early 1930s which appears to me to be more radical and probing in its social criticism than that of the much-acclaimed Fallada. My thesis is that this radical aspect of the novel led to its being ignored and forgotten. To substantiate my point it is useful to quote the views expressed by contemporary critics as they appeared in the respectable literary journals *Die literarische Welt* and *Die Weltbuhne*. The reviewer in *Die literarische Welt* states:

Irmgard Keun should soon be moving more into the foreground. Hopefully her enjoyable book will reach those it is meant to reach: the army of white collar workers (Angestellten).[1]

and Kurt Tucholsky writes in *Die Weltbuhne*:

*It is inadequate to translate "Angestellter" as "employee" since Angestellter refers specifically to employees working in shops, offices or banks.

An asterisk, because this woman has to be regarded as something special. A woman who writes and has a sense of humour. Just look! . . . Different, but very promising.[2]

But although it is obvious that both reviewers recognize the importance of Keun's book, they also share a common criticism of it. In *Die literarische Welt* the comment is made:

Irmgard Keun describes the life of a young girl, who, capable and unsentimental behind her typewriter, organised in her actions as well as her thoughts, *nonetheless fails in her love of a man* (italics LZW). She drowns in femininity until the certainty of pregnancy allows her to be delivered into a new awareness, into a narrow and once again restricted way of life. Some time in the future, after she has regained her strength, she hopes to be better able to stand up to her lover.[3]

These sentiments are echoed by Tucholsky in *Die Weltbuhne*:

Whenever women write about love something almost always goes wrong. It is either sour or sugar-sweet. The tone in the first half of this book is good. "It's nice lying quietly next to each other. You neither think nor speak separately, you melt together. Carefully she touches his thigh: there is the scar made by the crocodile bite. There's almost something exhalting about lying next to a man who was bitten by a crocodile in Colombia." Whenever women write about love something almost always goes wrong. The second half of this book does not have the right tone or feeling. It does not succeed. Pregnancy, complications . . . it does not succeed.[4]

From these excerpts it is obvious that these critics are sensitive to that aspect of Keun's novel which so clearly differentiates it from Fallada's, namely that it focuses on the relationship between the sexes.

Keun critically demonstrates contradictions as they exist in the dominant social and sexual morality as well as in economically determined social practices. She shows how these contradictions hinder real emancipation and thus prevents the two sexes from reaching a deeper understanding that is not restricted to the emotional sphere only. The conflicts engendered by the contradictions are manifested in an everyday story: the man is unable to provide for the beloved woman in a way that is in keeping with middle-class moral and social codes; pregnancy and the restrictive paragraph 218 which prohibits abortion, ruin the lives and destroy the love of millions of people in the time of unemployment. The fate of one couple, Hertha and Hans, foreshadows that of the other couple, Gilgi and Martin.

The unemployed white-collar worker, Hans, tells his story which is not dissimilar to that of Fallada's "Little Man":

"We got married. You know, she had such funny parents, they always kicked up a fuss if it was a bit late when she came home at night."
Gilgi nodded: "Well yes,—it's the same old story!"

"Yes, then we just got married. I was so happy that we had our own flat and everything—everything was wonderful—and as a young chap you really feel as if you've gone up in the world when you can say—my wife. And Hertha was a secretary at Brandt & Co., earned good money—yes, and then my salary on top of that. We were doing very well. And Hertha wanted to keep her job for another two years, until I earned enough for both of us. But then the first baby arrived and after that she had this terrible breast trouble for a long time. Then our firm went broke—I hung around for months with nothing to do. And we had to give up our flat and move into an attic room at the back of Friesenstrasse. And Hertha was such a good wife, Gilgi! She never complained or made a fuss. And the hardest times were the best—it was then that I learned what it means to really belong to someone. Then I got a job as a sales representative with an insurance company—I didn't like it much—having to be so hard and persuasive with people, but in these times you just can't afford not to like a job. I tried very hard—but just as I was starting to get the hang of it I got the sack again. And then Hertha had the second baby. We loved each other so much. It's terrible, Gilgi, when being in love can cause so much unhappiness. On her own, Hertha would have been much better off and if I had been on my own I would have been much better off too. But we were together, for better or for worse, and it would have killed us to separate. There's not meant to be any love in this world, Gilgi."[5]

It is a typical chain of events and a commonplace story of a family. The outcome of it does not change that fact: Hans finally embezzles money because he can no longer bear to watch his children starving. His only means of escape is to kill himself along with his entire family.

The previous quote reveals social criticism since it is obvious that people adopt the values of their society without questioning them. This leads then to a way of thinking which is quite false: "And the hardest times were the best" says Hans. This fleeting moment of wisdom is deprived of any value when it is seen in the context of his final act of desperation. The conclusion drawn by the unemployed white-collar worker, that one has to forego love under given circumstances, is an admission of his socio-political impotence. The case of Pit, the young socialist of bourgeois descent, is quite different because he deliberately sacrifices personal relationships and ties in order to further the revolutionary cause. The same problem presents itself to the women characters in the book in a way which is different again. For Hertha, Hans' wife, love is divided into two separate and conflicting components: sexuality and the need for tenderness. One annihilates the other. Hertha's confession has a strong impact on Gilgi:

"And Gilgi"—Hertha's voice grows even quieter—"there—in that little narrow bed is where we both sleep—and every, every evening when it gets dark, I'm seized by fear and anguish—my body has become so tired—I can't stand anyone to touch it any more. It used to be different—but sickness, tiredness and the constant fear of having a child—all of those things have made it so that—it—is torture—an awful torture. And a man has no idea and never guesses what's going on inside your head. Sometimes I think—if only he would wait and just leave me alone, until maybe I, myself—once I mentioned that to him—and when I did he broke down and cried: "I'm repulsive to you, you don't love me anymore." (*Gilgi*, p. 207)

A comparison with Fallada's Lammchen springs to mind. Just as Lammchen plays mother to Pinneberg, Hertha ostensibly plays the expected role of mother in comforting Hans, the fallen hero, and to some extent she has internalized this role. The decisive difference, however, is that Keun allows Hertha to reflect upon her situation. Thus, the passages in which Hertha discusses her feelings of guilt show that what is being dealt with here is the internalized notion of femininity as it is projected by the male imagination:

"I've had very bitter and very ugly and very, very unfair feelings, Gilgi—and what's more I knew that they were ugly and unfair—but I couldn't always stop myself. Only I've never said them out loud before, I've always kept them to myself. Oh, I shall never forget it was my second baby—how I lay there in that bed—the pains had started too soon—my whole body was being ripped apart—I screamed, screamed, screamed—and there was Hans sitting with a few of his friends in a bar drinking beer, unaware and happy. Poor chap! It was seldom enough that he had a chance for a few moments of pleasure, and he wasn't to know what I was going through—but I was almost out of my mind. The pain, Gilgi! I thought I was going crazy—at that moment I hated him,—you know—I could've killed him—you beast—I thought it over and over again—you beast, you beast—this is all your fault, your fault that I'm lying here like this. Yes, and afterwards, Gilgi,—as he sat on my bed—I just stroked his hair and kissed his hand—and it was sort of like asking for forgiveness and wanting to make everything all right again, and only a tiny bit untrue and dishonest." (*Gilgi*, p. 206)

It is not without significance that this confession is made solely to another woman. By means of this, a threatening reality is exposed to male readers and critics. If one recalls that contemporary criticism addressed itself to this point, namely that the woman fails in her love of a man, it would seem that the tabu area within the fiction presents a perilously exact mirror-image of social relationships as they exist in the non-fictional sphere. However, before final conclusions are drawn, the development of Keun's central character, who is called first "a girl" and later "a woman," should be examined in detail.

" . . . she is still young, and apart from marriage, becoming a movie star or a beauty queen, she takes into consideration every possible way of life." (*Gilgi*, p. 22). This is how she is described at the beginning of the book. She works as a secretary, very conscientiously, and at the end of her day at the office she learns three foreign languages. By using her typing skills she earns extra money so she can save enough to visit the three foreign countries and improve her language knowledge. "Perhaps later on she will be able to earn money by doing translations" (*Gilgi*, p. 22), or open a boutique, since she is an able and enthusiastic seamstress. She tells her friend Olga: " . . . the fact that my aspirations are no greater than the possibility of my attaining them gives me freedom. . . . "She is satisfied with herself and her life and has affairs which last as long as both partners want them to. In short, she manages her own life in a way that is sensible, practical and well-balanced and finds her work rewarding. That is, until she falls in love with a man twenty years her senior, a likeable drifter with a private income who wants to change her for the sake of his own pleasure:

"You dear, silly little girl, always so proper and middle-class—you are working so hard that you're getting a web of fine lines around your eyes. Why, for what? So much determination that's worth so little. So much dogged ambition for such a small goal." (*Gilgi*, p. 104)

This is what Martin tells her, and Gilgi tries unsuccessfully to explain to him that the work she does means something to her, and she values her independence. He does not really try to understand her:

"I'll take you away from this ugly country, little Gilgi—soon—what is there to keep you here? Only 150 Marks a month from the office?"—Oh, he's so sick and tired of this grey place where it rains all the time, of these depressing clock-work people—he wants to go away, and he wants to take his colorful little lady with him—if she's pretty enough already, just imagine how pretty she'll be somewhere else, set free from an eight-hour day with no more of those useless figures in her head. He'll simply take everything he's got left out of his brother's factory—they'll be able to enjoy the good life for a couple of years—and then? Well, what did that matter—his main talent was that he was always able to banish stupid, bothersome "and-thens" from his life. (*Gilgi*, p. 136)

Gilgi feels the physical and psychological strain of working during the day and trying to keep up with the demanding bohemian lifestyle of Martin at night. She progressively loses control over her own life—she no longer keeps up with her language studies and goes to work in the mornings after too little sleep. Gilgi has the feeling that she is merely allowing herself to drift along, so when she is given notice of dismissal from the office she accepts it with indifference. However, she plays the role of a "kept woman" with an uneasy conscience and that, together with her sense of alienation and the worry of Martin's ever-increasing debts, causes her considerable self-torment. Her depressing experiences in the dole queue fill her with fear at the prospect of the future. To her, the worst feature of the unemployed is not their misery and their poverty, but the fact that "all sense of responsibility has been taken away" from them. It is under these circumstances that she becomes pregnant. An abortion is out of the question. She sees the fate of Hans and Hertha ahead of her and knows, that if Martin were forced to work—as far as that was possible—because of the child, his feelings for her would soon change. In addition to that she feels guilty about the death of her friend, since Martin's jealousy prevented her from giving Hans the money he was unable to raise to save himself from being prosecuted for his embezzlement. She decides to leave Martin and go to Berlin where she will try and find a job with the help of her woman-friend. Gilgi wants to be herself again, despite the difficulties of bringing up a child on her own.

In *Gilgi—One of Us* there are many similarities to Fallada's *Little Man—What Now?*, but the reality presented by Keun is a much more threatening one. In her novel, the economic situation is seen to have an impact on even the most intimate aspects of life. Both novels deal with the social and material suffering of the white-collar worker, but in Keun's novel there is no room for idealization. Her critical description of the era is consistent and gives lie to the idealized final scene in Fallada's novel. Keun, in a way that is appropriate both artistically and socio-historically, postpones the utopian vision of personal happiness for the future. For even when a woman internalizes the male-created dichotomy of femininity as mother or whore, something remains that is neither. It is this remaining part of the self that Hertha reveals in her confession to Gilgi. But Fallada's Lammchen, in that she always plays the mother-comforter role in healing her wounded hero, is an idealized, utopian figure, a character-type who has been created in a way which has never reflected the real experiences of women but who nonetheless has a well-established place in the literary and artistic traditions of the Western world. But in order to do justice to Fallada one can categorize Lammchen as a traditional stereotype who is consistent with the imagined concept of femininity. The same is true of Cornelia in Kastner's *Fabian*. Countless women in the novel are whores and she is one of them. She prostitutes herself for the sake of money and success even though she loves Fabian. The entire novel is a showpiece of the previously mentioned dichotomy in the imagined concept of femininity, since the only woman character who is not greedy for sex or money is the hero's pure, mild, concerned mother, a constant source of comfort to her son.

Keun, however, bestows upon her female character so much determination to preserve her own identity that she leaves the man she loves rather than allow herself to be taken over by him. The reader is in no way under the illusion that this decision is an easy one or its consequences trivial. On the contrary. The woman suffers and struggles with herself before she takes this step and the reader is left with no doubt that the next phase of the heroine's life, although it is not described by the author, will be difficult.

The displeasure with which such an attempt at emancipation is viewed, even though it is won through suffering, is testified to by Kurt Tucholsky's reception of Alexandra Kollontai's book, *Pathways of Love*, three stories about love and marriage in Soviet Russia, the German translation of which appeared in Berlin in 1925. Tucholsky, liberal leftist and authoritative critic of the Weimar Republic, condemns the book in a review written in 1926 by describing it as "indifferent."[6] Accordingly, he fails to mention what the book is actually about despite his copious comment on the content of the stories. It is about the new chances women have of gaining self-awareness in a socialist state, which includes the sphere of love and sexuality. It is a state, too, where equality of the sexes before the law has already been made a reality.

In Kollontai's story "Wassilissa Maligyna," a woman leaves her husband after she discovers he loves someone else and she realizes her jealousy would jeopardize the friendship that exists between them. In addition to that she is uncomfortable in her role as a dependent wife, since she has always been accustomed to working independently as a party functionary. The fact that she is pregnant does not prevent her from carrying out her decision. In Russia in the 1920s, unlike Germany, abortion was legal, but she is happy about the expected child and chooses to keep it. Together with other women she decides to establish a crèche so that she can continue with her work.[7]

The story "Sisters" is also worth mentioning: a wife and a prostitute are able to talk to each other and they discover that they both feel themselves to be equally exploited by the same man. In *Gilgi—One of Us* there is also a reference to the sisterhood of women, especially in times of political fanaticism and repression:

"You know"—Olga's lively, blue operetta-eyes suddenly grow serious and thoughtful— "I really like men as such—but it's funny and it makes you a bit suspicious that you never find any real friendships between men anymore, no honest, obvious sticking together, and especially no unconditional solidarity. There are only "colleagues" or party comrades—that's mighty little. I would have a load of respect for a man who had a friend whom he preferred to me. Has it ever occurred to you, Gilgi, that we're living in a time when there's more real solidarity among women than men?"[8]

The only one of Kollontai's stories that Tucholsky approves of is "The Love of the Three Generations," which he lands for its "eternal truth": that of the difficulties different generations have in understanding each other. What he fails to mention, however, is that in the course of three generations—grandmother, mother and daughter—three radical steps are made in the sphere of sexual emancipation. The most radical of these takes place in the daughter's generation, since she rejects passionate love, the consequences of which she believes are destructive, and instead argues for a relationship based on friendship, without one partner claiming to own the other. The reason Tucholsky suppresses the actual content of this story as well is not likely to be because it offends romantic notions. One may come closer to the reason if one examines a piece of Tucholsky's own writing on the same theme in more detail. It appeared in 1931 under the title *Schloss Gripsholm* (Gripsholm Castle). Tucholsky playfully pretends it is both autobiography and fiction at the same time. The story is well-known, but the question is whether or not one has overlooked small but apparently not insignificant details. How indeed does the first person narrator sum up his views on the opposite sex?

How far it is from a man to a woman! But it is wonderful to submerge oneself in a woman as in an ocean. Not to think . . . many of them wear glasses, they have forgotten what it means, in the real sense of the word, to be a woman—and they have only a weak charm.[9]

He goes on to say about his mistress: "Sleep at least did not make this woman look simple." Or: " . . . in this head was so much man. The rest, thank God, was all women.''[10] And likewise he is not silent about the matter of possession. A binding code of honor, naturally strong between men, is presented to the reader: ''But this was an unwritten law between us—totem and tabu . . . and the others' women—never.''[11]

Such and similar revelations show us what it was about the second half of Keun's book that turned it sour for this influential critic. Keun exposes the foundation of patriarchal privileges and prejudices as questionable. And her female characters do not readily fit the accepted definition of femininity. They are much more concerned with preserving their identity.

It may be assumed that Irmgard Keun read Alexandra Kollontai's autobiography, which was first published in German and appeared in Munich in 1926 under the title: *Ziel und Wert meines Lebens* (The Aims and Worth of My Life). Kollontai writes:

Nevertheless we would have been able to create and achieve much more had our energies not been fragmented in the eternal struggle with our feelings for another. It was, in fact, an eternal defensive war against the intervention of the male into our ego, a struggle revolving around the problem-complex: work or marriage and love?

We, the older generation, did not yet understand, as most men do and as young women are learning today, that work and the longing for love can be harmoniously combined. Our mistake was that, the person with whom we believed we could blend our soul, one who was ready fully to recognize us as a spiritual-physical force.

But the man always tried to impose his ego upon us and adapt us fully to his purpose. Thus despite everything the inevitable inner rebellion ensued, over and over again since love became a fetter. We felt enslaved and tried to loosen the love-bond. And after the eternally recurring struggle with the beloved man, we finally tore ourselves away and rushed toward freedom. Thereupon we were alone, lonesome, but free—free to pursue our beloved, chosen ideal . . . work.[12]

The social criticism in *Gilgi—One of Us* is more complex and radical than that of *Little Man—What Now* and *Fabian*. It contains illuminating observations about the misery of the white-collar workers as it permeates the most intimate of relationships but does not attribute this misery exclusively to the economic crisis which only highlights the contradictions. It is also shown that women are sacrificed twofold by the prevailing social system, the patriarchal basis of which rejects equality of the sexes as a threat to the system. Although Russia was a country with a new beginning, Kollontai's concept of women's total emancipation from the oppressive mechanisms of the past was welcome for only a short time. It was not long before the revolutionaries of yesterday could be recognized as defenders of their privileges in a socialist patriarchy.[13] Without the efforts of the more recent American and German women's movement to re-evaluate the achievements of women, the works of Keun and Kollontai would have remained shamefully buried.

NOTES

1. *Die Literarische Welt*, No. 1, 1932.

2. *Die Weltbuhne*, No. 5, 1932.

3. *Die Literarische Welt*, No. 1, 1932.

4. *Die Weltbuhne*, No. 5, 1932.

5. Keun, *Gilgi—eine von uns*, p. 191 f. Further references are given in the text by page numbers.

6. Ignaz Wrobel, "Wege der Liebe," In: *Die Weltbuhne*, No. 33, 1926.

7. Cathy Porter, *Alexandra Kollontai*, London 1980, p. 407 f.

In Cathy Porter's summary: "She soon discovers that, as manager of one of the new enterprises created by the NEP, Volodya is enjoying all the material privileges of his position and expects her to live on his terms, in his house, wearing the clothes he buys for her, and dutifully supporting him in his disagreements with the Party. Surrounded by Volodya's servants and repulsive 'Nepman,' paralyzed by political inactivity and the slowly dawning suspicion of Volodya's unfaithfulness, Wasilisa struggles against illness and depression to understand the ways in which Volodya is exploiting her and to find a new independent life for herself outside the home he has created for her, with all its lies and luxury. When she does eventually leave him it is to embark on a more honest and optimistic life of hard-working independence."

8. Keun, *Gilgi—eine von uns*, p. 168 f. In her interview with Klaus Antes in the *Suddeutsche Zeitung* 21st and 22nd Nov. 1981, which appeared under the title "Einmal ist genug" (Once is Enough), Irmgard Keun remembers her own feelings when Hitler came to power:

And . . . oh God, oh God, I watched the parades of those pigs. That first time in Berlin I thought, I'm going to die . . . and at that time my hatred for Hitler wasn't yet as strong as my hatred for these repulsive men. I could only think, if I had the slightest capacity for being a lesbian I'd never look at another man. That's how repulsive those men were to me.

9. Kurt Tucholsky, *Gesammelte Werke* (Collected Works), Reinbek bei Hamburg, 1967, Vol. III, p. 671.

10. Ibid., p. 672.

11. Ibid., p. 704.

12. Alexandra Kollontai, *Autobiography of a Sexually Emancipated Woman*, London 1972, p. 7 f.

13. ref. Cathy Porter, *Alexandra Kollontai*, p. 400 f.

12

Charlotte Bronte, Emily Bronte and Jean Rhys: What Rhys's Letters Show about that Relationship

Joan Givner

It gives me wonder great as my content
To see you here before me. O my soul's joy!
If after every tempest come such calms,
May the winds blow till they have waken'd death,
And let the laboring bark climb hills of seas
Olympus-high and duck again as low
As hells from heaven. If I were now to die,
'Twere now to be most happy; for I fear
My soul hath her content so absolute
That not another comfort like to this
Succeeds in unknown fate.

Othello

But she could remember going cold with excitement and doing her hair in a kind of ecstasy (now the old feeling began to come back to her, as she took out her hairpins, laid them on the dressing-table, began to do her hair), with the rooks flaunting up and down in the pink evening light, and dressing, and going downstairs, and feeling as she crossed the hall 'if it were now to die, 'twere now to be most happy.' That was her feeling—Othello's feeling, and she felt it, she was convinced, as strongly as Shakespeare meant Othello to feel it, all because she was coming down to dinner in a white frock to meet Sally Seton!

Mrs. Dalloway

Jean Rhys's use of *Jane Eyre* has been well-documented. Critics have noted her use of the details of Bronte's story and the numerous echoes of her phrases.[1] Helen Nebeker has shown how the association of the two writers is mutually illuminating, Rhys giving back as much as she takes from Bronte.[2] Ellen Moers has cited the link between Rhys and Charlotte Bronte as a further example of the "productive pairings" between women writers.[3] While affirming, in general, the conclusions of these critics, I should like to modify some of the assumptions made about the Bronte connection.

That some revaluation of that connection and of her creative process in general is necessary is suggested by Rhys's letters to Selma Vaz Dias and to other friends.[4] In particular, the letters show how fiercely critical Rhys's attitude was toward *Jane Eyre*. Her motivation in writing her own account of the first Mrs. Rochester was not so much to amplify as to correct. She declared herself infuriated by Bronte's treatment, and described her own mood when she began to write her novel, as "fighting mad." She thought it was amazing that even sensitive people (like Charlotte Bronte) should be so blind to human misery.

The main target of her criticism was, of course, the portrait of the Creole heiress. She thought it a repulsive stock rendering of a mad woman, which never once came to life. She objected chiefly to the lack of reason or explanation given for her actions and her madness. Rhys wanted to give these reasons, make the character plausible and show why she lit the fire and burned down Thornfield Hall. (She thought the answer to that one was easy. Mrs. Rochester was cold and fire was the only warmth she ever knew in England.)

The second target of Rhys's anger was Rochester himself. She thought him a scoundrel, whom the writer had completely whitewashed. He had exploited a whole series of women, had pinched a huge sum of money from his wife and then kept her confined in a cold garret and fed her on sago pudding.

Inevitably, she read the novel carefully and frequently but if she absorbed certain details and echoes into her own work she did not do so deliberately out of eager admiration. She said she had done a stupid thing by reading it so much and that it was creeping into her own writing and she was afraid she might do a bad imitation. All told, she thought the novel overrated and wondered why people were so Jane Eyre conscious.

At the same time, and proportionately as her estimation of *Jane Eyre* declined, her admiration of another book increased. When she had acquired (with some difficulty on inter-library loan through the small Bude library) her copy of *Jane Eyre*, she had also requested *Wuthering Heights*. It was this novel which captured her imagination and dominated her thoughts as she worked on her own novel. She thought it magnificent and (mistakenly generalizing from her own experience) wondered why it was so neglected, while *Jane Eyre* was admired. She concluded that the answer lay in the very circumstance that accounted for her own preference. Heathcliff, who like Rochester, was a crude devil of a man, was not whitewashed but shown in his true colors as an unmitigated villain who had ruined the lives of several people.

Although Rhys does not analyze in detail her preferences between the two Brontes, her kinship with Emily is easily recognized. Neither is primarily interested in social concerns such as treatment of governesses, the corrupt administrations of girls' boarding schools or inheritance laws that discriminate against women. While they both deal with love and marriage, neither is interested in the peripheral trappings of love-making—in courtship, disguises, teasing, and lap-sitting. Catherine Earnshaw in *Wuthering Heights* makes a rough distinction between two characters.

Whatever our souls are made of, his and mine, are the same, and Linton's is as different as a moon beam from lightening or frost from fire.[5]

The distinction might be extended to the three writers. Rhys's women Annette and Antoinette, very different from the self-controlled Jane Eyre, might have said with Catherine Earnshaw's name-saint, "my nature is fire." Both Rhys and Emily Bronte write fiction that Katherine Anne Porter described thus:

Let me admit a deeply personal preference for this particular kind of story, where external act and the internal voiceless life of the human imagination almost meet and mingle on the mysterious threshold between dream and waking, one reality refusing to admit or confirm the existence of the other, yet both conspiring toward the same end.[6]

As the temperamental affinities between Jean Rhys and Emily Bronte might suggest, it is possible to chart as many correspondences of incident and phrase between *Wide Sargasso Sea* and *Wuthering Heights* as between it and *Jane Eyre*. These range from the titles (both suggesting freakish climactic disturbances) to the houses Wuthering Heights and Coulibri (both sparsely furnished and some-how dominated and diminished by their natural setting) to similar events (like the rock-throwing), a similar use of dreams, and many verbal echoes.

But more important than any of these, is the fact that from her absorption in *Wuthering Heights* Rhys struck the inspiration she needed to bring her own art to its ultimate fulfillment. In order to explain the nature and extent of that fulfillment, it is necessary to compare *Wide Sargasso Sea* with the novel published thirty-two years earlier under the title *Voyage in the Dark*.

Let me say at the outset that, while the earlier novel does contain many of the field-marks of Rhys's mature work and shares theme, characters and setting with *Wide Sargasso Sea*, it seems to me to be a somewhat unsatisfactory work, an under-developed blueprint for the triumphant last work but lacking its powerful tragic impact.

In part, the unsatisfactory nature of the earlier novel must be laid at the doorstep of the publisher rather than Rhys herself. Rhys had written a tragic ending, similar to the ending of *Wide Sargasso Sea*, in which her heroine moves irre-vocably into death. Her own ending is as follows:

And the concertina-music stopped and it was so still, so still and lovely like just before you go to sleep and it stopped and there was the ray of light along the floor like the last thrust of remembering before everything is blotted out and blackness comes.[7]

For the publishers whom Rhys approached, this ending with its description of death as the result of a botched abortion was too sordid. One publisher suggested that the woman recover and marry a rich man; another that Anna should recover and look forward to other love affairs, other pregnancies and other abortions in a—presumably—unsordid round of—perhaps—pleasure. This ending Rhys accepted as the price of having her work published, and this conclusion is still used:

"She'll be all right," he said, "Ready to start all over again in no time, I've no doubt."

When their voices stopped the ray of light came in again under the door like the last thrust of remembering before everything is blotted out. I lay and watched it and thought about starting all over again. And about being new and fresh. And about mornings, and misty days, when everything might happen. And about starting all over again, all over again. . . . [8]

Naturally, the ending lacks force as Rhys well knew. She wrote to a friend:

Evelyn I don't know what to do. I suppose I shall have to give in and cut the book and I'm afraid it will make it meaningless. The worst is that it is precisely the last part which I am most certain of that will have to be mutilated.

My dear it is so mad—really it is not a disgusting book—or even a very grey book. And I *know* the ending is the only possible ending.

I know if I tinker around with it I'll spoil it without helping myself a bit from this being popular point of view. [9]

As she says, the ending was the one thing she was sure about. There were many parts of the book about which she was not so sure:

Well Evelyn I don't know if I've got away with it. I don't know. It's written almost entirely in words of one syllable. Like a kitten mewing perhaps. The big idea—well I'm blowed if I can be sure what it is—Something to do with time being an illusion I think. I mean that the past exists side by side with the present not behind it—that what was—is—

I tried to do it by making the past (the West Indies) very vivid—the present (downward career of girl) the present dreamlike—Starting of course piano and ending fortissimo.

Perhaps I was simply trying to describe a girl going potty.

You see I don't know myself and am really trying to argue it out—Anyway it isn't very important. I didn't want to use any stunts and haven't. But I have no self-confidence— have cut too much and worried over things that were already done as well as I could do them with my one syllable mind. So there you are—(I expect I've made it sound even pottier than it is)—[10]

Rhys's own uncertainty results in two serious flaws in the novel. The first is the uneasy balancing of the two parts, the English experience and the West Indian experience. To a certain extent Rhys makes the problem of relating the two areas of experience Anna's own problem. Anna says:

Sometimes it was as if I were back there and as if England were a dream. At other times England was the real thing and out there was a dream, but I could never fit them together. (p. 8).

and again,

But when I began to talk about the flowers out there I got that feeling of a dream, of two things that I couldn't fit together, and it was as if I was making up the names. (p. 67).

These comments do not, I think, justify the many awkward and mechanical transitions throughout the novel. In the shower, Anna thinks:

I would put my head under the water and listen to the noise of the tap running. I would pretend it was a waterfall, like the one that falls into the pool where we bathed at Morgan's rest. (p. 77).

Similarly forced is the sandwiching of Walter Jeffries' letter severing the relationship between two flashbacks to the West Indies:

I thought, "But what's the matter with me?" That was years and years ago, ages and ages ago. Twelve years ago or something like that. What's this letter got to do with false teeth? (p. 79).
I thought, "What the hell's the matter with me?" I must be crazy. This letter has nothing to do with false teeth. (p. 81).

An early title which Rhys considered for this novel was *Two Tunes* and I think she never quite got the relationship between the two tunes effectively balanced.

Another unsatisfactory part of the novel is the lack of clarity about why, at a certain point in the relationship, Walter Jeffries tries to disengage himself from Anna. It has, of course, been clear from the beginning that the relationship will not be permanent, but the moment of dissolution is neither clarified nor dramatized. From other Rhys novels and from the circumstances that cause or precede the terminations of other relationships, I think some conclusion can be reached about what sends Walter Jeffries away. Katherine Anne Porter has spoken of "man's confused veneration for and terror of the fertility of women and vegetation."[11] Rhys's men manifest this confusion and terror and are frightened by sexually active women.

In *Quartet*, for instance, when Marva is sexually aroused, her state is physically indicated by a change in body temperature, heavy breathing and dilation of the eyes. Heidler looks at her in dismay and the phrase used to describe his reaction is "rather alarmed":

She collapsed on the bed and lay there breathing loudly and quickly as if she had been running. He stood looking down on her, feeling helpless and rather alarmed. He knelt down and stared at her. Her head had dropped backwards over the edge of the bed and from that angle her face seemed strange to him: the cheek-bones looked higher and more prominent, the nostrils wider, the lips thicker. A strange little Kalmuck face.

He whispered: "Open your eyes, savage. Open your eyes, savage." (p. 102).

In *Wide Sargasso Sea*, long before Mr. Rochester receives letters and hears rumors about his wife, he is predisposed to suspect her of something odd and unnatural by her sexual activity.

Similarly with Walter Jeffries: When he starts the affair with Anna, she is inexperienced, virginal, frightened. Very tenderly, he tells her "Be brave" and calls her "Shy Anna." But soon she is no longer shy. On two occasions, just before he ends the affair, it is she who suggests they go to bed. He mocks her sarcastically,

He imitated me, "Let's go upstairs, let's go upstairs. You really shock me sometimes, Miss Morgan!" (p. 76).

When they go to the country, he would like to make love outdoors. She also wishes to make love but prefers to do so back at the hotel. She thinks:

Laurie saying: Some women don't start liking it till they are getting old: that's a bit of bad luck if you like. I'd rather wear myself out while I'm young. (p. 68).

At this point in the novel, Anna is perfectly happy. But already it is too late. Walter Jeffries senses that she is sexually awakened, that he has lost control of the situation and no longer has the ability to dominate, intimidate, and subdue.

In *Wide Sargasso Sea*, so similar in theme and character to *Voyage in the Dark*, the weaknesses might have been repeated. Since the early part of the novel takes place in the West Indies and the last part in England, the two tunes might have been very uneasily balanced, the novel split into two uneasily yoked halves. The cause of Rochester's alienation from his wife might have been blurred or obscured. In this novel, however, his growing disenchantment is carefully traced and completely dramatized. This is achieved by Rhys's use of the West Indian background not merely as setting and not merely as a means of evoking Antoinette's past, but as the "objective correlative" by which the inarticulate emotions and sexual impulses of the characters are charted.

From time to time Rhys used this device for emphasis in her earlier novels. In *Quartet,* for example, the wallpaper suggests the sexual activity that takes place in the room:

As he dresses she would lie with one arm over her eyes and think: "A bedroom in hell might look rather like this one. Yellow-green and dullish mauve flowers crawling over black walls." (p. 92).

The atmosphere of departed and ephemeral loves hung about the bedroom like stale scent, for the hotel was one of unlimited hospitality, though quietly, discreetly and not more so than most of its neighbors. The wallpaper was vaguely erotic—huge and fantastically shaped mauve, green and yellow flowers sprawling on a black ground. (p. 87).

In Rhys's own original ending to *Voyage in the Dark* the insistent rhythms of the West Indian carnival and Anna's delirium come together to suggest wild sexuality that culminates, for the woman at least, in madness and death.

Wide Sargasso Sea, however, is the only novel in which landscape is used consistently and cumulatively throughout to reflect the emotional tenor of the characters. Again there are two tunes. The lush, fertile, hot West Indies suggest raw primary impulses. England, on the other hand, with its cold climate, tamed landscape and cultivated gardens, is associated with the controlled, over-civilized, domesticated world. (A similar contrast comes to Marlowe's mind as he sits on the Thames estuary in *Heart of Darkness*).

The first hint of the association of the West Indian landscape with the sexual comes early in the novel in the description of the garden at Coulibri:

The paths were overgrown and a smell of dead flowers mixed with the fresh living smell. Underneath the tree ferns, tall as forest tree ferns, the light was green. Orchids flourished out of reach or for some reason not to be touched. One was snaky looking, another like an octopus with long thin brown tentacles bare of leaves hanging from a twisted root. Twice a year the octopus orchid flowered—then not an inch of tentacle showed. It was a bell-shaped mass of white, mauve, deep purples, wonderful to see. The scent was very sweet and strong. I never went near it. (p. 17).

(This is reminiscent of the malarial jungle and undergrowth in Virginia Woolf's *The Voyage Out* and *The Waves*, and like the coffin-pit with its "pleasantly sweet, corrupt smell" in Porter's "The Grave."[12]) Coulibri is at first an all-female enclave—dominated by Annette, Christophine and Antoinette, until it is penetrated by Mr. Mason. Annette warns Mason that the place is dangerous but he is content and refuses to leave. Both are correct in their assessment of the situation. It is dangerous, but for her not for him. He escapes and she declines into madness.

In this early section Antoinette has two premonitions of disaster. She dreams that she is led into a deep forest by someone full of sly sinister malice towards her. In a second dream she is led again into the primeval forest but this time she is taken beyond it into a garden enclosed by a stone wall. She is following a person whose face is black with hatred and she awaits some unspecified fate. Her dress is dragged in the mud and she is abject and cringing. The act, like some kind of sacrifice is to happen at the top of a flight of steps.

The dreams prefigure the journey to Granbois—the great wood—to which Rochester and Antoinette journey for their honeymoon. The name of the nearby village is Massacre and Rochester asks who was massacred. She replies innocently "something must have happened a long time ago. Nobody remembers now." The images of male sexuality intensify. Cocks crow and the horses are led by a character called Young Bull. Christophine offers Bull's Blood to Rochester but he mistrusts her and her dress trailing in the dirt. He finds the place strange, does not like the scent and admits that he would be afraid of Christophine if she were "taller . . . one of these strapping women dressed up to the nines." (In *Jane Eyre* Rochester applies the word "strapping" to Blanche Ingram). A moth is singed in the candle flame and Rochester (echoes of *Jane Eyre*) sees it as a masculine victim, "a big fellow" and a "gay gentleman.")

At first, Rochester is not eager to take Antoinette to bed. He is debilitated by a fever which has afflicted him for most of his time in the West Indies and it is late before they go to bed. In the morning he is routed by a mocking Christophine offering Bull's Blood. Antoinette herself is lazy with the kind of relaxed will-less languor that overcomes Rachel and Terrence in Woolf's *The Voyage Out*. Gradually, however, Rochester too succumbs to the atmosphere and relaxes his attachment to social custom. Nevertheless there is something that disturbs him about the place. He feels that it evades him and holds a secret and he wants to seize that secret:

It was a beautiful place—wild, untouched, above all untouched, with an alien disturbing secret loveliness. And it kept its secret. I'd find myself thinking "What I see is nothing—I want what it *hides*—that is not nothing." (p. 73).

Antoinette, hot-blooded woman that she is, is very content with her honeymoon. She is developing strong sexual appetites that equal his and she is left even more satisfied and spent afterwards:

One night she whispered: If I could die. Now, when I am happy. Would you do that? You wouldn't have to kill me. Say die and I will die. You don't believe me? Then try, try, say die and watch me die.

"Die then! Die!" I watched her die many times. In my way, not in hers. In sunlight, in shadow, by moonlight, by candlelight. In the long afternoons when the house was empty. Only the sun was there to keep us company. We shut him out. And why not? Very soon she was as eager for what's called loving as I was—more lost and drowned afterwards. (p. 77).

But there is a hint of voracity in this description and he is more than a little alarmed. He plays on the Renaissance meaning of the word "die." When she experiences orgasm, he watches her and has the urge to destroy her:

Die then, Sleep. It is all that I can give you. . . . wonder if she ever guessed how near she came to dying. In her way, not in mine. (p. 79).

This is a primitive place they are living in and primary instincts and raw impulses are unleashed:

It is not a safe game to play—in that place. Desire, Hatred, Life, Death came very close in the darkness.

What repels and frightens him is that she is no longer submissive but becoming independent, inaccessible and not completely controllable by him. She says "I can do as I like here" and he grumbles, "Nothing that I told her influenced her at all." (p. 78). This is the crux: that when she is frightened and submissive she is not fulfilled but when she achieves fulfillment she is autonomous and excites his fury.

When the letter comes from Daniel Cosway it contains hints of sexual excess on the part of Antoinette's parents and particularly about her mother:

but you, an honorable man, know well that for marriage more is needed than all this. Which does not last. Old Mason bewitch so with her mother and look what happen to him. (p. 81).

For Rochester the letter simply confirms the inner doubts he already has about his wife. "I felt no surprise. It was as if I'd expected it, been waiting for it" (p. 82).

After Rochester's visit to Daniel Cosway, his mind is poisoned and destruction follows swiftly for Antoinette. As his early suspicions turned to hatred, she becomes desperate, irrational and (a word that he might have used) "hysterical." He avenges himself for her suspected liaison with Sandi by taking her maid, Amelie. Desperation and rage do their work and she is pushed towards madness. Since the association of female sexuality and madness is longstanding, Rochester is, once again, not surprised. Their union was doomed from the beginning. There might have been a way for them to leave the deep wood together but if such a path existed ever it has long been grown over. Both of them will retreat to separate worlds in which they will live like zombies, half-dead, unfulfilled. Of himself Rochester says: "A long deep sleep, mine will be, and very far away." (p. 126). Of Antoinette he says: "She'll have no lover, for I don't want her and she'll see no other" (p. 136). "She was only a ghost. A ghost in the grey daylight" (p. 140).

Emily Bronte at the end of *Wuthering Heights* could imagine a time in the future when the worlds of Thrushcross Grange and Wuthering Heights might harmoniously be united. Jean Rhys never imagined such a harmony. For her the two tunes, the West Indian and the English, the primitive and the civilized, the sexual and the social could never harmonize.

Early in Rhys's career, Ford Madox Ford advised her to inject more "local color" into her short stories. She resented this suggestion so much that she excised the few notations of the Left Bank setting that had crept into her work. He explained:

Her business was with passion, hardship, emotions: the locality in which these things are endured is immaterial.[13]

By the time she wrote her last novel, it was remarkable for just the kind of description she had cut from the short stories—"local color" or the vivid evocation of the West Indian setting. It seems to me that she recognized in Emily Bronte's novel, her method of using landscape, storms, tempests to show the powerful sexual energy of her characters. What she learned gave her a vocabulary and a set of images that allowed her to express her own powerfully felt ideas about female sexuality. Her use of such imagery to express such a theme places *Wide Sargasso Sea* alongside such works as Sylvia Plath's *Fever 106*, Eudora Welty's *Delta Wedding*, Virginia Woolf's *Mrs. Dalloway*. It also marks her kinship with such graphic artists as Georgia O'Keeffe and Judy Chicago.

NOTES

1. Dennis Porter, "Of Heroines and Victims: Jean Rhys and *Jane Eyre*," *The Massachusetts Review*, 17, no. 3 (Autumn 1976), pp. 450–51.

2. Helen Nebeker, *Jean Rhys: Woman in Passage* (Montreal: Eden Press Women's Publications, 1981), p. 171.

3. Ellen Moers, *Literary Women* (New York: Doubleday, 1977), p. 68.

4. The letters of Jean Rhys to Selma Vaz Dias are part of the Jean Rhys Collection at the University of Tulsa. The letters of Jean Rhys to Evelyn Scott are at the Humanities Research Center, the University of Texas, Austin, Texas.

5. Emily Bronte, *Wuthering Heights* (New York: Penguin Books), p. 121.

6. Katherine Anne Porter, *The Collected Essays and Occasional Writings* (New York: Delacourt Press, 1970), p. 289.

7. The original ending to *Voyage in the Dark* is part of the Jean Rhys Collection at the University of Tulsa.

8. I have used Penguin editions of Jean Rhys's novels.

9. Jean Rhys to Evelyn Scott, 10 June [no year], Humanities Research Center, Austin, Texas.

10. Jean Rhys to Evelyn Scott, 18 February [no year], Humanities Research Center, Austin, Texas.

11. Katherine Anne Porter, *The Collected Stories of Katherine Anne Porter* (New York: Harcourt Brace, 1965), p. 165.

12. *Collected Stories*, p. 363.

13. Ford Madox Ford, Preface to Jean Rhys, *Left Bank and Other Stories* (New York: Books for Libraries Press, Reprinted 1970).

13

Literary Criticism

Catharine R. Stimpson

I thought I would begin with a poem, by Emily Dickinson, which she wrote when she was 31, in 1861. It is about language. She begins by saying, "Many a phrase has the English language." She goes on, with the ironic modesty she does so well, that she has only heard one phrase, "Low as the laughter of the cricket/loud as the thunder's tongue." After this throw-away, she says the bright orthography of language breaks in upon her simple sleep, to make her cry, and weep, not for sorrow but "for the push of joy."

I begin with Emily Dickinson for several reasons. First, that poem gives me an image of my engagement with language. I think of all the engagements I have—with other people, with politics, with the falling leaves—the engagement with language is by far the most important. Dickinson also shows me that kind of stance the critics have, i.e., our dependency. I read Dickinson in order to be a critic, her texts in order to write my own. Beginning with Dickinson shows, too, the stance of the feminist critic. I turn, in my dependent ways, not simply to texts, but to those of the woman writer. The woman writer is my first source of authority.

However, if I am to talk about my sense of my own criticism, I cannot wholly submerge myself before this female figure. I must have a tiny bout of auto-biography, a tiny excursion into autobiography, because, as a critic, I am only one part of a divided linguistic self. For better, for worse, I also write fiction. This divided self, this mitosis, reflects itself in my two pen names. As a critic, I am Catharine R. Stimpson, "R" standing for Rosalind spelled after Shake-speare, if you believe my mother, and "R" standing for Roslyn, a coal mining town in which he was born, if you believe my father. My father controlled the birth certificate; my mother controlled my memory; I did not know I was not "Rosalind" on my birth certificate until I applied for my first passport. But those six syllables, Catharine R. Stimpson, have strength, sobriety, and a palpable respectability. But, as a novelist, I am Kate Stimpson. I became Kate not only because my friends call me that, but because my editor said Catharine R. is simply too big and unwieldy for a jacket cover. She also said, with the honesty you hope for in editors, "I'm sorry, Kate, but you know Catharine R. is really not a household word, and the difference between Catharine R. and Kate in bookstores in Flagstaff, Arizona, isn't big enough to control our sales." So I became Kate in print.

However, this was only the book jacket, a material cause. If you look at it semiotically, Kate is far livelier and far dirtier than Catharine R., Kate is a riskier name than Catharine R. Kate is a flute, and Catharine R. is a bass drum. But Kate is also far more frightened than Catharine R., far more aware of the abyss of silence and of blankness; Kate is far more conscious than Catharine R. of the perils of nothingness.

I speak today, not as Kate, but as Catharine R., and Catharine R., as a critic, has certain characteristics, which appear whether she is doing cultural criticism, theory, or journalism. First is that dependency I mentioned before, but my dependency is double-edged. All critics are infantile before the texts. We feel a kind of separation anxiety without them. We feel reassured, our need gratified, when we have our text before us. Yet to become a critic is to overlay this child with the adult. The word "critic," as we all know, comes from the Greek "to judge" and "to decide." The infantile dependency of the critic is masked by the adult judge. Secondly, when I write as a critic, my style is as clear and as taut as I can make it. I try to bring order into the prose, which is in itself the linguistic equivalent of the order I am bringing into the codification of the texts. Occasionally, I use a metaphor. When I use metaphors, I see them not as ornamentation, but more like a guide wire in a structure I am erecting. I want my style to have the kind of transparency that Sartre said was a characteristic of prose.

Something is now happening to my style; it is becoming closer to my speech, which is not without its ironic qualifications and timely rhythms. Perhaps under the guidance of Helene Cixous, writing is becoming closer to speaking. Unfortunately, this means that certain little throw-away lines that I can manage in speaking do not make sense when I write, and my ironies may either look like simplicities or snobberies. This style is, of course, the result of several drafts. I have this hard and refined style for several purposes. I think the first is psychological. I am simply pleased by these parsimonies, these purities. It is a way, this tight style, of shaping the world according to my desires for symbolic order. But I think, too, there may be something nastier afloat. So many of us who are both critics and academics know that our criticism is a form of credentialing. We are doing service to the texts, and to our careers. The purity of my style gives me a psychological *frisson* and dilutes a possible impurity of motive. A third reason for that style is pedagogical. Criticism is a public act, and so I write for others to read. I write rhetorical criticism. I wish to persuade. I see my criticism as a teaching act.

Needless to say, my relationship to criticism changed with my feminism. My style remained, but feminist criticism gave me three tasks. It gave me the job of exposing male cultural hegemonies, and that exposure, that shouting that the emperor had imperfect clothes on, is a lot of fun. Exposing male cultural hegemony can be an act of *Schadenfreude*, of taking joy in others' difficulties. I could use my simple style to say how bad John Milton was. The second task feminism gave me was, of course, to see the woman writer and to ask about her. But this was far more difficult, and is far more difficult, than exposing male cultural hegemony, because to write about male cultural hegemony is to make comparatively simple judgments. The difficulty of dealing is not in saying it is there, but in trying to figure out why it is there. But to ask about the woman writer; to do what Elaine Showalter called gynecriticism, to ask about women and their tradition is to ask difficult questions, among them the question of women's silence. Have women been co-conspirators with the ripping out of their own tongues? It is to ask difficult questions about the relationship to male tradition, and what we use and what we steal as we seek to create our own. In criticizing women writers, I also took on deviant subjects: Gertrude Stein; the lesbian novel. In writing about them, Catharine R. the critic joined Kate the novelist in an act of rather peripheral risk. I feared that in writing about tainted subjects that taint would spread from subject to critic, and not even the longest *vita* in the world would compensate for a *vita* that had such articles on it.

Feminism finally gave me the exploration of the cultural inscription of sexual difference, and whether culture reflects sexual difference because culture has had that male hegemony or because there is a transhistorical, acultural maleness and femaleness culture will ultimately reveal. Taking on these tasks, my style remained taut and clear, but I feel that style now under challenge from two sources. The first comes from two male Victorians who dominated my imagination when I was growing up. The first was the wild, prophetic, symbolic, crazed, magnificent Thomas Carlyle; the second was the wild, prophetic, symbolic, narrative-ridden and even more crazed Nietzsche. Their hold on my style remains through reminders that my own may be conservative. The second challenge is from French critical theory reminding us of the linguicity of language in the fiction of our criticisms, and the need for play as we speak sober truths. The French, primarily Helene Cixous, reinforced my sense of how conservative my style could be. "The Laugh of the Medusa," with all its passion and lyricism, its neologisms, its urgency, its wit, makes me doubt the way I write.

I fear giving up my old style. I fear that I cannot write the new way, that my style is not a matter of principle but of talent. I fear, if I adopt a new style, that I may be accepting the principle that there is a primordial female, a transhistorical, acultural, primordial female that will ultimately be revealed through language. If I change my style, if I can change, will I be wandering into theoretical swamps that I have previously disdained and argued against? In brief, if I change, is this to be more than a matter of the text? Am I going to have to make a horrible, metaphysical leap at once? As a critic I feel I have never before written with such assurance and self-confidence, but as a critic I have never before felt quite so strongly that the way in which I write can be abashing and defensive. In my current criticism this internal dialectic is not revealed, nor is it in the novel I am working on. My hunch is—if experimentation comes it will be worked out, not by Catharine R., but by Kate.

14

Miles Franklin: Chronicler of the Australian Bush and Early Feminist

Paulette Rose

Stella Maria Miles Franklin, born in 1879 into a fifth-generation pioneer family at Talbingo in New South Wales, drew the material for her novels from her own authentic experiences in the Australian bush. An unrelenting feminism and love of the land were to be the two poles around which her entire life and fictional world would revolve. Autobiographical in form and very Australian, *My Brilliant Career*, written when she was merely sixteen, determined both the direction of Franklin's literary works and her public life. Many years later when Franklin was an established literary personality she dismissed her first novel as a "girl's story . . . conceived and tossed off on impulse in a matter of weeks, spontaneously out of inexperience and consuming longings and discontents."[1] And yet this early work had the effect of a bombshell on the literary community. A. G. Stephens, critic of the weekly Sydney journal *The Bulletin*, heralded it as "the very first Australian novel to be published."[2] Another critic, H. M. Green, compared the heroine, Sybylla Penelope Melvyn, to Marie Bashkirtsef; the young Sybylla was "selfish and yet fervently idealistic in the cause of Australia, democracy and feminism."[3] And still another scholar, Ray Mathew, ventured to label it a classic in Australian literature, contending that after its publication in 1901 nothing more happened in Franklin's literary career.[4] If in fact Mathew's judgment is slightly exaggerated, it nevertheless underscores the novel's centrality in the life and work of the writer.

"Just a few lines to tell you that this story is all about myself," explains Sybylla in the introduction of *My Brilliant Career*.[5] "This is not a romance . . . neither is it a novel," she continues, "but a *real* yarn."[6] Thus unfolds the captivating story of a female adolescent growing up in the Australian outback, circa 1889. With a sense of urgency and authenticity, the fifteen-year-old Sybylla conceives the "idea of relieving" (p. 34) her feelings in writing when the drudgery of household duties becomes intolerable. Rebellious and moody, Sybylla struggles endlessly with the uneasy perception that she differs from other young girls, attributing her individuality to a "hot wild spirit which surged within" (p. 33). Her dreams of better things than dairying—her ambition to become a writer—are soon shattered when she awakens to the discovery that she is merely a girl, nothing more. She confesses:

It came home to me as a great blow that it was only men who could take the world by its ears and conquer their fate, while women, metaphorically speaking, were forced to sit with tied hands and patiently suffer as the waves of fate tossed them hither and thither, battering and bruising without mercy. (p. 39)

Even more devastating is the sudden realization that she is unattractive in a society where women are judged first and foremost by their youth and beauty and certainly not by their intellectual prowess. In this vein, Sybylla's special talent in music, her "hunger" for books and therapeutic need to write serve only to alienate her from family and neighbors. Restless, and above all lonely, Sybylla in a poignant self-analysis describes herself as misunderstood and solitary, "without a place in the world" (p. 54).

Imagining the reality of her mother's life—rising at two in the morning to make butter—Sybylla sees woman as "the helpless tool of man" (p. 17). She rails against the "curse of Eve" (p. 16)—the burden of unrestricted child bearing—and the disenchantment of marriage. Dismissing the custom as unfair and unfulfilling, she vows to remain "independent of the degradation of marriage" (p. 84), and despite her fondness for Harold Beecham, a neighboring "swell," and his tempting offers, Sybylla, after "momentary weakness" (p. 256), ultimately and definitively rejects the role of a wife.

The complexity and ambivalence of Miles Franklin's attitude toward love and marriage is first visible in this novel of adolescence. That Sybylla does not turn Harold away simply because marriage would interfere with her aspirations is made clear when he gently assures her that he would give her a study of her own to write in as often as it suited her. It would seem, then, that Sybylla, always distrustful of her feelings and repeatedly defining herself as "queer" or "different," cannot accept the traditional sex roles assigned in an adult relationship. Preferring "friendship" to the "hot fleeting passion . . . which is wrongfully designated love" (p. 56), Sybylla refuses marriage as escape from both the restrictive ambience of her home in Possum Gully and the suffocating demands of a man. As if to parody the Victorian novels of Austen in which marriage was almost always the ultimate reward for good behavior, a prize coveted by the female adolescent, Franklin presents us with an anti-heroine whose feminist inclinations clash with traditional canons of femininity.

But Franklin's Australianism, that brand of patriotism that flourished in the nineties, necessitated a belief in the institution of marriage as "the most sensible and respectable arrangement for the replenishing of a nation" (p. 257). Franklin, then, uncomfortable with the notion of sexuality in marriage perhaps for fear of giving up the autonomy she, herself, strove so hard to obtain, must nonetheless resolve the conflict in her fiction. On the whole, the novelist obstructs the matrimonial path for her heroines as if to spare them the disillusionment she associates with the practice. When marriage is conceded, however, singular couples result from bizarre and non-threatening combinations of seemingly mismatched individuals, often separated by great disparity in age or at times drawn together by blood ties.

In essence, Sybylla Melvyn, "a child of the mighty bush" (p. 265), became the archetypal female heroine in Franklin's fictional world and her love of "the weird rush of the stream and the Kookaburras' good-night"(p. 98) would reverberate throughout each of the major novels. The acute sense of alienation, the narcissism, the creative urge, were to be familiar concerns of most Franklin women.

Despite the acclaim surrounding *My Brilliant Career*, Miles Franklin could never feel comfortable with the first heroine she had so successfully created. Because her family and friends believed themselves travestied in its pages, Miles attempted a corrective in a companion piece, *My Career Goes Bung*.[7] Bristling with the same theme of rebellion that had characterized her earlier book, this novel bears mentioning because it brings Sybylla into sharper focus. She is now described as handsome, more poised and ready to be feted in Sydney after the publication of her first novel. Using the autobiographical form again, Franklin through Sybylla once more targets her attack against the inequitable position of women forced upon them by the social system. Familiar themes and attitudes recur, such as the indispensable need to write and probe the feelings of an Australian girl, an anti-heroine of sorts who differs from the conventional fictional heroine. So that her future books would not be interpreted literally and intrude upon her family's privacy, Sybylla announces her decision to adopt a "nom de plume," pointing the way to Franklin's own use of the pseudonym, Brent of Bin Bin.

If *My Brilliant Career* remains the cornerstone for all of Miles Franklin's subsequent novels, the Brent of Bin Bin series, published in England in the late 1920s and early 1930s, constitutes her masterpiece. The series comprises six books, five of which chronicle life in the Monaro over nearly a century.[8] They can best be understood as an almost perfect combination of the directions charted out by Miles Franklin in her early novel: feminist concerns wedded to her concept of Australianism of the nineties—all within the framework of her circular vision of life with its inevitable repetitions from one generation to another. Again we see her fiction of non-fiction focus on women who are spirited, rebellious, competent and always, like Sybylla, eager for a measure of autonomy. This time, however, the struggle for selfhood begins during an earlier period of Australian history and takes place within a comfortable society of squatters.

In the famous flood episode that opens *Up the Country*, the first in the series, Franklin introduces one of her favorite female characters. Mrs. Mazere is a small-statured, forty-two-year-old woman, mother of twelve, grandmother of five. Risking her life to save that of a neighboring squatter, despite the angry threats of her husband, she crosses a flooded river, delivers a baby and returns home triumphant. As the reigning matriarch in two of the five books of the epic saga, Mrs. Mazere represents the quintessential heroine facing the hardships of the Australian outback: loneliness resulting from the great distances between sheep and cattle stations, the "incessant child-bearing of the age"[9] and the merciless weather with its blistering heat in summer months and devastating winds during the monsoon season. Thus, the tone is set for a matriarchal society:

Up and down the country, as well as in the village and city, men often thought they were master in their own houses when their wives were too motherly to undeceive them. (p. 116).

Given Franklin's incessant preoccupation with selfhood and her uneasiness with sexuality, it is not surprising that her most haunting creations are widows and spinsters. Among the former is Rachel Labosseer (*Up the Country, Ten Creeks Run, Cockatoos*) who, second to her mother, Mrs. Mazere, leaves her imprint on successive generations. Widowed while still in her thirties and left with six children, she refuses to remarry, reasoning: "I have married once. I have done my duty. Nothing could induce me to go through it a second time. One husband and one family of children are enough for any woman" (p. 361). Energetic and made of "steel," Rachel is anxious to purchase and manage her own station. After hard work and prudent planning, she succeeds in proving that she can indeed fill a man's place in the outback.

We find an even more likeable and original representation of the single woman in Miss Jessie M'Eachern (*Up the Country, Ten Creeks Run, Cockatoos*). Once, on Leap Year, when she was younger, she had proposed marriage to Bert Poole—the most handsome and sympathetic of all the male characters in the saga. After being rejected, she chooses to remain single. Proud and feisty, Miss Jessie, as she is called, is judged eccentric by other squatters but nonetheless respected by all. "She was the acutest person on the Monaro in a horse or cattle deal," writes Franklin. "She asked searching and technical questions that only the bank or lawyer could answer."[10] When she is in her fifties Bert Poole proposes and Miss Jessie gingerly refuses, telling him he is twenty or thirty years too late. "Besides," she adds, "I'm too set in my ways. I could not settle down to domestic work completely. The station and the stock and buying and selling are my life now" (p. 142).

These two examples, along with others offered by Franklin, clearly show her vital interest in the single woman, unmarried or widowed. Despite the prevailing belief that women were not single by design, Franklin heroines go against the current, validating the choice women have to remain single. We are reminded of Sybylla's query in *My Career Goes Bung*: "Why are men so disturbed by a woman who escapes their spoliation? Is her refusal to capitulate unendurable to masculine egotism, or is it a symptom of something more fundamental?'' (p. 227).

It is evident that Franklin did not portray much love in the relationships between couples. Her attitude toward marriage had not changed essentially since *My Brilliant Career*. Although the Brent of Bin Bin books cover nearly a century (1830–1928), the paradigm never changes. In a telling question, Laleen Mazere in *Back to Bool Bool* asks: ''Did any of the pairs love the right ones?''[11] As if in perpetual motion, each character, male or female, loves someone who is inexorably connected to another.

The example of Milly Saunders in *Ten Creeks Run* typifies the novelist's solution to the conflict between sex and what her heroines prefer instead— ''friendship love'' or ''sweet friendship.'' Milly, lively and attractive, is surprised and disappointed by the inopportune sexual advances of her suitor, Larry Healy. She astonishes everyone by marrying Bert Poole, by now a man old enough to be her grandfather. Elsewhere, in a later novel, *All That Swagger*, Della Delacy marries a man young enough to be her son, while Clare Margaret marries a cousin. In each case, Franklin formulates a union based on mutual respect and compatibility, minimizing the role of sex.

If the author's attitude toward marriage and sex remains at best ambivalent, her position regarding female relationships in the Brent of Bin Bin novels is clearly indicated. Sybylla's outcry for companionship becomes a leitmotif for the concept of bonding, both physical and intellectual. The vacuum of isolation Sybylla so acutely feels is replaced by a web of camaraderie. The philosophy of ''mateship'' coined by the Australian writers Henry Lawson and Joseph Furphy is reread by Franklin as sororal bonding.[12] An intricate support system is established to encourage and promote unrecognized or misunderstood creativity. At the matrix of this structure is the figure of Ignez Milford, who first appears in *Cockatoos*, the third in the sequence.

A young girl of considerable talents, Ignez is strikingly similar to Sybylla in *My Brilliant Career* and questionably closest to Miles Franklin herself. With a precocious interest in politics, Ignez espouses the suffrage platform of Rose Scott, the feminist and philanthropist who had in fact introduced the author to the feminist movement in Sydney. Ignez is seen as ''mad'' and ''unsexed'' by the local residents of Oswald's Ridges because of her impatience with the usual talk of women centered on home and children. Ruling out marriage, she daydreams, in the manner of Sybylla, of a wider world where talk would focus on topics other than crops, poultry and weather.

In an effort to nurture the creative potential of little Nora Alfreda, her soulmate, and that of Dick Mazere, the only sensitive male member of the Mazere family, Ignez forms a literary salon. On Sunday afternoons, in a bush hideout, Ignez advises, criticizes and directs the writing of ''poetry about people like themselves, and vital with bush revelation.''[13] And like the heroine of *My Brilliant Career*, Ignez pens her first adolescent yarn entitled *Nita. The Story of a Real Girl*. The writing of that novel is perceived by its author as ''a kind of shouting at the top of her lungs into an uninhibited silence'' (p. 214). A familiar tale unfolds when a scandal follows the book's publication. Ignez ultimately decides to leave the district for America, as had Miles Franklin, in search of greater intellectual freedom.[14] Unlike Miles Franklin, Ignez never returns home; committing herself to all too many social causes, her literary and musical talents are stilled.

Considered by many readers her magnum opus, *All That Swagger*, winner of the coveted Prior Memorial Prize in 1936, is a final example of Franklin's raised feminist consciousness. To be sure, it is a sweeping romantic saga of Australia with its inimitable principal character, fearless Danny Delacy, the patriarchal leader of an impressive clan. And yet, it is also the tale of ''brave Johanna,'' the indomitable woman who portrays most searingly the hardships of pioneering women of mid-nineteenth-century Australia. As a young woman living in Ireland, Johanna elopes with the ambitious Danny Delacy. Envisioning a bright and comfortable future in Australia, the young bride accompanies her husband on the arduous trip to the far continent. A very different life from the one promised to her by Danny awaits Johanna. She is saddled with ''excessive childbearing'' and loses three children—one in a fire that completely destroys her home. Sympathizing with her heroine, Franklin writes: ''Hardship, suffering and loneliness had been her portion.''[15] Tired of landclearing and other grueling physical labor associated with pioneering, Johanna slowly begins to regard herself as deracinated and Australia as her ''territorial prison'' (p. 48). Never sharing her husband's enthusiasm for pioneering, she views his frequent absences from their station with relief. When Danny pushes farther west of their original homestead and builds a second station, she insists on maintaining an almost separate residence. She reconciles herself to the management of her own property, relegating Danny to the ''ind room''—guest quarters—whenever he returns home. Franklin's understanding of the disenchantment of her heroine is shown by the following description of Johanna in her middle years:

Her urge for man-flesh had dulled. She craved peace. . . . She saw Danny as an insignificant, ineffectual old man. . . . His once gallant daring now seemed foolhardiness . . . She had outgrown him or outworn him and was as careless of his feelings as though oblivious to them. (pp. 105–106)

Under her expertise, the property she manages during Danny's absence prospers. This accomplishment, she thinks, entitles her to some special recognition. From Danny's point of view, ''women's part in the struggle was accepted as their unpaid duty'' (p. 92). Danny never understands the anguish experienced by his wife in the early days of pioneering, nor does he look favorably upon her private battle to earn for herself a measure of independence. Johanna, the most embittered and least fulfilled of all the women in Franklin's galaxy of heroines, dies at ''the furthest extremity of the globe'' (p. 323), denied even her modest request of receiving last rites.

Even more powerful than Miss Jessie and Rachel Labosseer of the Brent of

Bin Bin saga is Clare Margaret Delacy, who along with Johanna, stands out as a key female character in *All That Swagger*. Distrustful of fleeting and fickle passion, Clare Margaret (the granddaughter of Johanna and Danny Delacy), like Sybylla and the majority of Franklin women, equates love with tenderness and friendship. For this reason, she marries her cousin Darcy, whom she endearingly and repeatedly refers to as a "real mate." But her happiness is abruptly terminated by his premature death. Widowed at thirty-three, Clare Margaret, as persistent as Rachel Labosseer and as shrewd as Miss Jessie, achieves financial success. Once independent, the young widow refuses to remarry for much the same reasons given by Miss Jessie and all the other single women in the Franklin novels—they have weathered hard times, earned their independence and are reluctant to concede their hard-won autonomy to any man.

In conclusion, the case of Miles Franklin remains worthy of re-examination today. Because her personality was so brilliant, there were some scholars who wondered if her works would outlive her memory.[16] Others believed her novels would indeed endure, especially *All That Swagger*, which one critic called "history for common man."[17] The Australianism, the passionate love of her country, was the quality most seized upon by the critics of her day. The Brent of Bin Bin books, the rambling and discursive saga, were judged favorably because of the resemblance to life in southeastern New South Wales. All critics joined in unanimous acclaim for *My Brilliant Career* because of its sheer originality. But unlike many critics who, upon Franklin's death in 1953, felt her feminism and social work to be wasted efforts, today's reader finds precisely these aspects of the author's life and work to be most appealing and significant.[18] Her clearsighted depiction of Australia's women in the environment she knew best and loved the most, the Monaro, warrants the increased attention of an international readership.

A surprisingly contemporary image of women emerges from the Franklin novels. *My Brilliant Career*, an indubitably feminist work with its accent on female narcissism and alienation, is still an exquisite and relevant study of female adolescence. Sybylla's awakening to early feminist and artistic yearnings coincided with Franklin's own development. And apart from the more apparent theme of the victimization of woman by man and Franklin's pleas for birth control, the notion of the single woman that the author treats in the Brent of Bin Bin sequence and in *All That Swagger* is an arresting one. Instead of portraying single women—widows or spinsters—as unfortunate or disadvantaged, Miles Franklin depicts them as independent, capable and in control of their lives. Moreover, the subtle suggestion of a support network for the artistic woman remains a valid concern for today's feminist scholars. Franklin is especially effective when describing the plight of the artist, singer, musician and above all the writer who, set apart from the mainstream of the community of women, attempts not only to survive as a woman in a man's world but to fulfill that creative urge which is as crucial to her as were the flow of the Murrumbidgee River and the song of the Kookaburras to Australia's pioneers.

NOTES

1. Miles Franklin, *Laughter, Not For a Cage: Notes on Australian Writing, with Biographical Emphasis on the Struggles, Function and Achievements of the Novel in Three Half-Centuries* (Sydney: Angus and Robertson, 1956), p. 119.

2. Quoted by Franklin in *Laughter, Not For a Cage*, p. 118.

3. Henry Mackenzie Green, *Outline of Australian Literature* (Sydney: Whitcombe and Tombs, 1930), p. 134.

4. Ray Mathew, *Miles Franklin* (Melbourne: Oxford University Press, 1963), p. 19.

5. Miles Franklin, *My Brilliant Career* (Edinburgh, 1901; rpt. New York: Pocket Books, 1981), p. xvii. Further quotations from this novel will be identified internally by page number.

6. The italics are Franklin's.

7. Miles Franklin, *My Career Goes Bung: Purporting to be the Autobiography of Sybylla Penelope Melvyn* (Melbourne: Georgian House, 1946). Because no publisher would accept the manuscript when it was first written circa 1903, Franklin put it aside during her years of exile. In the preface, obviously written later, she described the novel as having been "too audacious for publication." For more information, see Marjorie Barnard, *Miles Franklin* (Melbourne: Hill of Content, 1967), p. 60. All further quotations from this novel will be identified internally by page number.

8. They were published out of sequence. *Prelude to Waking* (1950) does not belong to the saga. The others in chronological order are: *Up the Country* (1928), *Ten Creeks Run* (1930), *Cockatoos* (1954), *Gentlemen at Gyang Gyang* (1936), *Back to Bool Bool* (1931). Through marriage and a host of events, the lives of several memorable pioneer families were linked together, forming the backbone of a sweeping saga.

9. Miles Franklin, *Up the Country: A Tale of the Early Australian Squattocracy by Brent of Bin Bin* (1928), (rpt. Edinburgh: Blackwood, 1931), p. 114. All further quotations from this novel will be identified internally by page numbers. Note that this work covers the period 1830–1860s.

10. Miles Franklin, *Ten Creeks Run: A Tale of the Horse and Cattle Stations of the Murrumbidgee by Brent of Bin Bin*. (Edinburgh: Blackwood, 1930), pp. 142–143. All further quotations from this novel will be identified internally by page numbers. The second book in the series covers the period 1870–1895.

11. Miles Franklin, *Back to Bool Bool: A Ramiparous Novel with Several Prominent Characters and a Hantle of Others Disposed as the Atolls of Oceania's Archipelagoes by Brent of Bin Bin* (Edinburgh: Blackwood, 1931), p. 76. The final book in the sequence covers the period 1927–1928.

12. For a concise but good history of Australia with a complete bibliography, see A. G. L. Shaw, *The Story of Australia* (New York: Roy n.d.).

13. Miles Franklin, *Cockatoos: A Story of Youth and Exodists by Brent of Bin Bin* (Sydney: Angus and Robertson, 1954), p. 67. All further quotations from this novel will be identified internally by page number. The third book in the sequence covers the period 1899–1906.

14. For an account of Franklin's years in exile and her involvement in social causes, like the labor movement in the United States, see Barnard, ch. V.

15. Miles Franklin, *All That Swagger* (Sydney: The Bulletin, 1936), p. 49. All further quotations from this novel will be identified internally by page number.

16. See Mathew, p. 5 and Cecil Hadgraft, *Australian Literature* (London: Heinemann, 1960), p. 166.

17. Colin Roderick, *Twenty Australian Novelists* (Sydney: Angus and Robertson, 1947), p. 219.

18. *"Miles Franklin": A Tribute by Some of Her Friends* (Melbourne: Bread and Cheese Club, 1955), pp. 32–40.

15

Edna St. Vincent Millay—Saint of the Modern Sonnet

Jean Gould

I call Millay the "Saint" of the modern sonnet because she strove for perfection
in a form that was considered old-fashioned, if not obsolete in the early part of
the twentieth century. More specifically, in the same sense that she was supportive
of a form that was being demeaned if not actually under attack, she was the
patron-saint of the modern sonnet. She wrote a good many individual love sonnets
that have immortalized her image as a celebrant of sexual love for its own sake,
plus a number of "intellectual sonnets," like the one on Beethoven's Fifth
Symphony, or the one on Euclid's vision of naked Beauty, or the tribute to all
women activists, dedicated to Inez Milholland, a dashing young Suffragist who
died while campaigning for the Cause. This was read by the poet herself in
Washington, D.C. at the unveiling of a statue of the three leaders in the cause
of equal rights for women.

But beyond these individual fourteen-line poems, Millay is the author of three
sonnet sequences, the first of which is notable for its homely language, its
narrative quality. This sequence is the only one that Millay ever wrote employing
the third person singular, and while an unusual genre piece composed with insight
into the stoical character of a woman, it did not have the appeal or the pure
artistry of her intimate yet objective personal sonnets, or those written out of
deep philosophical conviction, as the other two sequences were. I am referring
to "Fatal Interview," and "Epitaph for the Race of Man," which reach near-
perfection in the sustained intensity of an emotional experience found in the
former, and the powerful philosophic thought in the latter. I intend to trace the
origins of these two sequences as well as those of the single sonnets through the
events in the life of Millay that made her a twentieth-century sonneteer of the
first rank. I am not discounting the worth of many of the lyrics, ballads, and of
an early verse-play, *Aria da Capo*, that Millay wrote, but merely emphasizing

her most valuable contribution to twentieth-century poetry, and that is the modern sonnet. By "modern" I mean a fresh handling of the form while keeping the form itself intact—modern in language and feeling while still classical in form. Like Robert Frost,[1] Millay employed "language common to all"; except for one early sonnet, Millay rejected the classic *thee* and *thou*, and substituted the present-day *you*. The diction and images are twentieth-century: "only until this cigarette is ended"; "jazzing music"; the subway stations flying past. Twenty sonnets were published in *Reedy's Mirror* in April, 1920, and did much to increase Millay's reputation as a literary figure who spoke of her own times.

What was the source of Millay's inspiration? I have always held that the person who evoked her poetry more than any other was Arthur Davison Ficke; notice that I am speaking of inspiration, not influence, for Edna Millay maintained her individuality throughout her career as a poet, which began when she was very young. Her first source of encouragement was her mother, an early divorcee who was herself an unfulfilled poet, and prodded all three of her daughters into artistic endeavor, giving them an unusual appreciation of literature, music and drama. She recognized the gift for poetry that "Vincent," as the family called Edna, revealed from the age of five; and after the girl had won all the prizes offered by *St. Nicholas* magazine, her mother insisted that her daughter enter the latest and longest work Vincent had yet tried—a narrative allegorical poem in iambic tetrameter—in an unusual competition that would result in the one-hundred best poems appearing in an anthology entitled, *The Lyric Year*. The top three out of the hundred selected were to receive $500 first prize, and $250 second and third.

It is well known that Edna St. Vincent Millay narrowly missed winning the coveted first prize. The controversy caused by the fact that her remarkable poem, "Renascence," won no prize but placed fourth in that famous anthology is pertinent here because it led to her long, fluctuating, but always loyal relationship with Arthur Ficke. In November, 1912, Ficke, his best friend, poet Witter Bynner, and Ficke's then-wife, painter Evelyn Blunt, wrote to Millay a few days after publication of *The Lyric Year*, expressing their "thanks" (on Thanksgiving Day) to her for "Renascence," which, in their opinion lit up the entire anthology of far less luminous poetry. Millay was deeply moved by their tribute which arrived December 5. She answered with the brief note, "You are three dear people. This is Thanksgiving Day, too, and I thank you." After "Very truly yours," she signed her full name instead of "E. St. Vincent Millay" as it appeared in the anthology.[2] The men, in a separate letter to the editor, had voiced their suspicions of both the name and the bio-note. They doubted that a "sweet young thing of twenty" could have written a poem with the depth and vision of "Renascence." They claimed that "it takes a brawny male of forty-five to do that," a blatant instance of male chauvinism in the early attitude toward women poets.

The editor passed their remarks along to Millay, who was quick to defend her sex. She simply would not be a "brawny male," she let them know in a second letter. As proof, she included a snapshot of herself, adding, "The 'brawny male' sends his picture. I have to laugh." So began the exchange among the three poets. Between Ficke and Millay there was a communion at once. He was to be her spiritual advisor long before he became her "beloved," but from the first she asserted her strong individuality in regard to her work. When Arthur asked her if one of the lines in "Renascence" had its source in a book, she answered with a resounding, "I'll slap your face." Yet she could accept specific suggestions or criticisms from both Bynner and Ficke, and respected both poets for their scholarly, analytic viewpoints, their literary, artistic backgrounds, both oriental and occidental.

Although Millay met "H. Witter Bynner" at the February (1913) Poetry Society meeting in New York, and found in him a courtly, yet comforting friend among the myriad of new poets she was being introduced to all at once, it would be six years before she met Arthur Ficke face to face. By then—1918—the "sweet young thing" from Camden, Maine had become a sophisticated bohemian of Greenwich Village, struggling to earn her living as a poet and in any form of artistic endeavor she could find to augment her income from the sale of poems. Her first volume had been published in 1917 by Mitchell Kinnerly but no royalties had appeared as yet; she had dozens of admirers, some of them her lovers, some, suitors, but so far no one had touched her deeply enough to inspire her to write love poems. Her most ardent suitor, playwright, pacifist and free-thinker, Floyd Dell, a member of the Provincetown Players who discovered Edna, with her multiple gifts for acting as well as creative writing, and got her to join the Players, could not win her over. She would not marry him or share his ramshackle Village apartment. It was through Floyd Dell, however, that she finally met her fellow poet and spiritual advisor, Arthur Ficke, who, to her surprise, turned out to be an old friend of Dell's from Davenport, Iowa, their home town. Edna had long realized the spiritual affinity between herself and Ficke, but now he entered her life with the blinding impact of physical beauty. He "showed up wearing a Sam Browne belt and puttees, a *Major*, carrying dispatches from Washington to General Pershing,"[3] and asked Dell to introduce him to Millay. She was delighted, but not prepared for the tall, broad-shouldered, superlatively handsome man who came to her apartment on Waverly Place one evening in the early spring of 1918. For once in her life, she was dazzled by male physical perfection, combined in Ficke as she already knew, with a high order of intelligence and a gift for poetry. Before the evening was over, both had acknowledged the unspoken, profound feeling between them.

The hour of their love was brief. A night, a day, and part of another night was all they had together before Arthur sailed on his mission. During the days and weeks that followed his departure, there was a rapturous exchange of love sonnets such as probably never occurred before and has never been duplicated. Ficke's sonnets to Millay have been overlooked in the annals of poetry, but they are among his best. And the love sonnets of Edna St. Vincent Millay that were inspired by Arthur Ficke are among her most lyrical and spontaneous. To her line, "After the feet of Beauty fly my own," the fourth in a sonnet often cited: "Oh think not I am faithful to a vow!/Faithless am I save to love's self alone./ Were you not lovely I would leave you now:/" he answered with the sonnet beginning, "For Beauty kissed your lips when they were young . . . " And, in a sonnet he deemed almost "flawless," she wrote, knowing they could not be together, "Into the golden vessel of great song/Let us pour all our passion; . . . /" with its classic line, "Longing alone is singer to the lute."[4]

They intellectualized their love, and immortalized it, but that did not make it any less real, as some writers have suggested. One has only to read Millay's poignant, brooding lines in the sonnet beginning, "And you as well must die, beloved dust," which, by her own testimony was written to Arthur, and became a lasting bond between them, to realize that their meeting in person on that evening in 1918 was a momentous occurrence for both of them, although she was undoubtedly more affected by it than he. In any case, the deep feeling on both sides was not illusory. And it is essential in discussing Millay's gift as a modern sonneteer to point out that in this rare instance of an exchange of love poems between two poets of opposite sex, it is the woman's that have survived, because they are written with greater artistry.

Emotionally, the fourteen-line poems of Millay present a modern woman who was at times almost masculine in her attitude toward love. It is the woman who takes the initiative in ending a love affair, written to Floyd Dell or some unknown admirer: "I shall forget you presently, my dear/So make the most of this, your little day"; and, "Faithless am I except to love's self alone." Here was the "New" woman, free in her attitude toward love, yet "stern in her soul's chastity." Her loyalty was to her first love, Poetry, written as she considered appropriate to the subject matter, singing out unconventional ideas in traditional forms. As Floyd Dell said, "She learned the molds first, into which she later poured her emotions while hot."[5] Even the most avant-garde literary critics were outspoken in their admiration of these sonnets; and Edmund Wilson was one who never changed his mind about their merit, or in according Millay high status as a poet.

Her love for Ficke found expression not only in the sonnets, but in a general surge of creativity—short lyrics, odes, and verse plays flowed from Millay's fertile mind. She expanded her publication credits to *Poetry, The Dial*, and *Reedy's Mirror*. These magazines, however, paid so little that, after meeting W. A. Roberts, editor of the popular *Ainsley's*, labelled a "trashy magazine" by Edmund Wilson, she placed some of her poems there. When Roberts asked if she had any fiction, she dashed off a short story, but decided to use a pseudonym, Nancy Boyd, for this and all prose pieces in the future. The name of Edna St. Vincent Millay was to signify a poet only, and she rarely compromised her stand on this point. From mid-1918 *Ainsley's* proved a steady source of income for several years.

When the November 11th (1918) Armistice was signed, and the Americans in service who had survived came "marching home again," Arthur Ficke did not stop in New York, or if so, he did not call Edna Millay as he had promised. He wrote her from Davenport that he would come to New York soon, but instead he took his wife and son on a trip to the Orient with Hal Bynner. She knew from the letters of both poets that the Fickes' marriage was failing, and that this trip was an attempt at reconciliation, but she was bitterly disappointed that Arthur had not even stopped in New York long enough to call her.

In the meantime, she had to deal with Floyd Dell. As a pacifist and one of the editors of *The Masses*, the liberal publication founded by Max Eastman, he had been indicted, along with the entire staff, under the Sedition Act of 1918, for defending the rights of conscientious objectors. The arrest papers had been delivered shortly before Arthur appeared on the scene; and later the magazine had dissolved and the rights Dell had defended had been granted to "C.O.'s"; but it made no difference: they all had to stand trial, in the unreasoning wave of war hysteria. Edna Millay's strong sense of justice and loyalty was aroused; she made slight distinction between friendship and love. As Dell pointed out in his memoirs, "friendship had for her all the candor and fearlessness of love, as love had for her the gaiety and generosity of friendship."[6] No matter how irritated she was with him as an over-insistent suitor, she was outraged at the unfairness of his arrest; and, with some of the other members of the Provincetown group, she went down to the courtroom to lend moral support to the victims. In true pacifist spirit, she recited poetry to while away the tedious hours of waiting for the jury to give its verdict which, after two and a half days of debate, was "no agreement." The case was dismissed, pending a new trial.

Floyd Dell was more than delighted by Edna's staunch loyalty, and was quick to assume she had changed her mind about marrying him. She had put him off, parrying for time until she heard from Arthur.

The year 1920 marked Millay's meeting with Edmund Wilson, who was among the first to recognize the superior quality of her sonnets, and who indirectly altered the course of her life by elevating her status both as poet and as a figure to be reckoned with in the literary world.[7] He had been impressed with her work when he discovered it in *Reedy's Mirror*; and after he heard her recite "Renascence" and some of the sonnets at a party he attended with the poet John Peale Bishop, Wilson, like so many others, fell in love with the already legendary Edna St. Vincent Millay. Incidentally, it was Wilson who made the distinction between Millay's "suitors" and her "admirers": the former, who were serious about her, called her "Edna"; to most others, and significantly to Arthur Ficke, she was "Vincent." Wilson wooed her through *Vanity Fair* where he and Bishop were both staff contributors; he, as assistant editor, pointed out to Frank Crowninshield, editor-in-chief, that a writer like Edna Millay was far above the level of *Ainsley's*, and it was not long before she became a regular contributor to a prestigious instead of to a "trashy" magazine.

The love sonnets cited by Wilson as proof of her dexterity in the form are not those usually quoted; of those published in *Reedy's Mirror*, for example, he was especially attracted by one written before she was smitten by Arthur Ficke, while dozens of admirers swarmed around her and none fazed her cool acceptance of ardor. "Love, though for this you riddle me with darts," it begins, "And drag me at your chariot till I die,—/" and goes on to denounce as liars those who call Love "mighty," contains this provocative sextet: "I, that have bared me to your quiver's fire,/Lifted my face into its puny rain,/Do wreathe you impotent to Evoke Desire/As you are Powerless to Elicit Pain!" Then comes the "twist" in the final couplet, parenthetically: "(Now will the god, for blasphemy so brave,/Punish me surely with the shaft I crave!)." Wilson liked the impudence, the arrogance and impishness of her words, expressing a deep desire for love while denying it, quite apart from her skill in structuring the sonnet.

Another of these sonnets noted by Wilson was one that Edna recited to him and John Peale Bishop, who was also her eager escort, as they rode atop a Fifth Avenue bus on the way to the Claremont for dinner. She had just completed the fourteen lines, which Wilson implied might well have been directed to him. Starting off with the query: "Cherish you then the hope I shall forget/At length, my lord, Pieria? . . . " the lines give the lover to understand that she will never forsake "The Singing Mountain" for mortal love. Though he and Bishop with Millay formed a kind of triumvirate of poets for a time, discussing and exchanging their respective efforts at all hours and places, it was inevitable that rivalry sprang up between the two men. Edna herself was fond of them both, but not in love with either. And neither of them could know that she was longing for Arthur Ficke. A third sonnet cited by Wilson as one that always haunted him was not written until later, and states at the outset: "Here is a wound that never will heal, I know." It was written, as nearly as one can place it, in reference to Ficke and his highly questionable, ambivalent behavior toward Millay. One has only to read his love poems, openly dedicated to her in his fourth volume, now at the Beineke Library at Yale, to realize that his conflict must have been deeper than hers.[8]

Of the two young editors at *Vanity Fair*, "Bunny," as his intimates, including Edna, called Wilson, was more persistent than Bishop in courting the shining new contributor to the magazine, and saw her as often as he could. He kept finding new facets to her "swift mind," and was struck by what he termed her "tough intellectual side" one evening when she outlined for him a plan for a long poem dealing with the evolution and extinction of the human race, destroyed by its own kind. Here, as early as 1920 was the genesis of her extraordinary sonnet sequence, "Epitaph for the Race of Man." The fragments she read to him surprised Wilson "in being purely philosophical," giving him a new idea of her range. By the summer of 1920, Wilson was so enamoured of Millay's brilliant mind and mercurial charm that he proposed marriage to her one sweltering night in Truro, where the Millay sisters and their mother had the loan of a cottage. Edna was in a quandary on the question of marriage. She told Bunny she would consider his proposal. He thought he heard her murmur, "That might be the solution," and he was probably right, for she was still waiting for some definite word from Arthur Ficke.

That evocative but evasive advisor-lover kept sending her batches of poems written to or about her, asking her opinion of them as a colleague, but never declaring love for her as a person or planning for a future life together. Finally, in an impulsive moment on October 29, 1920, she took the initiative and sent him a note, an outright admission that she loved him "too," and always would, just as she did the first moment she saw him. This began a series of tender, touching letters from Edna Millay to Arthur Ficke. In a few eloquent paragraphs she set down her emotions, as both had done in their sonnets. In one prophetic sentence she stated openly that they "would never escape from each other." She closed with a quiet vow that he would never be lost to her in any way, and signed herself simply "Vincent."

Yet she did not go into seclusion. According to Wilson, who continued to court her, Edna was besieged by suitors or admirers, and she was working harder than ever to earn her living expenses, since she had moved into a more expensive apartment at 77 West 12th Street. Besides the poems Kinnerly was supposed to publish in her second book, entitled *Second April*, but which had not yet appeared, she was writing a regular series of satiric "Distressing Dialogues" for *Vanity Fair* under her pseudonym, Nancy Boyd. At the same time, by way of contrast and a change of pace, she was dashing off flippant light verse for a volume to follow *Second April*. She heard nothing from Kennerly about either one; he had gone into hiding somewhere and could not be reached. She was sick with fear that both books were gone a-glimmer. When Frank Shay, owner of a Village bookshop, offered to publish the light verse as a chapbook, she accepted hoping to prod Kennerly into producing *Second April*. However, when the little paper volume, entitled *A Few Figs from Thistles,* appeared in November, it brought a tremendous response from the public, particularly the defiant "First Fig," the famous, much quoted "candle quatrain."

Since this is a discussion of Millay's sonnets, I am not going to dwell on the cleverness of "My candle burns at both ends, / It will not last the night," except to say that it catapulted Edna St. Vincent Millay into an enormous popularity as "the poet laureate of the twenties," and a label she never completely lived down. She was also hailed as the mouthpiece for the "new woman" and the voice of rebellious, "flaming youth." The fact that the five sonnets in this small volume included two of those I have mentioned, cited by Wilson as among her best to date, was hardly heeded. Whatever the shadings of merit in the poetry, however, *A Few Figs . . .* was widely read and quoted. It was also often parodied. The poet was rather dismayed by its popularity, not to mention the notoriety the volume brought her over the years. The poems, especially the impudent love sonnets, were not carelessly constructed, and they expressed a certain side of her complex nature, the side that echoed the poetic wits of the past, including Suckling, Andrew Marvell, Robert Herrick and Oscar Wilde. Shakespearean excellence shines in the inverted epithets of the closing couplet of the third sonnet: "So wanton, light and false, my love, are you, / I am most faithless when I am most true," but it was lost on the neophytes of feminism who used it as their credo, voicing undying loyalty to Millay. Her decision to publish light verse separately was one of her undeniable mistakes. The volume created an image of Edna St. Vincent Millay that was not easily dispelled, and that was only a fragmentary view of her essentially serious art.

Moreover, she received little financial return from the wide circulation the volume enjoyed. That December her apartment was so chilly she could not stay up long enough to type her Nancy Boyd piece. Wilson brought her his electric heater and found her looking so forlorn and miserable, bundled up in a bathrobe under the covers, that he suggested she should have a complete change—perhaps join the general exodus of American literary lights who were all leaving for Europe. The idea appealed to Edna: she was tired of all the suitors that knocked on her door, and weary of waiting for word from Arthur. And so "it was decided she should go abroad," according to Wilson.[9] He helped her to arrange with Crowninshield to go as foreign correspondent for *Vanity Fair*; she was to send in two articles a month, which made it possible for her to be paid on an allowance basis. After hectic preparations for the journey (in the midst of which her sister Kathleen was married in Edna's apartment), and a hasty trip to see her mother in New England, Millay sailed for France on January 4, 1921.

She had assured her mother that her sudden plans "had nothing to do with any love affair, past or present." She was going as "a free woman, a business woman, because she wanted to travel." Bold words from a sorely aching heart. In spite of the whirl of activity she found in Paris, the company of compatriots at the cafes—poet brothers Stephen and William Rose Benét, Edgar Lee Masters and composer Deems Taylor, to name a few—she was still longing to see Arthur Ficke again; and she surprised herself with feelings of homesickness. Her letters at this time reveal a nostalgia amounting to neurosis. Those to her family, especially to her mother, are embarrassingly affectionate, effusive. It was inevitable that she should begin writing a ballad, half fairytale, half fable, in tribute to her mother, which, with the finest of her sonnets to Ficke, was to bring the poet her most prominent award. Europe had not brought the change of heart she had hoped for in regard to Ficke. Though she traveled to England, then back to the continent, and took a trip on horseback through Albania, she pined to be with Ficke and said as much in her letters. He had sent her a photograph of himself, which she carried everywhere, but he still had not answered her second declaration of love, mailed from Albania. When she did hear from him, it was to ask if she had returned a rare Japanese print he had lent her. Millay was puzzled and hurt.

In a series of circumstances too complicated to go into here, indicated in my comment that Wilson changed the course of her life, Millay learned that Arthur had come to New York; and it is likely that if Edna had not taken up Wilson's suggestion to go to Europe, she and Arthur would have been together and discovered whether their passionate relationship could endure. If you read the exchange of notes and letters—some of which are "restricted"—as I did in preparation for my biography, you will find a fascinating explanation of my remark. The core is that Ficke met and fell in love with a young painter, Gladys Brown, whom I interviewed several times before she died.[10]

The amazing thing was Millay's reaction when she finally learned the truth from Arthur himself. With unbelievable bravado, she wrote that it did not matter "with whom he fell in love, nor how often, nor how sweetly." It would in no way affect their relationship. They would love each other for all time. And Arthur Ficke took her at her word. *Second April* had appeared while Millay was in France, hailed with shouts of praise by the critics at home. He evidently wanted to keep the tie with a poet of Millay's stature, even to the point of introducing his new love to her. The account given to me by Gladys is revealing of Millay's spirit, her ability to make the most of any situation, no matter how she felt physically or emotionally.

The close of 1922, although a low point in her physical and emotional life, marked a high point in her career. "The Ballad of the Harp-Weaver," the poem written for, and dedicated to her mother, was published by Frank Shay in the same format as *A Few Figs* . . . It was later published by Harper's who became her permanent publishers. For this work, and eight of her sonnets, most of which were written to Ficke and published in *An American Miscellany of Poetry* (the anthology compiled by Amy Lowell and Louis Untermeyer) Millay was awarded the Pulitzer prize, the first in the field of poetry to be won by a woman. This was the only time she received the Pulitzer, although her next sonnet sequence was considered more deserving of award by Wilson and other critics.

And so we come to *Fatal Interview*. Shortly after her return from Europe, she had met for a third time Eugen Boissevain, who was the widower of Inez Milholland, a man who was a free-thinker, believer in women's rights and free love. Floyd Dell had introduced Millay to him previously, but nothing had come of their meeting. This time, at a party in Mt. Airy near Croton, where Millay was spending the weekend with Arthur and Gladys—who were not yet married— and Floyd Dell and the girl he finally found to marry, Edna and Eugen fell in love.[11] He saw that beneath her bright gaiety, Millay was actually ill, and persuaded her to stay at Mt. Airy while having tests to see if the doctors could diagnose her problem. Two months later, just before a serious operation, Edna Millay was married to Eugen Boissevain with Arthur and Gladys as witnesses. He was twelve years older than she, and was in a way, a father to her, since her own father, although friendly at times, had never shown much paternal interest in his daughters. Eugen was proud and pleased to be married to a famous poet, whom he called "Aidna" or "Vincie," depending on the situation. At any rate, he was the most understanding person she could have found as a husband. As she had predicted, she and Arthur Ficke never did escape from each other, and Eugen never questioned their relationship.

After Millay's success in winning the Pulitzer prize, she was offered a series of lectureships at colleges and universities every year. Sometime in 1929, fol- lowing publication of her fourth volume, *The Buck in the Snow*, a serious work, containing a sonnet to Sacco and Vanzetti and several poems reflecting her activism in their sad case, she spoke at the University of Chicago. She was introduced by George Dillon, already recognized as a distinguished scholar and poet of great promise. Their meeting before her lecture had been electric in its intensity. Both must have known they would meet soon again. Shortly thereafter, Millay entered into a love affair of tremendous impact, which inspired the first of her major sonnet sequences. Although Dillon was only twenty-one at the time—fifteen years younger than she—the attraction was so compelling that age made no difference to either. George, who had just been made associate editor of Harriet Monroe's *Poetry*, was known as one of the most charming men in literary circles, a reputation he never lost, and to Edna Millay, he was irresistible. Just when he and Millay realized and fulfilled their love is difficult to place, but from Dillon's letters to his sister in Virginia, and from the testimony of contemporary poets who knew him well, the affair followed her appearance at the university, and ran its course in about a year.

In any case, *Fatal Interview*, her volume of fifty-two sonnets in celebration of a recent love affair was published by Harper in May, 1931.[12] It was hailed by the critics generally for the sustained quality of its passionate lines and for its artistic maturity. Two decades after it was published, Edmund Wilson called the work "one of the great poems of this century." The sonnet sequence traces the course of a troubled and fervid love affair from its inception through its heady Olympian consummation to its deep, sorrowful, poignant close. Taking her title from the opening phrase of John Donne's sixteenth elegy in his celebrated series immortalizing a tragic love, which begins, "By our first strange and fatal interview," Millay sought to answer, in terms of her own experience, and in her own style, all the poets who had sung the praises and trials of love. She began by questioning the worth of her objective, wondering why she should want to "forsake her spiritual wings to journey barefoot with a mortal joy." As the Celtic pagan in her wins out over the New England puritan, she grows rapturous over an irrational and as yet unreturned love. This phase culminates in an outburst of disarming generosity toward her lover, the desire to give all, openly and without guile.

With lilting lyricism Sonnet XI begins, "Not in a silver casket cool with pearls / Or rich with red corundum or with blue," and leads to a figure as refreshing as a field of wildflowers in the morning. Here is an eloquence that seems to epitomize the poet's entire philosophy. The first phrase of the sextet, "Love in the open hand," which she read with deliberate emphasis, reveals the core of Millay's concept of sexual joy. To picture the gift of love as a "brimming hatful of freshly gathered cowslips or a skirtful of shining apples" is to see love as the constant and timeless rejuvenator; the ever-present child in the artist comes forward as Edna Millay in the often-quoted final couplet appears with overflowing arms, "calling out, as children do, 'Look what I have! And these are all for you.'"

The next sonnet is an ecstatic expression of joyful sexual consummation, a powerful paean to the pleasures of sexual joy, which endow the lover with the gifts of the gods. The images are in direct contrast to those of the preceding sonnet; the woman in the poet has superseded the child. The succeeding sonnets of the sequence present their own varied richness. Readers thrilled to simile in the twenty-sixth sonnet, "love like a burning city in the breast," one of Millay's most felicitous images. Perhaps the most celebrated of the fifty-two sonnets is the thirtieth, which begins: "Love is not all: it is not meat nor drink / nor slumber nor a roof against the rain." Her recorded reading of these lines is almost chilling in intensity. The sonnet is often cited in such books as *Love, Sex and Identity*, which is used as a text in a course on "The Erotic Impulse" at New York City's Pace University.[13] In the course of the narrative, certain psychological aspects of the poet's complex nature come to light. She frequently employs Freudian symbols, particularly in the 16th, 21st, and 33rd sonnets, in all of which she makes use of the Dream, each time in a different way. In the 16th, it is an idyll of sexual bliss following gratification; in the 21st the dream portrays a sexual longing for the departed lover, denoting the shadowy glimmer of a mirage in sleep; and the 33rd reveals "a dark and secret dolour," a foreboding of the final, sorrowful phase of the love affair. Both of these are rife with sexual symbols, consciously or unconsciously included. The subjective mood is sustained by the almost exclusive use of the first-person-singular throughout the sequence. The mid-way sonnet, the 27th, is addressed to the Moon, bidding her to "hold off the Sun," as she did on the Carian hill in Keats' *Endymion*. The 29th commands the heart to "have no pity—to shake the poet's house with dancing, break it down with joy." The 42nd counsels an ailing love to be "content to die"; and the 52nd, the last, addressed to Endymion, once more invokes the Moon, described in the third-person-singular. In this closing sonnet, the poet stands apart, viewing the entire episode with the contemplative eyes of a religious mourner for the dead. The finale could be called a hedonistic High Mass for a lost love, invoking the Moon gone mad, "being all unfit for mortal love, that might not die of it."

The immediate effect of *Fatal Interview* on Millay's public career was to increase her popularity, doubling the demands and the fees for her readings. Everyone was eager for a look at the poet who had written such an amazing book of love sonnets at a time when the form was being denounced and repudiated by such poets as T. S. Eliot and Ezra Pound. Millay scorned Eliot's edicts and paid no heed to her detractors; she had more than enough admirers. People everywhere jammed lecture halls to hear her. She received offers for a series of radio broadcasts, which soon materialized in a network series of poetry readings, an unheard-of venture in radio entertainment. Magazines and newspapers clamored for interviews. And all the time controversy ran wild over the "names and dates" of the principals in *Fatal Interview*.

Edna let Eugen handle everything and took no part in publicity matters aside from the readings. When the book came out, she was deep in sorrow over the death of her mother, who had died suddenly of a heart attack in March, 1931, while Edna was still mourning the loss of Elinor Wylie, her adored closest friend among poets of her sex, who had died suddenly also, in December, 1928. Edna wrote memorial poems that caught the spirit of both these women who had meant so much to her. The fact that she dedicated *Fatal Interview* to Wylie, whose work she held in high esteem, is indicative of the value she herself placed on the book. This volume, and the sonnet sequence that followed it, "Epitaph for the Race of Man," insured Edna Millay's literary reputation not only as a first-rank sonneteer, but also as a major American poet. She had put "Epitaph" aside ever since she had outlined the initial plan of the work for Wilson in 1920, but began to consider it again after she and Eugen moved to Steepletop, the country home they bought in the Berkshires. They often studied the stars with Arthur and Gladys, who, after their marriage had bought a home nearby. Sometimes Millay studied the stars by herself, and as her knowledge of astronomy increased, her study of the human race expanded to take in its behavior with relation to the universe.

Viewing Earth as a microscopic planet in the cosmos, "Epitaph for the Race of Man" starts with the prediction that long before its core is cold, Earth will be utterly still, and man and his engines gone. From there, the sonnets look backward in time to the age of dinosaurs, then proceed slowly forward "through fifty million years of jostling time," to man, "crawling out of ooze and climbing up the shore." Destined to stride across the sky like the sun, this strange, brilliant creature capable of laughter and "droll tears," of music and art and the invention of engines, is then mysteriously gone without a trace, and the silent Earth cannot tell the story of his demise. It is the poet who reveals the tragic reason for his eradication. Following him through the trials of the ages, the sonneteer tears away the veil of mystery to show him receiving destruction "at his brother's hand."

The last five sonnets in this sequence are the core of Millay's canon of anti-war poetry. The play on words is inadvertent but not inappropriate, for she waged a war of words against violence and destruction by the military until events in Europe leading up to World War II caused her to become an interventionist. The theme of man's inhumanity to man, of his cancerous greed, is sounded in eloquent powerful passages, until, in the 17th sonnet, the reader, with a sense of horror, sees man "set in brass on the swart thumb of Doom." In the closing sonnet, Millay sings with melodic phrasing a heart-breaking lament for "most various Man, cut down to spring no more," and all "the clamor that was he, silenced, and all the riveted pride he wore." Then with a masterful stroke, in answer to the wracking question, "What power brought you low? whose the heavy blade?" the poem ends with the tender admonition, "Strive not to speak, poor scattered Mouth; I know."

At the time "Epitaph" appeared, in the volume *Wine From These Grapes*, published in November, 1934,[14] it was usually lumped together with the rest of the social-problem poems in the book, like the acrid "Apostrophe to Man," mentioned earlier. The element that sets "Epitaph" apart from other poetry about social problems is its broad perspective and poetic excellence, which enables the work, while retaining its value as social commentary, to reach the realm of art. Yet the significance of ''Epitaph'' is rarely recognized. In fact, it is seldom mentioned by chroniclers or anthologists.

Fortunately, a few eminent critics—like Edmund Wilson, Robert Hillyer, and Max Eastman—and many discriminating admirers have been unafraid to place Edna Millay's mastery of the sonnet in its proper perspective. Though it is true that she has always been overplayed or underplayed, lauded beyond all bounds or dismissed as a youthful exponent of free love expressed in conventional forms, the sequence comprising ''Epitaph'' has been generally neglected in either case. But the timelessness of the theme, ironically more applicable today than it was in 1934; the flawlessness of the technique; and the depth of feeling combine to make this eighteen-sonnet poem profound and enduring.

At the end of her life, in her last volume, written when her world had fallen apart, Millay wrote a sonnet beginning, ''I will put chaos into fourteen lines. . . .''[15] It is significant as proof of the form to which she was deeply devoted. And it is proof, in the excellence of her posthumously published volume, *Mine the Harvest*, that her greatest contribution to twentieth-century poetry is the modern sonnet.

NOTES

1. Jean Gould, *Robert Frost: The Aim Was Song* (New York: Dodd, Mead & Company, 1964). Originally during an interview with Frost, July 27, 1962 in Ripton, Vermont.

2. *Letters of Edna St. Vincent Millay*. Edited by Allan Ross MacDougall (New York: Harper, 1952). Quotations from these letters and the early correspondence are contained in this collection.

3. Floyd Dell, *Homecoming: An Autobiography* (New York: Farrar & Rinehart, 1933). Most of the materials concerning Floyd Dell are from this book, and the one by Dell cited below.

4. This and the other early love sonnets quoted here were first published in *Second April* by Harper & Brothers, 1923. Harper's, which became Harper & Row in 1962, published all of Millay's volumes from 1922 on, including those posthumously published.

5. Floyd Dell, *Love in Greenwich Village* (New York: George H. Doran Company, 1926).

6. Ibid.

7. Edmund Wilson, *The Shores of Light: A Literary Chronicle of the Twenties and Thirties* (New York: Farrar, Straus & Young, 1952). Principally, Epilogue, 1952: ''Edna St. Vincent Millay,'' and ''Give That Beat Again!'' Most of the material and accounts of Wilson's relationship with Millay are to be found in this tribute to Millay. Cf. also correspondence between this author and Wilson when *The Poet and Her Book, A Biography of Edna St. Vincent Millay* was published in 1969. These letters are now in the Jean Gould Collection, Carlson Library Archives, University of Toledo, Toledo, Ohio.

8. Arthur Davison Ficke, *Sonnets of a Portrait Painter*, (New York: Mitchell Kennerly, 1922). ''Epitaph for the Poet V (Hymn to Intellectual Beauty), To Edna St. Vincent Millay.'' Also unpublished letters and notes at Beineke Library, Yale University.

9. Edmund Wilson, *The Shores of Light*; see note 7, above.

10. Interviews with Gladys Brown Ficke, 1967–68.

11. Ibid.

12. This first edition of *Fatal Interview* published by Harper's in May, 1931, was dedicated in a brief memorial poem to Elinor Wylie, never printed in subsequent editions, nor included in the series of six elegiac poems Millay later wrote for Wylie. *Fatal Interview* went into many printings and was, with "Epitaph for the Race of Man," the major section in *Collected Sonnets*, published by Harper's, New York and London, 1941, and in the final volume of *Collected Poems*, posthumously published in 1956, New York and London.

13. Jean Gould, *The Poet and Her Book, A Biography of Edna St. Vincent Millay* (New York: Dodd, Mead & Company, 1969).

14. There was one "gift edition" where "Epitaph" appeared in a slim volume separate from the other poems in *Wine From These Grapes*, both volumes packaged in an elegant black slipcase. As a gift item in December, 1934, it was not as successful as Harper's had hoped.

15. Edna St. Vincent Millay, *Mine the Harvest* (New York and London, Harper's, 1954).

16

Domestic Comedy, Black Comedy, and Real Life: Shirley Jackson, A Woman Writer

Lynette Carpenter

Shirley Jackson's short story, "The Lottery," published in 1948, was responsible for the greatest amount of mail ever received by *The New Yorker* up to that time in response to a piece of fiction. Jackson herself once said, "It was not my first published story, nor my last, but I have been assured over and over that if it had been the only story I ever wrote or published, there would be people who would not forget my name."[1] Now, seventeen years after her death in 1965, an informal survey will indicate that most people remember neither Jackson's name nor the name of her famous story, although most people can, with a little prodding, reconstruct a fairly accurate plot summary out of their memories of high school or college English. Jackson's story has become a part of our educational, and therefore cultural, heritage; her name has been forgotten. And despite her remarkable achievement of both critical acclaim and popular success during her lifetime, she has been virtually ignored by critics and written out of literary history since her death. I would like to suggest that the reasons for this neglect are also reasons for the reevaluation of Shirley Jackson by feminist critics. I will argue that traditional male critics could not, in the end, reconcile genre with gender in Jackson's case; unable to understand how a serious writer of gothic fiction could also be, to all outward appearances, a typical housewife, much less how she could publish housewife humor in *Good Housekeeping*, they dismissed her. Feminist critics, on the other hand, should be able to appreciate the variety of Jackson's writings and the range of her experiences as wife, mother, and Great American Novelist.

To the extent that she is remembered at all, Jackson is remembered for her gothic fiction or psychological thrillers, and one might well contend that writers of gothic fiction have rarely held a secure place in literary history. Worse for Jackson, she was a humorist as well; one of the distinguishing features of her work is a delicate balancing of humor and horror that is bound to make the reader uneasy. In *The Road Through the Wall* (1948), for example, when the comically portrayed thirteen-year-old neighborhood outcast hangs himself, our shock is compounded by our previous guilty participation in laughter at his expense. We may even feel betrayed because the author induced us to laugh at a character she knew to be tragically doomed. A similar situation occurs in *The Haunting of Hill House* (1959), in which the narrative's gentle mockery of the main character does not prepare us for her suicide at the end. Jackson's habit of mocking the doomed must have seemed to many traditional readers decidedly unfeminine.

Still, perhaps the literary historians would have accepted Jackson had she led the ill-fated life of an Edgar Allan Poe. But she did not conform to stereotype. Married to distinguished critic Stanley Edgar Hyman, she was, by published accounts, a model mother, hostess, PTA activist, cookie baker, and faculty wife. And if, in the end, she fell victim to severe nervous depression, no one considered it madness, since model wives and mothers did not, in those days, go mad. How could such a woman write stories about thirteen-year-old suicides, human sacrifice rituals, twelve-year-old girls who dispatched their families with arsenic? To make matters worse, she called herself a witch.

Historians might know less about Jackson's life had she not published numerous domestic sketches throughout her career, collected in *Life Among the Savages* (1953) and *Raising Demons* (1957). Although Jackson herself never called these sketches autobiographical, most readers take them to be slightly modified accounts of actual events. In the only book length study of Jackson to date, Lenemaja Friedman calls them "family chronicles."[2] They are humorous tales in the vein of Jean Kerr and Erma Bombeck about the everyday trials of managing a household and raising children. Stanley Edgar Hyman once wrote that critics did not understand Jackson because they could not reconcile these stories, published in such magazines as *Good Housekeeping, Woman's Day*, and *Woman's Home Companion* with what they considered her more serious work, published in such journals as the *Hudson Review*, the *Yale Review*, and *The New Yorker*.[3] In fact, the sketches display some of the same preoccupations as Jackson's fiction—her interest in the psychology of women and children, her fascination with fantasy worlds and characters, as well as with split or multiple personalities, and her appreciation of irony—but the tone is clearly different. Hyman's comment suggests that since critics were at a loss to explain how one writer could produce both gothic horror and cheerful housewife humor, they gave her up. We might also ask whether writers of domestic sketches have ever been taken seriously as writers. Is it not possible that Jackson's publication of housewife humor in the *Woman's Home Companion* hurt her literary reputation, caused critics, in the last analysis, to reconsider their estimation of her other work? If so, Jackson is overdue for a feminist reevaluation.

Increasingly, in the past decade, feminist scholars have challenged accusations of insignificance directed at women writers by traditional critics, and have made a new place in literary history for women of varied experiences and talents. Because feminist criticism recognizes the divided self that lies at the heart of the female experience in a patriarchal society, it has explored the variety of means by which women writers express multiple selves in their writing, reviving interest, for example in Louisa May Alcott's thrillers, Emily Dickinson's letters, and Ellen Glasgow's and Edith Wharton's ghost stories. In such company, Shirley Jackson appears perfectly normal. Moreover, feminist critics have recently begun to take a closer look at housewife humor, a mode Judith Wilt has labled "matriarchal comedy."[4]

If, as Wilt argues, matriarchal comics elect the safest way to express the frustrations of the female role in a sexist society, Jackson's uniqueness lies in her use of other more dangerous means as well. In fiction, she writes most often about women. The typical Jackson protagonist is a lonely young woman struggling toward maturity. She is a social misfit, not beautiful enough, charming enough, or articulate enough to get along well with other people, too introverted and awkward. In short, she does not fit any of the feminine stereotypes available to her. She is Harriet Merriam in *The Road Through the Wall* (1948), an overweight teenager who thinks to herself, "You'll always be fat, . . . never pretty, never charming, never dainty,"[5] and who may have been the one to murder pink and white, doll-like Caroline Desmond because the little girl was everything Harriet was not. She is Natalie Waite in *Hangsaman* (1951), whose feelings of isolation and alienation during her first few months away at college generate a fantasy other, an imaginary friend. She is Elizabeth Richmond in *The Bird's Nest* (1954), whose adolescent confusion about her mother and her mother's lover splits her at last into a tangle of discrete personalities. She is Eleanor Vance in *The Haunting of Hill House* (1959), whose feelings of rejection and social displacement ultimately lead her to suicide. She is Mary Katherine Blackwood in *We Have Always Lived in the Castle* (1962), who lives with her sister in a state of siege, barricaded against a town's hostility. She is Mrs. Angela Motorman in *Come Along With Me* (unfinished, 1965), whose world has always been peopled by creatures no one else can see. She is even Aunt Fanny in *The Sundial* (1958), whose life of uselessness as a maiden aunt is vindicated by a vision of doomsday.

These women are all victims, and several are clearly victimized by men. Elizabeth Richmond's split personality in *The Bird's Nest* is a result of her mother's neglect, but also of sexual exploitation by her mother's lover. Patriarchs, however, are often the villains. Natalie Waite's father in *Hangsaman* attempts to continue his proprietary control of her intellectual development even after she has gone off to college, just as Aunt Fanny's father presides over her life from beyond the grave by sending her visions of Armageddon. Mary Katherine Blackwood of *We Have Always Lived in the Castle* is the strongest of Jackson's heroines: she retaliates against her tyrannical father by poisoning him, along with most of the the rest of her family. Patriarchy is not beside the point in this novel; Mary Katherine's brother, heir to Blackwood male power, gets the most arsenic. The climax of the novel occurs when a male cousin, supported by the men of the town, attempts to assume her father's role as family head and dictator.

Equally interesting to the feminist critic should be Jackson's portrayal of women's relationships to other women, beginning with her portrayal of adolescent friendships in *The Road Through the Wall*. For most of the girls on Pepper Street, allegiances are drawn by intimidation; the most outspoken and audacious girls attract followers, until a tacitly understood hierarchy exists. Overweight Harriet Merriam, however, manages to develop a close friendship with the Jewish outcast Marilyn Perlman, until Mrs. Merriam intervenes. Without someone to share her ostracism, Harriet falls victim to despair. In *The Haunting of Hill House*, the lonely Eleanor Vance becomes infatuated with the beautiful Theodora when both are invited to a haunted house by a psychic investigator. The appearance of a young man introduces rivalry, tension, and cruelty into the relationship, as Eleanor struggles to maintain her favored status with Theodora. Eleanor kills herself when she is sent away and perceives that she is again to be excluded.

But the closest female friendship is that between the sisters, Mary Katherine and Constance Blackwood, in *We Have Always Lived in the Castle*. With all of the family dead from arsenic poisoning except Uncle Julian, who has been left a feeble-minded invalid by the attack, the Blackwood patriarchy has evolved into a matriarchy, and Constance Blackwood is its benign ruler. Mary Katherine, or Merricat, the narrator, says of her older sister, "She was the most precious person in my world, always,"[6] and the narrative is punctuated by their declarations of love for each other. Although Constance mothers Merricat, Merricat tries to protect Constance from the townspeople, who believe that Constance was the murderer despite her acquittal. The visit from a male Blackwood cousin signifies more than an attempt to reinstate the Blackwood patriarchy; it is also an attempt to undermine the love between the sisters upon which their matriarchal harmony depends. Cousin Charles tempts Constance with a romantic illusion of heterosexual happiness, a life more natural, in his eyes and in the eyes of the townspeople, than the life she is living with her sister. Merricat fights back and wins. After a cataclysmic confrontation which exposes Cousin Charles' greed and the murderous hostility of the townspeople, and which leaves Uncle Julian dead of a heart attack, the two women resolve to spend the rest of their lives together in isolation, and barricade themselves against intrusion from the outside world. In the final pages of the book, Constance tells her sister, "I am so happy" (*Castle*, p. 211).

The story about the persecution of two women who choose female companionship over heterosexual romance will sound familiar to many readers familiar with feminist writings on witchhunts and witchhunters. The connection is made explicit in the novel: Merricat aspires to be a witch, constantly devising spells and charms, but it is Constance who possesses the wise woman's knowledge of plants and their properties. Jackson herself owned a large collection of works on demonology. In the mid-fifties, she wrote *The Witchcraft of Salem Village* (1956) as a Landmark book for Random House. Yet even earlier, Jackson had established herself as a champion of the persecuted and the oppressed. At Syracuse University in the late thirties, she and Hyman had waged a bitter campaign against racial discrimination in campus housing. Her first novel, *The Road Through the Wall*, portrays discrimination against Jews and Orientals. And hindsight can suggest why Jackson wrote "The Lottery," a story about a scapegoat ritual, in the days of a cold war red scare and HUAC investigations.

Finally, a feminist critic should be better able to piece together Jackson's life and art than a traditional critic. Lenemaja Friedman's careful account of Jackson's life in *Shirley Jackson* does not attempt to speculate on the reasons for Jackson's attacks of anxiety and depression in the late fifties and early sixties, but a reader will not be able to resist the temptation to read between the lines. After Betty Friedan's analysis of the pathology of the feminine mystique, or even Erma Bombeck's witty commentary on Supermoms, how can we read a catalogue of Jackson's virtues as wife, mother, and great American writer without wondering how she kept her sanity? She was chauffeur to a family of six (her husband did not drive), PTA mother, Little League supporter, a wonderful cook, an energetic hostess, and a one-time president of the faculty wives' club at Bennington College. But she was also a prolific writer, and wrote every day, taking time out to serve refreshments at regular Thursday night poker games. *We Have Always Lived in the Castle* was written during the early years of Jackson's illness, when she found the company of others increasingly difficult to bear and began to withdraw into seclusion. She created Mary Katherine Blackwood, a narrator all contemporary reviewers labeled mad, shortly before beginning psychiatric treatment for her own anxieties.

Jackson's journals from 1963 will sound familiar to those who have read the personal writings of other women struggling to survive as individuals and as writers in a social context antithetical to female survival on those terms. About her career to that point, she muses: "insecure, uncontrolled, i wrote of neuroses and fear and i think all my books laid end to end would be one long documentation of anxiety. If i am cured and well and oh glorious alive then my books should be different. who wants to write about anxiety from a place of safety?"[7] She wants very badly to get well, but writes: "i must do it alone; do i have the courage? i am shaking." When she contemplates the "new life" she is battling to achieve, she sees it in terms of strength and independence: "to be separate, to be alone, to *stand* and *walk* alone, not to be different and weak and helpless and degraded . . . and shut out." Like many of her literary sisters, she believed in the power of her writing to create and affirm a new self: "writing is the way out writing is the way out writing is the way out." She looks forward to a time when she can write "perhaps a funny book. a happy book," and ends one entry, "laughter is possible laughter is possible laughter is possible."

Jackson's mental health improved. When she died of heart failure in 1965, she was working on a new novel, *Come Along with Me*—apparently a "happy book.'' It was the first Jackson novel to feature a female protagonist close to Jackson's own age. The narrator is a recent widow who buries her husband, sells her house, picks a city at random, and gleefully starts off for a new life under a new name. The book can be seen as a celebration of new beginnings. Ironically for Jackson, however, who had once been assured that her name would not be forgotten, the book marks the end of a distinguished career and the beginning of critical forgetfulness. Writing is the way out.

NOTES

1. ''Biography of a Story,'' in Shirley Jackson, *Come Along with Me*, ed. Stanley Edgar Hyman (New York: Viking, 1968), p. 211.

2. *Shirley Jackson*, Twayne United States Authors Series, No. 253 (Boston: Twayne, 1975), p. 145.

3. In Shirley Jackson, *The Magic of Shirley Jackson*, ed. Stanley Edgar Hyman (New York: Farrar, Straus, and Giroux, 1966), p. vii.

4. ''The Laughter of Maidens, the Cackle of Matriarchs: Notes on the Collision Between Comedy and Feminism,'' *Women and Literature*, NS 1 (1981).

5. *The Road Through the Wall* (New York: Popular Library, 1976), p. 214.

6. *We Have Always Lived in the Castle* (New York: Viking, 1962), p. 28. All subsequent references are to this edition of the text.

7. All subsequent journal references are to undated journals in the Library of Congress Manuscript Division.

17

Records of Survival: The Autobiographical Writings of Marieluise Fleisser and Marie Luise Kaschnitz

Ruth-Ellen B. Joeres

Aside from sharing a first name, Marieluise Fleisser and Marie Luise Kaschnitz seem in many other ways to have been uncannily alike. They were both born in 1901, both died in 1974; they spent most of their lives, including the dark years from 1933 to 1945, in Germany, yet they were neither Nazis nor Nazi sympathizers. As so-called "inner exiles," they belonged to that loosely defined group of writers who retreated into inner worlds as protest against the chaos and inhumanity around them. They concentrated as writers on particular genres in which they became well-known and respected. By the time of the Weimar Republic years, Fleisser was considered an important and controversial play-wright whose absurd view of a world gone mad seemed clearly reflected in the Germany of the 1920s and 1930s. Kaschnitz's personal and intense lyric poetry and short prose have become the subject of considerable discussion since the 1950s. The fame of both women has been largely confined to Germany; there are few translations of their works, only occasional book-length scholarly studies, yet they are considered to be among the most skilled German writers in this century.

Another habit shared by Fleisser and Kaschnitz involved the writing of au-tobiographical prose works—diaries, essays, and short stories heavily colored by personal detail—that appeared in great abundance in the later years of their lives. The personal politics these works display is neither overt nor obvious, but rather an effort to define a world in highly subjective fashion; the result is not only a collection of valuable source materials for the history of German women, but also a vivid look into the psyche of women whose role in that history was often uncertain and ambivalent. Born after the heyday of the radical feminists active at the end of the previous century and dying at the onset of the new feminism of the 1970s, Fleisser and Kaschnitz represent a vulnerable transitional group of writers caught up in two world wars. It saw itself at home nowhere. While logically it should have carried on in the progressive tradition that it had inherited, it often seemed bewildered and dislocated. The autobiographical writings of both women offer insight into a group that spent much of its energy trying just to stay alive: these records of survival seem appropriate introductions to two representative personalities whose importance should not be confined by barriers of language to a limited geographical sphere.

Despite the similarities between Kaschnitz and Fleisser, it becomes apparent as soon as one turns to the texts in question that their experience was shared only on certain levels. The most essential difference between them is socially determined. Kaschnitz, daughter of an upper-class family, married to a titled Viennese professor of archaeology, seems to share the philosophizing bent of her class and the tendency to take a broad world-view and to gain a perspective on her life as a whole. Fleisser, whose very birthdate, she tells us, was uncertain, whose father was a shopkeeper, remains particularistic, unable to concentrate on more than a short segment of her life at a time and tending instead to dwell on individual, often harsh details. There is divergence as well in the literary structures which the two women chose to define their lives: Kaschnitz developed to a finely-honed delicate art a form she called "Aufzeichnungen," sketches, diary-like entries in the first person, while Fleisser generally hid behind the third person and was most autobiographical in her ostensibly fictional short stories. But together, they illustrate a large segment of middle-class German women in this century. Either overtly or covertly, they give us information on their own perception of themselves as women, on the effect of war on their lives, and on the role played by others, especially men, in the shaping of their self-image. The resulting picture is both ambiguous and revealing.

The uncommitted and hesitant character of their generation is immediately apparent in their reactions to the more radical women of an earlier time. As Kaschnitz remarks in her last major autobiographical work, the 1973 *Orte* (Places) "I was not interested in the women's movement, whose great forerunners were already old by then, by the time of the First World War; I belonged instead to that group of women who recognized their accomplishments, but reneged on the inheritance."[1] Fleisser, in an answer to a question of what she had found to be the most significant characteristic of the first third of this century, wrote that it was the changing position of women. Yet she remained negative in her assessment, pessimistically commenting that male brutality prevents women from gaining by force what is their due.[2] Admiration of the strength and determination of their forerunners was not accompanied either by a desire to carry on the tradition or an optimistic belief that such a continuum was possible or indeed desirable.

In addition, the attitude of both women toward men imparts a sense of powerlessness and insecurity, or at the very least an impression of the secondary and dependent role to which they as women felt themselves consigned. The men who were so dominant in their lives often assumed a central position in their

autobiographical writings as well, in texts supposedly concentrating on the in-
nermost thoughts of their authors. In her later years, Kaschnitz wrote at length
on the effect of her husband's drawn-out illness and death upon her and her
understanding of her world. Similarly, Fleisser's descriptions in many of her
short stories and essays of her mentors Bertolt Brecht and Lion Feuchtwanger
and of Helmut Draws-Tychsen, a writer to whom she was briefly engaged, often
removed her from the major focus of the text. Particularly noteworthy in this
regard is her ambitious story "Avantgarde," an account of her devastating
relationship with Brecht. It abounds in sentences like the following:

The man was a power; he immediately broke her . . . She skipped her lectures and seminars
so that she could be available whenever the poet needed her. She took care of the daily
garbage for him. His time was worth more than hers, there was no argument about that
. . . Apparently, she could not manage at all without a male around . . . To get engaged
was horrible for a woman if she was a writer.[3]

For Fleisser, men are alternately saviors and monsters, but their role is vital to
her existence despite their always ruinous effect on her. In a less violent account
of her relationship with Brecht, the short sketch "Fruhe Begegnung (Early
Meeting)," she pointedly uses the first person: "And yet in my personal fate
Brecht was the enduring force that continued to pierce me—and it also brought
me bitter fruit."[4] Her report on the influence of Lion Feuchtwanger upon her is
equally insecure: in the short story "Aus der Augustenstrasse (From Augustus
Street)," she says that after Feuchtwanger had read all that she had written and
had labelled it "expressionism and convulsion," she burned everything except
the one story he had liked.[5] Draws-Tychsen is described by her as egotistical,
overpowering, and completely dictatorial in his relationship with her;[6] her later
husband Josef Haindl is depicted as a source of great misery and unhappiness
in her life. In an agonized tale entitled "Der Rauch (Smoke)," for example,
one senses no irony and only a maddening martyrdom when she comments: "If
I had run away from him, it would have been better for him, but I didn't know
where to go."[7] Patricia Meyer Spacks has described such an attitude as typical
for women autobiographers who see their vulnerability as virtuous, but Fleisser's
perception of herself is more like that of someone trapped in horror, who strikes
out at all those in power over her, but who is only ineffectual in her anger.[8]

Kaschnitz, whose gentility does not prevent her from being straightforward,
never presents the image of lesser woman cowed by male power that one finds
in Fleisser's writing. Fleisser is often the hapless, if wisecracking victim; Kaschnitz, on the other hand, obviously loved the man she married, was willing to
live very much for him, and was greatly damaged by his death. Her 1963 volume
of sketches, *Wohin denn ich* (Where Do I Go Now?), devotes its entire contents
to the attempt to emancipate herself from her grief, yet the results remain ambiguous: "I had drawn you deeper inside me and knew that I could not lose you
any more."[9] The idea of marriage as essential to her existence continues to

dominate Kaschnitz's autobiographical work even in her final volume *Orte* (*Places*) with its frequent references to her husband and to their married life. Whatever recovery takes place must occur within the framework of memory, of the still overpowering presence of a man long since dead.

In the relationships depicted by Fleisser and Kaschnitz with the men in their lives—whether devoted, beloved husband, strenuous mentor, or vicious dictator—there is a continuing impression of insecurity. At the time that all the texts referred to thus far were written, their authors were already important and respected writers, recipients of awards, widely published and reprinted. Where is their positive image of self, one is tempted to cry: what does it take to make a woman, even in this most progressive of centuries, grasp her own worth? Or is the peculiar situation of Germany during much of this era responsible for their uncertainty? Did the two wars that affected much of the globe have a particularly destructive effect on Germans, especially German women?

The resilience of youth helped Fleisser and Kaschnitz to survive the horrors of the war of 1914–18; it was the war of 1939–45 that made a far more lasting impression upon them. Both women withstood the pain of loss, the mental anguish, and the brutality caused by the men in their lives, albeit with mixed results. The same harsh honesty imbues their descriptions of the war, an unrelenting objectivity that emphasizes less their insecurity in the matter of personal relationships than their continuing effort to comprehend themselves against the background of the National Socialist dictatorship. Kaschnitz does not glorify the so-called "inner emigrants" among whom she was counted, and tries instead to analyze their role, to give it form and meaning without any sort of ameliorating embellishment:

Frankfurt in wartime, and what was it supposed to have consisted of, our so-called inner emigration? Was it that we listened to foreign radio stations, met and complained about the government, now and then shook hands with a Jew on the street, even when someone could observe us? Was it because we foretold the war, the total war, the defeat, and therewith the end of the Party? We didn't secretly print fliers in the basement, we didn't distribute them late at night, we didn't listen to resistance groups that one knew existed, but that one did not want to know too much about. Better to survive, better still to be around, to continue work when the spectre was past. We are not politicians, we are not heroes, we did something else. That other thing sustained us, research for him, the history of Mediterranean structures, for me the retelling of Greek myths, my poems, later on the life of the French painter Gustav Courbet, which I told anew. We never doubted the importance of our work: according to my view of things at the time, scholarly recognition, a felicitous line of verse, even one that would never be printed, could change the world, better it, that was our version of resistance, one that made us alien, indeed traitorous. National Socialism, however, anticipated something that would arise again later on, on an international, a global scale, namely the concept of the remoteness of pure science, of the superficiality of formalistic bourgeois art.[10]

The ability to see honestly the tentativeness of her position, to grasp in however weak a perspective the necessity of survival, takes her a step beyond the uncertain and dependent portrait she draws of herself as a widow. On a far more direct and concrete level Fleisser expresses a similar sentiment. Toward the end of the war she, like most remaining non-military Germans, was sent to a munitions factory to work, where the small and anonymous parts she assembled were, she was informed, essential to the survival of many: "I couldn't ignore what the supervisor said, I had no choice. I didn't want to cause anyone's death. Still, it was a killing machine on which we all had to work. The war had us in its grip. I had stayed in the country, that was my choice. I had a despairing love for this country, my roots were here, I felt myself bound to its language. To give up the language would mean that I would die off."[11] The need to come to grips with one's responsibility in that worst of wars is as essential for Fleisser and Kaschnitz as is the importance of finding a rationale to continue living. Accordingly, both women frequently use that most German of words, *Angst*: the pervasive *Angst* Fleisser claims did not leave her during the years of the war,[12] the concrete examples of *Angst* provided by Kaschnitz.[13]

Despite the fact that neither woman was threatened by more than the expected dangers of a war—neither was Jewish, neither was active in the resistance—the agony seems to have remained with them and to have become more intense with the passage of years. The oppression of the war was in many ways an extension of the omnipresent oppression of their anxiety and vulnerability: viewed abstractly, war provided them with the *Angst,* the sense of helplessness, that they also experienced during the less dramatic periods of their lives. The effect of the war upon them became the metaphor to describe much of their existence. The fear and impotence it brought forth in them were significant in the formation of a self-image that they carried with them for the rest of their lives.

As members of a generation characterized by suppression and defeat on many fronts, Kaschnitz and Fleisser illustrate how fragile the emancipation proclaimed with the enfranchisement of German women in 1919 really was. Germany's turn to National Socialism was, in fact, a direct blow to women's rights: women, as Fleisser tells us, became "Weiberfleisch," wares, more powerless even than the most impotent men around them.[14] But in addition to the concrete effect of the war upon their thinking about themselves is the sense of lasting insecurity that continuously encircled them. At the time of the war, they seem to have entered a sort of vacuum, a breath held that was not released again until the decade of their death, when their country had once again begun to take cognizance of women and their rightful place in the world.

Yet despite the fragility, despite the essentially gloomy portrait of vulnerable, often helpless women in a chaotic era that frequently did violence to them not only in physical, direct ways, there is an underlying current of power and optimism that becomes evident primarily through the telling of their lives. Kaschnitz claims that writers are born with an urge to express themselves autobiographically; she lends credence to such expression by making it representative of the many who, for reasons of hesitancy, tact, and inability to speak, or shame, cannot share of themselves as she is able to do.[15] The personal writings of both

Kaschnitz and Fleisser depict weakness in the face of oppression, but they expose a sense of durability as well. Both women were clearly diminished by the men who surrounded, indeed engulfed them, and by the world events that on occasion threatened to bury them. But by simultaneously exposing—and being exposed by—their accounts of a life in a difficult era, they have become representative of a generation caught in turmoil. The fact that they managed to write openly and with passionate involvement assures their survival and is a victory, however muted. Indeed, in their will to live on and to provide words that acknowledge and underline their existence, they serve as a bridge over the silent abyss that Germany has symbolized during much of this century: Kaschnitz, through an eloquent honesty that lent to her personal struggle to survive a larger relevance and importance for the twentieth-century German woman who has often needed a particular strength to go on; Fleisser, by means of a more accessible and equally determined will to describe and share her pain and by naming it, to transcend it. They show their strength in an act of accommodation rather than rebellion, in their ability to live within a given, yet not to be totally defeated by that given. They remain unrelenting, yet through their writing they share of themselves, and describe in their own histories an era that was often intent upon suppressing their hopes and ambitions. The mere recording of such histories is a step toward understanding, communicating, and providing perspective.

With the onset of age, Kaschnitz in particular became more confident and assertive and seemed to have found some optimism to temper her often dark view of her world, to have gained an independence of thought and action. In *Orte* (Places), for example, there are passages like the following that offer evidence of new strength:

I received a letter from somebody my age and it said that we all live in a death cell, no one visits us, we cannot leave the room, we only have to wait until somebody fetches us, and the scaffolding is already being erected in the prison yard. I don't understand the letter writer. I know that I am going to die, but I don't feel as if I am in a death cell. I hear the wild, heavy sounds of life and sense the sun and the icy rain on my skin. Age is no prison for me, but more like a balcony from which under certain circumstances one can fall, hit by lightning or overcome by vertigo, not because it is so dark and lonely, but because the sun is shining with such vehement power.[16]

Finally, a joyful and positive element that emerged in Kaschnitz's later autobiographical work was her effort to describe and define even the smallest, most basic parts that make up her being. There is an intense re-confirmation of her self in such descriptions, an affirmation of one who has found value and purpose in her existence:

I thought today about the fat marble hand of a child which once lay on a desk, not mine. It was the hand of a child that had died, a memory piece; I could not have owned it—I always would have dwelled on what the original looks like now, after ten years under the earth, twenty years under the earth, and that marbled hand still so dimpled, so well-nourished. I thought about that strange hand as I looked at my own, spread out but not stretched before me on the table, relaxed but not tired, ready to grasp my notebook, but then it just lay there, let itself be observed, my strong, no longer young hand. The veins emerge from the old hands, veins that once were concealed under smooth flesh, one long one stretching from the base of the hand up to the start of the middle finger, where it splits unclearly; a short broad one under the ring finger, ugly, almost like a bundle of veins. Another new feature, the small brown spots, freckles or liver spots appearing singly, but also in bunches, then disappearing again; they have nothing to do with the sun. Hold still, hand, don't start tapping your fingers, don't make yourself into a fist. Your skin is stretched over the bones in fine wrinkles, but that changes as soon as you make a fist, then the bones jump up as smooth as ivory like naked ridges out of the valleys, and when you tap your fingers another vein appears in the flatness. Your fingers are long but hardly thin; two of the ridges evidence what one in medical texts calls a spatula form, the others look younger, taper off. The nails are pinkish red and not very neatly polished, the great half moons at their base disappearing under the polish. The thumb has the rather unattractive ability of being able to bend at its lowest joint; it is then horizontal, a little joke that made quite an impression when I was a schoolchild, although naturally I don't do that any more. Like the fingers, the back of the hand is long and strong, it would be nice to look at if it weren't distorted by the blue veins and the brown spots I've already mentioned. One should also mention the two rings on the ring finger, two gold rings; one of them, my wedding ring, is narrow, the other is so broad that there is room enough for four small jewels, an old-fashioned piece of jewelry pleasing to me because it is so plain. Now turn over, hand, show your inner side, now you look rounder, softer, you cup yourself like a small basket or bowl; now the ring finger can no longer lie flat on its back, it juts above all the others in its uppermost part. I don't know anything about the lines; in the right hand there are very few in any case, no interesting ones as there are in the left hand, where the lines break off, then start again, then split like antlers, auxiliary lines, like the pale repetitions of a rainbow, a sense of disorder, unclear crosses, detailed root systems, deep furrows up to the index finger and the little finger. There are also furrows, weak ones, in the right hand. If, as I have been told, they indicate talent, and if, as I have also been told, the left hand is a mirror of inherited factors, and the right, the expression of one's own personality, then things look bad for me, a pitiful talent with accentuated vitality and harmony. Fat bumps, hills, and valleys are also visible in the right hand, which is as soft on the inner side as it is tense and hard on the outside. The hand for the cooking spoon, the garden hand, the piano hand, the writing hand, the hand for tenderness. How many movements are carried out in the course of a lifetime, how many pressing motions, and now it is lying there before me on the table, still, tan, yet strange, like anything else that one might observe for a long time and with such intensity. It is ever more peculiar, that bony piece of human flesh with its five grotesque extensions, its five stupid little faces, regulated by a part of my brain,—but it could also act independently, could rip out my hair, could scratch me until I bled, could grasp me by the throat, the frightening thing. So it is better to put a pen into its fingers, move, you thing, describe yourself, write.[17]

It is easier to write about women as heroes, to beable to view them in shining, positive light. It is, however, often unrealistic to do so. Marieluise Fleisser and Marie Luise Kaschnitz are believable representatives of their particular era, of the war-ridden years of this century that saw virtually no progress for German women. The historical reality of the Nazi suppression of women is illustrated vividly by the circumstances of Fleisser's existence, the almost constant victimization either at the hands of men or of a dictatorial government. Kaschnitz's struggle to survive not only the war, but also the sense of abandonment at the death of her husband, shows her insecurity as well as her effort to overcome a loss that diminished her greatly. The web of personal uncertainty that both women depict is symbolic of a larger problem, of a generation of women that did not, perhaps could not, carry on in the optimistic pattern established by previous generations.

Nevertheless, Fleisser remained tenacious despite her *Angst*, and Kaschnitz never abandoned her determination to understand and give meaning to her existence. Their greatest accomplishment is not so much in their use of the genres for which they are best known, but rather in their ability to paint an elusive, but important portrait of an unsettled age, a portrait neither radical nor expected, but representative of the great majority of contemporary German women. Above all, they allow us insight into the troubled psyche of a generation whose principal accomplishment—survival—is given worth and substance.

NOTES

1. Marie Luise Kaschnitz, *Orte. Aufzeichnungen* (Frankfurt: Insel, 1973), p. 91. All translations of Kaschnitz's and Fleisser's texts are my own.
2. In an essay entitled "Ruckblicke auf die ersten dreissig Jahre," reprinted in Gunther Ruhle, ed., *Materialien zum Leben und Schreiben der Marieluise Fleisser* (Frankfurt: Suhrkamp, 1973), pp. 176–77.
3. Marieluise Fleisser, "Avantgarde," *Gesammelte Werke* III (Frankfurt: Suhrkamp, 1972), found respectively on pp. 117, 117, 168, and 168.
4. Fleisser, "Frühe Begegnung," *Gesammelte Werke* II, p. 307.
5. Fleisser, "Aus der Augustenstrasse," *Gesammelte Werke* II, p. 309.
6. Fleisser, "Ich reise mit Draws nach Schweden," *Gesammelte Werke* II, p. 207 and elsewhere.
7. Fleisser, "Der Rauch," *Gesammelte Werke* III, p. 225.
8. Patricia Meyer Spacks, "Women's Stories, Women's Selves," *The Hudson Review* XXX, 1 (Spring, 1977), 27–46. See especially p. 44:

The dependency and need which both women confess and which help to determine their acting and their being do not exist merely as verbal formulations; they obviously represent genuine feelings. But they are among other things also ways of telling a story; the writer evokes such emotions, among the infinite number available to any autobiographer, partly because they provide useful methods of self-definition, self-reassurance, and particularly self-protection. The women [sic] who displays such feeling acknowledges her fear of being abandoned and accepts the moral consequences of that fear. The female concern with moral issues, as manifested in autobiographies and diaries, insistently associates itself with women's experiential awareness of lack of freedom, lack of social power. Women display their vulnerability and convert it into their virtue.

9. Kaschnitz, *Wohin denn ich* (Hamburg: Claassen, 1963), p. 224.
10. Kaschnitz, *Orte*, p. 112.

11. Fleisser, "Eine ganz gewohnliche Vorholle," *Gesammelte Werke* III, p. 207.

12. Fleisser, "Rauch," *Gesammelte Werke* III, p. 237.

13. Kaschnitz, *Orte*, p. 168. The specific examples she mentions are the climate of fear deliberately cultivated by the government in its attempts to control its subjects by spreading terrifying rumors, and the sleepless nights she suffered through after complaining to a friend, then lying awake thinking that she, too, could disappear.

14. Fleisser, "Eine ganz gewohnliche Vorholle," *Gesammelte Werke* III, p. 216.

15. Kaschnitz, *Tage, Tage, Jahre. Aufzeichnungen* (Frankfurt: Fischer, 1968), p. 152.

16. Kaschnitz, *Orte*, p. 145.

17. Kaschnitz, *Tage, Tage, Jahre*, pp. 196–97.

18

Jhabvala's Fiction: The Passage From India

Charmazel Dudt

It is a truism that woman today is caught between old strictures and new possibilities. She is well aware of her historical role and, therefore, struggles to establish a consistent, reliable identity as a member of a world which has not yet absorbed her as an integral part. When this struggle with temporal change is compounded with spatial and cultural challenges, what is written must be considered carefully for what it reveals of the struggle itself, and for the end it prophesies. The novels of Ruth Prawer Jhabvala, thus, have an immediate poignancy, for they reflect her personal journey from illusory myth to dusty reality.

Born of Polish parents in Germany in 1927, she went to England as a refugee at the age of twelve, achieving an easy transition from writing in German to composing stories in English about the lower-middle classes in England. She met an Indian architect while she was studying English Literature at Queen Mary College, London University, and married him. They moved to Delhi, where she has lived from 1951. "I have lived here for most of my adult life," she says, "and have an Indian family. This makes me not quite an insider but it does not leave me entirely an outsider either. I feel my position to be at a point in space where I have quite a good view of both sides but am myself left stranded in the middle."[1]

According to Jhabvala, her books are an attempt "to present India to myself in the hope of giving myself some kind of foothold. My books may appear objective, but really I think they are the opposite: for I describe the Indian scene not for its own sake but for mine. . . . My work can never claim to be a balanced or authoritative view of India but is only one individual European's attempt to compound the puzzling process of living in it."[2] A survey of four of her novels, written over nearly twenty years, from 1956 to 1975, reveals through her reaction to India, the difficulty in establishing a personhood and the price one has to pay for it.

When she first went to India, she wrote easily about the country and its people: "I did this quite instinctively. . . . It never struck me at that time that there was anything strange in my writing in this way about Indians as if I were an Indian."[3] In her first book, *Amrita*, the central character is the new woman who clashes directly with the old world.[4] She is fiercely determined to keep her job at the radio station despite her mother's desperate attempts to arrange for her marriage within her pseudo-European circle of friends; Amrita, however, is in love with Hari, a fellow-worker from a different caste. Yet she is neither a Nora nor a Hedda. Amrita delights in shocking her elders, but hesitates to go to a local restaurant in the company of two men. When compelled to go, she "kept her eyes lowered, and listlessly crumbled a small cream cake on her plate." (*Amrita*, p. 54). The boys enjoyed themselves thoroughly. One cannot avoid the impression that the westernized characters in the book are so only superficially. Her grandfather lives in a musty house surrounded by a litter of tastelessly chosen *objets d'art*, and dreams of the good old days when he was a barrister. One aunt has a wealthy husband who does nothing but affect boredom, while another aunt can only indulge her appetite for clothes and sweets. Both women are incapable of action, exactly like the grandfather's music box from Baden-Baden in Germany whose insides have long since ceased to move.

Hari's family, on the other hand, is life itself; simple and unspoiled, their ways are traditional. They are boisterous Punjabis who live in the center of town, and they are determined to marry their son to a "good" girl. Sushila Anand is their choice, for she knows how to cook and sew, and has wisely chosen to marry instead of developing her voice for the record market. The contrast between the feverish activity connected with the wedding and the languid humidity of Amrita's house where the servants do nothing but count and recount the silver cutlery, is almost too obvious for comment. The bias of the author towards the ancient and ritualistic seems undeniable in the last sentence of the novel: "It was all over, a high pitched voice sang a hymn. . . ; he had led her round the fire seven times and now she was his; and though he still could not see her . . . he was suddenly so happy, he felt he had/never been so happy in his life." (*Amrita*, p. 283).

In 1958, seven years after her own marriage, Jhabvala introduced into an increasingly bitter portrait of India, the theme of an East-West marriage. Each of the characters in *Esmond in India* is led by dreams towards destruction, and the conflict arising from Western influences is given strong statement. Ram Nath, the center of an admiring Cambridge crowd long ago, has sacrificed his life as a lawyer for the emergence of new India. His wife, prepared to live in a large house with many relatives and servants, does not understand the cause for which he forfeited his property and subjected himslf to prison.[5] He is no longer the bright, sharp little flame that conveyed a sense of urgency; instead, he has grown old, and his sister notices that life itself seems to have withdrawn from him

(*Esmond,* p. 177). The degree of his present ineffectiveness is emphasized in his inability even to arrange a marriage between his only son and the daughter of his once-best friend. "His past had been so full; and his present was nothing. He had lost contact, not with the world of affairs, of politics, meetings; he did not mean that, because that he had relinquished deliberately—but with all the world, all life." (*Esmond,* p. 193).

If Ram Nath represents the old world, then it is an unsatisfying one. Adherence to the classical prescription for Indian behavior that demands a retreat from things of this world has not brought an enlargement of the mind, but rather a narrow isolation. Can we then assume that those who throw themselves into the affairs of life have any sense of satisfaction? The answer again is "No." Har Dayal, the successful politician-litterateur is devoted to the Public Cause. He presides over never-ending meetings, advises Ministers, and allows himself to be garlanded at public functions. Surrounded as he is by adoration from friends and family, and busy as he may be with lectures and meetings and "many things to be arranged" he is, nevertheless, aware of the absence of spiritual satisfaction within (*Esmond,* p. 69). There is an ever-present sense of futility, and as he walks away from a successful lecture, he reminds himself of Shelley's Ozymandias.

That which has once served to inspire man, now appears to Har Dayal illusory and leaves him with little consolation. Even the central character, Esmond, is enticed into marrying India only to be trapped by her reality. His wife, whose eyes he had once thought "full of all the wisdom and sorrow of the East" was merely a dumb animal who did not even react to his brutality. "His senses revolted at the thought of her, of her greed and smell and languour, her passion for meat and for spices and strong perfumes. She was everywhere; everywhere he felt her—in the heat saturating the air which clung to him and enveloped him as in a sheath of perspiration . . . in the faint but penetrating smell of over-ripe fruit; everywhere, she was everywhere, and he felt himself stifling in her softness and her warmth." (*Esmond,* pp. 166–67). His only recourse is to escape, not into himself as Ram Nath has done, nor into frenetic activity as does Har Dayal; for Esmond the only escape is from India herself—furtively and secretly.

In 1959, Ruth Jhabvala, too, returned to England for the first time since her marriage. The impact of the visit was profound: "I saw people eating in London. Everyone had clothes. Everything in India was so different—you know, the way people have to live like that, from birth to death . . . . So after that visit to England I felt more and more alien in India."[6] It is, therefore, not surprising that her next novel, written in 1973, is entitled *Travelers.*[7] She is increasingly interested in those who seek enlightenment in India, for the country seems to have become a stronger and stronger adversary and travelers in it seem to get nowhere. The novel is an account of the journeys made in search of that spiritual core which seems to elude modern man. Some characters, like the Englishman Raymond, are prevented by their own Stoic background from ever becoming a part of India. That he should return to England disappointed, even frustrated by the realities of caste and dirt and bigotry is not surprising. What affects us is what happens to those who surrender to the demands of Indian life.

Asha, the spoiled sister of a successful politician, seems only to wish to indulge in the satisfactions of the flesh; surrounded by silk and lace negligés, swathed in foreign perfume, and gratified by a young boy, she seems too obviously in need of guidance. She flees to an old friend who has gained the reputation of a seer, only to feel uncomfortable if left alone with her, and to witness the indifferent advice given to those who suffer. To parents whose son has mysteriously disappeared, Banubai says: "If He [the One who has willed that it should happen so] wills it, He will bring him back; if not, then not." (*Travelers*, p. 127). Perhaps this detachment is commendable, for classical texts enjoin disinterest in action, yet one is compelled to question the fatalistic attitude recommended. Though it is one traditionally associated with India, it is empty of promise.

The other characters meet with similar discouragement. Lee, a young American, is free to travel in any direction, to stop at any station, and walk down any street. She allows herself to be taken to an ashram headed by a Swami of supposedly limitless power and knowledge. Here, Jhabvala succeeds brilliantly in creating the embodiment of brute power. The Swami compels his disciples to lose themselves in singing hymns to God—an action normally innocent, but here carefully controlled to create unusual excitement. Each of his devotees thinks he speaks only to him, looks only at her. One is literally mesmerized into his being for he will not brook any individuality. He is a loathsome character who demands abject surrender, and when questioned about its necessity, replies in a strange passionate way: "I want her [Lee] to be mine. She must be mine completely in heart and soul and . . . in body also, if I think it necessary." (*Travelers*, p. 140). When the surrender occurs, we feel only vile pain, and hear Lee's whimpering sounds against his animal breathing.

It is significant that though India is a country romantically associated with light and truth, travelers seeking those find neither. It is not as if the country identifies a wrong or a right path—what is devastating is that no path, no alternative proves satisfying. The soul, seeking itself, succumbs, eventually to futility. Jhabvala's novel, written in 1975, is delineated in its very title: the dominant image in *Heat and Dust* is that of disease, its smell is of decay.[8] The spirit is whirled around in the duststorms of late March and succumbs to the heat of midsummer. Early in the novel we are warned, "India always changes people," but they are not transformed into Shakespearean objects strange and new, but seem to be stripped of everything that is their identity and left to die, as if life itself is indifferent to their destiny. The cruelty of India seems more terrible, because it is inhuman. In this novel, most of all, we are reminded of the horrible aspect of Kali who dances on the bodies of her victims, who devours their very entrails in a macabre vision of the life cycle.

"Nothing human means anything here. Not a thing." (*Heat*, p. 6). A young English couple seem merely to repeat a never-changing experience: they came to find peace and all they get is dysentery. "They had been robbed of their watches in a house of devotion in Amritsar; cheated by a man they had met on the train to Kashmir who had promised them a cheap house-boat and had disappeared with their advance; . . . in Fatehpur Sikri the girl had been molested by a party of Sikh youths; the young man's pocket was picked on the way to Goa . . . '' (*Heat*, p. 21). If this seems a pathetically amusing account of naïve tourists, we are soon assured that similar ''robberies'' have taken place before, and the victims have been those who know India.

The very structure of the novel reminds us that history is, indeed, repeated. The narrator comes to India in search of the truth about her grandfather's first wife who ran away with an Indian prince in 1923. Clutching the journals she has inherited, she relives in fact and memory, the earlier journey. The English characters in the earlier story are puppets pulled by the strings of duty, stiff-upper-lipped propriety, and all the other shocks Empire was heir to. Amongst this sober lot of petty officials, Olivia seeks to ''feel'' India. She cannot understand how, surrounded by the exciting life outside, her circle can be satisfied discussing this year's trek to the hills or the washerman who ruins a crepe-de-chine blouse. She is gradually wooed away from this lifelessness by the Nawab who seems to promise her the excitement she craves. He is the charming sensualist who, in order to maintain his lifestyle, relies on thugs to plunder neighboring states. Olivia will not admit to this, and succumbs to him, even to the demand that her pregnancy be terminated in a primitive abortion. Ultimately, all that is left of her is a forlorn house in the hills containing an out-of-tune piano, and some tattered yellow cushions and curtains.

The story of her granddaughter is similarly disillusioning. As she retraces Olivia's journey, she is caught up in the charm of prayer-threads tied for fertility, and gets involved in the delicate problems of caste and personal relationships. Finally, she escapes to the mountainous village where Olivia spent her last days, but here there is no consolation or source of strength. As she looks out of the window of the old house, she can see nothing for it is raining heavily; ''it might have made a difference to know that,'' she murmurs, ''I'm impatient for it to stop raining because I want to move on, go higher up. I keep looking up all the time, but everything remains hidden.'' (*Heat*, p. 180).

If she has attained a solemn peace instead of a grand fulfillment, it may be because she has attained the only degree of contentment offered by contemporary India, and has acquired this only by a stark confrontation with, recognition, and rejection of the old. Is the Doctor's analysis correct that India is only for Indians? Does the Mother Goddess destroy any other who trespasses on her territory? Or does she enjoy a challenge? In a memoir written after his retirement, the English advisor to the Nawab warns, ''The most vulnerable are those who love her best . . . India always finds out the weak spot and presses on it . . . Yes, it is all very well to love and admire India but one should never, be warned, allow oneself to become softened by an excess of feeling; because the moment that happens— the moment one exceeds one's measure—one is in danger of being dragged over to the other side. . . . She always remained for him an opponent, even sometimes an enemy, to be guarded and if necessary fought against from without and, especially, from within; from within one's own being." (*Heat*, pp. 170–71).

This last sums up the journey made not only by Jhabvala's characters, but by the author herself. "India will exhaust physically and morally, any Westerner that tries to stay . . . the squalor, heat, indifference, smells and poverty will destroy those not born in the place." In self-defense, Mrs. Jhabvala left the country in 1976 and settled in New York. Significantly, she did not return to her home in England but chose the New World, not because of its promise, but because she feels it is a home for displaced persons. This sense of "immigrant awareness" is her inheritance—an absence of any nostalgia for what is left behind; she feels no ties to any particular country.⁹ Those who study her novels cannot avoid their lesson—the individual is left to shift for himself, for the old world provides little strength and the new mutters few words of consolation.

NOTES

1. "Jhabvala, Ruth," *Contemporary Novelists*, 2nd ed. (New York: St. Martin's Press, 1976).

2. Ibid., p. 720.

3. *World Authors, 1950–1970*, (New York: H. H. Wilson Co., 1975), p. 725.

4. Ruth Prawer Jhabvala, *Amrita*, (New York: W. W. Norton and Co., Inc., 1956). Further references to this edition will be given by page number in the text.

5. Ruth Prawer Jhabvala, *Esmond in India* (Middlesex: Penguin Books Ltd., 1958), p. 51. Further references to this edition will be given by page number in the text.

6. *New York Times*, May 15, 1976, p. 14.

7. Ruth Prawer Jhabvala, *Travelers* (New York: Harper and Row, 1973). Further references to this edition will be given by page number in the text.

8. Ruth Prawer Jhabvala, *Heat and Dust* (New York: Harper and Row, 1975). Further references to this edition will be given by page number in the text.

9. *Washington Post*, December 9, 1975, p. 2.

19

Luise Rinser's Autobiographical Prose: Political *Engagement* and Feminist Awareness

Elke Frederiksen

In German-speaking countries, Luise Rinser is known as one of the most successful contemporary writers. She has made the bestseller list three times, in the 1950s and early 1960s with her novels *Mitte des Lebens* (*Nina*) and *Die vollkommene Freude* (*Complete Joy*), and most recently, in 1981, with her autobiography *Den Wolf umarmen* (*To Embrace the Wolf*). *Nina* has been translated into 22 languages including Japanese and Hindu.

Despite this commercial success, literary critics have paid little attention to her works, a fate Rinser shares with most other German women writers even today. One exception may be Ingeborg Bachmann, for many years the only woman author mentioned by literary critics. Only very recently have the names Christa Wolf and Anna Seghers joined that of Bachmann as women authors worthy of merit. But there are others who wrote in the 1950s and 1960s, before the women's movement inspired many younger women, and who deserve much more recognition: they are Elisabeth Langgasser, Nelly Sachs, Marie Luise Kaschnitz, Hilde Domin, Ilse Aichinger to name just a few, and of course Rinser.

Who is Rinser? What are the characteristics of her work? And, since she has been on the literary scene since 1940, one must also ask: How did she deal with the immense political changes during these years? How did she realize herself as a writer and particularly as a woman writer in a patriarchal society? For there is no doubt that her experience as a woman and as a German under Fascism have shaped her literary expression. Her works, especially her autobiographical prose, demonstrate a strong political *engagement* and a keen awareness of the injustices towards women. These themes shall be the focus of my paper.

I would like to thank Katherine Goodman (Brown University) and Kirsten Frederiksen (Smith College) for helpful comments and editorial suggestions.

Rinser, who was born in Bavaria in 1911, published her first book *Die glas-ernen Ringe* (*Glass Rings*) in 1940, during the height of the Nazi regime. This short narrative was a tremendous success, which Rinser herself attributes in part to the need of the readers at that time for literature which differed from the "Blut- und Bodenliteratur" ("Blood and Fatherland literature") required by Hitler. And Rinser's *Glass Rings* was different: it showed the development of a young girl towards intellectual independence. Even Hermann Hesse, the well-known novelist and pacifist, sent her an enthusiastic letter of congratulations from Switzerland. He praised her polished German and her commitment to intellectual values, implying a significant difference from other works of that time. Hesse wrote: "I have wandered through your story as if it were a garden, appreciating every image, in agreement with everything, and it will not be long before I read it for the second time." (Letter to Rinser, May 1941). Nazi officials, however, were not as pleased. They responded by forbidding her to publish. Thus, although she continued to write, these texts were not published until after 1945.

In 1944, Rinser was imprisoned by the Nazis for high treason and sentenced to death. She was accused of undermining military morale. Rinser had tried to convince friends of the dangers of Hitler and of the uselessness of continuing the war, only to be betrayed by them. She was held in a women's prison in Traunstein for several months and would have been executed if the end of the war had not prevented it.

It was here that she wrote one of the most significant of her books, one of the earliest German works to be published immediately after the war and one of the few narrations of women's war experiences from a woman's perspective. *Gefangnistagebuch* (*Diary from Prison*) (1946) is a fascinating account of Rinser's prison experiences, but it focuses on the lives of other female inmates as well as on her own. In this diary the two recurring themes in Rinser's works are clearly discernible: her strong political *engagement*, which was unusual for a woman writer at that time, and her awareness of the plight of the oppressed, in this case women.

In the introduction Rinser emphasizes that her account is "fact, not fiction." She intends to portray "a completely true, photographically exact picture of life in a prison."[1] Being the writer that she is, she far exceeds that goal.

Rinser explains that this imprisonment changed her own life profoundly. As she recorded her new and strange experiences, she began to look at herself differently. For the first time in her life she felt like a suffering human being in great danger, someone who had to learn to deal calmly with this danger and who was utterly helpless without any of the security offered by bourgeois life. It is precisely this personal change which the author transmits so convincingly. And if the American feminist literary critic Cheri Register calls for a realistic representation of "female experience," "feminine consciousness" or "female reality" in order to win feminist acclaim, then Rinser's *Diary from Prison* certainly qualifies.[2]

Among the many tragic fates of other inmates related by Rinser, one of the most heartbreaking is the life of 33-year-old Lotte Sch, an intelligent, attractive, musically talented young woman. After a nervous breakdown years earlier she had been committed to a psychiatric hospital where she was used for experiments which destroyed her. A professor at the clinic had wanted to prove that injections of tubercular material into the uterus can produce mental illness. After other tortures the woman finally went insane, but she escaped when they wanted to gas her to death, only to be captured again.

It is the experience of women, but it is also the experience of Fascism, which Rinser describes. When the 26-year-old Betty, an outspoken communist, is put into her cell, it becomes quite obvious which political side the author adopts. After five years of suffering in the Auschwitz concentration camp, Betty fears nothing any more and loudly demands that Hitler be hanged. Rinser openly and courageously defends Betty when several other "upper class" inmates attack her communist views.

By skillfully combining descriptions of the prisoners' experiences and her own inner change, Rinser engages readers, like many of us, "who have never seen or experienced anything like this, who have probably never suffered from such diabiolical methods aimed at annihilating human freedom" (*Gefangnistagebuch*, p. 11). Indeed, she explicitly addresses those among us who do not want to understand that nationalism and militarism must lead directly to total destruction and who—in their undisturbed middle-class security—have never experienced the truth in Bertolt Brecht's *Three-Penny Opera*: "We would be good, instead of base/ But this old world is not that kind of place." (*Gefangnistagebuch*, p. 11).

During her imprisonment, Rinser became aware of a world she did not know existed. Half of these women were either divorced or separated. Many men divorced their imprisoned wives because they had become an embarrassment to them; some were afraid of the damage to their careers, others simply took advantage of the opportunity to get rid of wives they no longer wanted. Rinser exposes the reader to the despair and helplessness of these women who were always judged the guilty party in the divorce, and who therefore usually received neither alimony nor custody of the children. "The judges are men, after all!" comments the diarist, Rinser (*Gefangnistagebuch*, p. 49). Little by little she throws her remaining middle-class prejudices overboard. When one day she learns about eight methods of having an abortion, she closes her diary entry with the words: "I have never seen life the way I am seeing it here: Naked, ugly, hard, but true and real. If I ever return to normal life I shall be completely changed." (*Gefangnistagebuch*, p. 50).

Rinser's *Diary from Prison* is also significant because of its form. She wrote it in a fragmentary form as a diary, because that was the only possible means of expression for her, as she explained in a recent interview with me.[3] She emphasized the documentary character of the book and also the fact that she had nothing but scraps of toilet paper to write notes on, which she hid in her straw mattress. Moreover she only had fragments of time for writing because her days were occupied with prison duties and in the evenings her cell was only dimly lit. But writing gave her the strength to survive.

With the diary form, Rinser continued a tradition especially important for German women writers in the nineteenth century.[4] It was not until the late 1960s and early 1970s that the diary developed into one of the most popular German literary genres for both female and male writers.[5]

The diary form conveys immediacy, directness and truth, all undoubtedly reasons why Rinser developed it as an important structural element in her autobiographical and hitherto most successful novel *Mitte des Lebens* (*Nina*). Fictional diary entries and letters appear to interrupt and confuse the action of the novel, but at the same time they create, from various perspectives, a fascinating, intricate picture of Nina, the protagonist. The two themes pointed out at the beginning of the paper as characteristic of Rinser's works, are also clearly visible in this novel, even though in different form. The problems of a woman emancipating herself in all areas of life and struggling against middle-class norms predominate over the discussion of purely political issues, although these are also part of the protagonist's emancipatory process.

Although published in 1950, this novel focuses on questions which are particularly relevant for women today. It shows the desperate search for identity by an intelligent, strong-willed woman who, in spite of social pressures, achieves professional success and personal independence. She succeeds as a writer and has the courage to dissolve unhappy relationships with men in order to live by herself. Nina's political commitment, which expresses Rinser's own political philosophy, becomes evident in her selfless attitude towards a number of persecuted Jews whom she helps escape across the border at serious risk to her own life.

It is not surprising that this novel has been praised by feminists. Rinser herself sees as the main reason the fact that the emancipation question has still not been resolved. It is also not surprising that male critics have applied familiar sexual stereotypes in their evaluation of Nina. Karl Heinz Kramberg writes that this heroine seems to be "suspicious, almost monstrous, a male-killing vamp, a spiderwoman, whose sex appeal . . . captures her invariably weak men and often kills them."[6] In an all too familiar pattern, Rinser joins the many women writers in western society whose courageous and strong female protagonists are not interpreted as heroes but as villains.

Towards the end of the 1960s Rinser began to demand equal rights for women more consciously and more actively, and sought the raising of consciousness in a patriarchal society. In 1970 she published an essay *Unterentwickeltes Land Frau* (*Underdeveloped Country Woman*), which deserves a closer look although it is not autobiographical. Rinser expressed her ideas concerning the oppression of women earlier than any of the well-known West German feminists such as Alice Schwarzer (*Frauen gegen de 218*, 1971; *Women against 218*) or Jutta Menschik (*Gleichberechtigung oder Emanzipation?* 1971; *Equal Rights or Emancipation?*). Like these younger feminists Rinser criticizes discrimination against women, but in contrast to them she makes women themselves partly responsible for their oppression. She points out that objective lack of freedom can be perceived subjectively as freedom, if a woman lacks consciousness of sexual and social oppression. According to Rinser, many women are afraid of growing up, and change will only occur if women begin to question their identities by no longer taking their situations for granted. To change consciousness requires an analysis of women's history, and Rinser chooses the Christian church as a model for an authoritarian-patriarchal social structure in which to investigate the position of women. She demonstrates the treatment of women throughout history as "underdeveloped beings," a thesis carefully documented with texts from the earliest church fathers to Karl Barth. The main reason for this treatment, according to Rinser, is that two extreme Christian interpretations of femaleness exist: the adoration of Mary on one hand and the burning of the witches on the other. Both of these serve as a measure for the real image of women. Rinser pleads for a change in this tradition through gradual reform, which would replace male superiority with a partnership of women and men.

Although Rinser's essay expresses moderate feminism, and although even today she cannot be called a radical feminist, she nevertheless expressed strong solidarity with the successful West German feminist magazine *Emma*, when it took the magazine *Stern* to court for exploiting women as sex objects on its title pages.[7] But for Rinser the women's movement is only one part—although an important one—of a much larger irreversible emancipatory process of humankind. And for Germans in particular the events of the past will always play a role which they must never forget. For that reason, although she never ignores the contemporary political scene, Rinser's most important books of the 1970s and 1980s deal with the Nazi past.

In 1974 she published her novel *Der schwarze Esel* (*The Black Donkey*) and in 1981 her best-selling autobiography *Den Wolf umarmen* (*To Embrace the Wolf*). The author herself considers *The Black Donkey* her best book. Interestingly enough, reviews of the novel have been scarce in West Germany and Austria, in contrast to France and Italy where it was highly praised and awarded the Italian National Prize of Literature. In that novel the lives of six women are portrayed. Each must cope with the terrible events of the past in her own way. As in *Nina* and in *Diary from Prison*, Rinser prefers a multiple perspective not only in presenting the lives of six individuals rather than one, but also by viewing each through the double perspective of the first person narrator and the main protagonist. Moreover, although the main emphasis may be historical, she never loses the focus on women's experience in particular. The figure of Klara, the hunchback, is the most impressive, as this woman deals calmly, directly and courageously with the prejudices of the small middle-class Bavarian town depicted in the novel. Altogether the author succeeds in portraying a variety of individuals, whose lives she convincingly interweaves with the history of the time.

Rinser's concern with Germany's political past has made her a conscientious and critical observer of today's political events. She has spoken out against violence, war, and oppression, and she has done so in a typical fashion, in four diaries: *Baustelle (Construction Site)* 1970, *Grenzubergange (Border Crossing)* 1972, *Kriegsspielzeug (Toy of War)* 1978 and *Winterfrühling (Winter-spring)* 1982. She has also done so in a more overtly political way on lecture tours, at political meetings, and in radio and television programs. As a consequence many political conservatives in The Federal Republic of Germany consider her a thorn in their side. In 1977 she was forbidden to lecture in the small Bavarian town Gerlingen because they believed a spurious article in the magazine *Quick* which had accused her of sympathizing with German terrorists.[8] If one asks Rinser about her political beliefs, she answers that she declares herself in solidarity with all those "who want change for the sake of humanity, which seems to be of no importance in our capitalist world."[9]

Finally, I would like to take a brief look at Rinser's latest work, her autobiography *To Embrace the Wolf* (1981). This book represents an effort to express her political, literary and religious ideas through personal experiences. It recreates her own life from 1911 to 1950 and focuses to a large extent on the years between 1933 and 1945. The difference from her other works is, however, that she describes and analyzes more directly her own problems and difficulties with the Hitler regime, even before she was imprisoned.

The wolf Rinser embraces is life in general, life which is beautiful and at the same time full of obstacles. She emphasizes her development as a woman and a writer towards independence, but as in so many autobiographies by women writers, she continuously asserts her self-worth. Her clarifications and explanations with regard to her works at times give the impression of a defense of her writing. In part this defensive stance may be understood from her childhood. As a young woman, Rinser's development was severely hindered by her strict Catholic parents who almost drove her to commit suicide.[10] Her mother ridiculed her first literary attempts and removed the light bulbs from her room so that she could neither read nor write at night. Her father demanded that she swear to only marry a "respectable *Catholic* young man."[11] When she announced her engagement to the Protestant conductor Horst-Gunther Schnell, they threw her out of the house.

In her autobiography, Rinser distances herself from this domineering father figure. She places him on the stage of a Greek theatre. He becomes a figure in a tragedy; he is Creon. Rinser herself appears as Antigone, who in the ancient tragedy was sacrificed by Creon because she disobeyed his law which opposed a higher law. In contrast to Sophocles' female hero, however, this Rinser-Antigone does not die. She makes her way; she overcomes inferiority complexes and insecurity; she fights for intellectual freedom: in her early years for herself, today she is for humankind.

NOTES

1. Luise Rinser, *Gefangnistagebuch* (Frankfurt: Fischer Taschenbuch Verlag, 1976), p. 7. (Translation of all quotes from this text by Elke Frederiksen). Further references to this edition will be by page numbers in the text.

2. "American Feminist Literary Criticism: A Bibliographical Introduction," *Feminist Literary Criticism: Explorations in Theory*. Edited by Josephine Donovan (Lexington: The University Press of Kentucky, 1975), p. 12.

3. My interview with Luise Rinser took place in March, 1982, in Rome.

4. Some male German writers like Goethe also experimented with the diary form, but for women it was one of the primary forms of expression.

5. Several significant examples are Karin Struck's *Klassenliebe* (1973), Max Frisch's *Montauk* (1975) and Maxie Wander's *Leben war' eine prima Alternative* (1979).

6. *Das Schonste*, March 1962, p. 77. Quoted from Albert Scholz, *Luise Rinsers Leben und Werk. Eine Einfuhrung* (Syracuse: Peerless Press, 1968), p. 38. (Translation of quote by Elke Frederiksen).

7. See *Emma*, Nr. 4 (1979), pp. 12–13.

8. "Die Sympathisanten." *Quick*, 22 September 1977.

9. My interview with Luise Rinser in March, 1982.

10. Luise Rinser, *Den Wolf umarmen* (Frankfurt: S. Fischer, 1981), p. 92.

11. *Den Wolf umarmen*, p. 93.

20

Women and Choice—A New Look at Simone de Beauvoir and *The Second Sex*

Carol Ascher

How does the individual responsibility and choice that we assume for each woman dovetail with our belief that failure, disease, and psychological crippling are caused by oppression? In recent years, the women's movement has tended to accept the liberal connection between caring and an assumption of determinism. Because of this, we focus on the oppression side of the issue when we reach out to help a battered wife or someone who has just been raped. As if our sympathy might be blown away, we shout, "you're blaming the victim" at anyone who dares to raise the issue of choice. Though it may not seem useful to debate the abstract concepts of free will and determinism, the implications of these ideas live in the way we view, as well as act on, our lives.

These issues have crystallized for me in writing my book, *Simone de Beauvoir; a Life of Freedom*, and talking to other women across the country about her ideas. Though she has been called the mother of this wave of the women's movement the interest of American feminists in her existentialism has been negligible. In discussing *The Second Sex*, women have marveled at, or been exhausted by, her encyclopedic detailing of the patriarchy as it has shaped history as well as the chronological life of each female. But the dialectic of choice which is an integral (though imperfectly realized) part of that book has been almost totally ignored.

Freedom, as those who have read the memoirs know, has been a catapulting notion for Simone de Beauvoir throughout her life. As a personal vision, it has pulled at her as the wish for love or harmony might draw another. It has also been a tool by which she has judged (harshly at times) her life.

Reading the memoirs, however, one notes an idiosyncratic manner in which necessity and freedom combine at moments of particular contentment. She feels most free when she is at one with what she is doing and can't imagine doing or being anything else—that is, an inner necessity imparts her very feeling of freedom. For example, she writes of her pleasure as a child in being just who she was, inside her own family, with her younger sister Poupette at her side. It was all perfect; she couldn't imagine another life. Being a devout, bourgeois Catholic in the early years of this century was, of course, all part of this self-satisfied perfection. Or later, starting at the age of nine, her friendship with Elizabeth Mabille gave her a sense of freedom because of its feeling of being necessary to her existence. And when she met Sartre at the Sorbonne a dozen years later, she felt that, like Zaza, he too would "impose himself upon me, prove he was the right one otherwise I should always be wondering: why he and not another?"[1] A second quote about her early relationship with Sartre conveys this same overlay of freedom and necessity:

When I threw myself into a world of freedom, I found an unbroken sky above my head. I was free of all shackling restraint, and yet every moment of my existence possessed its own inevitability. All of my most remote and deep-felt longings were now fulfilled.[2]

Now de Beauvoir is being self-conscious and not a little self-ironic when she writes this (though she is also clear about the pleasure of her emotion), for the God who once granted her necessity is gone, and only the primitive wish to replace that necessity thrives on.

For the same reasons, philosophically speaking, de Beauvoir's most anguished moments are those when inner or outer necessity stands at the door, but is not answered by a freedom imported through either her acquiescence or circumstance. A moment alone on a train when she experiences the raw unfulfilled needs of her sexuality is one example from early adulthood. During World War II, and again during the French-Algerian War, the "force of circumstance" is unbearable to her because of the multitude of personal and political acts which go against her wishes and are beyond her control.

In reading Simone de Beauvoir, whether it is fiction, sociological treatise, or autobiography, however, one must remember that she is a philosopher at base, and words like freedom, even if ironically intended, convey the richness of a philosophical view. During the first decade of her relationship with Sartre (1929–39), their understanding of freedom was highly personal. With God unmasked as merely a "useless passion," society, as created by individual human beings, had nothing sacred about it. It could be changed to suit those individuals by mere acts of decision and will. As she writes of herself and Sartre:

The working plan which Sartre and I were pursuing for the annexation of the world around us did not fit in with those patterns and taboos established by society. Very well, then; we rejected the latter, on the supposition that man would have to create his world again from scratch. (*Prime*, p. 361)

In fact, in their view, the pretense that there was either a sacred quality to social laws or something immutable about them was an act of "bad faith."

Though the choice to be free was an individual one, it obviously had social repercussions. "Our liberties support each other like the stones of an arch," de Beauvoir argued in an early philosophical essay, *Pyrrhus et Cinéas*.[3] The choice had to be made. One had a moral duty to oneself and others to make it.

The war, and particularly her direct experience with the German occupation of France, gave to de Beauvoir the beginnings of a more complex view of the power of the world as it is and what might be needed for social change. Sartre, as she writes in her memoirs, was coming to consider himself an activist; and he would begin to try to reconcile his existentialism, for a short time, with the views of the French Communist Party and, in the long run, with a Marxist perspective.

The Ethics of Ambiguity, despite de Beauvoir's critical evaluation to the contrary, stands among her most interesting works. In this long philosophical essay, she began to speak to how oppression might curtail freedom—when an act of freedom "is condemned to fall uselessly back upon itself because it is cut off from its goals,"[4] this constitutes oppression—as well as to imagine how one might develop an ethics of revolution. (What does one do when one cannot convince the oppressor to yield his power; how does one evaluate violence?) One of the major contributions of this work is her distinction between freedom and liberation. Understanding that oppression for some people was such that they could not simply choose to be free, she argued that in those cases there had first to be social liberation. A slave, for example, might not even be aware of his or her servitude, and it would be "necessary to bring the seed of his liberation from the outside." (*Ethics*, p. 85) In this book, too, de Beauvoir tried to establish the criteria by which to distinguish oppression from acts of bad faith. "The less economic and social circumstances allow an individual to act upon the world, the more the world appears to him as given. This is the case of women who inherit a long tradition of submission, and those who are called 'the humble.' " (*Ethics*, p. 48) Yet, she warns, "There is often laziness and timidity in their resignation; their honesty is not complete." (*Ethics*, p. 49) Thus, though oppression was internalized in the individual, there were in a sense still free zones which could be called accountable to act.

In late 1946, at the age of 38, de Beauvoir began to write *The Second Sex*. She completed the book—1,000 pages in French—in 2½ years, taking out time to travel to the U.S. and to write her journalistic account, *America Day by Day*. To add to the accomplishment, it should be noted that, although women had recently been given the vote in France, and so the question of female emancipation was surely in the air, in the context of the devastation and deaths of World War II, news of Stalin's camps, the beginning of a nuclear world with the bombing of Hiroshima and Nagasaki, and the arming of Europe in the Cold War between the United States and Russia, a discussion of women from the beginning of civilization to the present did not appear on the front burner in the world of left Parisian intellectuals—or anywhere. Nor did de Beauvoir have a women's group, or even a woman friend, with whom to share her efforts.

The Second Sex opens with three sections focusing on theories of women's condition that to de Beauvoir are deterministic: biologism, psychoanalysis, and Marxism. To the first, she argues basically that, though our being finite and physical has an effect on how we see the world, the details of our body make no difference, and that "One is not born but becomes a woman."[5] To the second, she offers two arguments: that a Freudian explanation (penis envy) reduces to physiology what could be explained by power; and that psychoanalysis designates transcendence or freedom as normal for men, while condemning women to the "normalcy" of immanence and oppression. As for Marxism, the advent of private property is, to de Beauvoir, an insufficient explanation for women's oppression. In fact, class conflict itself need not exist and must be accounted for. Thus dispensing with the popular explanations for women's oppression, de Beauvoir would seem at the point of asserting a freedom which has merely been waiting to be acted upon. For if nothing has made the patriarchy a necessity, then why not simply lift it off?

Yet de Beauvoir does finally offer a grounding for men's power over women: it lies in what she sees as a basic category, "the other," and the primitive desire to dominate this other. Now this philosophical category has followed de Beauvoir through her early novels and theoretical works. (It is central to Sartre's *Being and Nothingness*.) The wish to dominate—or, at times, annihilate—the other is part of the same "bad faith" that makes some long for Gods and others want to be God. The lonely, separate, finiteness of the mortal individual is too hard to bear. Dominating and being dominated offer the escape from freedom into necessity. If men solve their fear of freedom by assuming power over women, women solve theirs by being that "other" which is dominated. In fact, with the introduction of this existentialist category of the Other, we are back, or still, in the realm of choice.

In *The Second Sex*, de Beauvoir expands the analysis of oppression, freedom, and morality she began in *The Ethics of Ambiguity*. "Every time transcendence falls back into immanence, stagnation, there is a degradation of existence into the 'en soi'—the brutish life of subjection to given conditions—and of liberty into constraint and contingence. At one time, in early civilization, there were material reasons for men becoming the dominators and women the dominated, but these reasons have long been obsolete. This downfall represents a moral fault if the subject consents to it; if it is inflicted upon him, it spells frustration and oppression." (*Second Sex*, p. XXXIII) Women who want to be the subject of their lives as much as do men, are confined to immanence, to being an object: "What particularly signalizes the situation of woman is that she—a free and autonomous being like all human creatures—nevertheless finds herself living in a world where men compel her to assume the status of Other." (*Second Sex*, p. XXXIII) Unable to reach out toward new liberties through projects in the world, women live unduly tied to their bodies, their physiology; through narcissism, they make projects of themselves, but they thereby only increase their situation as the Other.

In their status as Other, women are like Blacks and Jews—or any other oppressed people. "The eternal feminine corresponds to 'the black soul' and ,the Jewish character.' " (*Second Sex*, p. XXVII) Although the Jew is not so much inferior as the evil enemy, both women and Blacks "are being emancipated today from a like paternalism, and the former master class wishes to 'keep them in their place.' " (*Second Sex*, XXVII) The "good Negro" is childish, merry, submissive. The "true woman" is frivolous, infantile, irresponsible. By definition, the Other is not worthy of the responsibilities and benefits of full citizenship.

Still, de Beauvoir does not conceive of women's activities as fully determined. "I shall place woman in a world of values and give her behavior a dimension of liberty," she says. "I believe that she has the power to choose between the assertion of her transcendence and her alienation as object; she is not the plaything of contradictory drives; she devises solutions of diverse ranking in the ethical scale." (*Second Sex*, p. 56) Rather than her situation being imposed on her, as it is upon a child or a slave, "the western woman of today chooses it or at least consents to it." (*Ethics*, p. 38) This means that, unlike children or absolutely oppressed peoples, who have no opportunity to choose change, "once there appears a possibility of liberation, it is a resignation of freedom not to exploit the possibility, a resignation which implies dishonesty and which is a positive fault." (*Ethics*, p. 38) In fact, because all our liberties are mutually interdependent, de Beauvoir implies that women's complicity in their own oppression is also thwarting the liberty of men. Because women have some access to freedom, judgments about their acts should be based, not on "normalcy," but on "moral invention." These judgments should be positive, about where and when women have made choices within the confines of their circumstances.

Unfortunately, this enormously creative project of determining women's "moral inventiveness" within the framework of oppression is only unevenly accomplished. (In fact, more than thirty years later, the project awaits furthering by any writer.) Instead, *The Second Sex* has a lumpiness, in which oppression is described with great vigor for paragraphs or pages on end, and only at times interspersed with sections in which one sees how women choose or act upon their (greatly constricted) freedom, pushing it beyond its previous borders. Of course, the overweighting of the oppression side of the dialectic has also been emphasized in the English edition (and in the most current French edition, as well) by the omission of the lives of fifty French painters, writers, soldiers, doctors, etc., who pushed beyond the borders of their world and so created greater freedom for themselves and others. Still, the integration of freedom and oppression doesn't work perfectly on every page. One can imagine de Beauvoir in the Bibliothèque Nationale. She had begun the project, she says, not out of being a feminist, but merely to try to understand what it meant to be a woman. The impressions caused by her reading must have bowled her over! It must have been hard to remember the sense of freedom and choice she had sought to keep alive.

Simone de Beauvoir's pleasure in her memoirs when inner freedom and necessity seem contained within each other show both that she (like most others) finds comfort in being in harmony with herself, and that in her youth and early adulthood this inner harmony seemed most likely to be produced by loving someone who gave her life direction. Yet her life has not been one geared toward comfort; on the contrary, she had often sacrificed the least of the known in order to think and act in ways that grant herself and others greater freedom. If there is the anguish of this discomfort in her fiction and later memoirs, it is an honest anguish—of the price that everyone must pay.

In my talks about de Beauvoir I have been asked as often, "But she really hates men, doesn't she?" as "Don't you think she finally blames women for it all?" Like most books, *The Second Sex* may be seen as a Rorschach, for people do read what they want in it. And I must admit, ten years ago when I first read the book I saw the detailing of women's oppression only; I would have been astounded and disbelieving had someone pointed out the recurrent theme of choice. Yet de Beauvoir's requirement of determining oppression is a demanding one; if, and only if, one has *tried* to reach toward a goal, and that attempt has been definitively thwarted, can one speak of being oppressed. At a time when women are being asked to pull in the enlarged boundaries they have fought for over the past decade, it seems particularly important to hold onto this active notion of oppression, with its implications for responsibility and choice.

NOTES

1. Simone de Beauvoir, *Memoirs of a Dutiful Daughter*, trans. James Kirkup (Harmondsworth, England: Penguin Books, 1963), p. 33.

2. Simone de Beauvoir, *The Prime of Life*, trans. Peter Green (Harmondsworth, England: Penguin Books, 1965), p. 27. Further references will be given in the text.

3. Simone de Beauvoir, *Pyrrhus et Cinéas* (Paris: Gallimard, 1944), p. 120; my translation.

4. Simone de Beauvoir, *The Ethics of Ambiguity*, trans. Bernard Frechtman (New York: Citadel Press, 1964), p. 81. Further references will be given in the text.

5. Simone de Beauvoir, *The Second Sex*, trans. and ed. H. M. Parshley (New York: Vintage Books, 1974), p. 301. Further references will be given in the text.

21

Virginia, Virginius, Virginity

Louise A. DeSalvo

Virginia Woolf's apprentice novel, *The Voyage Out*, largely ignored or under-estimated by critics until recently, concerns Rachel Vinrace's voyage aboard the *Euphrosyne*, which is both an initiation voyage and a journey into the central character's death, just after she has become engaged to Terence Hewet.[1] An earlier and extremely curious first version of this first novel (a twenty-page fragment), probably written in 1908, describes the experiences of Cynthia Vinrace (Rachel, in the later and published versions), Captain Vinrace, Geranium and Lucilla Ambrose (later, Ridley and Helen Ambrose), antecedents of the characters in Virginia Woolf's published text.[2]

Perhaps the most important statement that one could make about this twenty-page fragment is that it presents a world that is extremely hostile to its central female character, Cynthia. In the draft, the fecundity of the earth has been poisoned; the fictive space is dominated by a hostile and malicious male god-like creature who has despoiled the natural order of things. Woolf describes the agony of a plant attempting to sustain itself in this hostile environment. After spending

whole months or winters close packed in the rich clods a small spike would burst the softened shell and quest so far as to feel the cold earth above it, all squeezed and compact, so that there was no airy crevice for plant or insect to pass up, sucking nourishment as they went. Finally, if it still adventured upwards, it would, though now maimed and blunted, knock its head against a flat sheet of some foreign substance, opaque, without pores, and subject moreover to terrible undulations of sound, to blows and crunchings, in which each separate atom of the substance seemed to grind against the other. After some futile assay . . . the sap would dry in the veins for no rain or sun would visit it, and it would lie there passive against the stone, white and soon shrivelled.[3]

The most frightening aspect of this description is that Woolf clearly intends it to represent Cynthia Vinrace's (and, in a predictive way, Rachel Vinrace's) fate in trying to come to fruitful womanhood. What Woolf seems to conclude in this first early fictional venture, is that there is something in the very air that will not allow women to grow boldly—that the natural order of things is inimical to them—that their growth will be maimed and stunted by natural forces.[4] In addition, their very families, even their very own mothers, deter their growth: Cynthia's mother "a great voluptuous woman"[5] does not very much like the members of her own sex, and one is forced to conclude that Cynthia Vinrace has not fared very well under the tutelage of such a mother. She has grown up to be a rather bookish young woman who obsessively reads and rereads the most blatantly misogynist passages of Sir Thomas Browne's *Religio Medici*, the passages in which all the evils of the world are attributed to women, as well as those excerpts in which the repulsive nature of heterosexual love is described. She reads these almost as if to confirm that her sex *is* vile and vulgar, an attitude that has been introduced, apparently, by her mother, and confirmed by her father, and by the world, in addition to writers like Sir Thomas Browne.

In a version of the novel, in progress from 1910 to 1912, which has recently been published under the title *Melymbrosia*,[6] Virginia Woolf picked up the threads of that earliest 1908 version and embellished them. The novel was still about the voyage of Rachel Vinrace aboard the *Euphrosyne*, but the novel now incorporated an enormous amount of topical social criticism, although it also contained the mythic doomed atmosphere of its predecessor. Its pages bristle with social commentary and reveal Woolf's engagement with the most pressing problems of Edwardian and Georgian England: the trade union movement and labor unrest; the suffrage movement; the effect of political leaders like Balfour and Lloyd George; the problem of reconciling humanism with empire building; the Irish nationalist movement, to name but a few.

These are the issues which permeate the text of *Melymbrosia*—they are the issues which the central characters discuss on their trip aboard the *Euphrosyne* to their destination in South America; they are the issues which the English colony in Santa Rosa discusses. Set against this socially conscious background, Rachel Vinrace meets and falls in love with one of the English visitors to Santa Rosa—Terence Hewet—but she dies shortly after her engagement.

The central issue of *Melymbrosia*, and the central issue of *The Voyage Out* revolves around the fact of Rachel Vinrace's death. I have written elsewhere that in "writing a female version of the Odyssey, a female reinterpretation of the hero's voyage of initiation, Woolf was suggesting that Rachel Vinrace would not come home alive to England because the negative attitudes towards women that prevailed there were so malevolent and so deeply ingrained that they now had the status and the sanction of myth."[7] Thus, in subverting the tradition of the journey of initiation, Woolf was pointing out that women are bred to fail, not to succeed; that, as Andrea Dworkin has observed in her *Woman Hating*, female victimization, often implemented by a woman's own mother and father, is the most salient feature of a patriarchal society.[8] *Melymbrosia* and *The Voyage Out* articulate how that victimization takes place in the context of one nuclear family, and in one particular society—Virginia Woolf's Edwardian and Georgian England. Many of the literary allusions that Woolf chooses to include in her texts indicate that "woman hating," that the institutionalization of the victimization of woman has a very, very long history.[9]

Melymbrosia and *The Voyage Out* describe how the ideal of virginity (age-old) murders women, even before they begin to grow, and how that murder has, as its willing accomplices, the mothers and fathers of Englishwomen, who instruct young women that virginity is necessary.[10] For Rachel Vinrace, learning about the necessity of virginity has been accompanied by learning about the restrictions on her behavior that would ensure that she would remain chaste. She is therefore kept at home, not allowed to roam, not allowed the freedom to learn and to grow apart from her restricted and altogether boring life with her aunts. She also learns, by extension, that her nature as a woman is so inherently vile and dangerous that she must be kept behind locked doors, in the company of her aunts. Her very presence in the world is enough to make grown men lose their own self control. Her very presence in the world is temptation. In her later work, *Orlando*, Woolf satirizes this attitude: "chastity is their jewel, their centre piece, which they run mad to protect, and die when ravished of."[11] In *Orlando*, Orlando, now a woman, realizes that the mere sight of her ankle is so disturbing that it causes a sailor a near-fatal fall from the rigging of a sailing ship: "If the sight of my ankles means death to an honest fellow who, no doubt, has a wife and family to support, I must, in all humanity, keep them covered."[12]

In *Orlando*, Woolf jests, even as she criticizes. In *Melymbrosia* and *The Voyage Out*, Woolf is deadly earnest. When Richard Dalloway kisses Rachel Vinrace on board the ship, he states that women have an enormous capacity for good and evil. "You tempt me,"[13] he says, and lays the blame for his act at her doorstep. He excuses his behavior, excuses his seduction of her. But Rachel has been so well-schooled that she is quick to blame herself, quick to think that she has been contaminated, quick to believe that she is inherently base. The mere illicit kiss of a lecherous married man is enough to defile in this society where chastity, where virginity is the ideal. It is no wonder, then, that Woolf chooses, as lynch-pin of the scene in which Rachel Vinrace dies, John Milton's *Comus*, that masque which acts as manual of instruction to young English girls in the necessity of maintaining their own chastity—without the assistance of any one; indeed, a significant lesson in *Comus* is that family is of no help, that family itself might not aid the young woman when she most sorely requires aid (the brothers are no help to the girl when she desperately needs them); that the responsibility for maintaining one's chastity is *one's own*.[14]

Thus, one of the hidden meanings in the death scene of Rachel Vinrace, indicated by the reference to *Comus* is that Rachel has not successfully maintained her chastity—not insofar as the strict rules of her society are concerned; and, without chastity, a young woman is as good as dead. When Milton's masque was performed for the first time at Ludlow Castle, the Lady Alice Egerton's mother and father were both present—the Lady Alice Egerton was the young girl performing the role of the Lady, the character who must traverse the temptations of Comus's wood. The masque, above all, is a lesson to a young woman about the necessity of a daughter's chastity and virginity. At the end of the masque, the young Lady, who has successfully negotiated Comus's wood and preserved her chastity, is reunited with her *actual* parents, is taken back into the social order. Thus, by extension, Rachel Vinrace cannot return home to England: she has not successfully negotiated Comus's wood.

The meaning of Milton's *Comus,* and Woolf's own critique of her society's insistence upon virginity as an ideal, form the subtext of *Melymbrosia* and *The Voyage Out.*

It is important, in this context, to note that although Virginia Woolf's first given name was "Adeline" (Adeline Virginia Stephen), her family insisted upon calling her *Virginia*.[15] It is, of course, impossible to speculate about the reason for this. But one thing can be sure: at some point in her reading, Virginia Stephen Woolf made the association between her own name and that name, "Virginia," which in the cultural history of Western civilization, was linked with the ideal of virginity.[16]

The story is told in Livy. It is quite possible that Virginia Woolf encountered it when she was fifteen years old. In a diary that she kept during that year, a very detailed account is given of her reading. In June, she entered that she was reading a *History of Rome*,[17] quite possibly that of Livy, for her personal library contained several volumes of his works.[18] The story of Virginius [Verginius] and Virginia [Verginia], as told in Livy, is one of the most overt statements of the virgin as property of her father, of the virgin as commodity to be exchanged in marriage, in all of history.[19] In Livy, one can see quite clearly what many contemporary feminists have claimed: that a virgin daughter acts as a counter in a system which values the private ownership of property; that virginity is a necessary commodity for one's father, so that he might advance his social and political position, even if virginity is not inherently important in and of itself. Thus, Livy's history indicates quite overtly that Virginia's virginity is more important to the men around her than it is to her; she has simply internalized their insistence upon it; she knows that unless she keeps her virginity intact, her family will turn on her. (Indeed, in Livy, one is not permitted inside her point of view. What she thinks of the events which transpire is, of course, insignificant.) But one suspects that she also knows that, like the Lady in *Comus*, she alone is responsible for herself, that no one will help her.

Livy's account is worth reiterating in some detail, not only because it is important in understanding an allusion that Woolf makes in *The Voyage Out* (which I will discuss shortly) to Thomas Babington Macaulay's *Lays of Ancient*

Rome, which were based upon Livy, but also because it is a moment of supreme cultural importance for all women and men who would like to understand our culture's fixation upon chastity. Livy's tale concerns:

A girl of humble birth whom Appius wished to debauch; her father Lucius Verginius [Virginius] . . . was a man with an excellent record in both military and civilian life, and his wife and children had been trained in the same high principles as himself.[20]

Verginia [Virginia] at this time, was a beautiful young woman and was betrothed to an ex-tribune, Lucius Icilius, "a keen and proven champion of the popular cause." (269). Although Appius could not seduce her, he claimed Verginius as his slave, taking advantage of her. The father responds ". . . I have no daughter—for, unable to live chaste, she met a piteous yet honourable end." (278)

That Virginia Woolf was aware that her own name was related to the ancient story of "Verginia" in Livy, and that her awareness might have shaped her thinking about the issues of chastity and virginity is, of course, sheer speculation. She might have read Livy. She probably did read Livy. But she also might have encountered the tale of her namesake in another, more contemporary version, in Thomas Babington Macaulay's more recent retellings of the events described in Livy about the foundation of Rome. We have an indication in *Melymbrosia* and in *The Voyage Out* that she might have, in fact, read Macaulay's "Virginia." Not a direct indication, but an indication nonetheless. It comes at the beginning of *Melymbrosia* and *The Voyage Out*, in a curious literary allusion to Thomas Babington Macaulay's "Horatius," also from the *Lays of Ancient Rome*.[21] If Woolf was conversant enough with Macaulay to use his "Horatius" as one of the first significant literary allusions in her novel, perhaps she knew of his "Virginia" as well—Macaulay's *Lays* begin with the "Horatius," which is followed by "Battle of Lake Regillus," which is followed, in turn, by the "Virginia." Wouldn't Virginia Woolf, insatiably curious as she was, have flipped forward in the volume and read the "Virginia?"

I will argue in the remainder of this essay that Macaulay's *Lays of Ancient Rome*, and quite possibly his "Virginia," inform our reading of *The Voyage Out* in ways as significant as Woolf's more famous and more well-discussed allusion to John Milton's *Comus* in Rachel Vinrace's death scene. I will suggest that her knowledge of this ancient story informed her own understanding of the way in which virginity and chastity operated in her own and other cultures and that she always saw virginity and chastity in the context of the power that they conferred upon those men related to the woman who remained chaste.

I have called this allusion to Macaulay's "Horatius" *curious* because although scholars have suggested good reasons why Woolf included lines from this lay at the beginning of her novel, it seems to be a *non sequitur*: Helen and Ridley Ambrose, the aunt and uncle of the heroine, Rachel Vinrace, are walking along the embankment to the *Euphrosyne*, soon after one of a group of small boys has called Ridley "Bluebeard" (10). The name communicates "something quite decisively negative . . . [It is a] forceful . . . image of cruelty and misogyny."[22] In the published text, Helen is teary-eyed for some unexplained reason as Ridley intones the lines from the first stanza of "Horatius":

> Lars Porsena of Clusium
> By the nine Gods he swore—
> . . . That the Great House of Tarquin
> Should suffer wrong no more. (10–11)

According to Beverly Ann Schlack: "This deftly chosen allusion to Macaulay's 'Horatius' reveals Ridley's proclivity for the heroic gesture and underscores his esoteric taste for the exotically unfamiliar, the remote in time and spirit. The lines strike the pose of the conquering hero. . . . Ridley obviously identifies with Macaulay's robust, virile imitations of the *Iliad* manner. But an admiration that borders on identification may indicate something of a bully lurking beneath the would-be hero."[23]

The lines that Ridley recites but which Woolf does not identify, are inextricably linked to Sextus Tarquinius' rape of Lucretia, to her suicide, and to her having extracted an oath of vengeance against Sextus from both her father and her husband before her death. Lars Porsena, king of Clusium, in defending Sextus, in trying to restore the power of the Tarquins, is the embodiment of a militaristic, amoral, political opportunist, who uses oaths to the nine gods for his own ends. In fact, the great house of Tarquin, in this instance, has not suffered wrongs so much as one of its members has inflicted one great and as yet unavenged wrong against Lucretia:

> But when the face of Sextus
>   Was seen among the foes,
> A yell that rent the firmament
>   From all the town arose.
> On the house-tops was no woman
>   But spat towards him and hissed,
> No child but screamed out curses,
>   And shook its little fist.[24]

Woolf alludes to a powerful leader of men, Lars Porsena of Clusium, who is able to sit by the side of Sextus, a man who has raped a woman, and invoke the gods on his behalf. One wonders why Woolf uses this allusion at the beginning of her novel, why Ridley recites the stanza, why Woolf abruptly curtails Helen's musings with his recital, and why the stanza is recited by Ridley while Helen cries. One wonders what it is that Helen must go back to; more importantly, what it is that Helen is departing from. Although it is left unspecified, one possible implication is that Helen and Ridley are leaving for six months because of an unspecified sexual wrong which Helen has been victim of, but this is left ambiguous, and it does not square with Helen's attitude to sexuality later in the novel. It is also possible that the life that she must go back to, which the voyage is allowing her to temporarily escape from, is the ordinary life of a woman of her class in England.

Equally ambiguous is whether one is to associate Ridley with Lars Porsena, the persecutor of Lucretia's kin, or with the wronged Lucretia's kin, or with the wronged Lucretia's father and husband, or, perhaps, even with Sextus. As soon as Ridley stops reciting the lines from Macaulay, he sees his wife crying:

Screening her face she sobbed more steadily than she had yet done. . . . It was this figure that her husband saw when, having reached the polished Sphinx . . . he turned; the stanza instantly stopped. (11)

In an extremely interesting recent reading of *The Voyage Out*, Stephen Trombley has argued that Richard Dalloway, in kissing Rachel, is a substitute for the experience of Virginia Woolf at the hands of her half-brothers:

Like George Duckworth seen from Virginia's point of view, Dalloway is a great hypocrite. He professes to stand for 'civilization', and a just and orderly society—with all of the philosophical baggage that accompanies social vision with a basis in 'morality.' Yet he is subject to uncontrollable desires which he allows to possess him momentarily, desires which he will later deny, or pretend do not exist.[25]

Trombley argues further that Rachel is caught "between the oppressive attitude of a Victorian matriarchy and the hypocrisy of Dalloway and his kind . . . " and so "Rachel's sexual identity does not manage to establish itself . . . "[26] Beverly Ann Schlack has argued that Ridley Ambrose's editing of the odes of Pindar indicates, as well, his covert "conventional praise for Establishment values."[27]

I have written elsewhere that *The Voyage Out* and its earlier version *Melymbrosia* are as covertly and fiercely seditious critiques of the English social order as many of Jane Austen's novels and that the novel is palimpsestic in the sense in which Sandra Gilbert and Susan Gubar use the term—that is, on the surface *Voyage* is using the conventional voyage structure to suggest that it is a novel about the initiation of a young woman into society. Yet the novel is, at the same time, a female version of the *Odyssey*—and Woolf even uses Greek lines from that work in the *Melymbrosia* text, although she has deleted them from the published version.[28] The lines which she uses come right at the beginning of the *Odyssey*, in Book I, in the discussion between Zeus and Athena about who is responsible for the woes of mankind, and more particularly, for the inability of Odysseus to get home. Zeus argues that women and men often blame the gods for events that are of their own doing: he cites the example of Aegisthus who made love to Agamemnon's wife unrighteously, who then killed Agamemnon, even though he knew it would be the death of him, as being himself responsible for his own fate. Athena responds that, in the case of Odysseus, it is the fault of the goddess Calypso that he cannot get home; it is simply not the fault of Odysseus, and the lines that Woolf quotes are from Zeus' response to his daughter, from Book I: "Then in answer to her, cloud-gathering Zeus said: My child, what a word has escaped thy teeth? How should I, then, forget god-like Odysseus, /who is beyond all mortals in wisdom and beyond all to the gods . . . '' (lines 63–66).[29] Woolf has deleted these lines from the *Odyssey* in her published text and has used, instead, lines from the *Antigone* in their place.

One of the themes of the *Odyssey*, of course, is whether Athena's view or Zeus' view about human responsibility is the more correct one. And another theme, probably the one to which Woolf refers here, is whether or not Odysseus can be properly termed an adulterer. Still another, to which Woolf no doubt also refers, is how women like Penelope must protect themselves by their chastity, a reenactment of their earlier virginal state, if they are to survive the rigors of war—a fierceness that they must have in their commitment to the ideal of chastity and virginity which their husbands need never have, and which, in fact, their husbands often traduce.

Now both the lines that Woolf uses from Macaulay's "Horatius," and the lines that she uses in *Melymbrosia* from the *Odyssey* alert us to the fact that there are similar sub-texts in *The Voyage Out*, sub-texts which indicate the necessity of a fierce commitment to chastity or virginity if one is a woman, and if one is to survive the rigors of a journey of initiation unscathed.

In Macaulay's *Lays of Ancient Rome*, the theme of the relationship between chastity, virginity and political turmoil is raised in lay after lay. The one that Woolf uses at the outset of *Voyage*, "Horatius," is only one of several, and in that one, the theme is of political turmoil ensuing after a man's forcible rape of a woman, and of a woman's necessary suicide, even though it is she who has been violated. The story of Lucretius is very much like that of the story of Helen of Troy—it is, in fact, a Roman analogue to that story, and it is no wonder that Woolf gives Helen Ambrose a first name that recalls the saga of the Trojan War and then uses the allusion to "Horatius" to underscore that she does have that Helen in mind. Both the war of Troy and the war of Regillus (recounted in Macaulay's "Battle of the Lake Regillus") were caused by the licentious passions of young princes and by their having victimized women. The conduct of Sextus at Regillus as described by Livy is so much like that of Paris in the third book of the *Iliad* that Macaulay was forced to conclude that the resemblance was not accidental.

Macaulay's "Virginia" repeats and enlarges upon Lucretius' story and upon the saga of Penelope, but it is a horrifying version of a story about the necessity of chastity because Virginia, who is entirely blameless, who has not so much as glanced at her intended seducer, is murdered by her own father, rather than protected by him, as a sacrifice to the republican ideal, and as a means of stirring up the equalitarian sensibilities of the members of his class by this dramatic act which he carries out in the presence of the whole Forum.

> With that he lifted high the steel, and smote
>   it in her side,
> And in her blood she sank to earth, and with
>   one sob she died.[30]

Saving a daughter from servitude and dishonor is one thing, stabbing her in the heart in order to incite one's comrades' revolutionary sensibilities is quite another, and one can imagine how Virginia Woolf must have felt when she read the story of a young girl who shared her name, whose father, Virginius, traded her innocence for a revolution which unseated the rule of the Ten. But it is a revolution which is intended to be a return to the old values, to the time when fathers did not need to worry about losing the services of their daughters, to the time when husbands did not need to worry whether or not their wives were virgins:

> Then leave the poor Plebian his single tie to
>   life—
> The sweet, sweet love of daughter, of sister,
>   and of wife,
> The gentle speech, the balm for all that his
>   vexed soul endures,
> The kiss, in which he half forgets even such
>   a yoke as yours.
> Still let the maiden's beauty swell the
>   father's breast with pride;
> Still let the bridegroom's arms infold an
>   unpolluted bride.[31]

Virginius' murder of Virginia, therefore, is not only a call to arms. It is also a warning to women that after the revolution, their fate will be no better than it was under the rule of the Ten, even though it will be better for their fathers and for their husbands. For Virginius is murdering Virginia to insist upon virginity as a necessary requirement for civilization to endure—the war against the Ten is a war against Virginius' women's wish to make their own way in the world as much as it is a war against the repression of an enemy. Virginius and his cohorts intend to restore what they consider to be the true and more appropriate nature of things—servile, sweet, gentle daughters; unpolluted, unspoiled brides. Their women have no recourse, the lay insists, none at all. They cannot even trust the men within their own families to protect them, just as they must not trust the enemies of their fathers and their husbands. They will be persecuted, they will begin wars, either because they have been seduced, or because someone might seduce them—their actions have nothing to do with it. They are murdered whether they are in fact adulteresses or whether they are blameless. Their own fathers are ready to sacrifice them for the ideal of chastity, for the ideal of virginity.

Given this sub-text, given this overt reference to "Horatius" and this covert reference to "Virginia," the use of the voyage motif in *The Voyage Out* is a macabre joke. Rachel Vinrace's death is akin to the murder of Virginia—it is a venomous uncovering of the impossibility of women to return from a journey of initiation unscathed—given a moral structure which insists upon virginity, which elevates chastity, a social structure which valorizes as a cultural hero worthy of emulation a man who has stabbed his own daughter in the heart for those ideals and which elevates that story to the level of a sacred text.

Given the meaning of the Macaulay lines in the context of *The Voyage Out*, it is no wonder, then, that Helen cries as she hears them.

NOTES

1. *The Voyage Out* (London: Duckworth, 1915); and see: Louise A. DeSalvo, *Virginia Woolf's First Voyage: A Novel in the Making* (Totowa, New Jersey: Rowman and Littlefield, 1980); Charles G. Hoffman, " 'From Lunch to Dinner': Virginia Woolf's Apprenticeship," *Texas Studies in Literature and Language* 10:4 (Winter 1969): 609–627; Mitchell A. Leaska, *The Novels of Virginia Woolf: From Beginning to End* (New York: The John Jay Press, 1977).

2. *Melymbrosia* by Virginia Woolf: An Early Version of *The Voyage Out*, edited with an Introduction by Louise A. DeSalvo (New York: The New York Public Library, 1982). The draft is presented in its entirety in Appendix B.

3. Ibid., 263–64.

4. For a more comprehensive discussion of this issue see my *Virginia Woolf's First Voyage* and my "Introduction" to *Melymbrosia*.

5. *Melymbrosia*, Appendix B, 264.

6. See Note 2.

7. DeSalvo, "Introduction" to *Melymbrosia*, xxxix.

8. Andrea Dworkin, *Woman Hating* (New York: E. P. Dutton, 1974).

9. See DeSalvo, "The Death of Rachel," *Virginia Woolf's First Voyage*, 126–53.

10. For a brilliant argument locating the origins of restrictive behavior for women as a deterrent to expectations for women's natural behavior, as induced from the evidence in primate behavior, see Sarah Blaffer Hrdy, "A Disputed Legacy," in *The Woman That Never Evolved* (Cambridge: Harvard University Press, 1981): "There can be no doubt from such evidence [the study of primate behavior] that the *expectation* of female 'promiscuity' has had a profound effect on human cultural institutions," 177.

11. Virginia Woolf, *Orlando* (New York: Harcourt Brace, 1928, 1956), 154.

12. Ibid., 157.

13. Virginia Woolf, *The Voyage Out* (New York and London: Harcourt Brace Jovanovich, 1920, 1948), 76. Further page references are to this easily available paperback edition, and will be placed within parentheses within the text.

14. For discussions about the relevance of Milton's *Comus* to the death of Rachel, see my own "The Death of Rachel" in *Virginia Woolf's First Voyage*; Mitchell A. Leaska's chapter on *The Voyage Out* in his previously cited work; Beverly Ann Schlack's

chapter on the novel in *Continuing Presences: Virginia Woolf's Use of Literary Allusion* (University Park and London: The Pennsylvania State University Press, 1979).

15. Quentin Bell, *Virginia Woolf: A Biography* (New York: Harcourt Brace Jovanovich, 1972), 2 vols., 1:8.

16. For companion discussion on Virginia Woolf's "valorization of chastity," see Jane Marcus, "The Niece of a Nun: Virginia Woolf, Caroline Emelia Stephen and the Cloistered Imagination," in *Virginia Woolf: A Feminist Slant* (Lincoln: The University of Nebraska Press, 1983).

17. See my "1897, Virginia Woolf at 15: 'the first really *lived* year of my life,' " in Marcus, *Virginia Woolf: A Feminist Slant*. The diary is in the Henry W. and Albert A. Berg Collection of English and American Literature of The New York Public Library, Astor, Lenox and Tilden Foundations. I am editing this diary with Mitchell A. Leaska for publication.

18. See: *Catalogue of Books from The Library of Leonard and Virginia Woolf*, taken from Monks House, Rodmell, Sussex and 24 Victoria Square, London and now in the possession of Washington State University, Pullman, Washington, U.S.A. (Brighton: Holleyman & Treacher, 1975). Woolf's library contained vols. 5 and 6 of the Everyman Library (n.d.) edition, in addition to a few other volumes.

19. The account is in Book Three, "The Patricians at Bay: (467–446 B.C.)", Livy, *The History of Early Rome*, trans. by Aubrey de Selincourt (Norwalk, Connecticut: The Easton Press, 1978).

20. Livy, 269. Further page references will be to the edition of Livy cited in note 20, above, and will be placed within parentheses in the text.

21. Thomas Babington Macaulay, *Lays of Ancient Rome* (London: Richard Edward King, n.d.).

22. Schlack, 8.

23. Ibid.

24. Macaulay, 35.

25. Stephen Trombley, *'All that Summer She was Mad,': Virginia Woolf and Her Doctors* (London: Junction Books, 1981), 15. Trombley's book excavates the writings of Woolf's doctors, among them, Savage, and documents that Savage at one time in his career experimented with drugs for the cure of "mental illness" (which he, incidentally, thought was caused by women receiving an education)—drugs which induce symptoms that are precisely those which Woolf describes as accompanying her illness. Trombley suggests that Woolf's illness was, in fact, drug induced, and his elucidation of Savage's beliefs about mental illness is extremely important.

26. Trombley, 30.

27. Schlack, 9.

28. I am indebted to Will Coakley of the Editor's Office of The New York Public Library for locating the source of the Greek lines which Woolf uses in the *Melymbrosia* text and for translating them.

29. See *Melymbrosia*, 31. Schlack has identified the Greek lines in *The Voyage Out* as a portion of the *Antigone*.

30. Macaulay, "Virginia," 96.

31. Ibid., 95.

22

Sexual Politics and Female Heroism in the Novels of Christina Stead

Louise Yelin

Christina Stead's career as a novelist spans three continents—Australia, Europe, and North America—and the middle half of the twentieth century. Her novels wander over territories as broad and varied as those she actually traversed, encompassing working-class life in Sydney in the 1920s (*Seven Poor Men of Sydney, For Love Alone*), international finance and politics in Paris in the 1930s (*House of All Nations*), the life of a middle-class family in New Deal Washington (*The Man Who Loved Children*), and the marginal existences of declassé rentiers in post-war Europe (*The Little Hotel*) and of working-class, women's, and bohemian subcultures in England in the 1950s and 1960s (*Cotters' England, Miss Herbert*). Yet underlying this evident diversity of character and setting is an imaginative terrain whose contours remain more or less constant.

Perhaps the most pervasive features of Stead's novelistic world are the political vision which shapes it and the delight she takes in language. Stead is surely a political writer, with a leftish disposition, as numerous critics have remarked and Stead herself has suggested.[1] Political in her case means a preoccupation with the ways that the familiar features of our world—love, say, or families, or finance, for that matter—are not given in nature but are rather products of struggle, arenas in which power is contested.[2] Conversely, *politics* for Stead also involves the tracing of what one of her characters somewhat cryptically identifies as "the influence of Marx on character,"[3] which I take to mean that view of the world that regards persons more or less as products of their circumstances. Stead's preoccupation with language links her with other contemporary writers. Her novels investigate, among other things, the processes of signification and the conditions and determinants of meaning. But their main energy lies in a linguistic excess that takes a number of different forms across an unusually wide stylistic register: intense lyricism coupled with closely observed descriptions, aphoristic brilliance, heightened reproduction of the ordinary speech of quite distinct groups of people.

While politics and language structure Stead's imaginative world and define it in relation to the world that she and her novels inhabit, they do so quite differently at different times. Indeed, the meanings of both *politics* and *language* as well as the relationship between them change in significant ways over the course of her long and distinguished career. Stead's early novels are concerned with explicitly social and political themes; the novels written during the 1940s transpose her political vision from public life to the more "private" world of the family and shift their focus from questions of class, loosely, to questions of gender; her late novels describe the commodification of both public and private life and represent the fragmentation of a world composed entirely of words. These changes, and especially the narrowing of Stead's novelistic world, mark the trajectory of a left-wing female intellectual through a literary culture initially somewhat receptive, later indifferent, and finally hostile to the left.

The novels Stead published in the early and mid–1940s occupy a central place in her *oeuvre*, both chronologically and thematically. In the early novels, the heroes, generally, are men whose heroism tends to involve public gestures of one kind or another. The late novels are lacking in both heroes and heroism, unless we consider as heroic the author's act of recording the disintegration of the novels' world. In the novels of the 1940s, however, the heroes are young women whose heroism is largely defined by their rebellion against the limitations of gender. Taken together, then, these novels examine the relationship of sexual politics and female heroism. But the changes in their notions of female heroism— from the heroic imagination of Louisa Pollit in *The Man Who Loved Children* to the romantic longings of Teresa Hawkins in *For Love Alone* (1944) to the satirical pragmatism of Letty Fox in *Letty Fox: Her Luck* (1946)—echo, in small, the evolution in Stead's vision from the exuberant if equivocal optimism of the early books to the growing pessimism of the later ones.

The Man Who Loved Children, the autobiographical novel rightly regarded as Stead's masterpiece, vividly portrays the life of a middle-class family in Washington, D.C., in the late 1930s. In dramatizing the struggles of its heroine, Louisa Pollit (age eleven when the novel begins) to grow up in a household whose members are constantly at war with each other, and to free herself from the sadistic tyranny of her father and the self-loathing of her mother, *The Man Who Loved Children* offers us a myth of feminine survival.

The portrayal of the Pollit family articulates a vision of radical sexual difference, manifesting the oppostion—in all senses—between the mother, Henny, and the father, Sam.[4] First, Stead at once evokes and parodies in Henny and Sam the conventional identification of woman and nature, man and culture: thus, Henny refers to her family as a brood, while Sam calls it a tribe but treats it as an extension of himself. In addition, Stead delineates feminine and masculine world-views, opposing Henny's particularity, imagination, and pessimism to Sam's moralizing abstraction and scientific optimism:

What a moral, high-minded world their father saw! But for Henny there was a wonderful, particular world, and when they went with her they saw it: they saw the fish eyes, the crocodile grins, the hair like a birch broom, the mean men crawling with maggots, and the children restless as an eel, that she saw. . . . Sam, their father, had endless tales of friends, enemies, but most often they were good citizens, married to good wives, with good children (though untaught), but never did Sam meet anyone out of Henny's world, grotesque, foul, loud-voiced, rude, uneducated, and insinuating, full of scandal, slander, and filth, financially deplorable and physically revolting, dubiously born and going awry to a desquamating end.[5]

These divergent visions, in turn, engender the Pollits' quite distinct verbal forms or discourses (as well as endow the novel with much of its linguistic richness): for Henny, the tirade and catalogue; for Sam, the secular sermon and a private, comic language composed out of the "verbal tatters of Artemus Ward" (p. 301).[6]

The novel's vision of the Pollits as polis is not only a fable of difference but also and equally one of domination. (One could profitably read *The Man Who Loved Children* as an illustration of Michel Foucault's notion that "the family" is an arena in which relations of knowledge and power are organized.)[7] Sam attempts to control his family by constant intrusions into Henny's and the children's lives, by repeated assertions of a will-to-knowledge that is also a will-to-power. Often, Sam's will is exercised through manipulation of language, as if by naming and renaming the inhabitants of his world he might denude them of their power to disturb his order and render them harmless. Although delight in language offers Sam a structure of illusions which mediates his attempts to alter his world and to create an alternative to it, Sam's word-play is defensive, ultimately a sign of his weakness and puerility. Indeed, Sam's children resist, revelling in the chaotic particularity of their mother's world, and an unspoken bond develops, in the course of the novel, between Henny and Louisa, Sam's daughter by his first wife. This bond, which Henny identifies as "the natural outlawry of womankind" (p. 244; the rhetoric of nature is singularly inappropriate), represents an alliance between the principal victims of Sam's tyranny. This tyranny, especially as it takes the form of apparently gratuitous sadism, suggests Sam's own weakness and, more generally, the obsolescence of the rule of the patriarch. (Stead comically evokes the latter in a slip of the pen made by Sam's daughter Evie, who begins a letter to him with the salutation "Dead Dad.")

While Stead is primarily concerned in *The Man Who Loved Children* with what might be called politics *in* the family, the novel is shaped by her characteristic social vision and depicts the Pollit family not in isolation but as it is inscribed within a wider network of social relations in a particular time and place. The novel's setting—Washington, Baltimore, Annapolis, and Harper's Ferry—is a politicized landscape marked by the Depression, the New Deal, and the intersection of the cultures of North and South.[8] Here we encounter Henny as a decayed Southern aristocrat from a fading Baltimore family and Sam as a

New Deal liberal, a government bureaucrat (a naturalist, like Stead's father) who believes that science and reason will enable him to raise his family above his own working-class origins.[9] From this vantage point, Sam's domination within the family is revealed as a function of his relative powerlessness in the world "outside." Thus, while Henny borrows money from anyone who will lend it, Sam blindly insists that the Pollits survive without credit, which he echoes his Puritan ancestors in equating with usury. His refusal to acknowledge that Henny's "sordid secrets" have been feeding the family (p. 477) is an act of bad faith which sustains him for a time, until bankruptcy finally forces him to confront the family's debts. While Stead uses the collapse of credit in *House of All Nations* to suggest the demise of the liberal political order, here, in the puncturing of Sam's illusions it delineates a crisis in liberal and patriarchal ideologies.

This crisis is vividly realized in Louisa's rebellion against her father's authority. Louisa's struggle is remarkable not only for its confidence and intensity, but also because it is carried out in writing—for example, in a play she writes in a language she invents for the occasion, a tragedy entitled *Herpes Rom* in which a father (Herpes Rom, or the snake man) murders his daughter. (When Sam angrily asks her why she does not write in English, she replies, in what might be the novel's greatest moment, "Did Euripides write in English?" (pp. 374–77).) If writing enables Louisa to articulate her anger, it is also a means of paying homage and a source of solace and delight—equipment for living, to borrow Kenneth Burke's phrase.[10] Louisa's writings—a cycle of poems she writes for a beloved teacher, the diary she keeps in code, so Sam cannot read it, the stories she tells her brothers and sisters—are among the novel's chief pleasures. Writing, moreover, Louisa surpasses both Henny and Sam, whose considerable verbal resources are dissipated in their vocal squabbling: by writing, that is, she transcends their *spoken* reality and, as her author does, successfully marries Henny's particularity to Sam's comedy.[11]

But writing alone cannot ensure Louisa's passage into adulthood; she must also overcome the crippling limitations of sexual difference, if not difference itself. In the novel's vision of how she does so lies its myth of feminine survival. On the one hand, Louisa appropriates the prerogatives of men, announcing, "I am triumphant, I am king." (p. 320) On the other hand, she invokes the solidarity of women, repudiating Sam's authority to speak for her mother by asking, "What do you know about my mother? She was a woman." (p. 488) To thrive, then, Louisa must be *both* woman and king. This resolution, which ignores the logical impossibility of the dyad woman/king, can be seen either as a symptom of the novel's central problem, a restatement of its question, "Can women have power?" or as a way of magically endowing women with the power of men.

The novel's climax is similarly ambiguous. Louisa, made wretched by the constant war between her parents, resolves to poison them, but changes her mind after placing cyanide in one teacup. Henny, though, notices what Louisa has done, seizes the poisoned cup, drinks the tea, and dies. For a girl to grow up, Stead seems to be saying, she must kill her mother. Or, alternatively, she must escape from her family and refuse the passivity and self-hatred that deform the feminine character, her own as well as her mother's. Thus, in the last pages of the novel, Louisa looks at her family as if from a great distance, and the book ends with her running away to take a "walk round the world" (p. 491). Unlike the heroines of nineteenth-century fiction, Louisa gets away with murder. By rewriting the nineteenth-century plot that punishes characters for their transgressions, Stead has invented a new mythology, a cultural script appropriate to a modern age.[12] But the myth belongs to the world of fantasy, as is evident in the way that the novel projects its resolution—Louisa's escape—into a future that it does not describe.

In fact, the meaning of Louisa's escape and therefore of the novel's denouement is rather more ambivalent than we have suggested and bears closer examination. The novel ends—quite conveniently—before Louisa actually reaches womanhood (she is still in her mid-teens), so that she can be said to evade the constraints of sexual difference by not having fully to experience them. Moreover, her escape is largely made possible—enacted in as well as enabled—by her writing. Literature, or vision, or the word is to be her mode of transcendence and also her way of solving the conundrum of women and power. As with so many characters in novels, her power is preeminently the power of narrative: that is, the power to tell her story or to make fictions. But Stead is not giving us a simple apotheosis of woman as author, for if *The Man Who Loved Children* manifests the power of the word, it just as surely indicates, for Louisa as for Henny and Sam, that the power of the word is poor compensation for powerlessness in the world. While Louisa's writing offers equipment for living, it does not substitute for the power to transform the world. In this respect, it suggests Stead's view, in 1940, of her own literary production.

Like *The Man Who Loved Children*, Stead's next two novels, the autobiographical *For Love Alone* and *Letty Fox: Her Luck* are preoccupied with relations between the sexes and with the question of women and power. The two novels present different versions of the future that is projected at the end of *The Man Who Loved Children*: the protagonists of both novels are young women facing conflicts involving their sexuality, their ambitions, and their circumstances. Although both Letty Fox and Teresa Hawkins, the heroine of *For Love Alone*, are survivors, neither is heroic in quite the manner of Louisa. Taken together, then, these two novels revise the myth of female heroism that underlies *The Man Who Loved Children*.

For Love Alone asks under what conditions it is possible to be both "woman and freeman"[13] and argues that love, in all its complexity, is one of the conditions in question. (Thus, the novel attempts, among other things, a provisional definition of *love*.) That Teresa sees herself as a *freeman* while Louisa insists that she is king can be read not only as a figure for the identification of power with masculinity, but also as a sign of the ever-contracting space in which Stead's characters enact their destinies. For Teresa, in any case, love represents the only possibility of escape from the stifling poverty of Sydney, from the tyranny of her father and the claustrophobic life of her family, and from the sterile existence of the old maid. But *love* in this novel is equivocal in somewhat the same way as writing is in the earlier book. For one thing, love often takes the form of domination and can hardly be imagined except as property relations or even fantasized except as it is represented in the canonical texts of the Western erotic tradition from Ovid to Sade: that is, love is inscribed within the discourse of European bourgeois and patriarchal hegemony.[14] (In this respect, love can be distinguished from writing in *The Man Who Loved Children* for in *For Love Alone* there is no movement beyond a gendered language such as we encountered in the earlier book.) In addition, although the novel seems to call for a transformation of bourgeois and patriarchal social relations,[15] it offers little hope of its being brought about. Accordingly, Teresa's heroism is limited more or less to the sphere accorded women within bourgeois and patriarchal social orders, the terrain of "private life," and takes the form of attempts to define for herself the meaning of love and a commitment to create, in love, an alternative to the exploitation and oppression that prevail in the world at large.

There is no such alternative or enclave in *Letty Fox: Her Luck*. Like its two predecessors, this novel asks whether (or how) its protagonist's ambitions can be realized. But Letty's desires are neither heroic, like Louisa's, nor romantic, like Teresa's, but pragmatic, in keeping with the cynicism that is the novel's dominant mood: Letty seeks "to get married and join organized society" and wants "to be a metropolitan."[16] In its scrutiny of these aspirations—Letty's scrutiny, for the most part, since the novel is told in the first person—the novel measures them not against ideal values like love or heroism but rather against the decadence and exploitation that pervade the world it describes.

Letty Fox, in short, is a satire which relentlessly exposes the commodification of culture, politics, and "personal life," especially in the world of the left-wing intelligentsia in New York in the 1930s and 1940s. Among the targets of Stead's satire is "radical chic," as one critic points out.[17] But *Letty Fox* also laments the degeneration, in the 1940s, of the idealism and activism that made the thirties a "younger, healthier world" (p. 476). Similarly, the novel's satire of the world of letters is an indictment of a literary culture that cannot accommodate Stead's apparently idiosyncratic talents. (Stead wrote *Letty Fox* soon after a stint as a screenwriter at MGM.) Although Letty herself is verbally inventive, words in *Letty Fox* lack the power they have for Louisa or even Sam Pollit. More important, most of what passes for culture in this novel is debased by the mass-production and marketing of words and images—as in Letty's work writing copy for advertisements—or is the sterile product of a quest for aesthetic purity. Finally, the law of the marketplace—illustrated in numerous kinds of traffic in flesh—and the universal exploitation of everyone by everyone else underlie the depiction of "private life" in *Letty Fox*. Here, parents neglect their children (abdication by both mothers and fathers replaces the paternal tyranny of the two previous books), and children desert their parents; men exploit women, and women victimize men. Marriage is the principal site of this parody of mutuality, but only briefly, for it is mainly important as an occasion for alimony—a form of legal extortion and therefore a paradigm for social relations generally in *Letty Fox*—and for divorce, which ensures that "the family" is little more than an aggregation of women who compete for attention from men.

While Letty does not share the values of the culture she inhabits, she does not, like Louisa or Teresa, actively confront it. But even though she appears to give in to the prevailing cynicism and despair, she wins our sympathy because she never yields completely. If Letty's complicity in a culture whose values she cannot endorse separates her from her author, the critical stance she adopts toward her world nevertheless defines the only possibility Stead sees for female heroism in a decidedly unheroic age. This critical stance, of course, resembles that of Stead herself, whose novels reveal the shabbiness of the dismal world we live in and at the same time insist that this is not the only imaginable world.

NOTES

1. See, for example, Terry Sturm, "Christina Stead's New Realism: *The Man Who Loved Children* and *Cotters' England*," in Don Anderson and Stephen Knight, eds., *Cunning Exiles: Studies of Modern Prose Writers* (Sydney: Angus and Robertson, 1974): 9–35; Grant McGregor, "*Seven Poor Men of Sydney*: The Historical Dimension," *Southerly* 38 (1978): 380–403; Jose Yglesias, review of *Dark Places of the Heart* (The American title of *Cotters' England*), *The Nation*, 24 October 1966, pp. 420–21; Yglesias, "Marx as Muse" (Review of the reissue of *The Man Who Loved Children*), *The Nation*, 5 April 1965, pp. 368–70; Michael Wilding, "Christina Stead's Australian Novels," *Southerly* 27 (1967): 20–33; Bell Gale Chevigny, "With Rake-offs for the Pope" (review of the reissue of *House of All Nations*), *Village Voice*, 4 October 1973, p. 21.

2. Here Stead can profitably be read in conjunction with feminist theory, particularly theories of feminism as politics. For recent examples, see Maria Ramos's reinterpretation of Freud in "Freud's Dora, Dora's Hysteria: The Negation of a Woman's Rebellion," *Feminist Studies* 6, no. 3 (Fall, 1980): 472–511, and Michele Barrett, *Women's Oppression Today: Problems in Marxist Feminist Analysis* (London: Verso editions, 1980).

3. *Seven Poor Men of Sydney* (1934; reprint ed., Sydney: Angus and Robertson, 1965), p. 120.

4. Stead took the name Pollit from Harry Pollit, a leader of the British Communist Party. Samuel Clemens was one of her father's favorite humorists (the other was Artemus Ward, whose linguistic style forms Sam's): thus, Samuel Clemens Pollit. Cf. John B. Beston, "An Interview with Christina Stead," *World Literature Written in English* 15 (1976): 93–94.

5. *The Man Who Loved Children* (reprint ed., New York: Avon, 1966), pp. 13–14. All subsequent references to this novel appear parenthetically in the text.

6. Henny's tirades are like the torrent of invective which Northrop Frye identifies as a feature of satire, in *Anatomy of Criticism* (1957; reprint ed., New York: Atheneum, 1965), pp. 223, 236. Joan Lidoff finds in the novel a "satiric realism of observation", cf. ("Home is Where the Heart Is," *Southerly* 38 (1978), p. 371).

7. See, for example, *History of Sexuality, Volume I: An Introduction*, trans. Robert

Hurley (New York: Pantheon, 1978), pp. 108–14; and Jacques Donzelot, *The Policing of Families*, trans. Robert Hurley (New York: Pantheon, 1980), pp. 217–34.

8. Jose Yglesias observes that the setting gives the novel political relevance ("Marx as Muse," p. 369).

9. Although Stead disavows any abstract intention in creating Sam Pollit, she does see some merit in Jonah Raskin's remark that Sam is the American liberal who is also totalitarian. ("Christina Stead in Washington Square," *London Magazine,* NS, 9, 11 [1970]: 74–75, 77; cf. Mary Kathleen Benet, who sees Sam as "the 'liberal' exemplar of the imperialist period of capitalist expansion.") (Introduction to the Virago edition of *Letty Fox: Her Luck*.)

10. Graham Burns sees Louisa's project as a challenge to Sam's monopoly of language, a moral struggle involving the "authority of the written word" ("The Moral Design of *The Man Who Loved Children*," *Critical Review*, no. 14 [1971]: 50–51, 55). Stead describes her own delight in writing—clearly the model for Louisa's—in "A Writer's Friends," *Southerly* 28 (1968):163–68.

11. Joan Lidoff points out that the novel is written with Henny's particularity ("Home is Where the Heart Is," p. 375).

12. This may be one reason for the interest in Stead on the part of feminist critics. Stead herself says of Louisa, "It's the child's viewpoint that I'm faithfully reproducing. We live through agonies and grow up perfectly straight. What happens to Louie doesn't upset her so much. She has some concept that what she's done is bad, but children are capable of very cool thinking. . . . People who do serious things are not necessarily scarred." (Beston, "Interview," p. 92).

13. *For Love Alone* (reprint ed., Virago Modern Classics, London: Virago, n.d.), p. 224. All subsequent references to this novel appear parenthetically in the text.

14. In the novel's most intensely lyrical passage, Teresa muses, in metaphors drawn from the language of land-tenure, on the "short season" woman has for love. She reads Ovid, Virgil, de Sade, etc., delighted to find her fantasies reflected there, "for she found nothing in the few words of women that was what they must have felt." (pp. 72–76).

15. Susan Higgins notes Stead's "radically critical insight into bourgeois social relations." See "Christina Stead's *For Love Alone*: A Female Odyssey?" *Southerly* 38 (1978), 429.

16. *Letty Fox: Her Luck* (reprint ed., Virago Modern Classics, London: Virago, n.d.), pp. 4, 235. All subsequent references to this novel appear parenthetically in the text.

17. Mary Kathleen Benet, Introduction to the Virago edition of the novel.

23

Agnes Smedley's "Cell Mates": A Writer's Discovery of Voice, Form, and Subject in Prison

Judith A. Scheffler

> I was one of the endless stream that passed in and out of the Tombs gates.
> It is good that I did. It is good that we should each know how others suffer;
> and if we have already known, that we should not forget; that we be forced
> to the level of the most miserable of men before we judge, and that we
> experience in our hearts again and again the suffering of the dispossessed.
> Agnes Smedley, *Daughter of Earth*

The current interest in feminist and China studies has introduced the work of Agnes Smedley to a growing, appreciative audience. Born in 1892[1] in northern Missouri and raised in poverty, Smedley longed to escape the economic slavery of marriage that killed her mother before age forty. Largely self-educated, Smedley combined the realism of her harsh childhood and adolescence with the idealism of the political, economic, and social reform movements of the early twentieth century. She became a writer, a journalist with a personal point of view, and began her life of political activism by supporting the Indian Nationalist movement. However, it was as a journalist traveling throughout China between 1928 and 1941, and reporting on her first-hand observation of the Chinese revolution, that Agnes Smedley was most well known. Ironically, it was this close association with and support of the Chinese communists that created much trouble for her[2] and that is largely responsible for the eclipse of her work since her death in 1950.

One especially obscure but intriguing series of early pieces is "Cell Mates," published in 1920 in the Sunday magazine section of the Socialist daily, the *New York Call*.[3] The series consists of four sketches, or "short stories," as Smedley herself described them.[4] Running from about 400 to about 1550 words, each focuses on an individual woman prisoner in the New York Tombs: Nellie, a prostitute; May, a forger; Mollie Steimer, anarchist supporting the Russian revolution; and Kitty Marion, British suffragette and birth control advocate associated with Margaret Sanger.

For students of Smedley's later writings, "Cell Mates" presents an early expression of her lifelong principles and an example of the young journalist's experimentation with the techniques of her craft. Fascinating reading in itself, "Cell Mates" reveals three significant points about Agnes Smedley. We see her finding her voice, her confidence as a writer, and her will to write; finding a mode or form of expression in character sketches, developing a personal brand of journalism, and assuming a dual role as participant/observer; and finding a subject in women's welfare, the rights of oppressed people, and revolution.

Agnes Smedley wrote these sketches from her personal meetings with these women when she, too, was a prisoner in the Tombs, "a monument of the savagery within man."[5] During World War I, Smedley lived in New York, studying with an Indian professor and meeting with young Indian nationalists who sought independence from Britain. In March 1918 she was arrested and held in the Tombs for six months on charges that she had violated the Espionage Act by assisting the Indians, who, unknown to her, had German connections, and that she had acted unlawfully as an agent for the Indian Nationalist Party. She was further charged with violating an anti–birth-control law, because a few copies of Margaret Sanger's pamphlet, *Family Limitation*, had been found in her possession. Her bail, set at $10,000, was raised by the Unitarian minister John Haynes Holmes, who supported Sanger's work. She was released but never tried, and charges were dropped in 1923.[6]

Agnes Smedley describes the effects this experience had upon her goals and her choice of writing as a vocation. Prison helped her to find her voice, to develop the confidence and determination that her message had to be communicated, and to recognize that writing was her proper medium.

Friends had sent me books, paper, and pencils, and for the first time in my life I had been able to study without being burdened with the necessity of earning my own living. My first short stories, *Cell Mates*, were written during that time.[7]

Of course, the darker side of prison touched her as well. "I came out of prison morose and miserable," she wrote many years later.[8] With her ingrained realism, the young Smedley bitterly acknowledged the limited choices of lifestyle available to her. Without an education or a husband, she saw that she might be doomed to a life of drudgery and a home in a gloomy, cheap room. She was at a critical point and was depressed, "for imprisonment does more to the mind, to the spirit, than to the body."[9] Her autobiographical character, Marie Rogers in *Daughter of Earth*, undergoes a similar experience and expresses Smedley's resolution:

Depressed by the spirit of the jail, my mind filled with the eyes of women who, from behind the great iron gates, had watched me go out of their lives, I walked along the street and watched the crowds of free people flow past. I felt that I should scream: "Stop! Think! Listen to the things I have learned and left behind!" They would have hurried faster, perhaps, had I done so, believing me to be insane. Behind towered the dark gray walls of the Tombs—the people did not even see it![10]

With idealism to match her realism, Smedley found her purpose in life—to serve as advocate for the oppressed, through action and through the power of the written word. Critic Susan J. Rosowski's classification of *Daughter of Earth* as a "novel of awakening"[11] is useful here, for Smedley, like her alter ego, Marie, was awakened not only to life's limitations for a young woman, but also to the intellectual and emotional richness possible through commitment to a cause. After working for a time on the *New York Call* staff and with Margaret Sanger, Smedley sailed to Germany and began a lifetime adventure in writing and revolution.

"Cell Mates" presents a second point of interest, in that it shows Smedley experimenting with the journalistic style that she would develop as her own. Examining this aspect of her work in light of theories from the current New Journalism helps to illuminate her techniques and reveals a remarkable parallel between her work and that of journalists practicing today. In his essay "The New Journalism," Tom Wolfe explains the theories of the New Journalism:

It seemed all-important to *be there* when dramatic scenes took place, to get the dialogue, the gestures, the facial expressions, the details of the environment. The idea was to give the full objective description, plus something that readers had always had to go to novels and short stories for: namely, the subjective or emotional life of the characters.[12]

Similarly, the sketches of "Cell Mates" convey the emotional impact of the scenes presented. However, in Smedley's work, considerable attention is paid to the narrator's point of view, as well as that of her subject. She is very much present in the sketches, where the interplay of her consciousness and that of her subject is important. She also liberally employs other devices cited by Wolfe as characteristic of the New Journalism: an emphasis upon scene construction as the vehicle of narration, the use of dialogue, and the recording of "*status life* . . . the entire pattern of behavior and possessions through which people express their position in the world or what they think it is or what they hope it to be."[13] The resemblance of Smedley's techniques to those of the New Journalism helps the reader identify the devices of her style, whose essence, as critics have noted, is a mixture of the personal and the political.[14]

Smedley fashioned for herself a journalistic role as participant/observer. Objectively observing the women prisoners, she notes that she was separated from them by her more highly developed ability to reason. As Marie Rogers, she writes:

They were physical women—as I had once been physical. But now I had some measure of thought, some measure of belief in the power of ideas; in this only did I differ from them. When the world, with its eating and sleeping, its dancing and singing, its colors and laughter, was taken from these women, they were without understanding or resistance. It was easy to make beasts of such women. They had nothing to support themselves with.[15]

The political prisoner Smedley differs from these inmates, but not because their crimes are sordid or their natures sinful. The difference is simply their lack of education, based upon social and economic circumstances beyond their control or understanding. Unlike a New Journalist who attempts to enter temporarily into the lifestyle of her subject, Smedley has a similar background of poverty and ignorance, and thus painfully identifies with her cell mates. She acts simultaneously as a participant and an observer of their dramas. Years later, marching with the Chinese Eighth Route Army, Smedley wistfully notes the duality of her role that prevents her from completely sharing the lives of those she describes:

I am still an onlooker and my position is privileged. I will always have food though these men hunger. I will have clothing and a warm bed though they freeze. They will fight and many of them will lie on frozen battlefields. I will be an onlooker. I watched them blend with the darkness of the street; they still sang. And I hungered for the spark of vision that would enable me to see in their minds and hearts and picture their convictions about the great struggle for which they give more than their lives.[16]

In "Cell Mates," Smedley repeatedly places herself in the position of naive observer, the better to draw the reader into the scene to share a growing awareness of the lives of the street-wise women who "educate" the writer. "My 'greenness' was very profound," Smedley admits, recounting how the clever forger May takes her money.[17] However, her respect for May's ability to survive a life of hardship is clear in this dialogue:

'How you worry about a $500 bail,' I exclaimed. 'Mine is $10,000.' 'Well,' May retorted, '*I* didn't try to swing the world by its tail. All I wanted was a little change.' 'Tell me,' I asked her, 'Why did you stop working in a factory?' 'Go work in a factory and find out,' was her reply.[18]

"Cell Mates," like Smedley's later piece on China, "Some Women of Mukden,"[19] uses the vignette to convey a vital, realistic description of her subject to the reader. Smedley, as naive observer, is most often present in the scene, learning from her cell mate so that she is later prepared to describe the encounter from a more sophisticated perspective, with editorial comment. We see such a scene unfold between Smedley and Mollie Steimer, a young immigrant whose sick mother has just come to tell her that her father and younger brother have died. Without tears, Steimer sits beside the narrator, who feels the "convulsive trembling of her body,"[20] and Steimer tells of her "fragile" dreams and her father's doomed life of poverty. Deftly, Smedley shifts the scene to the dirty prison windows, beyond which the "great stone wall" separates the misery inside from the bustle of New York. This movement makes a general statement from one individual's pain and anticipates the dual focus upon individual and mass suffering that characterizes Smedley's later work.

Smedley sprinkles her sketches with energetic, concentrated dialogue that accurately describes the lives and attitudes of her subjects and manages to celebrate life through humor. Consider for example, a conversation between Smedley and the prostitute Nellie. Morose and self-important, the journalist mumbles her doubt that Nellie could understand why Smedley is in jail. Nellie sadly agrees, but immediately bounces back:

"And how do ye like this hotel?"
I asked why she was there. She reflected for a moment.
"By the holy mother uv Jesus," she started, "I'm as innicent as a baby."
"What is the charge?"
" 'Hitting' a man on the head with a hammer," she replied.
"I didn't do it," she reiterated, to my back.
"Why didn't you?" I asked.
She chuckled and took some snuff. "Jest ye wait till I git out."[21]

One of Smedley's most effective techniques to enliven her sketches is the use of details of "status life," to use Tom Wolfe's term. With remarkable compactness, she describes a woman's personality and lifestyle through a gesture or a physical object. Consider May, the middle-aged forger who is once again doing time in order to protect her "man," even though he completely ignores her needs in prison. Forgiving him has become a habit, and her gesture as she draws his picture from her purse eloquently tells the story of her fate: "it was dim and worn from much handling, and she looked at it with mingled anger and compassion."[22] Nellie's Irish jig and "unprintable" songs, Mollie Steimer's cell wall, covered with newspaper photos of Eugene Debs and John Reed, and Kitty Marion's cheerful greeting to the prisoners as she mops the stone halls, "Three cheers for birth control,"[23] characterize the women with economy and precision.

"Cell Mates" shows Smedley finding her subject, as well as her voice, form, and vocation as a writer. The subject that captivates her interest and to which she dedicates her work and her entire life, is the welfare of all oppressed people. Controversy surrounded Smedley throughout her life, and she was increasingly criticized for her support of the Chinese communists. Though many critics considered her view of communism misguided, most acknowledged her sincerity and selfless dedication in aiding the poor,[24] and would agree with Emma Goldman's assessment of the young Smedley: "She is a striking girl, an earnest and true rebel. . . ."[25] Smedley herself commented in 1943 on her view of communism:

For years I listened to Communists with sympathy and in later years in China I gave them my active support, but I could never place my mind and life unquestioningly at the disposal of their leaders. I never believed that I myself was especially wise, but I could not become a mere instrument in the hands of men who believed that they held the one and only key to the truth.[26]

With her background of American Western individualism, Smedley could not accept any doctrine absolutely.

An essential point to note in considering the subject matter in "Cell Mates" is Smedley's feminism. It is clear, throughout her writings, that she is particularly concerned about improving the condition of women. In China, she worked with women revolutionaries, and often wrote of the traditional rules that restricted them, symbolized by the ancient custom of binding women's feet. Feminism, for Smedley, was a special interest, but she saw it as one aspect of the larger cause of all oppressed people. It is in this light that "Cell Mates" is best understood.

The four women here pictured represent various aspects of oppression: in Nellie and May we see its effects on simple women's lives; in Mollie Steimer and Kitty Marion we see portraits of two who serve the cause of human rights for men and women alike.

The portrait of the Irish-born, aging prostitute Nellie is perhaps the richest of the four in its implications about the development of Smedley's interests and attitudes. "Ugly and scarred, knotted, twisted and gnarled like an old oak,"[27] Nellie displays endurance through her humor, a quality Smedley herself possessed and obviously appreciated in others who suffered. Nellie appears in *Daughter of Earth* also, where, far from condemning her for her lifestyle, Smedley, as Marie Rogers, remarks, "But for the grace—not of God, but of the wildness and the selfishness within me—I would have been like her."[28] Because her own aunt had helped support Smedley's family through her earnings as a prostitute, she had a special interest in the fate of women like Nellie.[29] Although we see Nellie at the end of the sketch leaving prison alone, with no prospects of a better life, her refusal to be passive in an atmosphere that breeds passivity checks any sentimentality and elicits admiration instead. Smedley respects her spirit that cannot be imprisoned:

My first impression of Nellie was gained when I looked up from my luke-warm breakfast coffee to listen to an avalanche of profanity in an Irish brogue. Nellie was swearing at the food, and was showering blessings of wrath upon the wardens and matrons of the Tombs prison, who she swore by all the angels and the Blessed Virgin, had built the jail and ran it for their own pleasure and profit.

The matron spoke: 'Shut your mouth, Nellie, or I'll lock you in your cell.'

Nellie looked up, took up the matron's words, and set them to music. She sang hilariously and, finishing her coffee, two-stepped past the matron and looked her in the eye, still singing.[30]

The scene remarkably parallels a Chinese incident depicted much later, in which Smedley immortalizes an aged, foot-bound beggar woman who, after falling in the street rather ungracefully, shocks and even paralyzes a group of jeering men by cursing them, their ancestors, and their progeny forever. States Smedley pointedly, ". . . some women are passive and some are not. . . . "[31]

"About five feet high and five feet wide, yellow hair and an accordion pleated chin"[32]—this is the description of May, a forty-five-year-old "professional" forger, who committed her crime for Vic, who has now deserted her. While Smedley recognizes the strength that is the root of her fidelity, she notes the "tremulous voice" in which she tells her jokes. Together with Nellie, May represents the common woman, without education or security, whose circumstances bitterly reveal the connection between sexual and economic oppression.

Mollie Steimer, the third cell mate, was a Ukrainian immigrant, arrested in 1918 under the Espionage Act for distributing pro-Bolshevik leaflets.[33] Less than twenty-one years old, wearing a determined expression and a red Russian smock, she welcomes Smedley as a kindred spirit and fellow worker for the revolution. Smedley's admiration for this young woman is evident. She notes that Steimer is not of the *intelligentsia* but of the people, and that "She used English which the most humble could understand";[34] this point could not have been lost on a writer with Smedley's background. She notices the love between Steimer and her fellow inmates, evidenced by her selfless and often risky protest against the prison's treatment of the sick, insane, and outcast, whom she sees as "products of a diseased social system." The young Steimer served as a positive, outspoken role model for Smedley.

Kitty Marion, the fourth and last cell mate, was a veteran British suffragette who had joined Margaret Sanger's birth control movement in 1917, willingly accepting the humble duty of selling copies of the *Birth Control Review* on New York sidewalks. Her arrests were frequent and usually followed by her release as soon as Sanger appeared to bail her out, but she had been sentenced to a thirty-day term in the Tombs through the trickery of Charles Bamberger, of the Society for the Suppression of Vice, who had requested birth control information to aid his sick wife and promptly used the material as evidence against Kitty Marion.[35] Smedley sees Marion as a victim of deceit, but certainly not as passive. As a suffragette, she had withstood over two hundred forcible feedings and, in her fifties, she brought the same energy to her work with Sanger. The birth control issue was one that Smedley came to recognize as essential to the liberation of women worldwide. She saw that lack of birth control had contributed to her mother's hard life and early death, just as she later recognized the solution to this problem as basic to the improvement of life for Chinese women. Her sketch of Kitty Marion is relatively short, and there is no scene or dialogue between Smedley and the reformer.[36] Nevertheless, the narrator's admiration colors the scene. She seems particularly struck by the ability of all the women she pictures to endure their imprisonment with humor; in Kitty Marion she had a prime example of the power of sarcasm to vanquish fears and give strength:

The prison physician came to examine two infants.

"Three cheers for birth control," Kitty called to him from her kneeling position. She held her mop rag in mid air. He turned, and she, scrubbing away, remarked:

"Some way or other every time I see a man the more I believe in birth control."[37]

Readers and researchers of Agnes Smedley's work will find unexpected treasure in "Cell Mates." Its fresh and realistic personal portraits of these four women have much to contribute to feminist literature, and we can only regret that more sketches were not published. Despite its brevity, "Cell Mates" tells us a great deal about the growth of Agnes Smedley as a writer, a humanitarian, and a woman.

NOTES

1. Sources vary in their references to Smedley's date of birth. Jan and Stephen MacKinnon, who are currently working on Smedley's biography, accept the date 1892. See their article, "Agnes Smedley: A Working Introduction," *Bulletin of Concerned Asian Scholars* 7 (January-March 1975), 6–11.

2. In 1949, a report released by General MacArthur's staff of the U.S. Army accused Smedley of spy activity for the Soviet Union. The accusation was quickly withdrawn, but suspicion followed her until her death in 1950.

3. Agnes Smedley, "Cell Mates," *The Call Magazine*, Sunday supplement to the *New York Call*, 15 February, 1920; 22 February, 1920; 29 February, 1920; 14 March, 1920.

4. Smedley, *Battle Hymn of China* (New York: Knopf, 1943), p. 9.

5. Smedley, *Daughter of Earth* (1929; rpt. Old Westbury, New York: The Feminist Press, 1973), pp. 327–328.

6. Details of Smedley's arrest may be found in: Smedley, *Battle Hymn of China*, pp. 8–9; J. and S. MacKinnon, "Agnes Smedley's 'Cell Mates'," p. 531; MacKinnons, Introduction to Agnes Smedley, *Portraits of Chinese Women in Revolution* (Old Westbury, New York: The Feminist Press, 1976), p. xii; Obituary, *New York Times*, May 9, 1950, p. 29; Margaret Sanger, *An Autobiography* (1938; rpt. Elmsford, New York: Maxwell Reprint Co., 1970), pp. 252–253.

7. Smedley, *Battle Hymn of China*, p. 9.

8. Ibid., pp. 9–10.

9. *Daughter of Earth*, p. 330.

10. Ibid., pp. 333–334.

11. Susan J. Rosowski, "The Novel of Awakening," *Genre* 12 (Fall 1979), 313–332.

12. Tom Wolfe, "The New Journalism," in *The New Journalism*, ed. Tom Wolfe and E. W. Johnson (New York: Harper & Row, 1973), pp. 3–52, especially p. 21.

13. Ibid., pp. 31–34.

14. Paul Lauter, "Afterword," in *Daughter of Earth*, pp. 425–427; MacKinnons, "Agnes Smedley: A Working Introduction," pp. 6–11.

15. *Daughter of Earth*, pp. 329–330.

16. Smedley, *China Fights Back* (1938; rpt. Westbury, Conn.: Hyperion Press, 1977), 112.

17. Smedley, "My Cell Mate: No. 2," February 22, 1920.

18. Ibid.

19. Smedley, "Some Women of Mukden," in *Chinese Destinies: Sketches of Present-Day China* (New York: Vanguard Press, 1933), pp. 198–203.

20. "My Cell Mate: No. 3," February 29, 1920.

21. "My Cell Mate: No. 1," February 15, 1920.

22. "My Cell Mate: No. 2."

23. "My Cell Mate: No. 4," March 14, 1920.

24. See, for example, Freda Utley, *Odyssey of a Liberal: Memoirs* (Washington, D.C.: Washington National Press, 1970), p. 201; G. Venkatachalam, *Profiles* (Bombay, India: Malanda Publications, 1949), p. 258.

25. Emma Goldman, *Living My Life* (1931: rpt. New York: Dover, 1970), II, 905.

26. *Battle Hymn of China*, p. 10.

27. "My Cell Mate: No. 1."

28. *Daughter of Earth*, p. 330.

29. See Smedley's discussion of her aunt's lifestyle in *Daughter of Earth*, p. 142. The McKinnons note her mixed feelings on the subject, "Agnes Smedley: A Working Introduction," p. 6.

30. "My Cell Mate: No. 1."

31. "Some Women of Mukden," pp. 201–202.

32. "My Cell Mate: No. 2."

33. Margaret S. Marsh, *Anarchist Women 1870–1920* (Philadelphia: Temple University Press, 1981), pp. 32, 38–39.

34. "My Cell Mate: No. 3."

35. Sanger, *An Autobiography*, pp. 256–258.

36. Smedley did, however, know Marion. In a letter to Margaret Sanger, written from the Tombs, November 1, 1918, Smedley refers to "wonderful meetings" with Kitty Marion and Mollie Steimer. Margaret Sanger Papers (MSS in the Library of Congress).

37. Smedley, "My Cell Mate: No. 4."

24

The Transformation of Privilege in the Work of Elena Poniatowska

Bell Gale Chevigny

"We write in Latin America to reclaim a space to discover ourselves in the presence of others, of human community—so that they may see us, so that they may love us—to form the vision of the world, to acquire some dimension—so they cannot erase us so easily. We write so as not to disappear."[1]

These remarks of Elena Poniatowska at a conference at Wellesley College in the spring of 1980 drew their coloration from her anguish over the "disappearance" of Latin Americans by political forces, but they aptly characterize her most important work as well. The evanescent or invisible, the silent or the silenced, those who elude official history or vanish from it, make the subject of the two of Poniatowska's works from which her fame and influence chiefly derive. Her testimonial novel, *Hasta no verte Jesus mio* (1969, Until I see you, my Jesus) presents in first-person narration the story of an adventuring peasant woman, fighter in the Mexican revolution and survivor of its inhospitable aftermath. Hitherto such characters had been presented only externally, and Poniatowska's distillation of her subject's dense and highly-colored idiom became a new literary resource. *La Noche de Tlatelolco* (1971, translated as *Massacre in Mexico*) is a dramatic collage of interviews with participants in the 1968 student movement and with witnesses to the massacre of hundreds during a peaceful meeting in Mexico City, an event obfuscated by government agencies and the press alike.

A close reader of Poniatowska's work may also interpret her words at Wellesley to mean that as her writing brings Latin America into being, so has Latin America allowed Poniatowska to emerge as a writer; the two formations are intimately

Permission to reprint this chapter has been granted by *Latin American Literary Review*, published in XIII, #26, July-December 1985.

related. This interpretation gains force when we consider that Poniatowska's identification with Latin America and its language were both deliberate choices, the land and the tongue of her childhood being other. While her mother was Mexican, her father was Polish, and both were in many important ways French. Poniatowska was born and raised in Paris. Even after the family returned to Mexico when Poniatowska was nine, only French and English were spoken at home. Most of her family still identify themselves as European. Poniatowska's choosing to cast her lot with Latin America and to write in Spanish with a highly Mexican inflection, point to a deliberateness of self-formation that is reinforced by other choices. For Poniatowska's social roots are aristocratic and her political antecedents are conservative. Generations of exile from reform and revolution in Mexico and Poland produced in France Poniatowska's parents and Ponia-towska herself. Against such a background, her two most celebrated works stand in high relief; they delineate the dual trajectory of her career. In *Hasta no verte, Jesus mio*, she journeys to the opposite end of woman's world of social possibility and, in *La Noche de Tlatelolco*, she journeys to the alternate pole of political possibility. Each journey may be seen as metaphor and impetus of the other. Like her choice of Latin America, her choosing to write of a woman with no resources but herself and of political insurgents has everything to do with her authorial self-creation.

In this connection, her rejection in 1970 of Mexico's most prestigious literary award, the Xavier Villaurrutia Prize for *La Noche de Tlatelolco* takes on added significance. In an open letter to the new president, Luis Echevarria, Poniatowska asked who was going to give prizes to the dead. In 1968 Echevarria had been Minister of the Interior, responsible for all internal security forces. In Ponia-towska's rejection of the prize lie two refusals: a refusal to help Echevarria symbolically dissociate himself from the massacre and treat as settled the problem raised by the students, and a refusal to identify herself with established power. She rejects the implications of closure which the awarding and accepting of such a prize chiefly signify.

It is arguable that Poniatowska's rejection of the Villaurrutia Prize was an aesthetic as well as a political gesture; in refusing closure with the massacred subjects of her book, she acknowledges the sources of her art. I will try to show that the particular force of Poniatowska's work derives from the emptiness she found in her position as a woman of privilege and from her using that position to cultivate a readiness of imagination and spirit; when this readiness met with vivid exposure to the dispossessed, she converted equivocal privilege into real strength. Such an evolution would make her links to the dispossessed a continuing necessity.

I will trace this evolution by looking first at works of hers which treat women, seeking to discern in them her progressive identification of her career as a writer.[2] I will then look at the writings which treat more general political and social issues in an endeavor to show how her evolution as a woman informed her vision of these issues.

When socially privileged, Poniatowska's female characters are cursed with feverish instability. In *De noche vienes* (1979; You come at night) a volume of stories written over several years, the protagonist or narrator is almost always a woman. Sensuousness, an antic humor, and a lyrical eagerness stamp the stories which are also often edged with intimations of death or of isolation without remedy. Three of them offer patently autobiographical moments. In "Cancionde Cuna" (Cradle Song), dedicated to "una senorita bien educade," (a well-bred young lady), Poniatowska offers a paradigmatic image of that condition. An undefined narrator speaks fancifully to a woman disqualified from experience by her very position of privilege. She is counseled to march through her day with the steps of a sergeant, to end it with prayers and fall asleep to a lullaby:

> Lovely little sparrow
> with a coral beak
> I bring you a cage
> of pure crystal.[3]

But with her lids closed she feels beneath her body the earth and its grottos, its rivers with their crossing roads, its fire and its gold, its diamonds submerged in coal and still lower the deaf beat of the lava. She feels the elements which erupt in volcanos, and without opening her eyes she hears a voice whispering the most tender declarations of passion. It is important that the explosion of repressed love and longing comes from the earth, that one subterranean realm ignites the other, that despite her crystal cage, the senorita is not out of touch with earth. Although such women are cut off from life by sex, class, and rearing, their predicament does not jail their imaginations, their sense of the possible.

In "El limbo" (limbo), Monica, a kindred protagonist, tries to take action, carrying the unwanted infant of Rose, a housemaid, to the hospital, there trying absurdly first to get preferential treatment and then to organize a group of mothers to protest bad hospital conditions. At home, her aristocratic grandmother is repelled by the girl's raw indignation ("if you went about it a la Tolstoy, I would overlook it, but you are the most dreadful fabricator of commonplaces I have ever heard in my life"). Finally her mother half distracts her with thoughts of a dance, but Monica weeps over her supper:

She cried above all because she was Monica and no one else, because the death of Rose's baby was not her death and she couldn't experience it, because she knew very well she would dance Saturday in her red dress, o Bahia, ay, ay, tapping with her heels on the heart of the child, she would dance over the women whose babies fell between their legs like rotten fruit, she would dance . . . because after all, one's own life is stronger than that of the rest."[4]

The desperation underlying this self-assertion finds only ironic relief in the experience privilege affords mature women. In them the potential of the senorita is warped. The narrator of "El inventario" (the inventory), the young mistress of an ancestral house being dismantled, is one of those observers on whom nothing is lost. In an amazing scene, an Aunt Veronica, who lives to command the furniture and its care, loses herself in the miasma of sweet wood smells and turpentine oils in the shop of a furniture restorer.

Aunt Veronica stopped giving orders. I think she even forgot why she had come. She sniffed excitedly and hid behind the sound of the saw. Slowly, ever so slowly, she ran her slender fingers over the corners of a table, slipping them into this or that crack and leaving one of them inside with indescribable pleasure. Finger and cleft fit delicately together, immersed in each other, and, I don't know precisely how or why, my aunt's excitement was contagious. For the first time I was seeing something unknown and mysterious. Aunt Veronica was breathing hard, as if her body were brushing up against something alive and demanding, something inexhaustible which rose with her as her breathing filled with desire. . . . And then I understood that furniture is made to receive our bodies or for us to touch it lovingly. Not in vain did it have laps, backs, and quilted arms to play horsey on; not in vain were the shoulders so broad, the seats so cozy. Furniture was neither virgin nor innocent; on the contrary, it was heavy with awareness. Every piece was covered with sculpted flanks. There were corners filled with a secret light and an animal force rose unmistakably from the wood.[5]

Again, as with the senorita and Monica, imagination and the need to give and receive love have nowhere to go. They can offer only this delicious and perverse insight into chairs. It may forever alter our casual sense of furniture but is that enough? The flight of fancy here is both symptom and protest against the crystal cage of class and gender. And clearly here, the crystal cage is the stronger for being made in Europe. The narrator's family, troubled by her outbursts, determine to keep her more indoors—or to send her to Europe (two versions of the same idea, as it turns out, because for the narrator Europe is an old pullman car with dusty curtains, seats of wine-colored plush, toothless fringes; it is threadbare; it smells bad.)

It is tempting to read *Querido Diego, te abraza Quiela* (1978; Dear Diego, with hugs from Quiela) as that sort of covert autobiography which magically fends off possible destinies; in it Poniatowska, a Pole raised in Paris and in love with Mexico, seems to measure the cage she has had to flee. For Quiela is Angelina Beloff, a Russian painter who lived in Paris ten years with Diego Rivera before he left her for Mexico promising to write for her to follow. Drawn to this woman left on history's margin, Poniatowska has taken scraps of her letters and imagined them whole, imagined what Quiela felt, recalling the cold winter when their infant son died, living through another winter trying to keep her love alive and give new birth to her painting. All fails, motherhood, painting, and love—even the letters are (and were) never answered. Poniatowska has found a *form* that follows the contours of unrequited love and pathetically enduring hope, an epistolary novel of dead letters, a duet for one instrument. What is her object? Poniatowska explores the depths of female dependency, casting her light in that abyss to banish its terrors, for herself and the rest of us. In all these works Poniatowska demystifies privileged gentility so that it can no longer seduce any woman or be honored or used as weapon of control over them. Angelina's story may exorcise a ghost of Poniatowska's, but it is not her story. For she would have been already there in Mexico, like Rivera, but making her own mural of the revolution.

A mural of the revolution: that partly describes *Hasta no verte, Jesus mio*. Jesusa Palancares, the speaker of this extraordinary *novela-testimonio*, is the antithesis of Angelina Beloff, sharing with her only a will to survive and a need to break silence, to assert herself (Angelina before an indifferent man, Jesusa before an indifferent society). For Poniatowska sees in Angelina how one kind of female sensibility feeds dependence and in Jesusa how another kind feeds an independence that is almost complete.

The *novela-testimonio* lends itself peculiarly to a sort of symbiosis in which the author explores through the presentation of the subject her or his own potential strengths and weaknesses. As the writers become ventriloquists for their subjects, so is the reverse true.

What we know of Poniatowska's life bears out such an interpretation. When she was brought to Mexico at the age of nine, she was placed in an English school. As only French and English were spoken at home, she learned Spanish from the servants; her regard for these speakers and their world is bound up with her love for the language as they speak it. She has said that she feels that she is Mexican because this idiom comes now more definitively from within herself than any other.[6] When she first saw Jesusa, she was working as a journalist, interviewing important figures daily for the Mexican newspaper *Novedades*, but she was more attracted to Jesusa than to anyone else she says, ''because she spoke so coarsely, so vehemently—I loved her language—because she was always fighting and because she is very short like me.''[7] Jesusa did not want to be interviewed, however, and Poniatowska first visited Jesusa once a week in what appears a tacit understanding of an equalizing ritual. Jesusa would set her to the task of taking her thirteen hens, a little leash tied to a leg of each, out into the sun. Gradually Jesusa began to talk of her life, and after Poniatowska's period of initiation, reverted to the coarse and figurative speech that had so drawn the writer. The ensuing creative process was symbiotic. Although Poniatowska has said she made up details, her deference to Jesusa is patent in everything she says about her. For example, in speaking of Jesusa's wish to die alone, Poniatowska said, ''She needs no one, but I need her, and perhaps others need her.''[8]

The passage to which she refers ends the book and expresses as powerfully as any Jesusa's poignant self-sufficiency, in which the crucial relationships of her life form a part, and the mysteries of society, nature, and death are acknowledged and integrated:

It's really hard not dying when you're supposed to. . . . That's why I ask God to let me die up in the hills. If he answered my prayers, all I'd need would be the strength to climb to the top. But since He doesn't give scorpions wings, who knows? . . . I'd like to go back and die where I used to gallivant about when I was young and die under a tree over there, let the buzzards surround me, and that's it. Then if anyone came looking for me I'd be up there happy as can be flying in the buzzards' guts. Otherwise your neighbors come and peer in while you're dying, to see how horrible you look all twisted and tangled and bloated, with your legs splayed and your mouth gaping and your eyes popped out. Some life, to die like that! That's why I bolt myself in. . . . That's why I don't want to die in Mexico City. No. I want to be on a hillside or in a ditch like my father, who died under a tree in an open field. God give me the strength to get there! It's a good thing to know the hour of your death. I ask Him to let me know so I can get ready, and be on my way. I'll become fodder for the animals out there. For the coyotes, like Pedro, my husband. It's not that I don't want to be buried, but who's going to bury me? They'll say: "Praise the Lord, that old mule's finally bit the dust." I don't think people are good. Only Jesus Christ, but I never met him. And my father, who I never knew if he loved me or not. But here on earth, how can you expect people to be good? Now fuck off. Go away. Let me sleep.[9]

Here and throughout this book, Poniatowska's language becomes much more definitively Mexican than it has been in earlier work. She exploits the resources of Mexican campesino speech, making a thick brew of its errors and earthiness, its domesticating diminutives and strong images. For a European, she has said, writing is a way of belonging to one's adopted country, and in Jesusa's speech there is no trace of "the old Pullman."

Much of the power of *Hasta no verte* lies in the surprises it plays on official history, which has left Jesusa out of its accounting. Poniatowska not only adds her in, but gives us a Jesusa who recasts it wholly. That's one surprise. Another is that Jesusa gains prodigious authority from a range of activities on which society confers no authority. She is by turns a motherless child, a punching-bag for her father, a servant to her stepmothers, neglected by all but the revolutionary soldier-husband Pedro who likes to beat her; the pension she is promised after riding and fighting in the revolution, even leading Pedro's troops after his death, is later denied her; she lives in corners and vestibules, picking up work when she can in laundries, restaurants, factories, bars, fine houses; she becomes also a handy street-brawler and a protector, willing or not, of superfluous children and dogs. Orphaned, victimized, deluded, fired, cheated, beaten, and often jailed, Jesusa tells with unflagging zest of language how she fought back on each occasion; she delivers judgments as fresh as they are convincing on Mexican heroes, politics in general, marriage, the relation of men to women, of humans to the earth, to evil, and to death. How is this alchemy worked? I believe that Jesusa offered the anecdotal skeleton, that the styles of discourse are essentially hers, but that it was Poniatowska who heard what she said, who broke through the noise of disordered reminiscence (another kind of silence), and *saw* the strength hidden in weakness. Human gain buried in human loss, the diamond in the coal, these are the strengths granted woman in general that women artists are especially gifted in releasing. For a woman writing is converting her loss into gain. Poniatowska's writing moves her from the implosions of the haute-bourgeoisie—self-serenades, orgasms with furniture, dead letters—to the explosions of Jesusa. At the same time, the imaginative attention to things which distinguished the idle high-born ladies is now present in Jesusa's scrupulously detailed accounts of her work.

Poniatowska does not romanticize Jesusa's strength. When her difficulties seem overwhelming, Jesusa seeks consolation, from time to time, in confusion, in the mystifying light of the Obras Espirituales. This spiritualist sect, with its creed of reincarnation, plays on her naiveté and her desire for a more fulfilling past and future and a justification for her current suffering. Jesusa's engagement with the revolution responded in part to her quest for family, for community and for meaning; when it was foiled she sought them in individual terms, in the specious family and opportunistic meanings of the sect. In a sense, in her later work, Poniatowska makes Jesusa's quest her own.

Hasta no verte Jesus mio appears to have led Poniatowska past the impasse of adolescent Monica who felt, even while despising her own life, that it was stronger than that of the rest. Finding Jesusa's strength, she could begin to cultivate her own.

Listening to Jesusa in order to break the silence about her side of Mexican history prepared Poniatowska to understand the silence at the heart of contemporary Mexican political life. Profoundly shaken by the events of 1968, she brought to them, as to subsequent political events, imaginative resources developed in her evolving treatment of women. These include an uncanny ear and eye, and a vigilance for opportunities to identify the self in action and to locate the values of intimacy and family in a community which dominates no one.

In the summer of 1968 an escalating series of student demonstrations culminated in the call for a huge and public dialogue with the government. This last demand reveals the students' acumen with regard to the PRI, the Institutionalized Revolutionary Party—the bitter paradox of that name had become insufferable. The students saw that with its monolithic dominance of politics, of the economy, of the labor unions and of the press, the PRI offered less than a monologue—in effect, it offered only silence. The chants of the student movement were thus important but the dialogues they initiated were more so. The students of UNAM, the National Autonomous University of Mexico, bridged the chasms of class in making common cause with the students of the National Polytechnic Institute, women began to share positions of leadership with men; and their lightning meetings and imaginative street theatre began to tell in working-class districts.

The form of Poniatowska's chronicle *Massacre in Mexico* captures this excitement over dialogue itself.[10] Extracts of the testimony of student and faculty leaders, other participants, workers, passersby, journalists, critics and informers are interwoven with leaflets, slogans, and official statements. Poniatowska edits and orchestrates, but, adding no words to those of her sources, makes history seem to flow from the voices of the participants and gives us an uncanny experience of the simultaneous spontaneity and inevitability of events. And the feeling of immediacy is balanced by the historical sense of those who saw this movement against the backdrop of the railroad strike of 1958, the killing of Zapatista peasant organizer Ruben Jaramillo in 1962, and the repression of the doctors' movement in 1964. The euphoria of the movement at high tide is epitomized in the students' occupation of UNAM. They converted the university into a model or alternate society, an exemplary state, a self-proclaimed "territorio libre de Mexico." Poniatowska later wrote, with her characteristic susceptibility to dislocated domesticity, the university now "really functioned like an *alma mater*, an amorous mother who sheltered and covered with her protecting wings." Students fell asleep, she reports, to the cradle song of the mimeograph machine.[11]

The army's occupation of the free territory of UNAM on September 18 and later of the Polytechnical Institute brought an end to this dialogue. Although the students had promised not to interfere with the Olympic games scheduled to open October 12, the government grew frantic at the prospect of menace to this star in its crown, conclusive proof of Mexico's alleged superiority in the Hispanic world. The horror of Tlatelolco represents the loss of the trophy of world opinion in the effort to secure it. On October 2, while 10,000 people gathered to hear speeches from the National Strike Committee at the Tlatelolco housing unit, 5,000 soldiers and police surrounded the square. Flares in the sky gave the signal to open fire, and those who tried to flee were met by columns approaching in a pincer play. Over 2,000 were jailed, many of them for years. The dead proved harder to count; after careful investigation, the British newspaper, *The Guardian* offered what may be the best estimate: 325. On October 3, the Mexican press estimated variously 20 to 26 dead.

The press' irresponsibility was backed by deepened government silence as it refused to investigate the massacre. Poniatowska, who defines literature as "un largo grito" (a long shout),[12] constructed her narrative to amplify her protest against silence: the book's first part recounts the events before and after October 2; the second is the prolonged cry of anguish and rage which is the telling of the night of Tlatelolco.

Significantly, Poniatowska differs in her interpretation of that night from her good friend Octavio Paz, the poet and critic who in 1968 resigned his ambassadorial post in India in protest and also wrote the introduction to the United States edition of *Massacre in Mexico*. In his analysis, *The Other Mexico: A Critique of the Pyramid* (1972), he argues that the "invisible history" of the country, the survival in modern Mexico of Aztec hierarchical domination and ritual sacrifice, explains the blood-letting. As Poniatowska challenges the publicists who claim for Mexico an enlightenment that excepts it from the rest of Latin America, so she disputes the fatalism which for Paz distinguishes his land.[13]

Without making nationalist claims, Poniatowska discerns exceptional persons and moments which animate belief in change. Of the several massive marches on the Zocalo in 1968, she gives her sharpest attention in *Massacre In Mexico* to the silent march of September 13, which happened also to be the largest. On that date some 400,000 participants marched in silence, some with their mouths taped shut—a silence that ran counter to the fiesta-like abandon said to be the quintessence of Mexican public events. This show of the capacity for change, more than any other march, brought on-lookers off the benches and into the ranks. What engaged Poniatowska, I believe, is the power of silence transformed into silence *heard*: as such it is the emblem of her later work, and gives her most recent book its title.

Hearkening to the nuances of silence, speaking for those who answer "no one" to the preemptory question, "who goes there?"[14]—these are the disciplines that govern Poniatowska's five chronicles in *Fuerte es el silencio* (Silence is strong, 1980). Briefly, the first of these sketches the children who fly in and out of the capital selling Chiclets or Kleenex and make their cardboard homes in the hundreds of "lost cities" surrounding it. She calls them "angeles de la ciudad" (angels of the city) in a metaphoric strategy which makes visible those whom Mexico's miraculous "progress" brought into being and requires its proper citizens to ignore. We may recall the imaginative ingenuity by which Aunt Veronica transformed the furniture, but imagination is now and forever out of the house, discerning not the vitality of possessions but of the human dispossessed. The second chronicle traces the effects of 1968 in the next ten years, showing especially how Echevarria's attempt to co-opt the student movement without addressing its aims ended by reproducing 1968 in other forms; the picture of the PRI as a tightly-knit, self-indulgent family living in a blind fortress is fixed.

Poniatowska may have lived in crystal cages, but she never belonged to the PRI fortress. Through Jesusa's revolution and students' brigades, she had glimpsed the promise of better "families." Her remaining three chronicles are linked by her exploration of alternative organizations, the fragmentary "families" that emerged after 1968. Echevarria's equivocal liberalization worked both to politicize oppressed groups and to generate a stronger, more autonomous military. As student protests gave way to urban guerilla activities and peasant land seizures, Mexico learned practices—especially disappearance and torture— it had censured in dictatorships. In a third chronicle, Poniatowska tries through interviews to grasp the motives of jailed guerillas. In a fourth, the diary of a 1978 hunger strike, she describes the four-day bivouac in the Cathedral of the capital by eighty-three mothers of disappeared persons. While this makeshift family arouses more of Poniatowska's sympathy than the guerillas do, she remains ambivalent. She appears to be groping toward a new form, as she permits her own troubled musings and fantasies breaking the surface of documentary reportage. We feel again Monica's malaise over the tug between one's own life and that of others.

Far more successful as formal synthesis and as provocation to the reader is the last chronicle, the best in the book. While Poniatowska the interviewer disappears, she is perhaps more present than in any other work. The passionate force of this narrative derives partly from its temporary fulfillment of strivings expressed in other works. Here families of dispossessed "angels" find their home by making their own city in Morelos, the Colonia Ruben Jaramilo, (named for the assassinated peasant leader), as hundreds of Mexican groups were doing in the mid-seventies. The desire of the wellbred senorita to slip her cage and make her home in the earth here combines with Jesusa's search for a true revolutionary family. Indeed the populist idiom and spirit of this chronicle are more than any other work like that of *Hasta no verte Jesus mio*.

The extraordinary figure, Florencio Medrano, who leads the group, bears some resemblance to the better known Ruben Jaramillo, and other peasant leaders Genaro Vasquez Rojas and Lucio Cabanas killed in the seventies. Called "El Guero" (the blond), he combines the intimate knowledge of recipes and remedies of a Jesusa with the charisma of a Zapata and a rare compassion. Using a strategy he developed during a visit to China, he led families in 1973 to form a commune on *ejido* land outside Cuernavaca as the first in a contemplated series of land seizures which would culminate in armed revolution.

In a series of vignettes, Poniatowska offers moments which suggest the range and complexity of her vision. El Guero spurs thirty apprehensive families to leave Cuernavaca's slums for unused collective land; giving each a lot on condition they build their shanty in seventy-two hours and joining them in the work, he makes their very fear productive. In the name of Ruben Jaramillo, he then persuades them to divide their lots for late-comers. The guerilla patriarch inspires students to participate on his "Red Sundays" in construction of hospitals, roads, and plumbing in the "first free territory in America" since UNAM. In perhaps the most powerful episode, when the terrified governor comes to promise the settlers light, water, all services, El Guero shouts down their cheering, seeing in it evidence of their interiorized humiliation: "Don't thank them!" he insists. "The earth is yours, by legitimate right, you're not orphans, you're Mexicans, here you were sown and here you must grow . . . The light is yours, the water is yours, yours because they expelled you, don't go on being grateful, you have nothing to thank anyone for—nothing, nothing, *nothing*!—except yourselves and your own work."[15] And mysteriously his exhausted aspect gives those close to him an intuition of his death; it is as if the very absolutism of his claims for human justice promise to consume him.

Other episodes present growing contradictions. Over-confident, El Guero tolerates suspected spies. Scheming about collecting arms, he neglects the colonia, imperiling it. In long evenings of talk with women, he persuades them to speak their bitterness, and to assume responsibility, but he becomes possessively jealous of Elena, his secretary and confidante. Finally he flees, with Elena, from the encroachment of the police, hiding in the mountains to pursue his revolutionary dream, now reduced to kidnappings. Although his followers cannot believe the news of his death, they lose their revolutionary nerve. The chronicle ends with Poniatowska in 1980 watching a conventional beauty queen pageant, in which the children, without understanding it intone a song about the ultimate victory of Florencio Medrano. Only one in the crowd recalls Medrano and invites Elena Poniatowska to hear his story.

No other work of hers has more concentrated force and complexity than this. An explanation lies partly in her giving the intrinsically dramatic facts a particularity and emotional coloring of her own. As she could learn of only fragments of Medrano, she made him, she says, the way she wanted him to be.[16] Wholly fictional is the sheltered and faded Elena who comes as a secretary to help and writes at nights about "El Guero" and revolution, who learns the limitations of his scheme from the Colonia's thoughtful schoolteacher, and yet flees with him as his lover. As her name and her literary vocation broadly hint, she is a figure of autobiographical fantasy. But as Poniatowska both includes and goes beyond "Elena," this chronicle as a whole both embodies Mexican romanticism and points to its limits. All Poniatowska's work discloses reservations about the romanticism it depicts and expresses; here her irony also analyses it. The chronicle epitomizes Poniatowska's literary project: in naming and cultivating the lives and rights of others, the writer is naming and integrating herself in ever more complex ways. One's own life is stronger but imaginative familiarity with others gives meaning to its strength.

This compelling fable makes us perceive the shape of a terrible historical impasse. Damned by their own state, the people of the Colonia would never have fought without the fearless leadership of a Medrano, but that very revolutionary zeal dictated that he sacrifice the Colonia and abandon it to its fate. Poniatowska recognizes the heroic efforts of the marginal move toward the center of their own lives—to displace the heartless state,—and, when those efforts fail, she salvages the drama to seek out the issues which Medrano's successors must begin by addressing. Medrano sweeps through the lives of the people like a wind, moving them forward and going beyond them. What are the alternatives? The practical wisdom of the teacher (whom Poniatowska *did* meet) could not command the loyalty of the people as El Guero's daring could. With all that militates against them, can the people learn to define, and gain the strength to pursue, their own largest interests?

Poniatowska's work elicits such questions because her mixture of modes of knowing—investigative and empathetic—and of ways of telling—novelistic, testimonial, journalistic and confessional—engage the feelings and curiosity of the reader. The reader is implicated in pursuit of the story beyond its formal ending. To express it another way, Poniatowska herself practices a kind of alchemy related to that by which Jesusa derived great authority from her strong response to abuse. In Poniatowska's case an empty privilege is transformed into a full one—the fullest privilege is responsibility—but in the process, privilege and responsibility are stripped of their established social meanings. If Poniatowska's self-presentation is modest, her effect is not: for the reader, the conventional privilege is diminished as responsibility is enlarged.

NOTES

1. "Women's Literature in Latin America: Mexico," Wellesley College Conference, "Breaking the Sequence: Women, Literature, and the Future," April 30-May 2, 1981.

2. In my first section below, I violate chronology to present Poniatowska's writings about women in an order which dramatizes her dissatisfactions with the situation of women in the upper classes and her sympathetic attraction to women in positions of struggle. The fact that she wrote about Angelina Beloff after writing about Jesusa does not alter my point; doubtless her understanding of Jesusa gave Poniatowska new insight into the limitations of Angelina's situation. Indeed the project of coming to terms with women's class conditioning is a lifelong endeavor. In my second section, I follow chronology in discussing Poniatowska's writing about society and politics.

3. *De noche vienes* (Mexico: Editorial Grijalbo, 1979), p. 29.

4. Ibid., pp. 63, 65.

5. Ibid., pp. 89–90; translation by Magde Bogin for this essay.

6. Interview Margarita Garcia Flores, *Gartas Marcadas* (Mexico: Difusion Cultural, UNAM, 1979), p. 220; translation mine; all subsequent translations are mine, unless otherwise indicated.

7. From panel discussion at Wellesley conference, May 2, 1981.

8. Ibid.

9. *Hasta no verte, Jesus mio* (Mexico: Ediciones Era, 1969), pp. 315–16.

10. *Massacre in Mexico*, tr. Helen R. Lane (New York: Viking, 1975), is Poniatowska's only work translated into English.

11. "El movimiento estudiantil de 1968," *Fuerte es el silencio* (Mexico: Ediciones Era, 1980), p. 45.

12. Garcia Flores, p. 229.

13. Ibid., p. 225.

14. Prologo, *Fuerte es el silencio*, p. 11.

15. Ibid., pp. 227–28.

16. Panel discussion at Wellesley.

25

Marguerite Yourcenar's Sexual Politics in Fiction, 1939

Judith L. Johnston

Marguerite Yourcenar, the first woman elected to the Académie Française, is a French novelist and dramatist, born in Brussels in 1903, who resides on Mount Desert Island in Maine. She published her first play in 1921; her most famous novel in the United States is *Memoirs of Hadrian*; she translated Virginia Woolf's *The Waves* in 1937; and, since her election to the "immortals," she is beginning to receive the international critical attention her large body of work deserves. Her career as a twentieth-century writer spans more than half the century.

When I consider her place in literary history, I am amazed that she has received so little attention as a writer responding to the sexual and political crises of the twentieth century. Defining "political" broadly, to include all relations of power, I find that Yourcenar's political analysis of sexuality and modern culture shapes both her characters and her narratives. Here, I would like to explore sexual politics in her 1939 novel, *Coup de Grâce*, which is a confessional narrative set between the two world wars.

Although her preface to the 1981 translation denies any political value in this human document, the mutual bonding of authoritarian and submissive personalities portrayed in the love triangle of Erick, Sophie, and Conrad certainly derives from a political critique of her culture. In the same preface, she implicitly acknowledges the contemporary historical relevance of her 1939 novel, by alluding to Racine's *Bajazet* as "a tragedy of events close to his own time but occurring in what was then the closed world of the Ottoman Empire."[1] Yourcenar's own novel is a tragedy of events relevant to the impending second European war, but occurring two decades earlier, in 1919–20. Although she has refused to accept the concepts of "feminine discourse" or "feminine writing," her narrative nevertheless reveals that language reflects the gender-linked relations of power. The sexual identity of her narrator, Erick, shapes his "récit."

Coup de Grâce calls for a radical revisioning of culturally based gender stereotypes and requires the reader to envision alternatives to passivity when faced with the threat of violence.

Yourcenar has stated that she began writing *Coup de Grâce* in 1938, in response to the September Munich conference, at which Daladier and Chamberlain, the French and British prime ministers, hoping by their submission to gain peace in their time, yielded to Hitler's demand to "repatriate" Germanic peoples dwelling in the Sudentenland of Czechoslovakia. The conference raised questions about nationality, cultural history, and the proper response to the threat of force; *Coup de Grâce* demands consideration of these same three issues. The novel was published in May of 1939, after the failure of the Munich compromise was evident, but before the German invasion of Poland.

Yourcenar's historical fiction interprets the origin of the Nazi movement in the post-World War I *Freikorps* fighting in the Baltic against Bolshevik revolutionaries. The Baltic cross, or Swastika, those soldiers of fortune brought back to Germany symbolizes the continuity between the Baltic terror of 1919 and the threat of 1939. Like the broken string of pearls Erick carried with him as a memento of Sophie, the Baltic cross is a sign of past actions predicting and defining future character. *Coup de Grâce* is a contemporary historical parable, in which the events of 1919 forecast the events of 1939.

In 1939, reviewers failed to connect contemporary politics with the narrative of Yourcenar's historical novel. Edmond Jaloux, reviewing the novel in August 1939, in *Les Nouvelles Littéraires*, defined it as "une histoire vraie," and Jean Charpentier, in the September 1, 1939 issue of *Mercure de France*, noted "la vérité historique," but neither noted that Yourcenar's psychological tragedy might be relevant to France's moral dilemma of choosing submission or resistance to violent force. Her novel portrays individuals facing that dilemma, and the implications for her national culture in 1939 should have been sobering.

The narrator and principal character is Erick von Lhomond, a German soldier of fortune. In a brief preface, a third-person narrator introduces Erick in his late thirties, as he is returning wounded from fighting for Franco in Spain, specifically in the battle of Saragossa, which dates this part of the narrative in 1937. In a train station, Erick solicits unenthusiastic listeners for his Baltic war story; ominously, a nearly blind beggar also solicits the travelers, offering a tour of Pisa's famous Leaning Tower. As in *Madame Bovary*, the blind man's presence portends death, here the death of a culture. The narrative shifts into Erick's own voice as he tells his story, which he admits is a "text full of holes" (90).

Erick narrates a complicated tale of terrorist war and unrequited love. An impoverished aristocrat, born too late to have fought in World War I, Erick had allied himself with the Russian aristocracy displaced by the revolution. Erick describes his participation in the Baltic civil wars and in a love triangle with a brother and a sister, Conrad and Sophie, the Count and Countess de Reval. His story encompasses the ruin of their Edenic estate, and the deaths of both Sophie and Conrad in the war.

Erick's prejudices, his cult of force, and his self-deluding revision of history resemble those of other unreliable, biased characters of twentieth-century confessional fiction. Erick and his egocentric historical narrative most closely resemble Ernst von Salomon, the popular German fascist writer, and his autobiographical novel about his participation in the Baltic civil wars, *The Outlaws* (*Die Geächteten*, 1930). *Coup de Grâce* also invites comparison with André Gide's *The Immoralist* (1902), Louis-Ferdinand Céline's *Journey to the End of the Night* (1932), and Gunter Grass's *The Tin Drum* (1962), all novels in which narrators who are paradoxically both attractive and repulsive reflect the author's critical image of his own culture. Although Yourcenar, a French woman, chose a voice that was both German and male, her portrayal of Erick does not suggest that fascism was the symptom of a national neurosis, nor that it was peculiar to German culture; instead, Yourcenar's novel analyzes the authoritarian personality by presenting Erick's confession as a case history. His brutal first-person narrative provokes the reader's active, energetic, analytical response. This interplay between reader and narrator generates an alternative to the passive acceptance of authoritarian violence.

In Yourcenar's historical parable, Sophie may represent Russia, Conrad England and France, and Erick Germany; however, Sophie, Conrad, and Erick transcend national stereotypes. Their mixed national heritage signals their role as representative Europeans of the generation that became young adults in 1919. All three were orphaned by World War I. Erick is a "Prussian with French and Baltic blood," and Conrad and Sophie are "Balt with some Russian ancestry" (10). Separate national stereotypes dissolve in Erick's and Sophie's partial comprehension of each other, a comprehension both limited and empowered by their complex sexual relationship. Both Erick and Sophie are the age of their century; Conrad is a few years younger. Erick is not simply a proto-Fascist, but, as Carlos Baker vividly suggested, "a veritable Judas-goat of a stricken continent, a bad European leading his conferees toward the *coup de grâce*."[2] I agree, and wish to extend Baker's insight.

Erick is the European without roots after World War I, seeking identity in violent action. His lust for adventure is not satisfied in the Baltic civil war; throughout the 1920s and 1930s, he seeks out violent confrontations. He participates in the political agitations in central Europe which lead to Hitler's rise, and he takes part as well in the Japanese attack on Manchuria 1931–32, the Chaco war in Paraguay 1932–35, and the Spanish Civil War with Franco 1936–37. His active engagement in repressive military violence contradicts his claim to be apolitical. Although Erick asserts that fighting the Bolsheviks in 1919 was for him a "matter of caste" (10) and not an ideological commitment, his hostility toward "Jewish money-lenders everywhere" suggests a psychological complex that, in the 1930s, was being exploited for ideological ends. As he reconstructs his past, he envisions himself as a modern Napoleon, a great leader doomed to defeat at Waterloo.

Conrad is a "disciple" of this authoritarian leader, an "aide-de-camp" to

"Bonaparte" (52). He adopts his master's views (47), and he relinquishes his independent opinions when ridiculed (13). In the context of the 1930s, Conrad represents all those individual Europeans, in France and England as well as in Germany or Italy, who docilely welcomed a strong national leader.

Conrad's "susceptibility and softness" (13) also suggests France's and England's compliance with Germany's demand at Munich. Facing the threat of violence, they became impotent. Had Conrad survived into the 1920s, Erick contemptuously imagines he might have become "a poet cut to the pattern of T. S. Eliot or Jean Cocteau" (14).

Speaking in 1937, Erick pictures Conrad as resembling Rembrandt's portrait of a Polish cavalier, a youth on a pale horse, his anxious face turned toward the viewer (127–28), and the comparison seems the sign of a coming apocalypse. Yourcenar perhaps foresaw the tragedy of a second European war, but her narrator Erick exploits the apocalyptic image to prepare his listeners for his account of Conrad's slow, painful death. Erick considered "putting him out of his agony" (129), but could not deliver the *coup de grâce* to his friend. Wounded in the stomach, the Count de Reval spent his last hours in agony, but Erick idealizes and then immortalizes his body: "first he was like a wounded officer of the time of Charles the Twelfth, then like a medieval knight lying upon a tomb, and finally like any dying man" (129). Erick's nostalgia for "the time of Charles the Twelfth" colors his history, in which Conrad's death, prefaced by an evocation of the lost Polish cavalier, represents the downfall of European aristocracy.

Conrad's sister, though born an aristocrat, did not seek to preserve the domination of her class. Sophie, whose name recalls Dostoyevsky's Sophia in *Crime and Punishment*, believes in Marxism as Sophia believes in Christianity. Sophie represents the engaged European intellectual, but her ideological commitment is linked to her experience as a woman. Amid the death and terror of civil war, Sophie had been raped by a soldier. The rape ends her privileged and protected life, but for several months longer, she remains bound to her aristocratic past through Conrad and his friend Erick, with whom she had fallen in love. Her political sympathy for the Reds, which Erick acknowledges as "the one thing she had of her own" (48), remains steady, even against Erick's ridicule and criticism. Except in her political convictions, Sophie yields to Erick's mastery, and he manipulates "Sophie's subservience" (49). Her submissiveness ends only after she discovers the nature of his close relationship with her brother.[3] Then, she denounces Erick in obscenities, and responds to his calling her a streetwalker by spitting in his face. Abandoning her position as Countess de Reval and joining the workers' revolution, she acts on her convictions. Her rebellion against Erick's sadistic domination combines political and sexual liberation.

Yourcenar's portrayal of Sophie is a complex rendering of the possible responses to the threat of violence. Her irregular affair with an authoritarian figure seems to parallel Russia's changing relationship to Germany between 1917 and 1938. Sophie's early submissiveness to Erick represents Bolshevik Russia's 1917 armistice with Germany, and her later defiance suggests Russia's 1938 resistance to Hitler's demand for the partition of Czechoslovakia.

Sophie and Erick meet once more, after Conrad's death, but she refuses to submit to his mercy. She defies Erick's authority to the end. By requesting that Erick, not one of his subordinates, be her executioner, Sophie assumes the dominant role. Erick executes her as a revolutionary, and when his first shot fails to kill her, he delivers the *coup de grâce*.

At the end of her novel, Yourcenar chooses not to close the narrative frame, inflicting without mediation Erick's final self-justifying assertion: "One is always trapped, somehow, in dealings with women." The reader rejects his appropriation of the universal "one" and reinterprets the story just concluded.

Erick, in his self-deluding, falsely heroic narrative, seeks to intimidate his listeners into accepting his interpretation of events. He anticipates his audience's objections by admitting, "this summary that I am dishing up to you is made in retrospect, like History itself" (124), thus claiming the authority of History for his summary. Earlier, he had asserted, "I feel too strongly that each of our actions is an absolute, a thing complete, necessary and inevitable, although unforeseen a moment before and past history the moment after" (32), but his principle seems manufactured in retrospect to explain his executing Sophie. If Erick cannot foresee how he will act, if his violence has meaning only in retrospect, then he cannot be held responsible for killing Sophie, any more than he holds himself responsible for drunkenly taking a prostitute. The reader, however, is not trapped in Erick's persona.

Yourcenar, by forcing us to endure Erick's domineering voice, compels our active response. Her portrayal of his authoritarian personality, embodied in the form as well as the content of his confessional narrative, is so clearly defined that we recoil from it, appalled. The interplay between Erick's history and our response, guided by Sophie's acts and few words, explores the bond between domineering and submissive personalities. The tension is defined sexually, as well as politically, in terms of authority and power.

Erick's confession reveals his penchant for violence whenever his desires have been frustrated. Though he proudly rejects cruelty, his assertion unconsciously slips from killing to making love: "I preferred to deal out death without embellishment . . . . In the matter of love, too, I hold for perfection unadorned" (9). His sadism is revealed as he imagines Sophie as flesh yielding equally to his knife or his lips: "the ravishing sweetness of a fruit that is ripe for the cutting, or consuming" (41). His assertion that "Love had made her a glove in my hands" (41) reminds us of the peculiarly cruel torture of the Letts, which Erick had earlier described to deny its attraction for him: the "Chinese Hand" (8) involved slapping the victim "with the skin of his own hand stripped from him while he was alive" (9). The image of a slap becomes actual when Erick slaps Sophie so forcefully that he breaks her string of pearls.

In Erick, Yourcenar offers a savage caricature that is repulsive; and yet, Erick's personality is fascinating. He is as much a victim of his cult of force as is Sophie. Erick cannot imagine himself except as a victim, ''a crushed finger'' (10), or as a powerful leader, like Napoleon. He can envision Conrad as his disciple or brother, and therefore not threatening, but Sophie, in his fantasy, must be either an asexual saint or an eager whore.

He candidly admits: ''Between Sophie and me an intimacy swiftly sprang up like that between victim and executioner. The cruelty was not of my making . . . but it is not so certain that the whole situation was not to my liking'' (33– 34). Erick's comparison of their intimacy to ''that between victim and executioner'' predicts his final act, and his admission that he liked the situation is a truth that slips out, like others in his confession, as if by accident. The psychological source of his cruelty toward Sophie is his repulsion from female sexuality. He shudders just as he is about to kiss her, and at that moment recalls being terrified by a starfish thrust into his little hand by his mother. Since his fear and loathing of female genitalia are linked to his resentment of his mother's authority, his hostility toward Sophie finds expression in images of authoritative, destructive, passionate heroines.

Significantly, Erick compares Sophie to ''a heroine in Ibsen utterly fed up with life'' (22). He envisions her savagely poking a fire, so she embodies for him the volatile, threatening, and self-destructive Hedda Gabler. Though Sophie cannot burn Erick's confessional narrative, he nevertheless associates her with fire. Sophie, dancing, twirls ''like a flame'' (85). Asserting his mastery over her element, he notes, ''Fire may be trusted, provided one knows that its law is to burn, or to die'' (38). Because her desire threatens him, he tries to stand aloof, allowing her fire to consume herself alone. Like Dido and Aeneas, Sophie and Erick take shelter together during a rainstorm, but Sophie's well-lit fire dries their clothes without kindling Erick's desire or turning him aside from his aimless career as a soldier of fortune. On their journey home from this interlude, he put his ''arm round her, like a lover, to force her down beside me in a ditch'' (45), to shelter her from bullets, but he physically reasserts his mastery. The passionate Dido threw herself on a funeral pyre, but Sophie escapes.

Conrad also escapes, but only through his death. Linking his youthful docility to an inevitable decline, Erick imagines with dread an older Conrad, prey to an ''insidious dissolution, like the loathsome decay of iris; those sombre flowers, though nobly shaped like a lance, die miserably in their own sticky secretion, in marked contrast to the slow, heroic dying of the rose'' (125). This extraordinary passage, with its phallic iris and its genital rose, suggests the sexual roles Erick unconsciously assigns to himself and to Conrad.

Erick describes Conrad as ''pale and elated as Orestes in the opening of Racine's play,'' and he lovingly notes ''a small scar on his lip, like a dark violet'' (18). This allusion to the opening scene of *Andromache*, where the dialogue between Orestes and his comrade Pylades establishes them as a couple, hints at Erick's love for Conrad; however, the allusion also recalls the violence and the entrapment of Andromache's tragic passion.

The connection between sexuality, violence, and entrapment appears in a powerful image, which Erick once consciously employs as he defines the relationship between individual actions and history: "They say that fate excels in tightening the cord round the victim's neck, but to my knowledge her special skill is to break all ties" (121). Erick might wish all ties with his past were broken, but his narrative reveals only tightening cords. The image recurs without his explicit commentary in the pearl necklace he breaks from around Sophie's neck as he slaps her. Despite his disingenuous claim that the necklace was worthless (87–88), he carried it with him for years. The image also recurs in the torture suffered by one of Sophie's lovers: Franz von Aland, captured by the enemy, had a cord tied round his neck, and then set on fire; his body was found "with a charred wound round the neck" (61). Two explications of this image, one political and one sexual, are connected.

German diplomats and intellectuals justified both their aggression in the First World War and their 1938 demand for the Sudetenland by depicting the German nation surrounded by hostile rivals, seeking only to break free of the encirclement. The humiliation of German defeat in 1918 fueled support for the nationalistic claims on territory in 1938–39, as a buffer against the Communist Slavs in Russia. Fear of encirclement and the humiliation of defeat combine in Erick's actions at Gourna, where his leadership in the retreat is one of the blots on his military career.

In Yourcenar's psychological portrait of Erick, we see the child feeling trapped by the mother who gave birth. The son rebels against her authority and seeks to break free of the woman's body. The trap is linked to marriage in Erick's ambiguous admission, on his return from the Gourna retreat, "perhaps I was avoiding stepping back immediately into the trap where I now consented to be caught" (98), which alludes to his earlier assertion, "I was prepared to pledge myself to her immediately upon my return" (93). His frantic desire to escape from encirclement by the Bolsheviks at Gourna corresponds to his fear of entrapment by Sophie. By sending Volkmar back to Sophie's estate, Erick insures that she will learn of his homosexual relationship with Conrad. Such knowledge ends Sophie's desire for Erick and releases him from the trap. The connection between the political and the sexual may be seen in Erick's final assertion: "One is always trapped, somehow, in dealings with women." The trap, *piège*, is a noose, a circle used to catch the victim's head.

Yourcenar's timely and sensitive evaluation of the historical and psychological roots of fascism deserves critical appreciation. She has admitted that in writing this historical novel she immersed herself in documents about the Germans fighting in the Baltic in 1919–1920,[4] and, though she denies that the political confrontation was her subject, *Coup de Grâce* offers a political critique of modern culture. By defining her three characters in the context of their sexual identities and political history, she requires the reader's personal, intimate, judgment to make appropriate connections with contemporary events.

Yourcenar has stated, "In our epoch, more than in preceding epochs, politics plays a major role in our lives, whether we wish it and sense it or not. Consequently, even if we evoke a completely private adventure no more than five or ten years old, we encounter certain deeds which are already 'historical,' in the most official sense of the term, and of which we must take account."[5] Erick's apparently open confession of his private adventure requires the reader's collaborative, close study to determine the historical significance of his affair in 1919. Looking back, the reader must evaluate Erick's authoritarian domination by force, as well as Conrad's subservience and Sophie's defiance. In her portrait of these three complex personalities, Yourcenar held a mirror up to the European state of mind in 1939.

NOTES

1. The phrase appears on the second and third pages of the unpaginated 1981 preface; this and all subsequent quotations are from Grace Frick's and Marguerite Yourcenar's translation, *Coup de Grâce* (1957; rpt. New York: Farrar, Straus & Giroux, 1981).

2. *The New York Times Book Review*, 21 July 1957, p. 4.

3. Both in Erick's narrative and in Yourcenar's 1972 interview she refuses an explicit description of "son attachement plus ou moins charnel pour Conrad"—Patrick Rosbo, *Entretiens Radiophoniques avec Marguerite Yourcenar* (Paris: Mercure de France, 1972), p. 80.

4. Rosbo, p. 42.

5. Rosbo, p. 40.

26

A Way of Ordering Experience: A Study of Toni Morrison's *The Bluest Eye* and *Sula*

Robert Sargent

In the PBS series "The Writer in America" (1979) Toni Morrison said that in the lonely period after her divorce "writing became a thing to do" at night when her children were asleep. It was, she said, "a way of ordering." Her method of doing so, she said, was "always to push things to extremes." Her novels are organized around the interplay of characters who represent polar opposite values. The fact that the key representative of each pole has, what Morrison calls in *Sula*, a "craving for the other half of her equation"[1] suggests that a major theme of her novels is the need for balance or wholeness. These qualities may be acquired by the characters in the novels only through an act that is analogous to one involved in the creation of art—an act of the imagination which comes from a willingness to see the world as others see it.

The characters in Morrison's novels are types in the sense that they are associated with particular values, but they are not typical in the sense of being ordinary or common. In other words, another consequence of Morrison's decision "always to push things to extremes" is that she writes about characters that "are *un*common."[2] She has chosen to do so at least in part because as a black woman writer she is aware of the need to explode racial and sexual stereotypes.[3] In an interview in 1976 Morrison stressed that "the most extraordinary thing about any group, and particularly our group, is the fantastic variety of people and things and behavior and so on."[4]

In describing a course she taught at Yale University, Morrison said she had been "very much interested in how contemporary black women looked at the stereotype of black women. . . . Did the writers believe, in the works we studied, that that was pretty much the way we were? Were the characters representative of the mammy, whore, what ever? show-girl, what ever?"[5]

In her own novels Morrison attempts to destroy racial and sexual stereotypes through the two methods suggested here. She creates a sense of the variety within the black community by organizing her novels around characters that represent opposite attitudes towards life, and she makes her characters seem unique individuals by having them behave in exotic, bizarre, or brutal ways. The two techniques are interrelated: the character's behavior is symbolic of his or her attitudes and values.

The main contrast in values, for example, in Morrison's third novel *Song of Solomon* is conveyed through the struggle between a brother and sister, Macon and Pilate Dead, for the allegiance of Macon's son Milkman, the protagonist of the novel. Macon, who "fondled . . . from time to time"[6] his keys to the doors of the houses he owns, represents the Booker T. Washington approach to black progress, the importance of the individual achieving economic independence. Macon tells his son, "the one important thing you'll ever need to know: Own things. And let the things you own own other things. Then you'll own yourself and other people too" (p. 55).

Macon's sister Pilate, on the other hand, seems to represent the approach of W. E. B. DuBois, who emphasized the importance of maintaining the black family and a distinctive black culture. Pilate helps Ruth, Milkman's mother, to get pregnant (her husband had stopped having sex with her) and then to resist Macon's effort to abort the fetus. She sings a song, the song of Solomon, which Milkman later learns encapsulates the whole history of the family. In contrast to her brother's keys, she wears a little brass box strung from her left ear lobe, containing a scrap of paper on which is written the one word her father ever wrote, her name.

If the brass box is not exotic enough, Pilate can also claim the lack of a navel. Its absence not only gives Pilate an aura of magic and mystery, but gives Morrison a way of accounting for Pilate's experimental approach to life. From a naturalistic perspective the fact that Pilate has no navel shocks others and has the effect of isolating her from ordinary folk and therefore forcing her to see the world from her own point of view. From a symbolic perspective the lack of a navel suggests "that she had not come into this world through normal channels" (p. 28), that she has given birth to herself, in the sense that she has shaped herself as a unique individual.

On first seeing Pilate when he is twelve, Milkman is forced to abandon the stereotyped notions he had acquired about his "queer aunt" from his schoolmates and father:

And while she looked poor as everyone said she was, something was missing from her eyes that should have confirmed it. Nor was she dirty; unkempt, yes, but not dirty. The whites of her finger nails were like ivory. And unless he knew nothing, this woman was definitely not drunk. Of course she was anything but pretty, yet he knew he could have watched her all day: the fingers pulling thread veins from the orange sections, the berry-black lips that made her look as though she wore make-up, the earring. . . . And when she stood up, he all but gasped. She was as tall as his father, head and shoulders taller than himself. Her dress wasn't as long as he had thought; it came to just below her calf and now he could see her unlaced men's shoes and silvery-brown broken skin of her ankles (pp. 37–38).

This passage attacks racial stereotypes by attributing them to Milkman and indicating his surprise that his aunt, though a poor black woman, is not ashamed, dirty, drunk, or ugly. In addition, the wearing of men's shoes, with the physical strength and self-possession these imply, associates Pilate with qualities that are conventionally male and are in keeping with the fact that she has traveled alone around the country and has the courage to confront and defeat a man who beats her daughter Reba. On the other hand, the skillful separating of the orange recalls Pilate's making of a perfect soft boiled egg and this gift, along with her nurturing attitude towards her daughter, granddaughter, and Milkman, are qualities that are conventionally female. This combination of qualities breaks down sexual stereotypes.

Having discussed Morrison's method in general terms and having illustrated it briefly with an example from her third novel, I would now like to show its development in her first two novels, *The Bluest Eye* and *Sula*. Both novels are studies of the relationship between girlfriends of contrasting type, and of how and why the solidarity between them breaks down and then is partially reestablished. The two novels are continuous in the sense that the first novel concerns the crisis of puberty and the second moves from that point through the difficulties of adulthood. In *The Bluest Eye* the contrasting figures are somewhat obscured by a host of minor figures and by the shifting point of view, but in *Sula* the structure is clearly organized around a contrast between the two main characters.

The key event of *The Bluest Eye* (1970) is the rape of the eleven year old Pecola Breedlove by her father Cholly. The present time of the novel is organized around the seasons, from Autumn to Summer, from Pecola's first menstruation to her loss of the baby and her madness. Interwoven with these events are narrative summaries and flashbacks revealing the earlier experiences of Pecola's parents and of other members of the black community in order to suggest the social and psychological causes of the main action. The title *The Bluest Eye* indicates that the main cause of the tragedy is a negative attitude towards being black. Pecola is both the communal and familial scapegoat—she is continually defined by other characters as "Black and ugly."[7] She also embodies the insanity of trying to be white in order to be loved—in the end blue eyes are not sufficient; she must have the bluest eyes.

Morrison offers skillful psychological profiles of Pecola's parents and the negative influence on their marriage of the move to the North where there is more hostility between whites and blacks. Pecola's mother, Pauline Williams, comes under the influence of the movies, embracing white standards of physical beauty and romantic love; she stops having sex with her husband and becomes the "ideal servant" (p. 101) for whites, creating beauty, order, and cleanliness for the blue-eyed, yellow-haired Fisher girl and neglecting her own children, teaching them fear and self-hatred.

Pecola's father Cholly has the opposite response to oppression. Rather than introjecting the values of whites as his wife does, he is "dangerously free. Free to feel whatever he felt—fear, guilt, shame, love, grief, pity. Free to be tender or violent" (p. 125). "Abandoned in a junk heap by his mother, rejected for a crap game by his father," Cholly has "nothing to lose." (p. 126) By the time he meets Pauline Williams he has already killed three white men. His rape of his daughter is the final result of a complex sequence of emotions towards her: "revulsion, guilt, pity, then love" (p. 127). Though Cholly is free of the distortions of his wife who can only hate her daughter because she reminds her that she is also not white, he is able to love his daughter but only in a way that is destructive. Having had no parent himself, he has no idea how to raise children. As a "burned-out black man" he has nothing to give his daughter—there is no way to "earn him his own respect that would in turn allow him to accept her love" (p. 127). Thus, the rape is both an expression of tenderness, of love, and of a violent rebellion against all laws and taboos.

The extremes represented by Pecola's mother and father—the former who stands for those who allow the values of an alien community to dominate them and the latter who stands for those who operate out of lawless impulse—are both clearly negative. Against this bleak contrast in values is another contrast in the novel that suggests a somewhat more positive view of things. Pecola is placed between opposite types of peers. Maureen Peal, on one hand, is the "high-yellow," almost white, "dream child" (p. 52) of blacks like Pecola's mother. On the other hand, Claudia and Frieda McTeer are children who hate "all the Shirley Temples of the world" (p. 19); they break the fingers off and poke the eyes out of the blue-eyed Baby Dolls they are given for Christmas. Maureen Peal reinforces Pecola's negative self-image of being "Black and ugly." Frieda and Claudia, in contrast, are sympathetic because, as Claudia puts it,

Dolls we could destroy, but we could not destroy the honey voices of parents and aunts, the obedience in the eyes of our peers, the slippery light in the eyes of our teachers when they encountered the Maureen Peals of the world. What was the secret? What did we lack? Why was it so important? And so what? Guileless and without vanity, we were still in love with ourselves then. We felt comfortable in our skins, enjoyed the news that our sense released to us, admired our dirt, cultivated our scars, and could not comprehend this unworthiness. Jealousy we understood and thought natural—a desire to have what somebody else had; but envy was a strange, new feeling for us. And all the time we knew that Maureen Peal was not the Enemy and not worthy of such intense hatred. The *Thing* to fear was the *Thing* that made *her* beautiful, and not us (pp. 61–62).

Morrison illustrates the solidarity that Claudia and Frieda feel with Pecola in two episodes that express the two sides of the positive female character discussed earlier in reference to Pilate. First they show sympathy and understanding when Pecola is experiencing anxiety about her first menstruation. Then they defend her from being tormented by a group of boys who are projecting their own self-hatred for being black on Pecola. In doing so Frieda and Claudia are physically and verbally aggressive. In defending their friend they are expressing their own self-acceptance.

In the most difficult situation Pecola faces, being pregnant with her father's child, Claudia and Frieda are not able to do anything directly, but, in contrast to others, they wish that the baby will live. They go through a ritual of planting the seeds of marigolds as a magic act of solidarity with their pregnant friend. The baby comes too soon and dies (perhaps killed by the beating Pecola's mother gives her) and the seeds never sprout ("the land of the entire country was hostile to marigolds that year" [p. 160]). In wanting the baby to live, Claudia and Frieda have allied themselves with those who are committed to life, like Pilate in *Song of Solomon*, as opposed to those who are death oriented, like Macon Dead.

By making Claudia a point-of-view character, Morrison explores the imaginative act that is required to make a person whole. In the last pages of the novel Claudia expresses her own sense that she failed to help Pecola, that out of fear she never went near. She includes herself in the black community who used Pecola as a scapegoat: "All of our waste which we dumped on her and which she absorbed. . . . All of us—all who knew her—felt so wholesome after we cleaned ourselves on her. We were so beautiful when we stood astride her ugliness" (p. 159). Despite Claudia's identification with the community that was hostile to Pecola, her narrative implies that she was among the few who loved Pecola, the others being the prostitute called The Maginot Line, and Cholly. By associating Claudia with these characters, Morrison is suggesting that Claudia, like them, is free of the standards of the white world that the rest of the community has used to judge Pecola.

However, Claudia's narrative has a passage which implies that she, like Morrison, but unlike the Maginot Line and Cholly, has left this particular community far behind: "we were not free, merely licensed; we were not compassionate, we were polite; not good, but well behaved. . . . We substituted good grammar for intellect; we switched habits to simulate maturity; we rearranged lies and called it truth, seeing in the new pattern of an old idea the Revelation and the Word" (p. 159). Morrison has stated that in this her first novel she "was clearly pulling straight out of what autobiographical information" she had, that she "didn't create that town."[8] Like Morrison, Claudia is an artist who has been attempting to order her early experience.

It is possible, as Claudia fears, that in the attempt to see a "new pattern" there may be distortion, but it seems clear that both Claudia and Morrison are motivated by an effort to understand in a sympathetic way those numerous others. Earlier in the novel the omniscient narrator says that "the pieces of Cholly's life could become coherent only in the head of a musician. . . . Only a musician would sense, know, without ever knowing that he knew, that Cholly was free" (p. 125). Only the artist or the person who seeks to order experience like the artist (Claudia) is able to hold together the complex pieces that make up the "truth."

It is evident that Morrison discovered in the process of writing her first novel a method of ordering her fiction. The clarity of the pattern in her second novel *Sula* (1973) as well as her own comments in interviews suggests that she began that novel with the idea of using opposite kinds of characters to explore the difficulty of defining good and evil, that "Sometimes good looks like evil; sometimes evil looks like good."[9]

Morrison selected two only children, Sula Peace and Nel Wright to represent each side of this paradox. Sula comes from a house in which something is always cooking, where there is no scolding or direction. She grows up to be unconventional, breaking all the rules of the community, free of the need to please others and free to explore her own thoughts. Nel grows up in the opposite kind of atmosphere. Her mother Helene in order to avoid the wildness of her mother, a New Orleans prostitute, imposed a rigid order on the home and "succeeded in rubbing down to a dull glow any sparkle or splutter" (p. 72) her daughter had. Nel becomes a good woman in the conventional sense—she goes to church, she marries, she takes care of her children—but she is afraid of being alive. Sula sees Nel as "One of the spiders whose only thought was the next rung of the web, who dangled in the dark dry place suspended by their own spittle, more terrified of the free fall than the snake's breath below. . . . But the free fall, oh no, that required—demanded—invention . . . if they wished to . . . stay alive. But alive was what they, and now Nel, did not want to be. Too dangerous. Now Nel belonged to the town and all of its ways" (pp. 103–104).

The tragedy of *Sula* is the loss of the relief that Sula and Nel found as adolescents in each other's personality. Sula's influence enabled Nel to rebel against her mother who urged her to use beauty aids to make her look more conventionally beautiful (white). On the other hand, Nel gave Sula someone to care about; only in the defense of her friend was Sula able to sustain an emotion.

Because each had discovered years before that they were neither white nor male, and that all freedom and triumph was forbidden to them, they had set about creating something else to be. . . . Daughters of distant mothers and incomprehensible fathers (Sula's because he was dead; Nel's because he wasn't), they found in each other's eyes the intimacy they were looking for (pp. 44–45).

On becoming an adult Nel does the conventional thing—she marries a man who needed a wife to make him feel whole. Sula does the unconventional; she leaves the town for ten years, going to college and wandering around the country. On her return Sula has a series of sexual relations with various men, including Nel's husband, who abandons the town and Nel for good on realizing that Sula is unwilling to make him feel like a whole man. Nel breaks off her friendship with Sula, not understanding how Sula could have sex with "her man."

Morrison prepares for the reunion between Nel and Sula just before Sula's death by having Sula go through an experience the reverse of the one Nel had gone through and with Ajax, a man of opposite type to Nel's husband, Jude. Ajax is the first man to treat Sula like a person. They have genuine conversations; he refuses to baby or protect her, but assumes that she is both "tough and wise" (p. 110). Ironically as a result of this kind of relationship with Ajax, Sula discovers in herself the conventional desire to possess the man and she becomes domestic for the first time in her life. Naturally Ajax takes off for Dayton soon after seeing Sula "lying on fresh white sheets, wrapped in the deadly odor of freshly applied cologne" (p. 115). The imagery makes clear that the conventions of romantic love are deadly.

At Sula's death Nel and Sula come together and trade criticisms of each other's life. Nel tells Sula she can't have it all: " 'You a woman and a colored woman at that. You can't act like a man. You can't be walking around all independent-like, doing whatever you like, taking what you want, leaving what you don't' " (p. 123). Sula's retort is that unlike every other black woman in this country, at least she "sure did live in this world" (p. 123). It is evident here as in the other novels that though Morrison seems more sympathetic to the Sula type than to the Nel type, each is incomplete without "the other half" (p. 105). Without Nel, Sula like Cholly without the love of Pauline, is potentially dangerous, Morrison suggests, "like any artist with no art form." Had Sula "paints, or clay, or knew the discipline of the dance, or strings; had she anything to engage her tremendous curiosity and her gift for metaphor, she might have exchanged the restlessness and preoccupation with whim for an activity that provided her with all she yearned for" (p. 105). Morrison evidently found a way out of Sula's predicament through ordering her experience in her fiction.

Although less alive than Sula, Nel outlives her, but one senses at the end of the novel that in beginning to understand Sula again Nel is at the beginning of the process of becoming a whole person. The flat assertion of Sula's grandmother that no difference existed between the responsibility of Sula and Nel for the drowning of Chicken Little when they were girls forces Nel to reexamine the past and to reevaluate her secret pride that she was calm and controlled when Sula was uncontrollable. She must face the fact that Nel had cried about the death of the boy but she had remained calm, that is, unfeeling. As Nel returns to the graveyard in which Sula was buried but unmourned, she realizes that her real loss in life was not her husband who ran away but Sula. The novel ends with "a fine cry" and Nel's exclamation: " 'We was girls together,' she said as though explaining something" (p. 149).

Although the metaphor of the whole person's resemblance to the artist is not fully worked out in *Sula*, it is clear that the willingness to reevaluate the past and to embrace sympathetically the other, if only in memory, is crucial.

In *Song of Solomon* (1977) Milkman Dead becomes a whole person by the end of the novel. Although the process is too complex to go into here in detail, it involves a mechanism hinted at near the end of the first two novels. In the first half of the novel Milkman, in order to become "a whole man," is forced "to deal with the whole truth" (p. 70) about his father and mother. In the last half of the novel he leaves home for the first time, following in the footsteps of his aunt Pilate back in space and time and discovering finally the truth about his family history.

Morrison's metaphor in all three books for being whole is being able to fly. By the end Morrison implies that Milkman has learned to fly whereas earlier in the novel he is associated with a white, male peacock who can't fly because he has too much tail. Guitar, Milkman's friend, explains: " 'All that jewelry weighs it down. Like vanity. Can't nobody fly with all that shit. Wanna fly, you got to give up the shit that weighs you down' " (pp. 179–90). In order to fly Milkman must give up his egocentricity—his lack of concern about the lives of others— transcend his sense of masculine superiority that has made him feel he has the right to decide the lives of the women in his life, and shed the superficial trapping of white culture (his three piece suit, Florsheim shoes, and gold Longines watch). By the end of the novel Milkman has learned to see things for himself and yet also to care for others, therefore, affirming the value of life itself.

NOTES

1. Toni Morrison, *Sula* (1973; rpt. New York: Bantam, 1975), p. 105. Further references to this edition will be cited in the text.

2. Colette Dowling, "The Song of Toni Morrison," *The New York Times Magazine* (May 20, 1979), p. 56. See Diane Johnson, "The Oppressor in the Next Room," *New York Review of Books* (November 10, 1977), pp. 6, 8.

3. See Faith Pullin's "Landscapes of Reality: The Fiction of Contemporary Afro-American Women," *Black Fiction: New Studies in the Afro-American Novel Since 1945*, ed. A. Robert Lee (New York: Barnes & Noble, 1980), pp. 189–198, and Bonnie J. Barthold, "Women: Chaos and Redemption," *Black Times: Fiction of Africa, the Caribbean and the United States* (New Haven: Yale University Press, 1981), pp. 103, 121–123.

4. Robert B. Stepto, "Intimate Things in Place: A Conversation with Toni Morrison," *Massachusetts Review*, 18 (1977), 474.

5. Stepto, 485.

6. Toni Morrison, *Song of Solomon* (1977; rpt. New York: New American Library, 1978), p. 17. Further references to this editon will be cited in the text.

7. Toni Morrison, *The Bluest Eye* (1970; rpt. New York: Washington Square Press, 1972), p. 61. Further references to this edition will be cited in the text.

8. Stepto, 473.

9. Stepto, 476.

27

A Voice of Authority

Jane Marcus

I've always admired Rebecca West. She reminds me of my mother. Life was hard for her and we girls, and we often got out of hand. She used to say in the Irish brogue of her mother and grandmother, "I don't beat you 'cause I hate you; I beat you to show my authority."

For women brought up in strong female households, whose first social and intellectual models are mothers and teachers of abundant female strength, the experience of the real world, where women's voices are muffled and "female authority" is a contradiction in terms, is a shock. Rebecca West grew up in a household of strong women. Her mother supported her daughters as a professional pianist; the daughters distinguished themselves with scholarships and careers. Dame Rebecca told me she became a writer when she had the mumps at age nine alone in a room with a typewriter. She went from blood sisterhood to political sisterhood, sustained by both in her struggle as artist, political thinker and woman.

For seven decades Rebecca West's writing, fiction, essays, and literary and political criticism, has been a voice of female authority whose clear ringing tones have roused faint-hearted feminists during doldrums and bounced off the barricades in times of struggle. It is a voice of historical necessity and urgency, and we have heard it before, in Mme. de Stael and George Sand, in George Eliot and Harriet Beecher Stowe, in Mary Wollstonecraft and Olive Schreiner, in the Virginia Woolf of *Three Guineas*. The moral imperative in these voices of female authority, the political criticism of patriarchy and capitalism, is the backbone of their artistic bodies. Like the caryatids of a Greek temple, they stand out in bold relief as female figures bearing high the burden of art and ethical responsibility. They are our monuments.

Feminine fragility is enshrined on other pedestals. The saints and heroines of modern feminism show an eagle eye, a formidable body, a nose of character or a furrowed brow. The beholder is struck, not by their beauty, but by their authority. The pens of these women artists, as Ellen Moers eloquently argues in *Literary Women*,[1] were the voices of the oppressed, "literature was their pulpit, tribune, academy, commission, and parliament all in one." Meeting Rebecca West, at 89, with her intellectual powers blazing like the banners of all the causes she championed, was like meeting a head of state. She, I felt, not Mrs. Thatcher, should have been speaking in Parliament.

But she has spoken out, critically and forcefully, against British institutions, ever since she changed her name from Cicely Fairfield to Rebecca West, writing for the socialist and feminist journals, *The Clarion*, *The Freewoman*, and *The New Freewoman* in 1911. Her outspokenness drew the fire of many enemies and she was plagued by libel suits. Young American feminists who do not know her work may have been put off by an attack on her by Lillian Hellman in the *New York Times*. Lillian Hellman's fury was roused by Rebecca West's anti-communist books on treason trials. That many other socialists became anti-Stalinists, or sought to analyze the sources of political loyalties, did not concern Hellman. (Rebecca West was a public champion of feminist causes for 60 years. She insisted that Lillian Hellman is *not now nor ever has been* a feminist.)

A more recent attack by Leslie Garis in the *New York Times Sunday Magazine* in the spring of 1982 is symptomatic of the kind of enmity Rebecca West aroused.[2] Since her son Anthony West, who was fathered by H. G. Wells, began to write, he has attacked his mother in print. The *Times* essay gives a lot of space to public washing of this dirty baby linen, and I would like to address some of the problems this question of a woman's reputation raises, from a feminist perspective. Some reviewers of *The Young Rebecca* raised the issue of the absence of H. G. Wells from the text, except for a footnote, since he was her lover, on and off, during the early years of her career. The omission was a deliberate one, agreed to eagerly by Dame Rebecca herself, partly in answer to Gordon Ray's *H. G. Wells and Rebecca West*[3] which is clearly not in sympathy with West's feminist writing and treats her largely as the lover of "the great man."

Rebecca West died in 1983 at 90, and has produced a body of work which will last as long, if not longer, than H. G. Wells. Her brief relationship with him is not comparable to her literary achievements, and they ought not to be judged as the works of one of H. G. Wells' mistresses. This is not to say that the affair did not cause her great pain and personal suffering, but only that her contribution rests on her writing. And that, fortunately, survived the influence of H. G. Wells.

The question of her son's public hostility is even more crucial. When I raised with Dame Rebecca the thorny problem of the fact that like many women writers, she was both obscure and famous at the same time, that many people seemed to know her name who hadn't read her books, she faced the question directly and said that she did not expect posthumous fame. "History never forgives a woman whose son calls her a bad mother," she said. It was obviously a situation to which she had given much thought. The public has a great appetite for the family quarrels of public figures. But the public reviling of a mother by her son produces a strong sympathy for him and a strong antipathy for her. "How unnatural," people say, and the intellectual woman can be attacked with impunity if her son is the leader of the pack. I wonder how many women in public life at this moment fear an attack on this very vulnerable flank? I am not claiming that Rebecca West was a perfect mother or a perfect woman or a perfect writer. Perhaps Rebecca West's fearlessness and capacity for expressing anger made her a difficult lover and a difficult mother, but for seventy years no misogynist in government or the arts has been safe from her feminist indignation.

In an interview, Rebecca West discussed celibacy and feminism and that led to Shaw, whose antifeminism she battled in print for many years. In one of her first reviews for *The Freewoman* she compared Shaw unfavorably to Granville Barker: "For all Shaw's audacious discussions, there is not one character in all his eighteen plays who infringes the conventions in practice . . . Shaw never brought anything so anarchic as an unmarried mother on to his stage. Although he cultivates the flower of argument so well, he does not like the fruit of action."[4]

Dame Rebecca maintained that Shaw wasn't celibate, but like narcissists of either sex, must have been very boring as a lover. Meeting him on the street soon after her break up with H. G. Wells, she invited him for tea to see her newly-decorated flat. His wife, Charlotte, arrived alone, the unspoken message being that Shaw was not going to be seduced by the notorious Rebecca West. Michael Holyroyd, at work for some years on the biography of Bernard Shaw, had almost convinced me of Shaw's commitment to feminism, and I had been reading in the 1913 *Suffragette* several of Shaw's collected speeches and letters to editors against forcible feeding and the Cat and Mouse Act. But the stereotypes in his play *Press Cuttings* (written and produced for the cause) seem undeniably an insult to women. And as Dame Rebecca said, the intellectual paper dolls who pass for women in his plays are all the evidence one needs.

Music has been very important in Dame Rebecca's life and work, as readers of her autobiographical novel, *The Fountain Overflows* will note. A previous visitor had complained that her daughter couldn't get any work done at the university, since she was constantly fending off sexual advances from men. "Sex gets a better press than it deserves," said Dame Rebecca and gave me a message to bring to my daughter: "You can make love any time but you can only learn to play cello when you're young."

Rebecca West's masterpiece is *Black Lamb and Grey Falcon*, the supreme example of the 1930s form of anti-fascist documentary, at once a prime example of the visionary feminist travel book (like Rose Macauley's *Towers of Trebizond* or Ethel Smyth's A *Three-Legged Tour of Greece*) and a historical philosophic, poetic treatise on every imaginable subject. *Black Lamb and Grey Falcon* is a political and moral geography of Yugoslavia, but more than that, it is the map of a great twentieth-century mind in all its female force. Twice, like many others, I have followed her footsteps into the Balkans, never failing to find her spiritual journey the kind of guide and outline which forms a feminist intellectual's *Spiritual Exercises*. She had, among other gifts, the ancient and oracular talent of the storyteller and a powerful primitive eye for the symbolic in everyday life. One eloquent argument for the weight of Muslim oppression of women she found in an obscure cult which required that women wear huge heavy men's overcoats of black wool with sleeves sewn up and pinned across in front, confining and crushing the women within. It seems to be a prime characteristic of patriarchal societies to worship Womanhood while despising women.

Rebecca West's mind was indeed lofty in philosophic and moral thought, and deep with psychological and political insight. After one of these battles in print which make her literary career like the military career of a general, T. S. Eliot wrote in *Time and Tide* on February 2, 1935, "I admire Miss West as a sort of Mount Ararat, the first to rear her majestic head from the subsiding waters." This remark contains its own peculiar irony, given the association of the Ark with Freemasonry and exclusively male brotherhoods. We may indeed see her as a female Noah or his unsung wife, preserving the values of life and art against patriarchal ideas of war and death against the barbarian flood. She herself cared little for T. S. Eliot's poetry, although she says her husband had a great deal of it by heart; when she met Eliot in company with Auden, she found them "a scruffy pair." She noted that Gide, in his appeal to neurotic childishness, had moved from portraits of women as elemental evil, to equally intense portraits of criminal murderous children. This derives from man's guilt at what gives him pleasure, the transference of the myth of the origin of evil in female sexuality to a homosexual's hatred of the youths who give him pleasure. She extended this analysis to Cocteau and Richard Hughes' *High Wind in Jamaica*, not as a case against homosexuality but as an analysis of the male tendency to deny life and joy, a preoccupation with death and guilt. Hatred of women, derived from Paul and the patristic writers, leads ultimately to love of the male sex exclusively, then to a homosexuality which hates the object of pleasure, then the denial of life itself. I asked Dame Rebecca if she condemned all homosexuals and she replied that she merely disliked "professional" male homosexuals. We agreed on the brilliance of Wilde's plays and in particular his portrayal of women with a genius never achieved by Shaw.

Cicely Fairfield as a name suggests the genteel sweetness of a Shaw heroine with her head still above the waters of the life force or one of Wilde's society belles with backbone. It seems far more of a stage name than Ibsen's Rebecca West, which suited Dame Rebecca like a second skin. She never actually played the heroine of *Rosmersholm* on the stage, only in her life, she said darkly, and a cloud covered that eagle eye as she said it. A friend offered her the script just as she was beginning her brilliant career as a socialist feminist journalist for *The Clarion* and *The Freewoman*. In *Rosmersholm* Ibsen has written a sermon for socialist feminists with much more modern significance than *A Doll's House* or

Hedda Gabler. For Rebecca West sweeps out of the mountains radiant with radical feminist politics (as Cicely Fairfield herself swept into London) only to find out how bourgeois society can handle both free love and revolution. The "new woman" is undone by the suicide-as-revenge of the self-sacrificing wife. She is made to feel guilty about her sexuality by the impotent "great man" with whom she falls in love. His do-nothing idealism triumphs over revolutionary action. Because the conscience is conservative, she is trapped by Rosmer's demand that she drown herself in the millrace to prove her love is as strong as Beata's. The town is taken over by the liberals as reactionary Rosmer and radical Rebecca are dead, a dreadful lesson in how dissidents can be controlled by guilt about their own sexuality and their parents'.

Many women have had sons out of wedlock with great men, but few have brooked society's rules enough to demand public recognition in an independent career. Virginia Woolf was amazed at Rebecca West's strength of character. But the price she paid was too high for West to recommend it to younger women.

H. G. Wells was first attracted by her exposé of the anti-feminism of his early novels. She saw at once that he advocated free love and paid motherhood to provide men like himself with more interesting mistresses. It was not women's freedom he wanted, but the extension of men's sexual choice.

I would like to remedy the situation which has denied Rebecca West the readership of young feminists she deserves. For we have much to learn from her writing as well as her historical experience as a woman writer in a hostile world. She always fought back, refusing to fade into oblivion. Like the old mother eagle she was, even in old age she showed her claws. Attacked by a brilliant politician's charge that her review of another politician's diaries was too "savage" at a dinner party, she replied that she wasn't nearly savage enough. Few have seen beneath the savagery to the sensibility or the common sense. In this sense it has been possible for Rebecca West to be both obscure and famous at the same time, especially as she and her contemporary British women writers become conflated into one personality. She tells the story of an English novelist who has spent most of his life in exile. She was invited to a dinner in his honor. After many toasts he rose and recited, word for word, a review she had written. As he finished he said, "Rose Macaulay is the only person in England who has ever appreciated me."[5] (There is a double irony here, as Rose Macaulay is even less appreciated than Rebecca West.)

Britain has produced two different types of great feminist figures, the bold original fighting women like Caroline Norton and Mary Wollstonecraft, who demand an eye for an eye or a tooth for a tooth as they battle the patriarchy and are squelched by society as much for their sexual as their intellectual power. Then there are the saints, the Quaker pacifists like Virginia Woolf or Margaret Llewelyn Davies of the Cooperative Working Women's Guild. In my schooldays we used to differentiate between two types of heroines—the hunting amazons and the fishing amazons. Rebecca West is a hunting amazon. Her career, like that of the composer Dame Ethel Smyth, is one long battle. Virginia Woolf, in "Professions for Women,"[6] described Ethel Smyth as "among the ice-breakers, the window-smashers, the indomitable and irresistible armoured tanks; who went first, drew the enemy's fire, and left a pathway for those who came after her." Rebecca West, like Ethel Smyth, has drawn more than her share of the enemy's fire as she plowed through the patriarchal battlefields like an armored tank. Like Ethel Smyth, she accepted proudly the title of "Dame" from the government she had earlier fought like a tiger. Both Virginia Woolf and Margaret Llewelyn Davies refused these honors, steadfast in their conviction that capitalism and imperialism were the products of patriarchal government. But Ethel Smyth's music is rarely if ever played, and her memoirs are not in print.

I have always thought of Rebecca West as a general in the Feminist Church Militant, behind whom I would willingly march. She is like some ancient abbess of a powerful noncelibate convent, who has usurped the local bishop's authority, conferring sainthood, excommunicating heretics, with a voice of great moral authority. In these terms it is her boldly original psychobiography *St. Augustine* (1933) which is the key to her work.

As innovator of this new art form (as original in its scope for her psychological ideas as *Black Lamb* is for her political and philosophical ideas) she has avoided the pitfalls which have trapped her myriad followers in the field. Rare is the psychobiographer whose analysis can be separated from a feeling of superiority to the subject. Rebecca West's respect of the complexities of reality increases rather than diminishes as she investigates the unconscious. And she respects the reader as much as reality. Dame Rebecca unwinds the springs of Augustine's character and motivation, makes her examination and then carefully reassembles the delicate works, recoils the spring, so the reader not only may see what makes him tick, but experiences the tension and precision of Augustine's whole organism. Her critical and inquisitive spirit is balanced by human sympathy and kinship. Having figured him out, she does not despise him because his neuroses are exposed. An artist's eye for the symbolic, an investigator's nose for the critical moment, an outsider's ear for a fellow-outsider's clamor for recognition and aggressive self-pity, add to her equipment for telling a spell-binding story whose personal plot is nonetheless insistent because it also contains a critique of western culture's dualism. Duality disturbs her. In an essay on Joyce in *The Strange Necessity*, she writes, "In those who pursue unhappiness there is a profound Don Juanism, there is an incapacity to live monogamously with one tragedy, one must go on seducing events and getting them with fresh births of agony."[7]

In Augustine's life and work she found a thread of the love/hate relationship with Manichean ideas which both binds and loosens our culture. History as a battle between Good and Evil, God and Satan, spirit and matter, is still the staple of popular fiction. Augustine's painful rejection of the concept of free will and adoption of the ideas of predestination, salvation by grace and the election of the few have had a heady history of their own. Rebecca West traces Augustine's attraction to Manichean mysteries to the child's perception of duality in his parents as well as the artist's symbolic approach to reality. But by concentrating on the material world as evil and human sexuality as its most obnoxious form, Augustine becomes in Dame Rebecca's portrait, the father of modern guilt.

Driven to her analysis, one imagines, by self-conscious membership in the sex to which all the evils of the material world have been ascribed from ancient mythology through the Fathers of the Church, Rebecca West always maintained a feminist sense of humor. Augustine's unhappy attitude toward sex, consisting of an exaggerated sense of its importance combined with an unreasoning horror of it, which is not uncommon in men but rare among women may be caused by "the less dignified anatomy of man," a point on which Augustine copiously complained; but it may lie to some extent in the disadvantageous situation of man in the sexual act, who finds that for him it ends with physical collapse and the surrender of power, whereas for his partner it ends with motherhood and the increase of power.[8]

West saw Augustine as a great romantic artist whose hostility to art derives from guilt that it gives pleasure. His modern successors are Joyce and Lawrence; his death-wish denies art and life, like Tolstoy, and the concept of original sin springs from his sojourn with Manichean duality. He saw the universe in terms of his mother, Monica and himself. Spirituality was to be achieved by guilt, atonement and suffering. She sees Shakespeare as an Augustinian and Goethe as one of the few great artists who escaped his influence. Rebecca West's subsequent studies of traitors and criminals owe much to the example of Augustine rooting out heretics and may be seen as modern epistles to western man from a "mother" of the rational Church Militant attacking the death-wish in all its forms, affirming life and art, unity and reality.

Hers is a kind of "matristic" militancy attacking the still pernicious effects of patristic thought which produce sacrifice, victims and martyrs instead of joy, art and democracy. Borrowing the authority of the fathers for her critical tone of voice, she became neither a female patriarch nor a matriarch but a fighting feminist prophetess, stern and judgmental, yes, but always on the side of justice and the light. Like her hero, Ibsen, she saw the damage to personal and political life the Christian concept of original sin has caused. We must stop dividing the world into winners and losers, victims and conquerers, the saved and the damned. There will be a terrible confrontation when the victims take their revenge, "when we dead awaken," as Ibsen articulates.

This duality which she damns is, as she knew, reflected in her own work. *The Judge* (1922) seems cleft in two, the first half written by a new Jane Austen and the second by a new Charlotte Bronte. The rational, sunny first half includes a wonderful recreation of a young woman's experience of the suffrage movement in Edinburgh. *The Judge* belongs, in one sense, to an interesting genre of English fiction, the suffrage novel. It includes (leaving aside Lawrence's caricatures of suffragettes) Elizabeth Robins' *The Convert*, H. G. Wells' *Ann Veronica* and *The New Machiavelli*, Virginia Woolf's *Night and Day*, Evelyn Sharp's *Rebel*

Women, Ford Madox Ford's *Some Do Not* (the best of them all) and May Sinclair's *The Tree of Heaven*. Like *The Tree of Heaven*, *The Judge* is also an experimental "vorticist" novel. The doom and gloom of its second half is the landmark in English fiction between Bronte and Lawrence. Rebecca West believed she had expressed there her truest, "instinctive self" in its autobiographical force. "I damned near found myself in the millrace," she said of the tragic intensity of the passion for Wells which inspired it.[9] The novel is preceded by the lines "Every mother is a judge who sentences the children for the sins of the father," a prophecy that her own son seems to believe.[10] It is dedicated to her mother, and, like most great women's fiction, it contains powerful scenes of the death of the mother. The "good" mother and the "bad" mother are impressively drawn and the study of Marion's passion for her sons is a masterpiece of emotional force; the experience which prompted it is surely the precursor of her study of Monica and Augustine.

"Justicia" has been Rebecca West's muse, judgment her method, righteous indignation her tone. And so she has moved with confidence out of fiction and literary criticism, where women before her have worked with genius, on to paths where few female feet have left their mark, moral philosophy, psychobiography, political history. She and Virginia Woolf are English women of letters worthy of comparison to their French ancestresses. Their radical feminism is a common cause but the differences in techniques are profound. Gerald Brenan called Virginia Woolf a "Lapland witch," suggesting her self-styled coldness, and fierce intellect, as the lonely spellcasting outsider and feminist myth-maker of modern literature. Despite the snatching of her name from the great "Northern wizard," Rebecca West's witchery is more Celtic. If Virginia Woolf is a modern incarnation of Diana the huntress, equating chastity with freedom, Rebecca West reminds one of the vitality of the Irish heroine in one of Yeats' mythologies, Great-Bladdered Emir, elected queen because she could urinate the deepest hole in the snow. At 90 her presence still radiated an elemental female sexuality and creative power, what Hortense Calisher called "the feminism that comes straight from the belly, from the bed and from childbed."[11] The deepest difference is in the ability to express anger directly, the power to shout, curse, and laugh at male folly and persecution with no damage to her own ego. Her female family gave her self-confidence, high standards.

Virginia Woolf was bound by the deaths of her mother and stepsister, her famous father, her difficult life with brothers and stepbrothers to a wheel which demanded more subtle attacks on authority. Her desire for domination was directed at form; she broke it and made it new many times. Authority was a painful concept to her; she had bowed to it in men too often to want to see it in women. To her, there was only a very small gap between "authoritative" and "authoritarian."

But boldness was Rebecca West's forte. She polished the weapons of invective and denunciation into the tools of a fine art. She was never afraid of her own anger; it was justifiable. She turned its force against the enemy, not against herself. "Fie on the falsehood of men," she cried, like the sixteenth century "Jane Anger," who stretched "the veins of her brains, the strings of her fingers and the lists of her modesty" to lift up a pen in answer to them. We read with astonishment now the outpourings of rage, anger and resentment in Virginia Woolf's diaries and letters, and recognize just how she transformed it into art. Anger was the great well-spring of her genius, the record left behind her so we would see its source. She was full of admiration for Rebecca West's daring and Rebecca West was one of her earliest critics and champions. Few critics, even the most admiring, have seen in *Orlando* anything but what Louise Bogan called "a sapphic pastiche." But Rebecca West praised it as "a high fountain of genius," "the only successfully invented myth in English literature of our time," and "a poetic masterpiece of the first rank."

She saw the courage it took to publish *A Room of One's Own* in 1928, when women could vote and male "antifeminism is so strikingly the fashion of the day among intellectuals." Woolf's own admirers were worse and she risked losing what reputation she had: "the men who despised us for our specifically female organs chastized us with whips; but those to whom they are a matter for envy chastize us with scorpions." *A Room* she found "an uncompromising piece of feminist propaganda," "the ablest yet written." When Quentin Bell's biography appeared, she denounced it as "the conversion of biography from a form of literature to a blood sport. Virginia Woolf's official biography is to me a scene of carnage."[12]

Rebecca West may have been Britain's foremost champion of women artists, but that does not prevent her from demanding the very best from them. "And They All Lived Unhappily Ever After"[13] praised Doris Lessing as "the English George Sand," she "would try anything twice, and her strength is the strength of ten" in a "Mississippian flow of being." Margaret Drabble was given a severe lecture and Iris Murdoch was told in no uncertain terms that all human beings possess knowledge of good and evil as natural equipment, that simple observation is a better tool for the novelist than all the philosophies women have dreamed of.

Hungering and thirsting after righteousness, Rebecca West's appetite for justice did not diminish over the decades. Nor had she the slightest hesitation in expressing unpopular views. "I'm dead to Dante," she told me, "Beatrice is the great boring female of all time." She is not interested in woman as object or woman as subject, but in woman as she acts and thinks in history. She laughed at an American critic who wrote that Norman Mailer was her successor as political journalist; "Norman Mailer is a peacock without any tail," she said. And then she asked me what did I think of the "territorial imperative?" "I'll give men all the territory they want if they'd only leave us alone," she said—though I doubt if she would have given up an inch of territory without a fight.

All her life Dame Rebecca wrote in praise of virtue and condemned wickedness. She found moral relativism ridiculous and said so in essay and fiction. Men don't like women who act as their judges; they are intimidated by this appropriation of their own Old Testament thunder. Such wrath belongs to Jehovah and Jove. Can this really be a woman's voice, with such an authoritative tone? A woman's fist raised in anger against injustice? Not only does Rebecca West beat and berate the oppressors of women, her actions have a classical female beauty of style, an energetic grace. She beats with the great bold strokes of an archetypal figure of a woman beating a carpet. All the accumulated dust of centuries is blown away. The figures appear in bold relief and the colors are now sharp and bright. The voice is a voice of female authority. Long may its echoes be heard.

NOTES

This paper is part of the original introduction written for *The Young Rebecca: Writings of Rebecca West 1911–1917* (London: Macmillan/Virago, New York: Viking, 1982). Quotations from Rebecca West's *Freewoman* and *Clarion* essays may be found in that volume. Other quotations are from the author's interviews with Dame Rebecca in 1977 and 1978.

1. Ellen Moers, *Literary Women* (New York: Doubleday, 1976).

2. *New York Times Sunday Magazine*, April 4, 1982. For further contributions to the vilification of Rebecca West, see Anthony West, "Pursued by Rebecca West," *New York Review of Books*, March 1, 1984, which is the introduction to his *roman à clef, Heritage* (New York: Washington Square Press, 1984). A review of his 1984 *H. G. Wells: Aspects of A Life*, with further comments on his mother, appears in the *New York Times Book Review*, May 6, 1984.

3. Yale, 1974.

4. *The Young Rebecca West*.

5. Interview with the author.

6. Virginia Woolf's original speech, "Professions for Women," is printed in *The Pargiters,* ed. Mitchell Leaska (New York: New York Public Library and Readex Books, 1980).

7. Rebecca West, *The Strange Necessity* (London: Cape, 1928).

8. Rebecca West, *Saint Augustine* (New York: Appleton, 1933).

9. Interview with the author.

10. Quoted in Joan Goulianos, *By a Woman Writ* (Baltimore: Penguin, 1974).

11. Rebecca West, New York Herald Tribune, October 21, 1928.

12. Rebecca West, *Vogue* (September 1972): 274–75.

13. Rebecca West, *Times Literary Supplement*, July 26, 1974, p. 779.

28

Charlotte Delbo, A Woman/Book

Rosette C. Lamont

In 1943, when Charlotte Delbo was taken to Auschwitz, her deepest human roots had been severed. Her husband, Georges Dudach had been shot in prison after the couple's arrest as members of the Resistance. Dudach had been given the choice of going to work in one of the labor forces recruited for Germany, or death; he chose the latter. His wife was invited to visit him in his cell for a final farewell, perhaps in the hope that she might dissuade him at the last moment. This she never attempted to do. The young couple knew that this was to be their last encounter.

Charlotte Delbo never remarried; her life as a wife ended before she left for camp. For Charlotte, the severing of these gender-related roots provided an essential step in a rite of passage. She has since often declared: "I must not be discussed as a woman writer. I am not a woman in my writing." Although Delbo has described vividly various forms of female heroism in camp, and under Nazi occupation, she denies that there is such a thing as a distinctive female experience of the Holocaust. As Cynthia Haft—one of Delbo's closest young friends—has pointed out in her published dissertation: "the camp system grants complete equality to men and women."[1]

Camp made of Delbo a heroically strong human being, one with an imperishable sense of self, but also a genderless human being, or perhaps one ought to say a person who chose to transcend gender. Her connection with other women, however, became all the stronger. In her mind she would often return to thoughts of her mother, back home, waiting for her, hoping for her daughter's survival. She also felt at one with the women who shared her condition; they became members of a single family.

Today, the few survivors continue to meet in Paris. Their ties are deeper than those of relatives, or friends. They have shared an indelible experience, one which Delbo calls "the major event of the twentieth century."

In her own writing Delbo uses the first person singular sparingly. Most of the time she will speak through a collective "nous." This is not to be taken as "a self-effacing style," as is suggested by Marlene E. Heinemann in her recently completed but still unpublished study, *Women Prose Writers of the Nazi Holocaust*. Rather one ought to view the collective pronoun as a self-conscious attempt to transmit what the Russian dissident writer Andrey Siniavsky calls "A Voice from the Chorus." The great writers who have emerged from "l'univers concentrationnaire" are natural classicists, and moralists: they do not seek individual expression; they are the sacred interpreters of the dead and the survivors.

Delbo does not wish to write a personal memoir, but to create a series of prose poems that will speak for all those who were with her. She addresses the universal consciousness of today, and that of thinking people in the centuries to come. "Il faut donner a voir," she says with passionate intensity. Her purpose is to raise the image of the camps for all to see.

Delbo's style is clear, pure, well-balanced. She needs to do little or even no rewriting. By the time a text pours out of her it seems to have assumed its final form within her wonderfully lucid mind. This does not mean, however, that it is ready for publication. In the case of *None of Us Will Return (Aucun de nous ne reviendra)*, Charlotte had the supreme courage, self-control, and strength of purpose to hold on to it for twenty years in order to put the text to the test of time. If surviving is part courage, part instinct, the determination to convey, or crystallize the unforgettable image of camp life without being hasty, vengeful, or simply didactic, takes a wrenching kind of honesty.

Each one of Charlotte Delbo's prose poems is a quintessential concentrate of an extreme situation or condition: nudity (the result of forced public disrobing), hunger, thirst, fear, powerless pity, bloodless exhaustion, illness, a slow dying. As Elie Wiesel once stated in the course of a public lecture: "Words, simple, every day words such as 'bread,' 'water,' 'sleep' did not signify the same thing in camp as they did and do outside. Nor can they ever mean the same to those of us who have issued from *l'univers concentrationnaire*."

The Holocaust writer faces a dilemma: to compose a tragic work, classical in its intention to address each and every one, and yet raise the image of what Dante could only paint in Hell. In the work of Wiesel, Semprun, Delbo, the incidental, the contingent evaporate leaving in the alchemical *vas* of literary language something so powerfully direct and physical that it becomes, paradoxically, metaphysical. This can only happen when the intention of the writer is to produce a work of art, something beyond bearing witness.

L'univers concentrationnaire made a natural metaphysician of each thinking creature. Charlotte Delbo had been a student of philosophy at the Sorbonne before she began to work full time for Louis Jouvet who had been delighted by the interview he had given her for a student paper. Before she was arrested, Delbo had been committed to political activism—she participated with her husband, a Communist, in the Resistance movement. It was in solitary confinement, and later, in the camps that she discovered solitude. There was also the shared solitude of those who, like herself, had been cut off from the social context. They were forgotten, abandoned, given up for lost dead. Because the universe of the camp was a locus outside society, separated from the rest of the world, it placed every prisoner within his or her vulnerability. As to the community of the imprisoned, it existed somewhere outside history and politics in a space where death reigned supreme, and where life was tolerated only so long as it could be put to some use, however absurd the activity.

When Delbo describes her companions, she sees them as both tragic and strangely comical. They wear their long coats backwards in order to carry in the stretched out bottom part the earth and stones needed to create a garden at the camp's gate. This additional work, mortal to those already weakened, was performed on the day of the Lord, Sunday. The women, Charlotte notes, particularly the Jewish prisoners who had no special aprons, looked like penguins. It was impossible to preserve a feeling of one's humanity, to recall a world in which one had used a toothbrush, purchased a piece of soap, reached for a breakfast croissant, and—most unthinkable of all—applied perfume as a kind of floating, invisible dress, a veil of scent. Women tried to remember they had once been women, and people, but this was almost beyond the reach of their memory. They had become beasts of burden, and the cogwheels of the immense, and senseless technological machinery of the Nazi state. Nothing brings this fact more closely to mind than a visit to the Auschwitz Museum where one can view in an immense glass display case thousands of blond, black, grey curls and tresses, women's hair shorn from the heads of the living. Close by, in a smaller case, the visitor can see a rolled piece of brownish cloth, almost a homespun: the cloth was one of many such rolls manufactured from the hair of women prisoners.

The women of Delbo's trilogy (*Aucun de nous ne reviendra, Mesure de nos jours, Une connaissance inutile*) seem to move in a dream dreamt by some evil force that holds them in thralldom, a nightmare from which they cannot awaken since they are not the dreamers, since the evil dreamer is out of reach.

Within this unreality which had become their only reality, a light remained— for some—a memory of the other life. It came from words, from literature. For Charlotte who knew that literature, drama, theatre were all aspects of life, a deeper, more intense kind of life, this universe of art held the real. They (her captors) could imprison her, send her to forced labor, plan to end her life, but they could not take from her that world peopled by characters she knew as well if not better than her family and friends.

In her novella, "Phantoms, My Companions" ("Spectres mes compagnons"),[2] Delbo evokes what it means to be in touch with these vivid ghosts, literary characters. The story is written in the form of a letter to Charlotte's great friend and master, Louis Jouvet. It begins with a recreation of the many walks she took with Jouvet through the countryside surrounding Vallauris. The great director obviously enjoyed discussing novels and plays with this intelligent, sensitive young woman who had become his assistant, and the faithful recorder of his classes at the Conservatoire (long before the invention of the tape recorder). They walked and spoke of Stendhal, Dickens, of Giraudoux's *Electre*, and Moliere's *Misanthrope*. One of the questions they raised was that of the difference between a character in a novel and a *dramatis persona*. Jouvet thought that a character in a play is defined by his acts, that he is an essence defying introspection. Thus, in his opinion, many interpretations are possible when you deal with a dramatic work, many diverse incarnations can take place upon the stage.

Later, in camp, Charlotte recalled the great director's teachings as she recreated for the women of her *blockhaus* the plays she had seen Jouvet direct. In her own words she also narrated some of the great novels she had read. Late at night, despite a day of murderous work, the women who had discovered Charlotte's gift for storytelling begged her to share her knowledge with them. She became their Woman/Book.

Delbo had always enjoyed committing to memory poetry and dramatic texts; it came naturally as she watched a play being rehearsed. Now she was able to recite to her friends whole plays, acting out various characters. Moliere, Racine, Giraudoux came to life within the walls of the narrow *blockhaus*. Charlotte also evoked the life of the Paris theatres: *La Comédie Française*, *l'Opéra*, *l'Odéon* and Jouvet's own theatre, *L'Athénée*. Even from the highest balcony (*le paradis*) a student could enjoy a wonderful performance at some of these fine houses.

Most of Delbo's blockmates had never had a chance to go to the theatre, or had not been tempted to secure an inexpensive seat, Now, for the first time in their lives, they were being taken to the theatre, a magic place. Paris rose before the eyes and ears of an eager audience: the painted ceilings of the great houses, the red velvet seats, the chandeliers glittering like the diamonds on the bare arms and necks of lovely, spoiled women. Charlotte's friends vowed that if they were to survive they would read all the novels she told them about, see all the plays, go to museums. The oasis of peace was no longer a mirage; it was more than a distant memory of the past, it became a future possibility, a goal for survival.

It was while she was in solitary that Charlotte Delbo began to be visited by literary characters. In "Phantoms, My Companions" the writer speaks of her isolation:

At the beginning I was locked up in a high room where nothing could come close to me except faceless voices and a pallid light which projected shadows on a wall spotted by humidity. In this light the third dimension was abolished. Thoughts as well as objects were but shadows on a wall. Shadows of my thoughts, shadow of my life, these were projected on the screen of my memory while sentient remembrance failed. For days and nights, I struggled to lend these shadows contour and relief. Their reticent, fugitive presences slid by silently.[3]

A little later, Charlotte is "visited" by Stendhal's hero, Fabrice del Dongo, the protagonist of *The Charterhouse of Parma*. He is the perfect cell mate since he

spent much of his life—perhaps the best days—in a dungeon. Delbo tells us that
Fabrice enters her prison cell by means of a rope, the perfect daredevil act for
this adventurous, gallant youth. We understand that this is a metaphor for the
charitable offering of Stendhal's novel by a woman fellow-prisoner confined to
a cell below that of Charlotte, and who, on account of some inexplicable prison
regulation, is allowed the use of the prison library which is forbidden to Charlotte.
Charlotte tells her reader how she fashioned a slender rope from the threads of
the blanket, and, having lowered that rope through her window, was able to pull
up the precious volume. The book and its protagonist become the companions
of her solitary cell.

When the time comes for leaving her jail in order to board the train that is to
take her to the camp, neither the book, nor its hero can accompany her on that
journey. Fabrice del Dongo is much too civilized to travel on a cattle train with
human beings treated like beasts. For a while Delbo believes she is alone on
that train, alone with her fellow-prisoners, until she hears a voice whispering in
her ear. It says: "Why be so fearful of solitude? It is often richer in company,
and less disappointing. . . . "[4] Delbo recognizes at once the ironic, bitter voice
of Alceste, the accents of Jouvet. Moliere's protagonist seems to have embarked
at last on his own cherished flight from the hypocrites, flatterers and coquettes
who turn Paris into what he considers to be a living hell. Yet, when the train
reaches its destination, and the doors slide open revealing a ravaged site, barracks,
chimneys, arid ground, Alceste is unable to recognize the desert he was seeking;
this wasteland is too bare, too horrifying for him. Charlotte tells us that he slips
away, hastening back to the man who gave him new life on the stage, to his recreator if not his creator, Louis Jouvet.

Who will endure the horror of camp life? What literary character might share
this extreme form of exile. Charlotte is certain at first that she is now irretrievably
alone. But, at that very moment, she catches a glimpse of Electra. Delbo writes:
"She stood at the edge of a line formed by reeds, and it seemed to me that she
wore a proud, resolute smile."[5]

Electra heralds in other "resurrections": Giraudoux's Ondine, Moliere's Don
Juan, even Proust's Oriane. These ghosts made of words will live side by side
with women whose flesh is melting from their bones, turning them into ghost-
like creatures. Words can be as palpable as flesh; they can lend dignity to those
who have been stripped of pride and hope.

Charlotte Delbo tells her readers that the books we peruse, the plays we see,
are not "irrelevant" art objects, but friends who can assist us in the hour of our
greatest need. In a recently written piece, Delbo states:

Characters in novels and drama, creatures of fiction, are nevertheless real. They are alive.
They live in our minds and are part and parcel of our private universe in the same way
as our intimate friends, or the members of our family we feel closest to. Some are so
dear to us that we are in love with them, that we love them. This is the case for Tolstoy's
Natasha and Prince Andrei, for Fabrice and Lucien Leuwen, for Berenice and Violaine.

We share in their passions, identify with them, we refer to their feelings when we wish to give expression to our own. They are endowed with a magnified kind of existence, a dimension which exceeds by far that of human beings.[6]

When we study the literature that has issued from the camps, we realize with a special intensity that great art helps people survive because survival in dire circumstances can be a matter of spirit. Hope cannot cure malnutrition, but for a young, basically strong person the desire to live was often stirred by memory, that of one's personal past, and that of the collective past we find in works of art. Only memory makes it possible to envision shaping a future.

By upholding literary values, by believing in literature, Charlotte Delbo made her apprenticeship as a poet; she became one of the living voices of the Holocaust. Her companions in camp—the other phantoms, soon to become wispy ghosts— begged her to remember, to be their voice if she survived. Charlotte took her mission as a sacred trust. If she waited to publish her first book it was not negligence on her part, but the imperatives of her demanding spirit. If she was "self-effacing," it was only in this sense; she effaced the self in order for the world to glow.

Heroic in the Resistance, heroic in the camps, it is as a literary artist that Charlotte Delbo proved herself a true hero.

NOTES

Charlotte Delbo's works are easily available in French. Her publisher is Les Editions de Minuit. Her plays *La Sentence* and *Qui rapporters ces paroles*? have been published by Pierre Jean Oswald.

1. Cynthia Haft published the first Ph.D. dissertation in this country on the literature of the Holocaust: *The Theme of Nazi Concentration Camps in French Literature* (The Hague, Paris: Mouton, 1973). Haft also introduced the work of Charlotte Delbo to this country. Charlotte Delbo died on March 1,1985.

2. "Phantoms, My Companions" was translated by the author of this essay. It was published in this country many years before it came out in French in Europe. "Phantoms, My Companions," *The Massachusetts Review*, Vol. 7, no. 1, pp. 10–30, was followed by "Phantoms, My Faithful Ones," *The Massachusetts Review*, Vol. 4, no. 2, pp. 310– 315. Delbo's novella (Part 1 and 2) was given the MR Quill Award in Fiction.

3. Ibid., "Phantoms, My Companions," p. 15.

4. Ibid., p. 23.

5. Ibid., p. 30.

6. *Le Monde*, October 15, 1981.

29

The Case of the Dangling Signifier: Phallic Imagery in Eudora Welty's "Moon Lake"

Patricia S. Yaeger

How should we read phallic imagery when it is incorporated within women's texts? If the phallus is, as Lacan suggests, the central signifier of patriarchal culture, is the woman writer who gives phallic imagery a prominent place in her fictions reinstating our culture's patriarchal orientations? In this essay I will argue that the phallus can function as a misplaced signifier in women's writings. It becomes, that is, a signifier which is clearly out of place, which dominates and speaks out of turn, and yet by its very displacement, controls and disturbs those patterns of culture which women themselves have begun to initiate. In "Moon Lake," a story from *The Golden Apples*, Eudora Welty explores the ways in which the dominant sex/gender system[1] erases woman's past and endangers her future. Ostensibly a story about a group of young girls on their first camping expedition and a boy scout who saves one of them from drowning, on a more primary level "Moon Lake" describes the ways in which these young women, barely aware of their own sexuality, begin to adjust to, even before they can react against, a male-dominated world. Welty's use of phallic imagery keeps us continually aware of the tensions between the young girls' desires and the society which tries to shape their desires. Before examining the use of phallic imagery in "Moon Lake," however, I wish, for contrast, to examine its use in a familiar, patriarchal text: Herman Melville's *Moby-Dick*.

In *Moby-Dick* it is the donning of the "hassock" or skin from the whale's penis which defines the human dimensions of the demonic and helps to give the men aboard the *Pequod* an illusion of power over the creaturely world. In Melville's book man's delusive quest for economic and metaphysical power is described in terms of a search for the sperm whale, a search for the meta-creative source which the castrated Ahab regards as the transcendental signifier itself. In his *Écrits* Lacan has constructed a psychoanalytic system which can help us to analyze some of these narrative themes in *Moby-Dick*. The phallus, Lacan argues, is the "central signifier" of human culture: a sign of biological difference between man and woman which also comes to represent the difference between culture and nature, power and powerlessness, order and chaos.[2] As Gayle Rubin explains Lacan's system in "The Traffic in Women":

The phallus is, as it were, a distinctive feature differentiating "castrated" and "noncastrated." The presence or absence of the phallus carries the differences between two sexual statuses, "man" and "woman." Since these are not equal, the phallus also carries a meaning of the dominance of men over women, and it may be inferred that "penis envy" is a recognition thereof. Moreover, as long as men have rights in women which women do not have in themselves, the phallus also carries the meaning of the difference between "exchanger" and "exchanged," gift and giver. Ultimately, neither the classical Freudian nor the rephrased Lacanian theories of the Oedipal process make sense unless at least this much of the paleolithic relations of sexuality are still with us. We still live in a "phallic" culture. (TW, p. 191)

Rubin suggests that this "phallic" culture is not simply outmoded, but destructive as well "[T]he creation of 'femininity' in women in the course of socialization is an act of psychic brutality," she argues, that "leaves in women an immense resentment of the suppression to which they were subjected." Our culture sees the phallus as the mark of difference between man and woman and therefore as the mark of privilege which not only validates the repression of woman, but signifies her inferiority to man.

Melville does temper the cultural meaning of phallic imagery in *Moby-Dick* by contrasting Ahab's singular drive for power with Ishmael's good-humored bookishness. Ahab's view of the whale's brutality is further tempered by the narrator's ecstatic descriptions of whaling and by Ishmael's plural readings of cetology. In fact, Ishmael's increasingly clear recognition of multiplicity, of the individual and discrete creativity of each person's perceptions, establishes a background against which the delusions of Ahab's phallic quest can be partially measured. Still, Ahab's tragedy not only usurps the final third of *Moby-Dick*, creating within the naive reader a lasting impression of Ahab's evil splendor, but Melville also masks Ahab's delusions with the sublimity and romance of high tragedy. The reader is invited to see Ahab's mistaken reading of the world as a noble misprision; his tragedy, in point of fact, exonerates his quest. *Moby-Dick*, I would argue, is a book which simultaneously challenges the patriarchal order and covertly reinstates it by virtue of the approbation inherent in the narrator's description and valorization of Ahab. Though maternal discourse finally emerges as the source of survival in the novel's final scene with Ishmael's discovery by "the devious-cruising Rachel," the maternal or feminine is, for the most part, a buried presence in *Moby-Dick*, surfacing most often in scenes associated with the fear or fact of castration. In the extended comic scene where Ishmael first becomes acquainted with Queequeg, for example, it is precisely the overcoming of this fear which allows a sense of equality between self and other to emerge. In their first night together at the Spouter-Inn, just as Ishmael is about to introduce himself, Queequeg leaps precipitously into bed and Ishmael—fearing some mortal wound—cries out.

But the interval I spent in deliberating what to say, was a fatal one. Taking up his tomahawk from the table, he examined the head of it for an instant, and then holding it to the light, with his mouth at the handle, he puffed out great clouds of tobacco smoke. The next moment the light was extinguished, and this wild cannibal, tomahawk between his teeth, sprang into bed with me. I sang out, I could not help it now; and giving a sudden grunt of astonishment he began feeling me.[3]

After Ishmael's fears have been allayed, these companions embark upon a journey of unabashed camaraderie: "Upon waking next morning about daylight, I found Queequeg's arm thrown over me in the most loving and affectionate manner. You had almost thought I had been his wife" (M-D, p. 52). The willingness to overcome one's fear of symbolic mutilation and to subordinate feelings of hierarchy for those of inquisitive cooperation suggests that Ishmael may have learned something about phallocentrism from Queequeg's casual treatment of his wooden idol, "a curious little deformed image with a hunch on its back, and exactly the color of a three days' old Congo baby" (M-D, p. 49): "[a]t last extinguishing the fire, he took the idol up very unceremoniously, and bagged it again in his grego coat pocket as carelessly as if he were a sportsman bagging a dead woodcock" (M-D, p. 50). Both the diminutive shape and the irreverent treatment received by this small homunculus begin to work upon Ishmael's world view. Ishmael survives, it could be argued, by virtue of the androgynous identity which is both created and brought to the reader's attention in this scene where Queequeg, initially perceived as a figure of death, finally embraces Ishmael as "wife." But despite this counterplot which insists on the dangers of phallocentrism and the symbolic pleasures of "feminization," Melville's focus eventually strays in other directions. He gives phallic imagery and the quest for the father a privileged position in his writing, thereby reinscribing the centrality of his symbol within the very culture his novel interrogates.[4] Must we say the same of Eudora Welty's "Moon Lake," in which phallic imagery also plays a prominent part?

"Moon Lake" begins as a comic story describing the chill, lackadaisical rhythms of a week-long summer camp for girls. The camp itself is set against the backdrop of a *masculine* landscape—an odd reversal of the traditional associations of pastoral nature and femininity. From the beginning Welty describes the campers' lives as a dialogue between "girlish" activity and the masculine principle inscribed in this landscape. " 'Good morning, Mr. Dip, Dip, Dip with your water just as cold as ice!' sang Mrs. Gruenwald hoarsely. She took them for the dip, for Miss Moody said she couldn't simply couldn't.'"[5] Although the validity of the camp's gender-oriented setting and mythology is quickly called in question, this mythology is nevertheless reinstated in a less figurative and more substantial form. Listening to Mrs. Gruenwald,

Nina Carmichael thought, There is nobody and nothing named Mr. Dip, it is not a good morning until you have had coffee, and the water is the temperature of a just-cooling biscuit, thank Goodness. I hate this little parade of us girls, Nina thought, trotting fiercely in the center of it. It ruins the woods, all right. "Gee, we think you're mighty nice," they sang to Mr. Dip, while the Boy Scout, waiting at the lake, watched them go in. (ML, p. 110)

While Nina may be skeptical about the mythical Mr. Dip, she is certain of her own feminine insignificance. In fact, the sense of dominant male presence, of Mr. Dip's chill fingers, is not dispelled by Nina's meditation, but heightened. Every morning not only begins with a dip in the lake, a seductive encounter, as we will see later, with masculine otherness, but with the boy scout's proscriptive reveille:

From the beginning his martyred presence seriously affected them. They had a disquieting familiarity with it, hearing the spit of his despising that went into his bugle. At times they could hardly recognize what he thought he was playing. Loch Morrison, Boy Scout and Life Saver, was under the ordeal of a week's camp on Moon Lake with girls. (ML, p. 112).

This sound not only signals the beginning or origin of the campers' day, but its melody is marred by Loch's "phallic" anger at their presence, by the "spit of his despising that went into his bugle."

Reveille was his. He harangued the woods when the little minnows were trembling and running wizardlike in the water's edge. And how lovely and altered the trees were then, weighted with dew, leaning on one another's shoulders and smelling like big wet flowers. He blew his horn into their presence—trees' and girls'—and then watched the Dip. (ML, p. 113).

The erotic intent of this imagery is obvious enough; what is startling is its lyric tone. Loch Morrison, boy scout and enemy, is also the beloved. As he watches them disrobe: " 'Watch out for mosquitoes,' they called to one another . . . as they walked out of their kimonos and dropped them like the petals of one big scattered flower on the bank behind them, and exposing themselves felt in a hundred places at once the little pangs" (ML, p. 114). But although the derisive and masculine presence of "Loch" Morrison, demigod of the woods and companion to the lake itself, is at first described in a comic-lyric tone, the description both of Loch and of the generalized masculine presence in the landscape and in the lake grows more aggressively sexual as the story continues:

"Gee, we think you're mighty nice," they sang to Mr. Dip, gasping, pounding their legs in him. If they let their feet go down, the invisible bottom of the lake felt like soft, knee-deep fur. The sharp hard knobs came up where least expected. The Morgana girls of course wore bathing slippers, and the mud loved to suck them off. (ML, p. 116).

Although the camp's rituals focus repeatedly on matters of gender, the children (despite their "little pangs," despite their exposure before Loch Morrison and their figurative deflowering) are essentially blind to what threatens them.[6] These young girls define their difference from one another in terms of class, not gender. The status-conscious girls from the town of Morgana voice their open contempt for the country orphans. " 'Let's let the orphans go in the water first and get the snakes stirred up, Mrs. Gruenwald,' Jinny Love Star suggested . . . 'Then they'll be chased away by the time *we* go in.' " By the end of the story, however, just as the campers are beginning to form cautious friendships across class lines, an incident occurs in which class becomes irrelevant. The children come together in horror as an orphan is dragged from the water and hauled to a picnic table where she is gradually resuscitated. This is a "life-saving" Eudora Welty describes as if it were a rape:

The Boy Scout reached in and gouged out her mouth with his hand, an unbelievable act. She did not alter. He lifted up, screwed his toes, and with a groan of his own fell upon her and drove up and down upon her, into her, gouging the heels of his hands into her ribs again and again. She did not alter except that she let a thin stream of water out of her mouth, a dark stain down the fixed cheek. The children drew together. Life-saving was much worse than they had dreamed. (ML, p. 145).

Welty lightens the gothic tone of this text by focusing on the reaction of the drowned child's companions, creating within her reader a bemused contemplation, a detachment the true gothic never permits. But what Welty asks us to contemplate is not at all amusing. Her text intimates that it is not the segregation of classes, but the hierarchical relation between man and woman—and beyond this the symbolic status of the phallus as arbiter and fetish of masculine power—which is the creator of difference within our culture.

Phallic imagery not only provides the dominant set of metaphors in "Moon Lake," but also presides over the plot of this story in unexpected ways. We have seen, for instance, that the bugle controls the young girls' rhythms of waking and sleeping as well as the erotic apparitions in the woods and the "little minnows" at the water's edge which resemble, in their funny "trembling and running," the marginality and the vulnerability of the campers themselves. This bugle, or rather, its miniature, appears again in a scene where Nina Carmichael is trying to write her name in the sand. "The sand was coarse like beads and full of minute shells, some shaped exactly like bugles" (ML, p. 129). Nina and Jinny Love Stark and the orphan Easter have run away from the silly and gender-specific activity of basket-weaving. But even here, far from camp and its sexually biased rituals, the law of the father, imaged in these pervasive if diminutive shells, prevails. Hoping for an adventure Nina tries, like the young Wordsworth in Book I of *The Prelude*, to steal a boat—but fails, unlike him, to leave the shore. Wordsworth's journey in the "elfin pinnace" is self-delusive, but it is also self-constructive, permitting him to internalize and to shape his own still-to-be-recognized powers. These powers at first have ominous and possibly phallic attributes:

> And growing still in stature the grim shape
> Towered up between me and the stars, and still,
> For so it seemed, with purpose of its own
> And measured motion like a living thing,
> Strode after me.[7]

Wordsworth's sexuality, his autonomy, and his creativity appear to him at this early age as "other," later they are discovered to be self-possessed and self-inspired. But these young girls are not allowed to venture beyond themselves into this psychological region in which the "other" is gradually discovered to be a complex version of the self and its fictions. Instead of experiencing nature, as Wordsworth does, as the sublime arena of her hidden creativity, Nina finds herself displaced and delayed; she becomes nature's erotic object. "Firming her feet in the sucking, minnowy mud, Nina put her weight against the boat. Soon her legs were half hidden, the mud like some awful kiss pulled at her toes, and all over she tautened and felt the sweat start out of her body. Roots laced her feet, knotty and streaming." Freeing the boat is hard, but the discovery that it is permanently chained is harder still. (" 'You thought we'd all be out in the middle of Moon Lake by now, didn't you?' Jinny Love said from her lady's seat. 'Well, look where we are.' " But Nina can only reply: "Oh, Easter! Easter! I wish you still had your knife!" (ML, p. 132).

A second game—the game of writing their names in the grainy, bugle-shelled sand, also ends in disappointment. The knife, an arbitrary but culturally inscribed tool of masculine culture, can be taken away from young girls, but a simple writing stick should easily remain the children's own. But the writing stick is also designated as a "masculine" tool in this story; it provides Nina with a blissful but forbidden experiment in identity. Nina's "own hand was writing in the sand. Nina, Nina, Nina. Writing, she could dream that her self might get away from her—that here in this faraway place she could tell herself, by name, to go or to stay" (ML, p. 130).[8] But the freedom to imagine is soon dispelled. "Spell it right and it's real!" Nina calls to Easter who, though she misspells her name, claims in a realization of Nina's fantasy, to have named herself. In the midst of this argument Nina flings the writing stick into the lake—already the repository of a multitude of roots and snakes and vines and electric eels. As repository of the children's pen and a medium resisting their adventures, the lake begins to acquire an increasingly dangerous aura. It is, as we will see, more instrumental in the orphan's drowning than one would expect in a story about the pleasures of summer camp.

The girl who drowns in this masculine lake, who is metaphorically raped even as she is "literally" saved, is Easter herself—the most tomboyish and headstrong of the orphans. The only girl in camp whose body has begun to show signs of biological womanhood, Easter refuses to act in a "womanly" fashion. She not only bites the hand of Mr. Nesbitt, the Sunday School teacher who has noticed that Easter "had started her breasts," but she possesses a formidable collection of male accoutrements herself, ranging from her sense of self-origination to the jackknife she uses to win at mumblety-peg to a secret cache of cigarettes. But Easter's defiance and her set of forbidden and "phallic" attributes can be said to create the conditions for her gender-defined crucifixion at the story's end. Rescued as Easter is from the masculine lake by the masculine "Loch," Welty suggests that Easter must become the patriarchy's first victim.[9] It is as if she has traveled too far into masculine territory and must learn "feminine" passivity through the violence of a ritual rape. This "rape," which is also a life-saving, defines Easter's rite of passage from an active, androgynous life to the stunted and conventional life defined by a masculine hierarchy.[10] Easter's newly imposed passivity, however, elucidates a new realm of dangerous feminine activity in the eyes of her beholders.

"Keep away. Keep away, I told you you better keep away. Leave me alone," Loch Morrison was saying with short breaths. "I dove for her, didn't I?"

They hated him, Nina most of all. Almost, they hated Easter.

They looked at Easter's mouth and at the eyes where they were contemplating without sense the back side of the light. Though she had bullied and repulsed them earlier, they began to speculate in another kind of allurement: was there danger that Easter, turned in on herself, might call out to them after all, from the other, worse side of it? Her secret voice, if soundless then possibly visible, might work, out of her terrible mouth like a vine, preening and sprung with flowers. Or a snake would come out. (ML, p. 150).

The text turns back upon itself in an unpredictable manner and gathers those attributes into Easter's persona which had been ascribed to the "masculine" landscape. As snakes and vines seem to twine out of her mouth, Easter has suddenly acquired phallic power. Her "terrible" language is figured forth in those organic forms which have populated the masculine landscape. And yet, this description does not match the description of masculine prowess attributed to Loch Morrison, nor does it match the tone of those erotic and playful dangers which lurk in Moon Lake's patriarchal depths.

Beyond lay the deep part, some bottomless parts, said Moody. Here and there was the quicksand that stirred your footprint and kissed your heel. All snakes, harmless and harmful, were freely playing now; they put a trailing, moony division between weed and weed—bright, turning, bright and turning. (ML, p. 138).

The dangerous but playful sexuality of this environment undergoes a metamorphosis in the scene where Easter's life is saved, so that the erotic energies that have characterized the phallic landscape are no longer ascribed to the environment, but to woman's inner space. Easter herself comes to resemble a prolific form of nature. She is transformed, that is, from human status into a primitive and frighteningly sexualized form.

> Easter lay in a mold of wetness from Moon Lake, on her side; sharp as a flatiron her hipbone pointed up. She was arm to arm and leg to leg in a long fold, wrong-colored and pressed together as unopen leaves are. Her breasts, too, faced together. Out of the water Easter's hair was darkened, and lay over her face in long fern shapes. Miss Moody laid it back. (ML, p. 144).

Easter's elongated fetal posture, her reincarnation as a less-than-human form, signifies both the beginning of a process of being molded or shaped and a return to a status of vegetal and spore-like fecundity. Moreover, the emphasis on hips and breasts marks her birth as anonymous (or even monstrous) sexual being.[11]

Welty, then, is collapsing the gradual and customary event of a child's passage into our culture's definition of "womanhood" into a brief span of time. The erotic images which had been ascribed to a threatening masculine nature are suddenly applicable to woman alone. Feminized, interiorized, these images cease to be playful or erotic, as if it were not the violent man, but the silent woman who is dangerous:

> Easter's body lay up on the table to receive anything that was done to it. If *he* was brutal, her self, her body, the withheld life, was brutal too. While the Boy Scout as if he rode a runaway horse clung momently to her and arched himself off her back, dug his knees and fists into her and was flung back careening by his own tactics, she lay there. (ML, p. 146).[12]

Her "terrible mouth" a cruel metonymy for woman's genitals, Easter has come to represent woman's "dangerous" creative functioning, her "evil" power of generation: associations which characterize our culture's fear of female sexuality. Paradoxically, in losing her autonomy and becoming an object of masculine possession ("Keep away . . . " Loch insists), Easter herself becomes an object of dread. She is regarded as a source of power which is overtly feared because it is overly mystified. From a feminist perspective it is clear that Easter frightens not simply her fellow campers, but the patriarchy itself (which is, in fact, inscribed within the campers). She is feared because her real and human power—which will come to maturity as she comes of age—carries with it a capacity for rebellion against that law which has been unable, before puberty, to define her. As she passes puberty and approaches a realization of her own forbidden adult identity, woman necessarily represents a revolutionary capacity for self-creation and self-naming, for raising ideas or children who are made in her own image. Woman's sexuality, then, is fetishized in Welty's story as it is in her society, in its most malignant and destructive form. Figuring death for her society, woman is made into a "figure" of death, an icon, a unit of discourse which effectively reinscribes and represses the creative and revolutionary power it contains.

Ironically, it is the young girls themselves who seem—quite spontaneously—to discover this dread of Easter's body. "The Boy Scout crushed in her body and blood came out of her mouth. For them all, it was like being spoken to. 'Nina, you! Come stand right here in my skirt,' Miss Lizzie called. Nina went and stood under the big bosom that started down, at the neck of her dress, like a big cloven white hide."[13] The barely veiled reference to menstrual blood as something frightening and unmentionable, as something which is finally deforming (note, for example, the peculiar description of Miss Lizzie's adult anatomy), is emphasized in Miss Lizzie's "maternal" reaction— but before the children can voice their reaction they are returned to the silence of the womb, enfolded in Miss Lizzie's skirt. This fear of Easter has been pre-inscribed; it does not emerge with the force of a new idea, but with the evidence of an old one. While Loch Morrison's masculine "ordeal"—a week on Moon Lake with girls—becomes a fairly painless source of initiation upward into the world of male power, Easter's ordeal is an initiation downward—into the nether world of feminine sexuality as it has been patriarchally inscribed and maligned. Unfortunately, this ordeal is a representative initiation. " 'I know another Moon Lake,' one girl had said yesterday. 'Oh, my child, Moon Lakes are all over the world,' Mrs. Gruenwald had interrupted. 'I know of one in Austria. . . . ' And into each fell a girl, they dared, now, to think" (ML, p. 154).

Easter, then, is paradoxically true to both her names. Christened "Esther," the powerful queen of the Jews (a people who are, nevertheless, historically defined through their "otherness"), she renames herself "Easter," exercising the masculine prerogative to name or figure herself within the central cultural tradition. But this power redounds upon her; she not only loses Esther's capacities for active leadership, she becomes a parodically feminine version of the masculine Christ. Spread out on the communal picnic table, Easter is unable, despite the former power of her tomboy dignity, to save either herself or the young girls who look up to her. Brought to life by Loch Morrison, she is resurrected into a state of helpless passivity: "Easter lifted one arm and shaded her eyes, but the arm fell in her lap like a clod . . . 'Carry me.' Easter's words had no inflection. Again, 'Carry me.' She held out her arms to them, stupidly" (ML, p. 153). Her hands, which have been so dextrous and nimble, grow passive, heavy with the weight of earth itself, and, as the story draws to a close, we are given a final glimpse of Easter entombed in the close space of her tent: "Easter slept; Twosie watched her" (ML, p. 155). Sexually crucified, Easter becomes a symbol for woman's otherness as sexual object.

But if "Moon Lake" reiterates the sexual mythology of patriarchal culture, how does Welty escape the charge of complicity with this culture? Though Welty asks her readers to witness and to mourn the disempowerment of woman within phallocentric society, she also seems to accept the necessity of such disempowerment. Miss Lizzie Stark, Jinny Love's mother, does punctuate the rhythms of resuscitation with her militant asseverations: "But what's he doing to her? Stop that . . . He ought to be put out of business" (ML, pp. 146–47). But to stop would also be to put an end to Easter's life. Welty has created the cruelest possible entry into the world of sexuality for her characters; she has created a situation requiring protest that admits no protestation, for to rebel against Loch's ministrations would be to rebel against life itself. And yet the images describing Easter grow more leprous and impersonal as the story continues: "they took in sharply for memory's sake that berated figure, the mask formed and set on the face, one hand displayed, one jealously clawed under the waist, as if a secret handful had been groveled for, the spread and spotted legs. It was a betrayed figure . . . " (ML, p. 152). The images move toward a definition of woman which is more terrifying than mere subordination should require.

Is "Moon Lake," then, not only an exploration, but a grudging affirmation of those collective neuroses which result in woman's subordination? But we have examined neither the end of Welty's story nor her exploration of the collective and personal patterns of preadolescent sexuality which these young girls enjoy before their stories are disrupted by the dominant sex/gender system. Before examining these patterns, however, we should note that Welty's style— especially her hyperbolic use of phallic imagery—can serve as one index of her story's meaning. Just as the power of the phallus is portrayed as a disruption of feminine power or energy, so the very stylization of phallic imagery in Welty's story disrupts an easy affirmation of the patriarchal code. The world she has created is one of such plurality, of so many menacing, if symbolic, penises, that a word like "phallocentrism" loses its descriptive power. Welty's intent in overinscribing the phallus as referent is comically serious, as if to make us aware that culture's preoccupation with the phallus to the exclusion of other symbolic matrices is not simply comic or tragic, but fetishistic and reductive. Hyperbole, then, becomes a method of mimesis and de-centering. The phallus is revealed as a fantasy object, a cultural construct which is textually as well as socially intrusive. It is only "intrusive" however, insofar as these children possess another way of organizing and exploring their sexuality.

Over against the power that the dominant sex/gender system possesses to inscribe these children's lives, Welty gives us a counterplot—a description of the ways in which these children have a creative power over their own erotic energies. Immersed in her private world, each girl possesses a sexual orientation that is self-structured and self-sufficient: a sexuality which does not exclude the possibility of otherness, but which does not include intimations of self-violation or of brutality.

Nina stood and bent over from the waist. Calmly, she held her cup in the spring and watched it fill. They could all see how it spangled like a cold star in the curling water. The water tasted the silver cool of the rim it went over running to her lips, and at moments the cup gave her teeth a pang. Nina heard her own throat swallowing. She paused and threw a smile about her. After she had drunk she wiped the cup on her tie and collapsed it, and put the little top on, and its ring over her finger. With that, Easter, one arm tilted, charged against the green bank and mounted it. Nina felt her surveying the spring and all from above Jinny Love was down drinking like a chicken, kissing the water only. (ML, p. 118).

Nina's spring worship is described with beautifully detailed realism, and yet the cup has obvious symbolic properties. Filling with the capacity of the female genitals, collapsing at the end of its usefulness like the male genitals, the sensation it gives the drinker is erotic and disturbing at the same time. Nina's embarrassed imaginings of her own audible sensations, her flirtatious and reassuring smile to her companions, fill the margins of this "collapsible" version of the erotic plot, which ends with Nina closing the cup and putting its ring over her finger. Both a parody and a prefiguration of the marriage rite, the gesture signifies Nina's ease and innocence of self-gratification. While it could be argued that this is the beginning of woman's end—of an acquiescence to materialism (later the girls gamble for the cup) and a male-defined eroticism (the water *is* the locus of sexual loss in this story), such a reading would ignore Welty's affectionate and temperate tone. The cup is not a symbol of feminine receptivity, but of childlike androgyny prefiguring a possible adult androgyny. Nina possesses, in miniature, a complete cycle of sexual fulfillment all her own. Nor is this cycle subsumed by a fetish. Nina is no more concerned with the loss of the cup when Jinny Love Stark loses it to Easter in a game of mumblety-peg, than Easter is with the gaining of it. The universe, even for civilized children, is a source of endless and simple erotic pleasures. It is only with the advent of social maturity, of the sex/gender system imposed on older children by a patriarchal culture, that this pleasure is brought to its unnatural end.

Easter's role in this scene seems, on the other hand, more aggressive and precarious than Nina's. Her playful jousting up the green bank could be seen as a measure of how far she must, eventually, fall. But the inevitability of such a fall is neither a function of Easter's spontaneity nor her will-to-power, but of our society's gender-bound concept of the nature of social transgression. Easter's "sin" consists in her energy and self-completeness. She possesses the attributes of male and female, god and goddess, knight and lady: "The color in Easter's eyes could have been found somewhere, away—away under lost leaves—strange as the painted color of the ants. Instead of round black holes in the center of her eyes, there might have been women's heads, ancient" (ML, p. 120). Because Easter possesses this odd and archaic power of mutability, her dominance does not come from her aggression, but from her self-sufficiency. "Easter was dominant among the orphans. It was not that she was so bad. The one called Geneva stole, for example, but Easter was dominant for what she was in herself—for the way she held still, sometimes" (ML, p. 118).

It is the narrator's awareness of the children's spontaneity and autonomy that sets the stage for the second scene of the counterplot in "Moon Lake," a scene which invokes both male and female principles and allows the female principle to preside. Several nights after Nina and Jinny Love and Easter fail in their attempt to steal the boat, "the campers built a fire up above the spring . . . and poured a last song into the woods—'Little Sir Echo.' " Summer camp is almost over and so, perhaps, is girlhood. "The fire was put out and there was no bright point to look into, no circle. The presence of night was beside them—a beast

in gossamer, with no shine of outline, only of ornament—rings, ear rings. . . . ''
It is within this dark and plural world that the children ''worm'' into their tents
''which were hot as cloth pockets,'' and Miss Moody rubs them all with ''Sweet
Dreams''—''pulling to her girls all just alike, as if girlhood itself were not an
infinity, but a commodity'' (ML, pp. 135–37). Half aware of this perilous
economy in which women are exchanged and interchangeable, Nina Carmichael
wakes in the night and finds herself imagining an alternate story:

> The orphan! she thought, exultantly. The other way to live. There were secret ways. She
> thought, Time's really short, I've been only thinking like the others. It's only interesting,
> only worthy, to try for the fiercest secrets. To slip into them all—to change. To change
> for a moment into Gertrude, into Mrs. Gruenwald, into Twosie—into a boy. To *have
> been* an orphan. (ML, pp. 138–39).

The fantasy of self-transformation (though still within economic limits), of playing roles which deepen and multiply the options available to the self and permit
a knowledge of otherness: this is Nina's dream; her burden consists of an inability
to achieve the freedom from culture and gender which she is able to imagine.
But her fantasy, as it continues, offers some measure of an alternative story in
which woman might possess her own power, her own ''fiercest secrets'' in the
midst of her debate with man. ''Nina sat up on the cot and stared passionately
before her at the night—the pale dark roaring night with its secret step, the
Indian night. She felt the forehead, the beaded stars, look in thoughtfully at
her'' (ML, p. 139). Initially night has the capacity to translate Nina's own power
of gazing, her own private and libidinal subjectivity, into the opposite sense of
being gazed upon, of becoming someone else's object. (As Lacan says in *The
Four Fundamental Concepts of Psycho-Analysis*: ''From the moment that this
gaze appears, the subject tries to adapt himself to it . . . he becomes that punc-
tiform object.'')[14] But as Nina redirects her imagination toward Easter, her sense
of becoming an object is momentarily disrupted. The ominous play of forces
begins to change into a more beneficent drama:

> The pondering night stood rude at the tent door, the opening fold would let it stoop in—
> it, him—he had risen up inside. Long-armed, or long-winged, he stood in the center
> there where the pole went up. Nina lay back, drawn quietly from him. But the night
> knew about Easter. All about her. Geneva had pushed her to the very edge of the cot.
> Easter's hand hung down, opened outward. Come here, night, Easter might say, tender
> to a giant, to such a dark thing. And the night, obedient and graceful, would kneel to
> her. Easter's calloused hand hung open there to the night that had got wholly into the
> tent. (ML, p. 139).

Night is now figured as a masculine power—a dark energy which enters the
feminine or ''opening fold'' of the tent and not only grows erect, but becomes
the center of what had before been imaged as pensively feminine space.
    If there is something ominously sexual not only in night's intrusion, but in

its initial gaze, this power is partially tamed. Nina sees Easter as someone who possesses, even as she approaches the borders of "otherness," a dimension of selfhood which is inviolate and unperturbed. It is, in fact, at this very edge of experience that the image of danger suddenly reverses itself as Easter seems to speak, her voice a simpler echo of Juliet's "Gallop apace" speech from Act III of *Romeo and Juliet*. Juliet, like Easter, addresses night:

> Come, civil night,
> Thou sober-suited matron all in black,
> And learn me how to lose a winning match.
> Played for a pair of stainless maidenhoods,
> Hood my unmanned blood, bating in my cheeks,
> With thy black mantle till strange love,
>   grown bold,
> Think true love acted simple modesty.
> Come, night; come, Romeo; come, thou day in night;
> For thou wilt lie upon the wings of night
> Whiter than new snow upon a raven's back.
> Come, gentle night; come, loving, black-browed night;
> Give me my Romeo; and, when he shall die,
> Take him and cut him out in little stars,
> And he will make the face of heaven so fine
> That all the world will be in love with night
> And pay no worship to the garish sun.[15]

Juliet, a child who is also on the verge of discovering an adult identity, embraces her newfound sexuality with confident sorrow. She sees that to enter the sexual world is to enter a world not only of ecstasy, but of dark sobriety in which woman must lose all she is and has in order to live by man's imperfect if celestial-seeming lights. Welty, however, has appropriated Juliet's speech to suit her own authorial purposes. While Shakespeare's night is, primarily, a feminine figure, a mother and widow who will educate Juliet in the "womanly" rituals of self-abnegation, the night that Welty describes is masculine, and Easter's speech is not only about desire, but about the need for personal and verbal power over this masculine "other" which threatens to redefine her humanity. Juliet's growing maturity is associated, then, with a capacity for self-abnegation which is disguised or "aestheticized" by the rhetoric of paradox. Finally, the simple imperative of Easter's speech contributes to our sense of her androgyny rather than her femininity (or "unmanned blood"): an androgynous identity which is further suggested by her "calloused" yet open hand. Easter's gesture seems to promise an initial solution to the trauma of difference: a trauma which is largely tamed through Easter's own plural fierceness and tenderness. "Come here night, Easter might say, tender to a giant, to such a dark thing, and the night, obedient and graceful, would kneel to her." Drawn toward Easter's strength, "night" is transformed simultaneously into a homonymic association and a character, night becoming "knight," a naively constructed but assimilable figure of thought as well as of speech. The counterplot, however, is now twice removed from the story's primary reality; it presents a fiction within another fiction. Can we still credit Nina's fantasy with any validity?

Almost immediately the dominant story which has begun to prepare us for woman's disempowerment reasserts itself; the counterplot seems to disappear.

Nina let her own arm stretch forward opposite Easter's. Her hand too opened, of itself. She lay there a long time motionless, under the night's gaze, its black cheek, looking immovably at her hand, the only part of her now which was not asleep. Its gesture was like Easter's, but Easter's hand slept and her own hand knew—shrank and knew, yet offered still.

"Instead . . . me instead. . . . "

In the cup of her hand, in her filling skin, in the fingers' bursting weight and stillness, Nina felt it: compassion and a kind of competing that were all one, a single ecstasy, a single longing. For the night loved some more than others, served some more than others. Nina's hand lay open there for a long time, as if its fingers would be its eyes. Then it too slept. She dreamed her hand was helpless to the tearing teeth of wild beasts. At reveille she woke up lying on it. She could not move it. She hit it and bit it until like a cluster of bees it stung back and came to life. (ML, p. 139).

Even Nina cannot transform the world by sleight of words. The transfigured image of the "cup" as source of pain, or the hand as a womb which is finally "helpless to the tearing teeth of wild beasts," moves us from the counterplot in which these children experience the power their own imaginations might have in transforming the dominant sex/gender system into something more harmonious with woman's needs, into a plot that is more ominous. And yet Nina, through her writing on the sand, her self-consciousness, and her imaginative seeing, represents the woman writer in embryo, and through her Welty begins to reveal the arbitrary and culturally inscribed nature of the phallic plot. Later in the story, worn out with the experience of Easter's figurative rape, Nina begins once more to imagine an alternate story: "Nina had spotted three little shells in the sand she wanted to pick up when she could. And suddenly this seemed to her one of those moments out of the future . . . this was far, far ahead of her—picking up the shells, one, another, another, without time moving any more, and Easter abandoned on a little edifice, beyond dying and beyond being remembered about" (ML, p. 151). Nina's desire to gather these tiny shells and to preserve them suggests a covert but insistent reaction to her friend's violation and a generalized wish for symbols which reflect her own anatomy. And yet, for all woman's capacity to construct gestures of self-preservation or to construct roles for themselves transcending those which have been socially defined, it is still the over-inscription of male sexuality which prevents the enactment of these alternate stories. It is therefore in the final section of "Moon Lake" that Welty finally deconstructs the very image of masculine power which has dominated her story and interrupted her heroine's plots.

The Boy Scout, little old Loch Morrison, was undressing in his tent for the whole world to see. He took his time wrenching off each garment; then he threw it to the floor as hard as he would throw a ball; yet that seemed, in him, meditative.

His candle—for that was all it was—jumping a little now, he stood there studying and touching his case of sunburn in a Kress mirror like theirs. He was naked and there was his little tickling thing hung on him like the last drop on the pitcher's lip. He ceased or exhausted study and came to the tent opening again and stood leaning on one raised arm with his weight on one foot—just looking out into the night, which was clamorous.

. . . Minnowy thing that matched his candle flame, naked as he was with that, he thought he shone forth too. Didn't he?

Nevertheless standing there with the tent slanting over him and his arm knobby as it reached up and his head bent a little, he looked rather at loose ends. (ML, pp. 155–56).

In a story which contains such vehement phallic imagery, this mimetic and metaphoric diminishment of the phallus can only come as a surprise. Why does Welty readjust her emphasis so abruptly? To understand her narrative strategies in greater detail we should return to the psychoanalytic strategies of Lacan. In his *Écrits* Lacan is careful to distingush between the male genitals as cultural symbol and as biological organ. The phallus, he explains, is a cultural construct, a symbol for something other than its physical analogue; specifically, for the transcendent power of the father. The penis, on the other hand, is a physical organ which is not the effective cause of the father's power, but is, rather, an object fetishized by culture as a symbol of man's power over nature, over himself, and over woman. As Sherry Turkle explains in *Psychoanalytic Politics: Freud's French Revolution*:

The infant does not just want to be cared for, touched and fed, but wants to actually complete the mother, to be what she lacks and can be presumed to want above all else: the phallus. In Lacan's work, the phallus does not stand for the penis itself. It stands for the infant's absolute and irreducible desire to be a part of the mother, to be what she most desires. . . .

. . . What Lacan has done is to translate repression into linguistic terms as a process of metaphor formation. One signifier (father's name) comes to substitute for another (desire for the mother and desire to be the object of her desire). Of course, what is being signified, the phallus, remains the same. But two important things have happened. The relationship between signifier and signified has been mediated: they are now more distanced from each other. And the old signifier (desire for the mother) and what it signifies are "pushed down" to a deeper level: they are now unconscious. The father's name now only signifies the phallus through a chain of signification that has an invisible link, the desire for the mother.[16]

Lacan asserts that the child's creation or realization of the phallic metaphor signals that child's necessary separation from the desire for the mother and his or her inevitable insertion into the "Symbolic," that realm of culture created and controlled by the father or name-of-the-Father.

But Lacan's account seems incomplete. It does not explain the desire which

Welty ascribes to her feminine characters, nor does it provide an account of Welty's own deconstruction of phallocentrism. We need, then, to make a series of discriminations. First, Lacan's ideas about the centrality of the phallus can be useful — but only insofar as his distinctions between the male genitals and their socially prescribed meaning permits this difference to become more socially legible. For Lacan to argue that phallocentrism is inevitable and that woman's repression is necessary for the maintenance of a lawful society is to reinscribe the very repression that Lacan himself has begun, in the act of naming, to deconstruct. If Lacan's ideas about our sexual construction are worth considering it is because they show us the directions that feminist demystifications must take.[17] As Evlyn Gould comments in her essay "The Enigma of Woman and the Enigmas She Creates: on Sarah Kofman's *L'Énigme de la femme*": "Why does psychoanalytic theory only create a series of enigmas which allow biological fact to corroborate social prejudice against women? The point is that ultimately psychoanalysis becomes as much the creating of enigmas as the solving of them."[18] It is fitting, then, that at the end of "Moon Lake" Eudora Welty begins to deconstruct the enigma of the phallus; man's power to control woman is neither a biological nor a beneficent cultural power. It is, instead, an ongoing or inscriptive power that is mystical only because it is self-perpetuating. As Gayle Rubin says in "The Traffic in Women": "The Organization of sex and gender once had functions other than itself—it organized society. Now, it only organizes and reproduces itself" (TW, p. 199). While Lacan's analysis is deliberately a-historical or synchronic, Rubin asks for an analysis that is diachronic as well: an analysis which will begin to account for woman's continued repression. The character of Jessie in Lois Gould's *A Sea-Change* begins to see the discontinuities between our most common words and ideas and the things they describe:

But look at the real one. Roy's is real. Feel it. Taste . . . Soft, vulnerable. Nothing like a gun, really. Nothing like the words. Buildings, guns, words. Blown up out of proportion so you forget how soft, how vulnerable. Think phallus is a monster, destroyer. See it in the movie ads. Long, black, loaded, aiming at you. Fire when ready. Always ready. They never show the real one—can't. You'd notice the actual size, softness, limited striking power. When they do want to show a real one, they find a monster. Shock of seeing it enlarges it in your mind. They count on that.[19]

Like the makers of movie ads Welty avoids showing "the real one" until the moment its appearance will have maximum effect: "little tickling thing [that] hung on him like the last drop on the pitcher's lip . . . Minnowy thing that matched his candle flame. . . . " Welty removes the phallus from the overinscribed realm of patriarchal myth; she undoes the power of the phallic environment which has menaced these children with an extra-erotic intent. And yet Easter's death, her rebirth into a passive and feminine life, is hardly a myth. The power of sexual patriarchy, Welty tells us, is all too real, but its putative source, its central and symbolic instrument of feminine disempowerment, is a cultural delusion, a sham. Phallic power emanates, as Welty demonstrates in "Moon Lake," from the cultural enshrinement of a biological apparatus. The phallus must be seen, finally, as a dangling signifier, a "minnowy thing," a peevish light which is attached loosely and vulnerably to the male body and cannot be described in terms of itself, but only through the unstable mediations of metaphor.

NOTES

1. The phrase "sex/gender system" is derived from Gayle Rubin's essay "The Traffic in Women," in *Toward an Anthropology of Women*, ed. Rayna R. Reiter (New York: Monthly Review Press, 1975), pp. 157–69. As Rubin explains, "A 'sex/gender system' is the set of arrangements by which a society transforms biological sexuality into products of human activity, and in which these transformed needs are satisfied" (p 159). "Other names have been proposed for the sex/gender system. The most common alternatives are 'mode of reproduction' and 'patriarchy.' It may be foolish to quibble about terms, but both of these can lead to confusion. All three proposals have been made in order to introduce a distinction between 'economic' systems and 'sexual' systems, and to indicate that sexual systems have a certain autonomy . . . a sex/gender system is not simply the reproductive moment of a 'mode of production.' The formation of gender identity is an example of production in the realm of the sexual system" (p. 167). Throughout the rest of this essay I will use the term "patriarchy" primarily as a term which also refers to sexism or to a sexual system dominated by male rather than female interests. All further references to Rubin's essay will be cited parenthetically in the text as TW.

2. See Jacques Lacan, *Écrits: A Selection*, trans. Alan Sheridan (New York: Norton, 1977), especially "The Signification of the Phallus." See also Fredric Jameson, "Imaginary and Symbolic in Lacan: Marxism, Psychoanalytic Criticism, and the Problem of the Subject," in *Literature and Psychoanalysis / The Question of Reading: Otherwise*, ed. Shoshana Felman, No. 55/56.

3. Herman Melville, *Moby-Dick or The Whale*, ed. Charles Feidelson, Jr. (New York: Bobbs-Merrill, 1964), p. 50. All further references to *Moby-Dick* will be cited parenthetically in the text as M-D.

4. For a similar point of view see Regis Durand, " 'The Captive King': The Absent Father in Melville's Text" in *The Fictional Father: Lacanian Readings of the Text*, ed. Robert Con Davis (Amherst: University of Massachusetts Press, 1981). Durand's analysis of the figure of the absent father as part of an endless and empty signifying chain is excellent. He ignores, however, the ways in which—in chapters like "The Grand Armada"—the loss of generative vision is associated with the phallic intrusions of the quest. Melville does imagine the symbol of the whale line to have, at least, a double function. It is both a signifier of death and a substitution for the umbilical cord which might attach the whalers to the mother they seek to recover and to repress. This paradigm is partially developed in Melville's chapter on "The Monkey-rope" and in the recurring image of the coffin which becomes the orphan's cradle. While the obsession with paternity subsumes a majority of Melville's themes and metaphors, as Durand says, still, maternal discourse is not entirely repressed. It does not serve as a corrective in Melville's text, but rather as a reminder of that which, like the image of the father, remains unresolved.

5. Eudora Welty, "Moon Lake," in *The Golden Apples* (New York: Harcourt, 1947). All further references to "Moon Lake" will be cited parenthetically in the text as ML.

6. The critics who have written about "Moon Lake" also seem oblivious to the gender-defined drama that Welty develops in this story. In *Eudora Welty's Achievement of Order* (Baton Rouge: Louisiana State University Press, 1980), Michael Kreyling focuses on the difference between Nina Carmichael's "overloaded" consciousness and her friend Easter's "unreflective power and mystery." "Nina's stalemate is not happy; like Cassie, she is sharply aware of her own incompleteness. The impenetrable wall between her sense of herself and her sense of fulfillment remains. She has tried to answer the summons addressed to the unified self, body and heart, but too often she finds in herself a second presence, the one that thinks and paralyzes her instinctive self by watching it" (p. 91). We will see that Nina's "Paralysis" and incompleteness are the result of the sex/gender system she inhabits and that her intense consciousness is the only thing that will save her, since it represents an incipient awareness of the need to reform or to rebel against this self-alienating system. Kreyling's desire to analyze "the impression of unity" that emerges when (as he says) he reads Welty, creates an overtly moral tone in his book and a covert disapprobation of the moments of self-division or textual fragmentation that occur so frequently in Welty's texts. In *The Faraway Country: Writers of the Modern South* (Seattle: University of Washington Press, 1963), Louis Rubin emphasizes the "intensity and heroism" that presages Loch's "coming estrangement from Morgana" (p. 148). While Loch's determination and persistence in diving for and resuscitating Easter are noble, to focus on this aspect of his behavior is to ignore the disturbing tone and darkening imagery which Welty uses to describe his actions. Rubin's analysis of Welty generally comes closer to the mark than King's (see especially his analysis of Virgie Rainey and "The Wanderers," pp 143f). Still, his evaluation of Welty's style helps him to miss the sexual aspects of her plot and the gender-specific nature of her themes: "The most startling quality of Eudora Welty's art is her style: shimmering, hovering, elusive, fanciful, fastening on little things. Entirely feminine . . . " (p. 133).

7. William Wordsworth, *Selected Poems and Prefaces*, ed. Jack Stillinger (Boston: Houghton Mifflin, 1965), *The Prelude*, I, 381–85.

8. Notice the importance of names throughout this story as an index of character (Jinny Love Stark, Mrs. Gruenwald). Only Loch Morrison has accumulated names which are linked not only to gender, but to a social capacity for self-transcendence ("Boy Scout," "Life Saver").

9. I would like to suggest that "Moon Lake" is designed as a "masculine" force in this story because it is associated with the simultaneous onset of menses and the social trauma associated with maturity which women feel helpless to change. Easter's solution (until she is pushed in by Exum, who "constantly moved along an even further fringe of landscape than Loch, wearing the man's stiff straw hat . . . " [ML, p. 140]) is to stay *out* of the water. ("Easter was through drinking—wiping her mouth and flinging her hand as if to break the bones, to get rid of the drops . . . "[ML, p. 118].)

10. In *Eudora Walty's Achievement of Order*, Kreyling's insistence that Easter is one of "King MacLain's children," that she is an unconscious and happy child of Morgana's spiritual patrilineage, seems very strange, considering the extent of her suffering and victimization in the final third of the story. Kreyling's claim for Easter is that, unlike Nina, she is not self-divided: "The essence of Easter's King-like charm is its freedom from such reflective thought. Easter, like all King's progeny, does not stand outside of herself or see herself in two times, being and having been" (p. 90). "The children of

King possess the gift of living in a present moment unencumbered by any past or future time. . . . The word that King prophesies to Morgana is that time is not a gauntlet but a splendid moment, a 'shower of gold' that transforms those willing to stand in it'' (p. 91). But Easter's story does not end in an escape from time nor in a "shower of gold." Welty's earlier allusion to Danae's story must be regarded in the light of Easter's accumulating deformities:

The Boy Scout, nodding, took Easter's hair and turned her head. He left her face looking at them. Her eyes were neither open nor altogether shut but as if her ears heard a great noise, back from the time she fell; the whites showed under the lids pale and slick as watermelon seeds. Her lips were parted to the same degree; her teeth could be seen smeared with black mud. (ML, p. 145).

11. Oddly, Kreyling, in *Eudora Welty's Achievement of Order*, defines Easter's plunge into Moon Lake as "the adventure that Nina must only watch." This plunge is defined as "the orphan's renewed claim to mystery. No one can follow her to the bottom" (p. 90). If "Moon Lake" has any moral it is that all of these young women must "take the plunge" and endure the sense of deformity, of victimization, and of otherness that Easter endures. Critics who define rape as a "renewed claim to mystery" should examine both their sexual politics and their techniques of close reading.

12. In this passage two struggles occur simultaneously. On a realistic level Loch Morrison is struggling to save Easter's life while she continues to drown. On a symbolic level, however, "the Boy Scout" is trying to tame Easter's spirit into quiescence and "fertility." Easter's "brutality" is a measure of her continuing resistence to this plot; the image of the "runaway horse" signifies both her fighting spirit and her gradual regression.

13. Although Kreyling quotes these lines he does not gloss them; he once again ignores the story's obvious sexual implications.

14. Jacques Lacan, *The Four Fundamental Concepts of Psycho-Analysis*, trans. Alan Sheridan (New York: Norton, 1977), p. 83.

15. William Shakespeare, *Romeo and Juliet*, ed. J. A. Bryant, Jr. (New York: Signet, 1964), III.ii 10–25.

16. Sherry Turkle, *Psychoanalytic Politics: Freud's French Revolution* (Cambridge, Mass.: MIT Press, 1981), pp. 55–56.

17. See Ann Rosalind Jones, "Writing the Body: Toward an Understanding of *L'Écriture féminine*," in *Feminist Studies*, 7 (Summer 1981), 247–61, for a feminist account of this problem, and Fredric Jameson "Imaginary and Symbolic in Lacan" in *Literature and Psychoanalysis*, ed. Shoshana Felman, No. 55/56, 338–95, for a Marxist analysis.

18. Evlyn Gould, "On Sarah Kofman's *L'Énigme de la femme*," in *Discourse*, 4 (Winter 1981/82), p. 33.

19. Lois Gould, *A Sea-Change* (New York: Simon and Schuster, 1976), pp. 28–29.

30

An End to Torment: H.D.'s Metonymic Course

Paul Smith

In April 1958, attended by much indignation and sentiment and amid much debate about the moral connections between poetry and politics, Ezra Pound, perhaps the most important patriarchal influence on the whole of twentieth-century poetry, was released from his home of fourteen years—St. Elizabeths Hospital for the criminally insane. His case merited extensive public airing and caused great perturbation, not least for H.D., a lifelong contact, colleague and sometime fiancée. She was at this time at Küsnacht in Switzerland recovering from a debilitating accident. At the instigation of two men, Erich Heydt and Norman Holmes Pearson, she employed some of her time in the sanatorium writing a personal memoir of Pound. This memoir was called *End to Torment*, taking its name from a phrase Pearson used to describe Pound's release. The phrase might be regarded as no more than an ironic reflection on Pound's situation; indeed, Pound himself thought the phrase "optimistic."[1] But for H.D. it was more pertinent. For many years she had resisted the urge to write about Pound because of the pain that her memories caused her; her torment resided in her repression of such memories, and the end to torment resides in the process of exorcising them by writing them down. It is in this writing-down that H.D. presents an exploration that seems to me almost emblematically to represent a typical female struggle in the poetic writing of this century.

End to Torment is concerned to tackle squarely the wound that patriarchal influences inflict upon the female experience. It deals not only with the lasting personal pain (caused by Pound's abandoning H.D. and breaking off their adolescent engagement) but deals too with the lasting mark that Pound made upon H.D.'s literary production. That mark, made in 1912 in the tea-room of the British Museum, consists in the very sigil H.D., a sigil given to Hilda Doolittle by her poetic father, slashed by "his creative pencil" (*ETT*, p. 40) across her poetry which he was editing for publication. H.D. there becomes marked by the male, given a name that delimits her as the discovery of the male and brands her as his invention. Given this original, almost paternal naming, it is hardly surprising that from then on H.D. felt constrained by Pound's shadow and was forced to recognize that "consciously or unconsciously, it seems that we have been bound with him, bound up with him and his fate." (ETT, p. 37) The 'we' of that remark might refer, not only to H.D. and her friends and colleagues or to anyone concerned with the condition of poetic writing in the twentieth century, but more specifically to woman, adjectivised and conditioned, bound with 'Him' and 'His fate.'

So writing about Pound is, for H.D., an attempt to explicate a connectedness that is also a bind: she, as woman, is bound by the prescriptions of Pound who represents the patriarchal hold on poetic creativity. She tries to reproduce that sense of connectedness almost in rivalry with Pound's Cantos which offer her a technique in that they "weave over and back." (ETT, p. 29) H.D.'s own weaving in End to Torment begins with the memory of Pound's face and his fiery red hair. That fiery head is set off by the "snow on his beard" and the coldness emanating from his "pebble-green" eyes. (ETT, p. 3) A polarity of fire and cold is thus established immediately, instituted on Pound's very body. This polarity presides over the memoir in a variety of forms; continually, the passion and the "perfection of the fiery moment" (ETT, p. 11) is contrasted to the cold "rigor mortis," (ETT, p. 3) the frozen sensation that had been inserted into H.D.'s experience by Pound's actual and metaphorical gaze. The structure of the memoir depends upon the slow proliferation of words and images that will attach to that basic polarity and thicken it, but without ever proposing any exact limits for its meaning. The cold appears in H.D.'s associations with her father, or in the freezing experience of being spied upon by prurient schoolfriends, or with the death of the androgynous being in Balzac's Seraphita, even in the fact that on March 9, 1958, it was "too bitter cold to go out." And on the other hand there is the fire, in the blazing head of H.D.'s fantasized son glimpsed at a station, in the virtuosity of the explosive pianist Van Cliburn, in a book shared by Pound and H.D. in the early days—May Sinclair's The Divine Fire. And these qualities stand as an antithetical pair: for example, remembering a 1913 meeting with Pound in Venice, H.D. remarks on the oppressive heat outside, contrasted with the church of Santa Maria dei Miracoli which is "cool, with a balcony of icy mermaids." (ETT, p. 6) Generally, this cold seems to be attached to a state of enfeebled and dominated femininity and to the notion of death, whereas fire is capable of unfreezing and giving access to passion, fulfillment and creativity.

It is clearly such a fire that H.D. craved—not only in her work but in her personal life. Pearson says a lot about her when he stresses that she "always reached out in an almost hungry fashion for friendships,"[2] often seeing them as routes to creativity. Pound, of course, acted for her as a crucial contact with the world of creative power. End to Torment can be seen as the working-out of this unanswered desire, as an almost bemused investigation of the apparent impossibility of being reinstated in the "perfection of the fiery moment" that the teenage affair with Pound represented. That impossibility is formally set into the very process of its discovery: If H.D.'s torment resides in an unrealized desire, the writing of it is both situated by that desire and surpasses it.

On one level it would be easy to regard the memoir as the equivalent of the final embrace given to the exhausted and beaten Peer Gynt by Solveig after she has waited "spinning and weaving" (*ETT*, p. 20) for the return of her lover, for her end to torment. But H.D.'s *End to Torment* is not simply the passive, consolatory gesture of a waiting and faithful mother-wife, nor is it the secure resting place for an errant son-lover. H.D.'s enterprise is rather more active: she establishes herself as less the object of the male hero's quest, and rather more as the seeker herself.[3] Pound, in fact, might function here as the very object of H.D.'s "lifelong Isis search": (*ETT*, p. 32) he is the dismembered lover whose limbs must be re-collected and laid to rest. H.D.'s Isis search is, by analogy, an *assemblage* in much the same way as the structure of her writing is an assemblage or the active forging of metonymic links that are a binding together but not a bondage.

The element of bringing together that H.D. takes pleasure in so often is perhaps best illustrated in her straightforward assertion that "To recall Ezra is to recall my father" (*ETT*, p. 48). This is an example of her tendency to conflate real people and to allow any given person a number of symbolic representations. She herself is referred to in *End to Torment* under many different guises— Penelope, Solveig, satyr, dryad, Lady Loba of the Pierre Vidal legend, Isis, Athene and so on. The multi-identification of real male figures seems to involve Erich Heydt, her doctor at Küsnacht and whose insistence helped H.D. produce the memoir. In a telling incident Heydt is seen pressing H.D. to tell him another of her memories, despite her fear of their being seen "huddled on a bench together," hand in hand. Her fear here is related not only to her memory of "myself and Ezra, standing before my father, caught 'in the very act' " of their "*demi-vierge* embraces," (*ETT*, p. 18/19) but it also heralds the appearance of "A small male child with short red-gold curls" (*ETT*, p. 21) who is the offspring that she continually fantasizes about, the symbol as it were of the lover's re-constituted body.

This whole sense of the conflation and connection of personalities and roles is reinforced if we consider Heydt's continual probing of H.D.'s memory. His insistence is reminiscent of nothing so much as the psychoanalytical intervention, and so calls to mind H.D.'s earlier book *Tribute to Freud*: indeed, Michael King's foreword to *End to Torment* views the latter "as a personal sequel" to the former. (*ETT*, p. x) This is perhaps because Freud became for H.D. a sort of ideal father representing the phallic power that she herself did not possess; and H.D.'s stance toward Pound in *End to Torment* is of a similar kind. In that earlier text H.D. tells of Freud's flaunting before her a figure of Pallas Athene, "perfect . . . *only she has lost her spear*." Athene and Greece (Hellas) are important identificatory symbols for the whole of H.D.'s work; Freud "knew that I loved Hellas" and that Athene and her winged attribute Nike (victory) represented for H.D. the possible overcoming of obstacles.[4] What Freud seemed not to know, of course, in his eagerness to point out H.D.'s *Penisneid*, was the extent to which his phallocentric propositions formed a crucial part of those obstacles for H.D.

On one level, of course, it might be easy to recognize the symptoms of *Penisneid* in many places in H.D.'s work. Her continual fantasies about a son, "a small yet sturdy male object," (*ETT*, p. 33) complete with a fiery head of Poundian hair, are significant in the light of H.D.'s determination that "If I was not the Child, as I obviously was not (as a child), I would have the Child." (*ETT*, p. 51) Denied closeness as a child to her mother (because of her brother's superior ability to act as the phallus for the mother's desire), the little girl— according to Freudian thinking—would turn to her father. After all "there are things, not altogether negligible to be said for him."[5] The girl experiences the unconscious desire to encompass the father's phallus and keep it inside her body, as the Child. This movement mimed in H.D.'s reflections, seems to corroborate Freud's notion that unconsciously the woman slips "along the lines of a symbolic equation—from the penis to the baby."[6] And there are many other registering marks of penis envy in H.D.'s writing, and each such registration is a moment of coldness for H.D., or a moment of confusion and terror. For example, she alludes to the "terror one cannot speak of" that she attaches to the prospect of having an X-ray performed on her broken limbs: (*ETT*, p. 7) not only is the X-ray the epitome of the male's searching gaze, capable of revealing the most secret defects of her anatomy, but 'X-ray' is also how the young Ezra Pound used to sign his letters.[7]

Everywhere that such penis envy appears in H.D.'s writing it marks the state of enfeebled or deficient femininity from which release must be sought; feminine victory would consist in overcoming the obstacle that the whole notion of penis envy constitutes. Thus it is that H.D. can begin to work toward a resistance to masculine entrapment of the female, confronting the "pounding, (Pounding)" (*ETT*, p. 8) of male power.

This is the fundamental tension in H.D.'s writing. While the mark of female subjugation is registered, it is also explored and resisted. Even in that original mark of Hilda Doolittle's powerlessness, the sigil H.D., there is a resistance. Far from simply registering a truncation or a castration, the siglum might also be reminiscent of the active goddess Isis who wears the Hieroglyph of her name above her head as an emblem of her own peculiar and mysterious power; it is precisely such a hieroglyph, an "undecipherable script"[8] that H.D. proposes must be *read* by women writers. A specifically feminine power must be arrived at. The question, of course remains: in what does such a feminine victory consist?

I think an important clue can be gleaned from *Tribute to Freud*. There a certain victory emerges from a transmutation of a masculine name. Sigmund Freud's name is played upon so that it becomes a cipher of victorious language; *Sieg* (victory) and *Mund* (mouth).[9] That disruption of Freud's name acts first to dispel the legal identity of the male subject. The masculine name is *metonymised* and led into the very area of connectedness and play that constitutes the locus of all of H.D.'s nominal transformations. The disruption of fixed and entire identity is crucial to, for example, H.D.'s novel *Palimpsest* with its overlaying of very many female names and characters, all connected; or central to a work like *Helen in Egypt* with its rapid and ceaseless metamorphoses of Helen herself. So, for another example, when H.D. writes in *Trilogy*, "I am Mary . . . ," it is precisely the solidity, the legal fixity, of the 'I am' that is undermined. Mary Magdalene becomes a metonymic exploration of her own name: "Magdala is a tower . . . Mary shall be myrrh . . . will weep bitterly (*mara*)" and so on.[10]

I have argued elsewhere that patriarchal literature, as epitomized for me in the work of Ezra Pound, is constituted fundamentally upon the postulation and defense of a fixed, legalistic identity in the male, and that the linguistic mode specific to that foundation is metaphor.[11] Against this, and in an explicit resistance to masculine power generally and to Pound's creative power in particular, H.D. offers another course—a metonymic course. This is a writing that does not attempt to emulate the traditional metaphoric procedures of male writing, but one that veers off into the other of those two fundamental poles of language. H.D. takes us into the realm of metonymy which, as Lacan suggests, is the realm of desire itself, unfettered. Her writing aims toward "a rhythm as yet unheard,"[12] a writing that is expansive like "the spread of wings"[13]—Nike's wings, perhaps. But, most importantly I think, in its embracing of "oneness lost" it *enacts* a radical disruption of the notion of identity that supports patriarchal systems of exchange.

It is here that I find the most compelling aspect of H.D.'s writing as a feminist. Instead of trying to establish a kind of rivalrous identity with which to confront the male (which would be, as Irigaray says, to dream grammatically an inversion, merely, of current systems), H.D. attempts to metonymically unfold a series of overlapping and unfixed identities that respond to her desire. Hers is an attempt to exorcize the identical spectre of the whole and wholesome fixity that underlies patriarchy, just as in *End to Torment* she exorcizes the threatening spectre of Ezra Pound, allowing him to leave and never be reconstituted. Happily enough, it is after the writing of *End to Torment* that H.D. can reflesh and re-empower the mutilated sigil that Pound bequeathed her: H.D. becomes *Hermetic Definition*, perhaps her most powerful work. And at the time of writing H.D. confides to a friend that "I can't think that I *must* be Pound-Eliot in my writing."[14] The metaphorical lures and laws of male identity and of identifying with the male are cast aside in favor of a new and metonymic definition.

NOTES

1. *End to Torment* (New York: New Directions, 1979), p. xi. All further references to this work will be by *ETT* plus page number in the text.

2. N. H. Pearson, "H.D.: An Interview," *Contemporary Literature*, vol. 10, no. 4, p. 436.

3. This is the gist of Susan Friedman's argument in *Psyche Reborn*, Bloomington: Indiana University Press, 1981.

4. *Tribute to Freud* (Oxford: Oxford University Press, 1971), p. 74.

5. *Tribute to Freud*, p. 40.

6. Freud, *Standard Edition*, vol. 19, p. 179.

7. See Noel Stock, *The Life of Ezra Pound* (London: Routledge & Kegan Paul, 1974), p. 11/12.

8. *Helen in Egypt* (New York: Grove Press, 1961), p. 86.

9. *Tribute to Freud*, p. 110.

10. *Trilogy*, Cheadle, Cheshire, 1974, p. 135.

11. See my *Pound Revised* (London: Croom Helm, 1983), which also includes a chapter on H.D.'s post-imagist poetry. The present article constitutes in part a critical reflection on what I said in that chapter. An article which draws on both pieces of work will appear in *Women's Studies* under the title, "The Signature of H.D.'s Feminism."

12. *Helen in Egypt*, p. 229.

13. Ibid., p. 24.

14. *Hermetic Definition* (Oxford: Oxford University Press, 1972), introduction (no pagination).

31

Leslie Stephen Revisited: A New Fragment of Virginia Woolf's "A Sketch of the Past"

Katherine C. Hill-Miller

Leslie Stephen has become a hot issue in Virginia Woolf criticism. As the first influential man in Virginia Woolf's life, he has been variously described as squelching her genius because she was only a girl, nurturing her genius because she was his favorite daughter, and ignoring her because he had his own interests to pursue. Whichever of these versions comes closest to the truth, one thing is certain about Virginia Woolf's feelings for her gifted father: complicated and powerful, they troubled and consoled her until the end of her life. The discovery of a new fragment of "A Sketch of the Past" makes the complexity and high pitch of her feelings yet more apparent. With the exception of *To the Lighthouse*, this new fragment, which analyzes Leslie Stephen and Virginia's relation to him, is more sustained and eloquent than any other piece Virginia Woolf wrote about her father.

The new fragment is 77 pages long, and was written at intervals from 19 June, 1940, until 15 November, 1940. The first fourteen pages discuss Leslie Stephen exclusively. The next thirteen pages paint a portrait of the Stephen home at 22 Hyde Park Gate and describe Virginia's room. The remaining fifty pages are very similar to the text of "A Sketch of the Past" as it appears in Jeanne Schulkind's edition of *Moments of Being*.[1] While Jeanne Schulkind and the Hogarth Press have known about the existence of this typescript for about two years, the fragment was a part of the property of Mrs. Trekkie Parsons, and was sold at auction at Sotheby's in July of 1981. It will be published in a new and expanded edition of *Moments of Being* at some point in the future.

The most striking feature of the new fragment is the Leslie Stephen who emerges: a Leslie Stephen who is more human and complex than he is in Woolf's other essays about him. Her 1904 memoir, conceived as a tribute in F. W. Maitland's commemorative biography of Sir Leslie, was designed for public consumption. It does little more than portray a Leslie Stephen who reads books to his children and shares with them his ideas about literary masterpieces. The Stephen of the fragment is also not the Leslie Stephen who emerges from Woolf's 1908 "Reminiscences." "Reminiscences," though ostensibly directed to Julian Bell, was actually addressed to Clive and Vanessa Bell, the parents of the unborn Julian. Vanessa felt little for her father except anger, and Virginia's 1908 portrait meets Vanessa's expectations: it presents a Leslie Stephen who is harsh, angry and victimizes his daughters. The 1908 portrait is lopsided, too, perhaps because Virginia was still suffering from the pressure of Leslie Stephen's long last illness only a few years earlier. The Leslie Stephen of the new fragment is also strikingly different from the Leslie Stephen of Woolf's 1932 centenary essay. In the centenary essay, perhaps the most flattering of the lot, Woolf depicts him as a smiling, if eccentric, public man. But in the new fragment, written shortly before Woolf's death, she tries to confront her relation to her father head-on, and the result is both eloquent and moving. In April, 1940, a few months before Woolf turned to describing Leslie Stephen in "Sketch of the Past," she wrote in her diary that she condemned her father as a child, but saw him with more understanding and tolerance as a woman of 58. These are just the qualities that characterize this new fragment: understanding and tolerance. Not surprisingly, we can also detect some affectionate envy, an identification that results from Woolf's desire to possess her father's power.

In the beginning of the fragment, what strikes Woolf most about her relation to Leslie Stephen is her ambivalence to him. She notes that she, unlike Vanessa, always reacted to him with a violently disturbing, deeply embedded complex of love and hate. Woolf also says that she learned ambivalence was a common feeling only a few days earlier, when she read Freud for the first time. Woolf's comment about reading Freud for the first time, made here in June of 1940, is puzzling: she also writes about reading Freud in a diary entry of December, 1939. The inconsistency may be psychologically significant: has Woolf repressed her earlier reading of Freud, finding his observations too pertinent and unsettling? Whatever her reasons for forgetting her prior encounter with Freud, in June of 1940 Woolf seems to feel relief that Freud has told her ambivalence toward her father is entirely common, even in its violent extremes.

Woolf finds Leslie Stephen disturbingly puzzling. To solve the enigma and reinhabit her old relation to him, she uses tactics that build him up from various points of view. To the public eye, Woolf says, he was the perfect type of the Cambridge intellectual. But at home, at 22 Hyde Park Gate, Stephen was, alternately, what she calls the tyrant father, the writer father and the social father. Woolf also creates and analyzes, though she does not name, a fourth category. In this last category, Woolf examines the sources of her love for and identification with her father.

Woolf's description of Leslie Stephen as the tyrant father does not differ materially from her depiction of him in her 1908 "Reminiscences." He is violent, self-pitying, self-centered and histrionic, and he expects his wife and daughters to bear his fury silently and then forgive him immediately. Virginia notes that this tyrant father, alternately loved and hated, dominated her entirely when she was 15, and that living with him was like being shut up in a cage with a dangerous, dejected and injured old lion. She pictures herself as a nervous little monkey, flying from side to side of the same cage in alternating terror and rapture. This portrait of Leslie Stephen as family tyrant is completely consistent with Woolf's other descriptions of his overbearing behavior.

Leslie Stephen as the writer father is not surprising either, though the portrait does present him as a more positive influence on Woolf's literary criticism. She says

I always read *Hours in a Library* by way of filling out my ideas, say of Coleridge, if I'm reading Coleridge: and always find something to fill out; to correct; to stiffen my fluid vision.[2]

Her choice of words suggests Virginia feels she has assumed some privileges of male literary power through her father. She says further that Stephen's mind might not be imaginative or suggestive, but that it is a strong mind, a healthy, out-of-doors mind. He is not a writer for whom she has a natural taste, but she admires him, and feels a reader's, rather than a daughter's affection for his books. It is clear from Woolf's description that she has distanced herself from her father, and can describe him as a peer, rather than a rival, in the world of letters.

In fact, Woolf's accounts of Leslie Stephen as her tyrant father and writer father in the 1940 fragment both seem detached, as if cooled by the passage of time. Woolf struggles more with her descriptions of him as her social father, and as the father she loved passionately. This increased struggle can be explained partly by the method Woolf uses to portray Stephen's less familiar social and beloved aspects. In her diary of April, 1940, and in "A Sketch of the Past" entry of May, 1940, Woolf talks about both her parents as having two characters or personalities. One character is created by the platform of Woolf's adult vision. The other character is created by her child's vision, a vision that is much more difficult to reenter and recapture. When Woolf portrays Leslie Stephen as tyrant father and writer father in the fragment, she writes from her adult angle of vision. But when she recreates her social father and the father she loved passionately, she tries to reinhabit and relive the relation she had to him as a child. In the process, she burrows beneath her automatic adult recollections and responses, and discovers bits of memories about him that make him a more rounded character, and her relation to him more complex.

Even though Woolf insists she never really knew her social father, since all his sociability vanished with Julia Stephen's death in 1895, Woolf is able to recreate him by piecing together snippets of memories and deducing from them how he must have been. Woolf reveals a less austere and more human side of Leslie Stephen. She remembers that he was, before Julia died, an attractive man of fifty, with four small children and a beautiful wife, who attended dinner parties regularly and graciously, and who was often attracted to lovely young women. Woolf recreates a sexualized and flirtatious side of Leslie Stephen, a Leslie Stephen who went to see Lily Langtry in a play simply because he was affected by her beauty, and who flirted with an American woman named Mrs. Grey. Woolf tells a story about Julia Stephen prodding Virginia to tease her father over his flirting with pretty ladies. Virginia promptly climbed up on his lap, began to pull the crumbs from his beard, and asked him about his pretty women. Stephen was shocked, and made it clear that he didn't want to be teased about *that* above all. Woolf concludes that he cannot really have been, at least before Julia died, as severe, melancholy and morose as she usually makes him out to herself. She realizes that the pressure of her anger at him makes her color her picture too darkly sometimes.

But Woolf perhaps burrows deepest when she tries to analyze her feelings of love for her father. Again she struggles to reinhabit her child's relation to him. Her analysis of these feelings is revealing because it confronts what is perhaps most confused and least distanced for Woolf. She can't even find, at first, the right language to name what accounts for her love for him. She refers to some picturesque element, to something that can't be analyzed. This element arises, perhaps, from some of the random good aspects of his character she enumerates: his simplicity, integrity, eccentricity. But none of those words seems to get at it, and Woolf is finally left with a vague sense of his general attractiveness, a sense that she traces to three things: the force of his physical presence, his ability to make her feel as if the two of them are in league together, and his privileged position in the family structure.

Woolf's description of Leslie Stephen's appearance is fascinating because it reveals her lively appreciation of his physical attractions. He was magnificent, Woolf remembers, with his lean figure, his shining blue eyes and his thick hair wound in a lock behind his ear. Even more important as a source of Woolf's love for her father though, was Stephen's ability to make Virginia feel in league with him, particularly as an intellectual being. As Woolf puts it, she felt much pleasure

When he fixed . . . his eyes upon me and somehow made me feel that we two were in league together. There was something we had in common. 'What have you got hold of,' he would say looking over my shoulder at the book I was reading; and how proud, priggishly, I was, if he gave his little amused, surprised snort, when he found me reading some book that no child my age could understand. I was a snob no doubt, and read partly to make him think me a very clever little brat.[3]

In this passage Woolf identifies Stephen as one source of her desire to read books: she enjoyed pleasing him by exercising her intellectual talents.

Woolf remembers that she felt in league with her father not only as an intellectual being, but as an emotional being too. She remembers that she was often on her father's side even when he was throwing one of the hideous tantrums she later grew to find completely reprehensible. She recalls a scene in which Julia impulsively invited a friend to stay to dinner, and Leslie Stephen, coming home from a day's walk, would have no part of it. He raged; he argued within clear earshot of the young friend. He was possessed by his genius mood, and he wouldn't be stopped. Woolf says that she, meanwhile, stood on a step observing the scene: "I affirmed my sympathy, felt my likeness."[4] Though there are several spots in Woolf's letters she mentions to Ethel Smythe or Julian Bell that she inherited her father's irritable headpiece, this comment in the new fragment may be Woolf's clearest and most forthright statement that, as a child, she identified with her father specifically when he threw his angry tantrums. This identification must have been formidably confusing for her, especially when Leslie Stephen attacked the women she loved: she hated what he did, yet she was like him. Even more suggestive is the connection this passage makes between Leslie Stephen's violent temper and his genius: it implies that as a child, Virginia identified with her father's genius whenever she identified with his rage. This conflation of genius and rage, a connection that Woolf criticizes elsewhere in the fragment, must also have confused Virginia terrifically. As she puts it, Leslie Stephen's status in his family was both godlike and childlike, and as such he was accorded extraordinary license—a license Virginia must have both coveted and abhorred.

When placed in the context of the whole of "A Sketch of the Past," the new fragment shows us a Virginia Woolf who has moved far in the direction of understanding and tolerating her father's sins. It also sheds light on Woolf's ambivalent attitude toward her father's influence—on the way in which she often identified with her father and resists identifying with him at the same time. Finally, and perhaps most important, the new fragment makes clearer to us why Virginia Woolf loved and hated Leslie Stephen so intently, and why the battle between her contradictory emotions raged in her psyche for most of her life.

NOTES

1. The new fragment picks up where the Sussex A 5.a manuscript breaks off and the Sussex A 5.d manuscript of "A Sketch of the Past" begins. The fragment was purchased by the British Library, and is housed there as additional manuscript 61973. It will be incorporated into a new edition of *Moments of Being*, edited by Jeanne Schulkind, and published by the Hogarth Press in London and Harcourt, Brace, Jovanovich in the United States.

2. "A Sketch of the Past I," British Library Additional Manuscript 61973. For permission to quote from this typescript, I am grateful to Quentin Bell, the Hogarth Press and the British Library.

3. Ibid., p. 8.

4. Ibid., p. 9.

32

Defeating the False God: Janie's Self-Determination in Zora Neale Hurston's *Their Eyes Were Watching God*

Gay Wilentz

> The devil is not the terror that he is in European folklore. He is a powerful trickster who often competes successfully with God. There is a strong suspicion that the devil is an extension of the story-makers while God is the supposedly impregnable white masters, who are nevertheless defeated by the negroes.
>
> Zora Neale Hurston[1]

Aspects of Afro-American culture in the U.S. have been formed by a necessity of those in the oppressed group to confront and in some way control the oppressor from the white slave masters to the later dominant white culture. "With tongues cocked and loaded," folktales were "the only killing tool they [were] allowed to use in the presence of white folks."[2] The folktales and the folk culture provided the black folks with a source of "power and knowledge alternative to those existing within the world of the master class."[3] Therefore, for blacks, the God of the white man takes on a sinister role in contradistinction as well as in addition to the savior God of the community church. Within the context of an oppressive society, "God" is viewed ironically, if often surreptitiously, as the strict slave master determined to keep the dominated culture in its place.

In *Their Eyes Were Watching God*, Zora Neale Hurston takes the supposition quoted above from the glossary of her anthropological study, *Mules and Men*, and weaves a larger folktale of the white man as a false "god" who must eventually be defeated. The novel is about Janie, an independent black woman, who does not, as her community does, watch God; she is looking elsewhere. Janie fights her way out of the constricting conventions of the dominant culture and, through her quest for self-determination, comes to find her own values in life. These spiritual values are paramount to Janie's growth and well-being, unlike the materialistic, middle-class values imposed on a group which by color alone cannot realize the "ideal." At each stage of Janie's development, certain characters pressure her to deify the white culture. First there is her grandmother Nanny's materialism; later, her husband Jody's bourgeois aspirations; and finally, Mrs. Turner's worship of white features. As the pressure of this imposing white culture increases, the ability of each character involved to exert influence over Janie decreases as she progresses towards what is real. What is *real* in this novel are Janie's self-determination, her love for Tea Cake, and the folk culture.

Hurston has received criticism, from both black and white critics, for ignoring racial issues in her novels.[4] It is true that she does not document the tragic history of social injustice as did Richard Wright (who compared Hurston to Jane Austen and said she did not look at race or class struggles).[5] Yet by the very absence of explicit racial conflict, the pressure of the dominant culture on the thoughts and actions of the all-black community of Eatonville as well as blacks as a whole, is detailed throughout the novel. Robert Hemenway, in his biography of Hurston, states that Hurston "triumphs over the racist environment without political propaganda but by turning inward and turning around the folktale. . . . "[6] By breaking away from the racist atmosphere in which she was brought up, Janie loses a false god and finds herself. And Hurston, through the medium of the folk culture, creates a world in which Janie defeats the oppressor.

The title of the novel strikes us as strange when it becomes apparent that the story is about one woman rather than the "they" mentioned in the title. The reference to the title comes when there is a hurricane on the "muck" (the Florida everglades). The seasonal workers in the community are debating whether or not to leave the area: "They seemed to be staring in the dark, but their eyes were watching God" (p. 236). I am not suggesting that the "God" of the passage is the white man; certainly the concept of a supreme being governing humanity is present in the novel. But Hurston gives us a second reading of "God" which indicates that it may refer not only to an absolute spirit but to the white hegemony. In the section describing the hurricane in the everglades, numerous references are made to God as "bossman" and "Ole Massa." God appears at times as capricious slave master whose whims and dangerous acts are incontrollable. Yet Hurston constantly keeps us aware of the duality of the Christian God for the black folks as they make their decision to leave the muck: "The time was past for asking the white folks what to look for outside that door. Six eyes were questioning God" (p. 235). Therefore, the title and the word "God" incorporates a double, yet contradictory meaning: There is the God to whom we look for answers and pray for help and there is the other god, the cruel, false god who definitely needs watching.

As a young girl, Janie is confronted with her grandmother's desires that Janie have everything she did not have. This is the first stage of Janie's development when she is totally under Nanny's control. Janie doesn't understand why she is marrying ancient Logan Killicks but listens to her grandmother. To Nanny, "being married is just being like white folks."[7] It will protect Janie and help her to achieve certain middle-class values, particularly since Logan has 60 acres of land and will not beat her. Although an independent woman herself, Nanny becomes, as Lillie Howard says, "The chief spokesman for prosaic materialism" because of her experiences with the white world.[8] She tells Janie, "Honey, de white man is de ruler of everything as fur as Ah been able tuh find out," (p. 29) and what she wants for Janie is a life that is protected from, as well as a position that is safely within the framework of that culture. She uses a version of the tale, "Why the Sisters in Black Works Hardest" in which "de white man tells de nigger to work and he takes and tells his wife,"[9] to try to make Janie understand. Yet Logan treats Janie exactly like the black man in the folk tale. The life that Nanny wants for Janie is the life that she saw the plantation owner's wife had: "Ah was born back due in slavery so it wasn't for me to fulfill my dreams of whut a woman oughta be and do" (p. 31).

Nanny dies before Janie runs off with Jody Starks, but it is he who secures and even furthers Nanny's dream for Janie. Nanny's basic materialism is transformed into Jody's bourgeois aspirations. Jody is an example of the "Black Bourgeoisie" who believed that acquisitions of wealth and status would in some way make them closer to the white culture which thought them inferior. In the all-black community of Eatonville, Jody quickly rises to success, becoming what one French sociologist termed a "colored Babbit."[10] It is important to note that Janie did not leave Logan for Jody because of any material gains; she went because of a sense of adventure and because she was sure "the change was bound to do her good" (p. 54). At this point, Janie begins to make choices concerning her own life.

Jody is a hard-working, ambitious person and basically good-natured, but he is bourgeois and conventional in the way that he sees the world. He gains many possessions, the finest of these being his wife. He believes, as Nanny did, that the life for Janie is one in which she can "class off." Jody is confused by Janie's desire to thwart his attempts to put her "on the porch." The notion is that Janie, being the mayor's wife, should act more like a white woman. Jody, like the Black bourgeoisie "who strove to make themselves over in the image of the white man,"[11] wanted to change his community into one which would be comparable to the white town up the road. The "white" imagery in the Eatonville section is striking. Jody builds a "gloaty, sparkly white" house (p. 75) in the tradition of the old plantations and a large white porch for Janie to sit on. He buys a street lamp for the town and keeps it on show for a week. It was the first "light" brought to the colored town although some felt it a useless notion (p. 73). He does not understand Janie's disillusionment with their relationship because he did what he promised—made a "big woman" out of her. Although at this stage Jody has a greater identification with white middle-class values than Nanny did, his power over Janie is less complete.

Janie's values are different from Jody's and what she wants is a spiritual partnership which has nothing to do with material things: "She got nothing from

Jody except what money could buy, and she was giving away what she didn't value'' (p. 118). Janie realizes that the life determined for her by Nanny which she lived with Jody was not for her. ''[Nanny] was born in slavery time when folks, dat is black folks, didn't sit down anytime dey felt lak it. So sittin' on porches lak de white madam looked like a mighty fine thing tuh her. . . . So Ah got on de high stool lak she told me, but Phoeby, Ah done nearly languished tuh death up dere'' (p. 172). Janie has been living a life that was not her choice and with the death of Jody, she is determined to follow her own judgment. She has found out what love is not and that leads her to make a positive step towards Tea Cake and spiritual fulfillment.

Even after Janie goes with Tea Cake to the muck—which unlike the town is rich and black and big and free—she still must deal with the white world seen through the eyes of the mulatto Mrs. Turner. This woman exemplifies the final stage of white identification: idol worship. Of the three characters, Mrs. Turner has the least effect on Janie; her main function is to show how warped an individual can become when she chooses the white man as her god. Janie's caucasian features, which are incidental to her, become paramount to Mrs. Turner. She separates Janie and herself from dark ones like Tea Cake. Janie does not understand why this is important and in answer to Mrs. Turner's suggestion that they ''class off,'' Janie replies, ''Us can't *do* it. We'se a mingled people and all of us got black kinfolks as well as yaller kinfolks'' (p. 210). Mrs. Turner is horrified that Janie lets her whiteness be ''defiled'' by Tea Cake's blackness, because Mrs. Turner had deified white features and now is prepared to worship them in anyone who fits this description:

Anyone who looked more white folkish than herself was better than she was in her criteria, therefore it was right that they should be cruel to her at times, just as she was cruel to those more negroid than her in direct ratio to their negroness. . . . Once having set up her idols and built altars to them it was inevitable that she would worship there. It was inevitable that she should accept any inconsistency and cruelty from her deity as all good worshippers do from theirs. All gods who receive homage are cruel. All gods dispense suffering without reason. Otherwise they would not be worshipped. . . .

Mrs. Turner, like all other believers had built an altar to the unattainable—Caucasian characteristics for all. Her god would smite her, would hurl her from pinnacles and lose her in deserts. But she would not forsake his altars. (p. 215–16)

Even though Mrs. Turner's views ''didn't affect Tea Cake and Janie too much'' (p. 27), ironically, it is Mrs. Turner's brother who is the object of Tea Cake's jealousy when he goes mad at the end.

After Janie and Tea Cake leave the muck during the hurricane, they end up in Palm Beach. Since Tea Cake has been bitten by a dog (they do not know it's rabid) while saving Janie from the flooding waters, they remain in a hotel for a few days attending to Tea Cake's wounds. Finally Tea Cake wanders out to find out what has happened to his friends. While he is out on the streets of Palm Beach, he encounters two white men with guns who *force* him to recover and bury the victims of the flood. When he objects, one man shoves the rifle in his face and says, "Git on down de road dere, suh! Don't look out somebody'll be buryin' you!" (p. 252). The Palm Beach incident, which has been viewed as an isolated example of racial injustice,[12] appears in light of this analysis to be a concrete representation of what has been happening all along: the imposition of a dominant culture on an oppressed group, whether the oppression be physical or psychological. Roger Rosenblatt notes that Tea Cake and Janie flourish only when they avoid the white world.[13] This world implies white cultural values as well. When Janie and Tea Cake are pushed off the bridge in the storm to make room for the white folks and later in Palm Beach when Tea Cake is forced to throw the black corpses in a pit while he buries the white ones, we see their lives violated by the white world; yet, equally destructive to their sense of well-being are the Mrs. Turners and the materialistic considerations in the Eatonville community. Janie resists these pressures and looks to Tea Cake and their love so that her soul can crawl out of its hiding place (p. 192).

Life on the muck is very different from life in Eatonville. Janie has left her "white" house and all the trappings of the false "white" god and has gone to find her own values in the rich, black soil, the stories and the folk tales, and the warm feeling of friendship shared there. Janie, through the rejection of the white values, becomes self-determining:

Sometimes Janie would think of the old days in the big white house and the store and laugh to herself. What if Eatonville could see her now in her blue denim overalls and heavy shoes? The crowd of people around her and a dice game on her floor! She was sorry for her friends back there and scornful of the others. The men held arguments here like they used to do on the store porch. Only here she could listen and laugh and even talk some herself if she wanted to (p. 200).

Through their love and spiritual partnership, Tea Cake and Janie find an alternative to the white culture which is not only hostile and unattainable, but also sterile and confining. They are not like Mrs. Turner; they make no distinctions concerning the folks. They bring the West Indians into their group of friends, and their house is a center of activity. Unlike the big, white house in Eatonville which became a center by power and fear, Tea Cake and Janie's place on the muck is a center fashioned from love. Even as the storm threatens to break up this close-knit community, Janie and Tea Cake retain allegiance to the folk culture and the black world. As their Bahamian friend Lias leaves the glades, he tells them "If Ah never see you no mo' on Earth, Ah'll meet you in Africa" (p. 231). They will not meet in the cold, hard heaven of the white man; they will find each other in the rich, black fields of their African heaven.

The story makes it clear that the heaven which is controlled by the white man does not include black folks. We see this in Janie's thoughts about help from God when Tea Cake is dying. Since he was bitten by a rabid dog while trying to save her from drowning, Janie realizes that he will "die for loving her" (p.

264). Janie, questioning their fate, looks up into the "blue ether" of the sky and waits for a sign. Like the cold, blue eyes of the slave master, "the sky stayed hard looking and quiet so she went into the house. God would do less than He had in His heart" (p. 264). Janie sees no recourse in the "god" of the white man nor in the dominant culture. Certainly the white doctor who tells her how dangerous Tea Cake is, never sends the medicine to make Tea Cake's dying easier for him and less threatening to Janie. After Janie is forced to kill the rabid Tea Cake in self-defense, she thanks him "wordlessly for giving her the chance for loving service" (p. 273). Janie realizes that she need not look to external sources to save Tea Cake, since love is stronger than death: "If you kin see de light at daybreak, you don't keer if you die at dusk" (p. 236).

When Janie returns to Eatonville after Tea Cake's death, without him and without the "fine clothes" she left with, she feels no need to justify herself to the community. Perhaps they think Tea Cake stole her money and left her for another woman (which happened to one woman who turned her back on the community), but Janie is satisfied that she knows the truth. She comes back in her overalls to a house once filled with the loneliness of Jody's dreams and now filled with the rich memory of Tea Cake's love. She shares this with Phoeby, not to explain her position to the community but because Phoeby is her friend. And Phoeby hears and learns: "Ah done growed ten feet higher from jus' listening tuh you, Janie. Ah ain't satisfied wid mah-self no mo'. Ah means tuh make Sam take me fishin wid him after this" (p. 284). The community of Eatonville showed her what love was *not*, but by looking into herself, she found what it was. Janie's advice to the town is that they better stop watching "god" and find out what their own lives are about before they go to God. "Two things everybody's got tuh do fuh themselves. They got tuh go tuh God, and they got tuh find out about livin' fuh theyselves" (p. 285).

Janie does just that. She finds her humanity against all odds. "The enormous effort she must make in order to feel human only serves to demonstrate how strong the opposition to her humanity is."[14] And Janie pays a price for finding her humanity. She loses Tea Cake and is alone at the end. But by negating a false system of values, she becomes one of the few women characters in early Afro-American fiction to emerge whole. "Here was peace. She pulled in her horizon like a great fish-net. Pulled it from around the waist of the world and draped it over her shoulders. So much of life in its meshes! She called her soul to come and see" (p. 286).

Robert Bone in *The Negro Novel in America* states, "In true [Negro] Renaissance spirit, it is the folk culture, through Tea Cake, which provides the means of spiritual fulfillment."[15] Folk tales often have a moral at the end to point out quirks in human nature or to give a new perspective on an old problem. If we look at *Their Eyes Were Watching God* as a broader type of folk tale, or perhaps folk novel, Hurston's moral is that black folks can be proud of their cultural heritage, presented in this novel by the folk culture, tales and language, and should not look to the false "gods" of the white world. And Hurston herself seems to have taken on the role of the folk trickster: She tricks the white readership by her own positive resistance—her ability to negate the values of the dominant culture in this novel without once saying it outright.

For finally, this is a novel of resistance. It is not negative in tone but it details Janie's fight for self-determination by negating the values imposed by the white culture. And although Janie's own values are not concretely articulated in the novel, they are real and fluid creations of self. Janie's resistance to the dominant culture is in itself a positive step, a life-affirming process which has evolved from the folk culture—a culture which has sought to keep its humanity in a hostile and life-opposing world.

NOTES

1. Zora Neale Hurston, *Mules and Men* (New York: Harper & Row, 1935), p. 306.

2. Zora Neale Hurston, *Their Eyes Were Watching God* (Urbana: University of Illinois Press, 1937), p. 275. All further references to this work appear in the text.

3. Lawrence W. Levine, *Black Culture and Black Consciousness* (New York: Oxford University Press, 1977), p. 63.

4. See, for example, Nick Aaron Ford, *The Contemporary Negro Novel* (Boston: Meador Publishing, 1936), and James Byrd, "Zora Neale Hurston: A Folk Novelist," *Tennessee Folklore Society Bulletin*, 21 (1955), pp. 37–41.

5. Lillie Howard, "Marriage: Zora Neale Hurston's System of Values," *CLA Journal*, 21 (1980), pp. 256–68.

6. Robert Hemenway, *Zora Neale Hurston* (Urbana: University of Illinois Press, 1977), p. 51.

7. Lillie Howard, *Zora Neale Hurston* (Boston: Twayne Publishing, 1980), p. 95.

8. Ibid., p. 108.

9. Hurston, *Mules and Men*, p. 101.

10. E. Franklin Frazier, *Black Bourgeoisie* (London: Collier Books, 1957), p. 109.

11. Ibid., p. 112.

12. Hugh Gloster, *Negro Voices in American Fiction* (Chapel Hill: University of North Carolina Press, 1948), p. 236.

13. Roger Rosenblatt, *Black Fiction* (Cambridge: Harvard University Press, 1974), p. 89.

14. Ibid.

15. Robert Bone, *The Negro Novel in America* (New Haven: Yale University Press, 1958), p. 131.

33

The Woman Warrior: Claiming Narrative Power, Recreating Female Selfhood

Joanne S. Frye

One of the compelling insights of feminist literary criticism has been the recognition that the literary traditions we inherit have often denied women the power of naming and the power of narrative: women have inherited a sense of story in which action and affirming self-definition seem precluded not only by social environment but also by expectations of how stories work.[1] Neither the mythic nor the realistic mode, as traditionally used, has seemed capable of adequately portraying the possibilities for a strong female selfhood.

In response to this apparent preclusion, recent women writers have sought to develop alternate narrative modes for the literary interpretation of female experience. And, as Suzanne Juhasz points out in her analysis of form in feminist autobiography, some particularly fruitful development of form has been done by women autobiographers. Associating these formal responses with versions of reality that are "characteristically" female, Juhasz identifies two possible patterns of response to female experience: the personal, factual, diary-like form chosen by Kate Millett and the imaginative, fantastic, novelistic form chosen by Maxine Hong Kingston in *The Woman Warrior*. Kingston's style, argues Juhasz, develops "from the notion that fantasy, the life of the imagination, creates female identity."[2] The argument is as follows: Millett's choice of the diary-like form is appropriate to women because "women's lives are traditionally private lives" (237); Kingston's choice of the fantastic is appropriate because "women also live, traditionally, another kind of private life, an inner life of the imagination that has special significance for them due to the outright conflict between societal possibility and imaginative possibility" (237). "Kingston's approach," Juhasz says, "makes creating rather than recording, the significant autobiographical act" (237).

Juhasz's assertions and her analysis are perceptive, particularly her assessment of the formal restructuring which women are developing in response to claiming and recreating their own lived experience. But, without disputing the overall argument, I want to point out the dangers implicit in building an analysis on the antithesis between the fantastic and the realistic and to argue that Kingston's achievement lies rather in her use of the narrative process to refuse this antithesis and to develop a female identity within a social context. To claim fantasy as an autobiographical mode—i.e., to withdraw into what Juhasz calls the "inner life of the imagination" as a reaction to an oppressive reality—is to risk leaving the oppressive reality untouched, unaltered, and also to leave one's shaped identity without a basis for action within that reality. Kingston, I think, is *not* withdrawing from reality. Rather, by drawing upon the possibilities of Chinese narrative tradition as well as the English language tradition to which she contributes, she is offering both an imaginative construction of self and also a realistic affirming of self within a societal context.

In my view, Kingston's reaction to female experience is centered in simultaneously claiming new possibilities and integrating a knowledge of actual lived reality—claiming fantasy not as a separate inner world of the imagination but as a powerful tool for reshaping lived experience beyond the repressions of personal daily life. For it seems to me that the power of *The Woman Warrior* lies not in the invisible force of fantasy as distinct from reality but in the powerful interaction of fantasy with reality—without refusing to differentiate[3]—in determining new possibilities for female selfhood. Through this interaction, the narrative process, then, enables Kingston to develop a strong female identity, grounded—as is narrative itself—in the capacity to choose and to interpret and in the ability to act in a social context.[4]

The most immediate reality in Kingston's childhood is extremely oppressive: not only the isolation of a bi-cultural context in which she can claim neither Chinese identity nor American identity but also the immediate misogyny of much of that context. Kingston grows up haunted by a vague fear of being sold into slavery or wifehood and a more immediate awareness that her brothers are more valued than she and her sisters, as is clearly evident in the rituals and celebrations of their lives. She knows fully the traditions of feet-binding and the capacity of the language to reinforce self-hatred; as she says, "There is a Chinese word for the female I—which is 'slave.' Break the women with their own tongues!"[5] She is surrounded, too, by the villagers' voices sadly noting, "One girl—and another girl," and her great-uncle's voice roaring his refusal: "No girls!" (55). And the misogynist sayings fill the air around her: "Feeding girls is feeding cowbirds"; "There's no profit in raising girls. Better to raise geese than girls"; "When you raise girls, you're raising children for strangers" (54).

Her own femaleness thus becomes itself a negation to be overcome. At times in her childhood, Kingston attempts resistance by trying to deny her femaleness, especially by breaking the established codes for female behavior: achieving academic success, behaving clumsily, breaking dishes, refusing to cook. And her resistance to the norms gives her reason to gloat when accused of being a "bad girl": for, she says, "Isn't a bad girl almost a boy?" (56). But the resistance is difficult, if not impossible, to achieve when immersed in daily reality since she is confronted not only with the repressive norms from her Chinese heritage but also with the conflicting and differently repressive norms of American femininity.

The attempts to reject her own femaleness imply a kind of self-hatred, which is even more evident in a story of factual reality from her childhood, told in the final section of the autobiography. Following the portrayal of her own shrouded childhood silence in American public schools, she tells of her physical and psychological abuse of another Chinese American girl with whom Kingston herself obviously identifies, for the "quiet one" (201) shares Kingston's own earlier refusal to speak aloud in public and her inability to participate in American life. But Kingston is also making every effort to differentiate herself from this girl by claiming her own hatred of neatness and pastel colors, her own desire to be tough rather than soft. The actual abuse is clearly an effort to expunge those parts of her Chinese-female identity which she abhors and to mark out her own possibilities for strength in resisting that identity. The experience is followed by a "mysterious illness" (211) and with it an eighteen-month period of social isolation, after which she must relearn "how to talk" and come to recognize that the other girl has different ways of surviving, different protections than are available to Kingston (212). The painful retelling of the abuse and of her subsequent healing solitude becomes the attempt now to reinterpret her own past, to free herself from both the silence and the aggression, to alleviate the evident guilt she feels, and to understand the sources of the person she has become, somehow straddling Chinese and American realities and accepting her female identity.

But this effort cannot succeed through simple documentation of either the repressive reality or her attempts to resist it. Rather she must claim her female identity by shaping her narrative interpretation of self through the interpenetration of fantasy with reality. The dominant fantasy in the autobiography is, of course, that of the woman warrior, told in the second section, titled "White Tigers." The tale is a retelling of the story of a legendary Chinese woman, Fa Mu Lan, who replaced her father in battle, fought with courage and strength, and then returned to live peacefully in the village. Kingston uses it as an old legend with roots in reality; but she also uses it as a powerful personal story, transforming the legend of Fa Mu Lan—which, as a child, she had sung over and over with her mother—into a personal myth of being herself chosen to be the salvation of her people. Telling it in the first person indicative, she claims for herself all the mythical powers of Fa Mu Lan. But in the final paragraph, she returns to the subjunctive—no longer "I did," but rather "I would"—and concludes the tale: "From the words on my back, and how they were fulfilled, the villagers would make a legend about my perfect filiality" (54).

The framing of the legend-as-personal myth—introduced and concluded in the subjunctive mood but told throughout in the indicative—is confusing to some readers: students have asked me, "What really did happen? What does she mean, she carried her baby inside her armor? Did she really meet an old man and woman who taught her magical survival techniques?" The power of the fantastic event told as actual is hard to resist. But the tale gains its real power through the simultaneous knowledge that it is not actual and that it is grounded in what *is* actual: though the tale itself is framed in the subjunctive mood, its larger frame is the highly conscious narrative of lived experience both preceding and following it. The section begins, for example, with a clear assessment of the uses of fantasy: "When we Chinese girls listened to the adults talk-story, we learned that we failed if we grew up to be but wives or slaves. We could be heroines, swordswomen. . . . Perhaps women were once so dangerous that they had to have their feet bound" (23). And the presentation of the legend is followed abruptly by the statement, "My American life has been such a disappointment" (54) and the reiteration of the misogynist sayings which surrounded her childhood.

The tale becomes her protection against her hostile surroundings, but it is not a fantastic escape from a harsh reality, as might be implied in the contrast between "slaves" and "swordswomen" or in the allusion to women's once dangerous powers.[6] Rather the tale is itself rooted in her harsh daily reality and assumes for itself and for her a reality of its own. Early in the section she recalls the stories of her childhood: "Night after night my mother would talk-story until we fell asleep. I couldn't tell where the stories left off and the dreams began, her voice the voice of the heroines in my sleep." And then, "At last I saw that I too had been in the presence of great power, my other talking-story. . . . She said I would grow up a wife and a slave, but she taught me the song of the warrior woman, Fa Mu Lan. I would have to grow up a warrior woman" (24). This reality then—the power of her mother as a real woman and as a story-teller[7]—is the source of the knowledge present in the subjunctive become indicative, the impetus for the personal legend, and the basis for creating a powerful selfhood rooted in reality, strengthened through fantasy, and evolved through the narrative process. She understands the limits of the real—"I mustn't feel bad that I haven't done as well as the swordswoman did; after all, no bird called me, no wise old people tutored me. I have no magic beads . . . " (58)—but she also understands the strength available through both the mythic perception and the lived reality.

The conclusion of the section draws fully on this integration of a painful reality and an infusion of strength. Kingston evokes her present distance from the American-Chinese villagers of her childhood: "When I visit the family now, I wrap my American successes around me like a private shawl;. . . I refuse to shy my way anymore through our Chinatown, which tasks me with the old sayings and the stories" (62). But the concluding paragraph reveals precisely how this refusal has become possible—and it is not simply a question of "American successes," but rather of finding a use for the Chinese legend in the context of a successful American reality:

The swordswoman and I are not so dissimilar. May my people understand the resemblance soon so that I can return to them. What we have in common are the words at our backs. The ideographs for *revenge* are "report a crime" and "report to five families." The reporting is the vengeance—not the beheading, not the gutting, but the words. And I have so many words—"chink" words and "gook" words too—that they do not fit on my skin. (62–63)

The woman warrior, with the words of vengeance carved into the skin of her back, and the mother's daily talking-story merge for Kingston into a powerful source of female identity—beyond the bound feet and the cries of "maggot" which haunt her childhood on the other side of this reality.

This use of fantasy is not precisely an "inner life" as distinct from "societal possibility." Rather it is a restructuring of societal possibility through the dailiness of stories told and stories remembered. The fantasy, in other words, is not distinct from the reporting of fact—it is itself a kind of reporting from the dailiness of both childhood and adulthood: vengeance for the abuse inherent in "chink" words and "gook" words—the claiming of the power of language through a heritage of power in fantasy. In this way, Kingston can merge her "American successes" as a writer with the heritage of the fantastic from her Chinese-American childhood: as a writer she claims the power to avenge the wrongs done to her people and to herself—to be the woman warrior. In claiming the power of the legend, she has simultaneously claimed her own personal strength and her ability to act in a social context.

The centrality of narrative and the power of imagination are established even before the introduction of the central fantasy of the woman warrior. The book opens in a section titled "No Name Woman" with Kingston's mother telling her a story in confidence, a real life story of an aunt who had been expunged from the family history for her sexual sins, her illegitimate pregnancy. Kingston's mother concludes her narrative with a warning: "Now that you have started to menstruate, what happened to her could happen to you. Don't humiliate us. You wouldn't like to be forgotten as if you had never been born. The villagers are watchful" (5). Kingston calls this narrative "a story to grow up on" by which her mother "tested our strength to establish realities" (5). She goes on, "Those of us in the first American generations have had to figure out how the invisible world the emigrants built around our childhoods fit in solid America" (6). Kingston's own immediate response to the problem is to recreate for herself in vivid detail the story of her aunt, thereby making it her own to experience fully, to live out for her aunt. In the midst of this narrative Kingston, somewhat incongruously, addresses her own specific problems in growing up and trying "to turn myself American-feminine" (13); but the conclusion brings her back to the imagined subjective experience of the aunt and the painful recognition of outsiderness focussed in her aunt's suicide and the family's denial. The issue of femininity and more, of female sexuality, however, finally does provide a kind of coherence: it is because of her sexuality that Kingston's mother tells her the story, and it is through the knowledge of her own sexuality that Kingston creates the story of her aunt's painful death. The need for a female heritage by which to assess and develop her own female selfhood is the driving force: "Unless I see her life branching into mine, she gives me no ancestral help" (10). Through telling the aunt's story and thus rescuing her from the family silence which had denied her existence, Kingston has created the branches of her own female ancestry.

There are other women, too, both real and fantastic, whose stories shape Kingston's emerging female identity: another aunt, Lovely Orchid, who does not, cannot, endure the culture shock in her arrival in America; the other "crazy women," who in various ways have lost their control over language as a shaping force—"Insane people were the ones who couldn't explain themselves" (216); her sister, whom she wants to protect from the marriage-making assaults on her selfhood; the other Chinese girls in her school, hated for their shared silence in public; her grandmother who loved the theater and refused to fear the bandits; and finally the legendary poet Ts'ai Yen. Each provides yet another lens on Kingston's own immediate reality: the possibility of seeing it more clearly and claiming it more forcefully. And each participates in establishing an awareness of female vulnerability to cultural expectations and female strength through language and especially through narrative power.

The stories, then, become interpretive strategies for her own lived experience as a female and are never severed from that experience. Each story—legendary fantasy or imaginative construction of another's life—interacts profoundly with the foundation narrative of her own immediate experience: the autobiography of fact, of daily lived reality. As she has told us in the opening section, her mother explicitly gave her stories—both fantastic and actual—in order to heighten her awareness of perceived reality.

The third section thus assumes a pivotal significance as Kingston's sympathetic reconstruction of her mother's own story of her life in China as a woman alone and independent, a woman who establishes her identity through her work as a student and then a doctor but who also engages in fantastic encounters with ghosts and monsters. The experience, as told, is both alien to the teller and personally real and powerful to her. Through telling her mother's story, she understands her own Chinese roots, the reality of a deeply misogynist heritage which nonetheless has fed her mother's strength and autonomy. The conclusion of this section provides us with the most recent event in the autobiography: a conversation between mother and daughter—"when I last visited my parents" (116)—a conversation in which they affirm a shared identity in being both Dragons, born in dragon years, and in being both fully committed to the work they do, however different it is: "She sends me on my way, working always and now old . . ." (127). As the most direct branching of ancestral lives, Kingston's mother provides the personal integration of fantasy and reality through which Kingston can claim her strength in femaleness.

But before she can claim the strength she shares with her mother, she must find the uses of narrative which will effectively assess her own reality; and these cannot be the same as her mother's easy blend of fantasy and reality. The process by which she works this through for herself is analogous to the writing of the autobiography itself: the taking on for herself the story-telling and the listening functions which she has previously attributed to her mother.[8] In the final section of the book she tells of a childhood confrontation with her mother, based on her own need to gain absolution through confessing to her mother: "I had grown inside me a list of over two hundred things that I had to tell my mother so that she would know the true things about me and to stop the pain in my throat" (229). When she actually undertakes this confession process, she and her mother end up shouting at each other from the confusion of Kingston's need and their difficulties of cross-cultural, cross-generational communication: "And suddenly I got very confused and lonely because I was at that moment telling her my list, and in telling, it grew. No higher listener. No listener but myself" (237). Thus she confronts her own essential aloneness and attempts to overcome it through the imposition of language and explanation, the naming of realities and the imagining of possibilities: making herself the confirming listener and integrating her mother's reality into her own become the basis of her autobiographical process.

While claiming the listening function for herself, she must also claim and redefine the story-telling function. She ends one segment of her childhood confessional outpouring by saying, "And I don't want to listen to any more of your stories; they have no logic. They scramble me up. You lie with stories.... I can't tell what's real and what you make up" (235). Her mother's story-telling—which so clearly branches into her own life and her own identity—must be redefined for her own uses, but it cannot be entirely relinquished. Where her mother had felt no need to distinguish between fantasy and reality in her narratives, Kingston feels impelled to begin with reality and to hold onto the distinction and yet to allow them to interpenetrate as a part of the truth-telling process. The necessity of defining her reality and her cultural roots, the need to contain and overcome the negations of her culturally perceived femaleness drives her to write the autobiography—to be teller, as well as listener—and in it to claim the power of narrative explanation: "Be careful what you say. It comes true. It comes true. I had to leave home in order to see the world logically, logic the new way of seeing. I learned to think that mysteries are for explanation" (237). And two pages later: "Perhaps ... what I once had was not Chinese-sight at all but child-sight that would have disappeared eventually without struggle. The throat pain always returns, though, unless I tell what I really think..." (239). The need to make sense of her life—lived reality and imaginative construction—is what motivates the autobiography and what defines the rich and complex form it takes: "I continue to sort out what's just my childhood, just my imagination, just my family, just the village, just movies, just living" (239). And the sorting out is a new integration of her mother's uses of fantasy with her own lived reality.

The final story, then, is a merging of these needs from an adult perspective, and, significantly, a merging of her mother's story-telling with her own. She introduces it, saying, "Here is a story my mother told me, not when I was young, but recently, when I told her I also talk-story. The beginning is hers, the ending, mine" (240). Like the story of the woman warrior, this story focuses on a woman from Chinese legend: Ts'ai Yen, a poet. But this story is given Kingston's own family history, as related by her mother, and is given its "branches" into Kingston's own life through the implicit meaning of the narrative rather than through the narrative transfiguration of selfhood, as with the woman warrior. Captured by the barbarians, Ts'ai Yen gave music and form to her experiences among them, thus communicating to both the barbarians and her own people, somehow bridging those cultural differences and also transmitting meaning in a different language eighteen centuries later. Kingston ends the story and the autobiography with the meaningful understatement about one of the songs, which survives in modern China and in Kingston's personal history: "It translated well" (243); like Kingston's own story, the verse has bridged the cultures and infused the experience with meaning for its listeners.

Thus does Kingston claim for herself the power of Ts'ai Yen, the power of language both to shape and to convey reality:[9] the power of narrative to bridge cultural barriers and to reinfuse the female identity with the strength of an affirmed selfhood. In merging the realistic with the fantastic, *The Woman Warrior* demonstrates the centrality of the narrative process to interpreting lives and its special capacity to overcome the isolation of being an outsider—without a cultural identity and refusing identity in femininity as prescribed by either culture. Through the interpenetration of fantasy and reality in a multi-layered narrative, she has moved beyond her misogynistic heritage and overcome what she elsewhere calls her own "woman-hatred."[10] In her autobiography, Maxine Hong Kingston has been able to use the narrative process itself to refuse the cultural negations she describes and to claim her femaleness as a source of strength both rooted in her cultural heritage and affirmed beyond that heritage. In doing so, she enriches her bi-cultural literary heritage and makes it truly her own.

NOTES

1. See, for example, Joanna Russ's analysis of the limitations on female plots, "What Can a Heroine Do? or Why Women Can't Write?" in *Images of Women in Fiction*, ed. Susan Koppelman Cornillon (Bowling Green, Ohio: Bowling Green University Popular Press, 1973), pp. 3–20; and Jean Kennard's analysis of the conventions which limit the portrayal of female experience in *Victims of Convention* (Hamden, Connecticut: Archon Books, 1978).

2. Juhasz, "Towards a Theory of Form in Feminist Autobiography: Kate Millett's *Flying* and *Sita*; Maxine Hong Kingston's *The Woman Warrior*," in Estelle C. Jelinek, ed., *Women's Autobiography: Essays in Criticism* (Bloomington, Indiana: Indiana University Press, 1980), p. 222. Subsequent references will be indicated within the text.

3. Deborah Homsher sees *The Woman Warrior* as having a larger commitment to fantasy and as "break[ing] up the usual distinctions between fact and fantasy"; "*The*

Woman Warrior, by Maxine Hong Kingston: A Bridging of Autobiography and Fiction,'' *Iowa Review* 10, iv (1979): 92.

4. In its insistence on choice and continual redefinition, this view of female identity is processual but it differs from the ''processual identity'' which Judith Kegan Gardiner sees as central in female writing; for Gardiner the idea of ''female identity'' derives largely from Nancy Chodorow's view that women's identities tend to be fluid and relationally defined. See Gardiner, ''On Female Identity and Writing by Women,'' *Critical Inquiry* 8, 2 (Winter 1981): 347–61.

5. Kingston, *The Woman Warrior: Memoirs of a Girlhood Among Ghosts* (New York: Vintage, 1977), p. 56. Subsequent references will be indicated within the text.

6. It is interesting that Kingston's potentially escapist sentence—''Perhaps women were once so dangerous that they had to have their feet bound''—serves as epigraph for Nina Auerbach's *Woman and the Demon: The Life of a Victorian Myth* (Cambridge: Harvard University Press, 1982). But in my view, Auerbach's argument that the negative images of women in the Victorian period were, in fact, a tribute to female strength reinforces the escapist possibilities and risks showing women images of power with no clear arena for action in a social context. By contrast, Kingston's complex narrative process reveals the interpretive usefulness of integrating mythic and real in understanding female experience.

7. Although I think the basis of Kingston's evolving strength lies in reclaiming her own narrative power over reality rather than in relating to her mother through ''archetypal aspects of the woman's psyche,'' I agree with Stephanie A. Demetrakopoulos that Kingston's mother sent her an ''underground message of the possibility of freedom for a woman''; see ''The Metaphysics of Matrilinearism in Women's Autobiography: Studies of Mead's *Blackberry Winter*, Hellman's *Pentimento*, Angelou's *I Know Why the Caged Bird Sings*, and Kingston's *The Woman Warrior*,'' in Jelinek, ed. pp. 183, 203.

8. In her analysis of the mother-daughter relationship in several autobiographies, including *The Woman Warrior*, Lynn Z. Bloom points out that ''not only . . . does the daughter-as-autobiographer become her own mother, she also becomes the recreator of her maternal parent and the controlling adult in their literary relationship''; see ''Heritages: Dimensions of Mother-Daughter Relationships in Women's Autobiographies,'' in Cathy N. Davidson and E. M. Broner, ed., *The Lost Tradition: Mothers and Daughters in Literature* (New York: Ungar, 1980), p. 292.

9. Cf. Annette Kolodny's belief that the ''radical alteration'' in human experience through feminism must include the critique of literature's reification of male power structures *and* the continuing focus on ''the power of the word to both structure and mirror human experience''; ''Dancing through the Minefield: Some Observations on the Theory, Practice and Politics of a Feminist Criticism,'' *Feminist Studies* 6,1 (Spring 1980); 17.

10. Kingston, ''Reservations About China,'' *Ms.* 7 (October 1978): 67.

34

In Search of "Ordinary Human Happiness": Rebellion and Affirmation in Mary Gordon's Novels

Susan Ward

Felicitas Maria Taylor, Mary Gordon tells us in the first line of *The Company of Women*, is christened after "the one virgin martyr whose name contained some hope for ordinary human happiness."[1] She yearns for the happiness her name represents. So does Isabel Moore, the heroine of *Final Payments*, Gordon's earlier novel. But both heroines find ordinary happiness extraordinarily difficult to attain. Their separate searches determine the plots of the novels and give rise to some of Gordon's most important themes.

Because they give us heroines caught in webs of conflicting values, each trying to disentangle an old and strong affiliation with the Catholic Church from her desire to establish herself as a free, modern woman, it is tempting to view the two novels as discussions of Catholicism. In part, they are. But the novels finally assert and illustrate three themes which cut across the lines of religious denomination. First, they affirm that self-assertive, intelligent young women must rebel against or at least reevaluate their allegiance to any code to which they are wont to give unthinking loyalty. Second, they suggest that the fathers of such young women are often dominant influences in their lives and that their growing-up process must involve a rebellion, replacement, and reconciliation with the father as well as a reevaluation of ties to old authorities. And third, they illustrate that the Catholic Church, and by extension any other institution founded on patriarchal values, offers little hope to modern women. The world is in need, the novels imply, of a new system of values. And they offer an alternative which enables Isabel and Felicitas, at least, a chance to discover some of the "ordinary" happiness they seek.

The laws of the Catholic Church make up the code to which both Isabel and Felicitas, brought up by religious parents, give their uncritical childhood allegiance. Rebellion against this authority unfolds straightforwardly in both novels.

Isabel begins by lying to her father about her weekly attendance at Mass, sells her house and moves out of her Irish Catholic neighborhood after her father's death when old family friends would be only too happy to keep an eye on her, is fitted for an IUD and has affairs with married men. Felicitas refuses to be taken in by the morality of "St. Peggy of the Tennis Courts," the pamphlet Muriel brings her from the Church rack, transfers from Catholic St. Anne's to Columbia School of General Studies, has an affair with a professor and another with a student, and winds up pregnant. Though each has a moment of reembracing Catholic mores—Felicitas when she returns to the "company" surrounding Father Cyprian, and Isabel when she volunteers to live with Margaret Casey as a penance for indulging in illicit sex—each, finally, discards her old allegiance to Catholicism for a more carefully thought out morality. Isabel will probably marry the divorced Hugh after the close of *Final Payments*, and Felicitas, at the end of *The Company of Women*, attends Mass and receives Communion after spending the night with her lover. Though neither action is likely to be officially sanctioned by the Catholic Church, these actions make the most sense.

The senselessness of the Church's official attitude is perhaps best summed up in Father Cyprian's difficulty in explaining the rationale which bars women from the priesthood to Felicitas' small daughter.

I thought of all the foolish mediocre men who were permitted ordination because of the accident of their sex. And I thought of this child, obviously superior to all others of her age in beauty, grace, and wisdom [the priest recalls]. I told her to pray that the Church would change its mind.

And so each morning, at my Mass, I pray for the ordination of women. (288–89)

Cyprian's confusion here and his and Father Mulcahy's willingness to sanction Felicitas' and Isabel's actions even when they lie outside the perimeters of Church law betray more than any other factor Gordon's idea that the Church must change if it wishes to number intelligent women among its followers. Church law is a major obstacle to a woman's self-worth. Throughout the novels, it keeps Felicitas and Isabel from happiness. Therefore, it must be left behind. This realization underlies the first rebellion theme in both novels.

The relationship between father or father-figure and daughter gives rise to a second rebellion theme which further shapes the plots of both novels. Both heroines have grown up in situations in which a father or father-figure is an extremely dominating influence, and this fact exaggerates the father-daughter bond. Isabel, whose father is widowed when she is very young and who dismisses the housekeeper so that she can live alone with him at the age of thirteen, moves almost into the role of helpmeet when she nurses him singlehandedly for the last eleven years of his life. Felicitas, whose mother is widowed, cannot help but see Father Cyprian, her own "father-confessor" and the spiritual center of the company of single women who are her mother's friends, in a fatherly and dominating light.

In each novel, the heroine worships, rebels against, and replaces the father-figure with another man in a near-perfect illustration of Freud's Electra complex.[2] In childhood, both heroines betray traces of almost lover-like attachment to the "fathers." Isabel becomes upset at both her friend Eleanor's and Margaret Casey's daring to entertain sexual notions about her father; Felicitas, gazing at the soles of Father Cyprian's feet, thinks that she wanted "always to be there kneeling, looking at his black shoes . . . They were at the center of things." (6) Both heroines rebel against the fathers by elevating other men to the central positions in their lives. Isabel begins when she sleeps with her father's student, denies her father outright when she refuses to cry at his funeral, and falls in love with Hugh, who, she realizes, "had authority . . . " like her father's.[3] Felicitas denies Father Cyprian when she refuses to acknowledge him as her teacher, and in a passage reminiscent of the one in which she designates Cyprian the center of her pre-teenage universe, replaces him with Robert, who seems, for the moment, "life, . . . the one essential." (146) In gestures of contrition, both heroines reject men and re-embrace the influence of the fathers halfway through the novels. Felicitas, pregnant, goes to live with the company surrounding Father Cyprian; Isabel, convinced of her selfishness by Hugh's wife, goes to live with Margaret Casey in the spirit of her father's charity. And both heroines accept men at the ends of the novels whose good qualities remind them of their father-figures. Isabel is reconciled to Hugh at least partly because his sternness reminds her of her father and "I needed a man I could love for his rigor" (301); Felicitas accepts Leo because his nurturing qualities reflect one good aspect of the father role and she needs a father for Linda. In the end, memory of their fathers' influences equalizes the heroines' choices of mates.

This playing out of the father-daughter conflict and resolution forces us to see that accepting the good as well as the bad in fathers and in men in general is part of the "ordinary" happiness both heroines seek. Felicitas talks to, although she does not fully love, Cyprian at the end of *The Company of Women*; Isabel finally cries over the death of her father at the end of *Final Payments*. Accepting the notion of one's own sexuality as non-sinful is another. Both heroines are ready to make presumably happy sexual commitments at the ends of the novels. Even Cyprian, though he does not understand it, approves Felicitas' upcoming marriage. At the end of *The Company of Women*, Felicitas tells us: "Now I will be married; I will do this ordinary thing." (261) These words most clearly articulate the notion implicit in both novels that a heterosexual union is part of the ordinary way to happiness for most women.

But the novels do more than simply assert that the mindless allegiance to authority stifles the individuality of intelligent women and that the process of growth for women includes the separation from the correct assessment of one's relationship with one's father. They contrast male and female value systems and suggest that women must live by their own, even though they may lie counter to the "higher" values of men. Gordon introduces this idea by building male and female value systems, exactly counter in every tenet, into each novel. Finally, her heroines must choose between them. Only when they have done so can they find complete and ordinary happiness.

The Catholic Church, which is the starting point for each heroine because it is the value system each espouses at the beginning of her life, is depicted in each novel as an authoritarian, male-dominated institution. In each novel, the heroine's father-figure hands down the Church's precepts, and the precepts are remarkably masculine in tone. Professor Moore and Father Cyprian preach denial of the physical self and of nature and the triumph of the spirit. "My father always said that Catholics did not believe in nature," Isabel recalls (171); Felicitas remembers Father Cyprian's teaching her the corruption of the flesh by forcing her to smell piles of rotting manure (42–44). Moore and Cyprian adhere to old and strict interpretations of Church law. Moore works to reestablish the celebration of the Latin Mass; Father Cyprian leaves his order when a modernization trend allows priests to wear chinos, read paperbacks, and practice golf swings in the cloister. They believe in reason and revelation and deny the possibility of coming to truth on the basis of instinct. "Your father, for all his brains, had the faith of a child," Father Mulcahy tells Isabel (219); "[T]hey have dragged me down to the middling terrain of their conception of the world, half blood-instinct, half the impulse of the womb," thinks Father Cyprian of the women (185). They propose that the individual live only for spiritual rewards and that pleasure has no place in the life of the orthodox believer. "[My father] believed that truth and beauty could be achieved only by a process of chastening and exclusion."

One did not look for happiness on earth, recalls Isabel (2). "You must hate the world and love God," says Father Cyprian (45). They are allies with the concept of universal charity rather than that of love of the individual. Father Cyprian yearns all his life for "the great ideal . . . impersonal, restrained, available, utterly public and yet full of solitude" (280); Father Mulcahy, whose ideas on love Isabel associates with her father's, forgives Margaret Casey, who tries to ruin him, with "an engaged love for one of God's poor." (64) They are stern, rather than merciful. Isabel's father is a figure of wrath when he discovers her in bed with his prize student; Father Cyprian punishes swiftly and terribly when Felicitas remarks that she is in love with smell. Divorced from their Catholic applications, these precepts—spirituality, strict interpretation of law, belief in reason at the expense of instinct, the application of truths on universal levels, and belief in retributive punishment—all stem from traditional male values.

The counter female value system is practiced in *The Company of Women* by Isabel's mother's friends and in *Final Payments* by Liz and Eleanor. This value system revolves around principles which are the exact opposite of the orthodox, masculine code. Women love nature and physical objects and accept these things as good. Eleanor, with her beautiful clothes and melons for breakfast and the silver bowl of holly she gives Isabel for Christmas; Charlotte, always associated with soft flesh, round white arms, and perfume; Clare, who runs a fine leather goods store and "love[s] most in life . . . objects, perfectly crafted, for specific use," (20) embody this principle. Women are flexible in matters of religion and in personal and public politics. Liz loves a woman, Mary Rose works in a Times Square porn parlor, Clare brushes elbows with adultery, abortion and homosexuality as she runs her leather business, and all three accept these aspects of life, irregular at best to their Catholic eyes, without discarding the entire Catholic value system. Women arrive at the truth through instinct. Charlotte, musing on the differences between herself, on the one hand, and Felicitas and Father Cyprian, on the other, thinks "For those two I would die," (19), and she is right. Women acknowledge love of the individual and its attendant danger—loss. "I never wanted anyone. But I want her," Liz says of Erica (86), and admits later "She will probably leave me one day for a man who can give her babies." (225) Women object to the notion of forcing personal love in the name of charity. "Why do you want to *conquer* yourself? And why pure acts?" asks Eleanor when Isabel speaks of going to live with Margaret Casey (119). And women are, above all, merciful. Eleanor and Liz, after all the discouragement their overtures have met with, drive to meet Isabel the day she calls them; Felicitas' mothers' friends welcome her back, pregnant, without a harsh word. The value system the women represent, finally, is the only positive one in the novels. And it alone offers any hope for the novels' young, female protagonists.

But for Felicitas and Isabel, progress toward this realization is painfully slow. Coached by their spiritual fathers to admire "masculine" values as versions of extraordinary Catholicism, they are also encouraged in roles which are counter to the roles of ordinary women. Both Professor Moore and Father Cyprian bring up the parable of Mary and Martha and counsel their charges to adopt the Mary, or less traditionally female role. Isabel and Felicitas are encouraged to be intellectual rather than instinctive. They are not encouraged to learn the intricacies of running households or to think of themselves as wives and mothers. In a telling passage at the end of *The Company of Women*, Father Cyprian reveals that he "never meant for [Felicitas] to marry . . . . [S]he is not simple enough to make an ordinary wife, . . . "(286) One wonders, as one might wonder if one stopped to consider the outcome of Professor Moore's training of Isabel, what he *did* mean. Both young women are convinced by their mentors of the inferiority of the feminine role, yet they are barred by virtue of their femininity from the masculine. Their "training" has left them with no positive role-models and in a state of confusion over positive values of any kind.

At the ends of the novels, when Isabel and Felicitas return to the company of their female friends, they adopt, with qualifications, the female value system. Both realize that it is women and feminine values that save them. "I loved them for their solidity, for their real and possible existences, . . . For they had come the moment I called them," thinks Isabel as Liz and Eleanor rescue her (307). "They stood by me and defended me . . . . Kindness is a rare thing," thinks Felicitas after her pregnancy (252). At the ends of the novels, both Isabel and Felicitas are ready to affirm their own femininity. This, as well as rebellion, is a necessary step in their search for happiness.

Thus, Gordon implies, for modern young women like Isabel and Felicitas, feminine values hold the most hope. But Isabel's and Felicitas' alignment with the feminine is, at best, qualified. They will never embrace the secondary role of women within the Catholic Church. They will never yield unthinkingly to men or to authority of any kind.[4] They will never be the kind of women society wholeheartedly embraces.

This last, too, is a part of Gordon's point. Isabel and Felicitas are part of a new breed of women who discard the bad and extract the good from old values. They fashion new codes, applicable to themselves and the moment in which they live. Their struggles will not end with the ending of the novels. The struggles of such women, trying to find their places in "ordinary" society, very rarely end.

NOTES

1. Mary Gordon, *The Company of Women* (New York: Ballantine Books, 1980), p. 3. All further page references are included in the text and are to this edition.

2. Most of Freud's commentary on the father-daughter relationship occurs in three essays: "Some Physical Consequences of the Anatomical Distinction Between the Sexes" (1925), "Female Sexuality" (1931), and "Femininity" (1933). Points most relevant to Gordon's novels include his description of the daughter's early identification of the father as a love object (the Oedipal or Electra complex) and his replacement by another male. Freud also posits that, should the replacement male resemble the father, the daughter may struggle before accepting him for that very reason. As noted above, both Isabel and Felicitas follow this pattern.

3. Mary Gordon, *Final Payments* (New York: Ballantine Books, 1978), p. 167. All further page references are included in the text and are to this edition.

4. In an interview with Le Anne Schreiber in *The New York Times Book Review*, Gordon points out that a central issue in *The Company of Women* is "the phenomenon of women who are very powerful with each other and in their own lives and . . . in their outside accomplishments, but who will suddenly buckle to the authority of a male mentor." It is precisely this tendency which Isabel and Felicitas react against. See Le Anne Schreiber, "A Talk with Mary Gordon," *The New York Times Book Review*, February 15, 1981, pp. 26–28.

Twentieth-Century
Women Writers'
International Conference

November 4 - 7, 1982

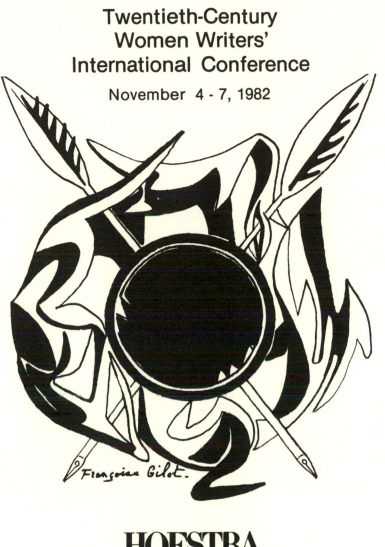

HOFSTRA
UNIVERSITY
HEMPSTEAD, NEW YORK 11550

UNIVERSITY CENTER FOR CULTURAL & INTERCULTURAL STUDIES (UCCIS)

SPECIAL THANKS

It is with the deepest gratitude that the Hofstra University community, in general,

and the University Center for Cultural & Intercultural Studies, in particular,

acknowledge the significant role played by

FRANCOISE GILOT

for her magnanimous contributions to

the Twentieth-Century Women Writers' International Conference.

We are grateful, as well, to those individuals, corporations, and institutions

listed below, who so generously supported this conference.

Co-Sponsoring Institution:

Lufthansa German Airlines
East Meadow, NY

Patrons:

Mr. & Mrs. Rubin Bass

Mr. & Mrs. Jerome L. Clair

Mr. Irving Feinman

Mr. & Mrs. Samuel Gross

Mr. & Mrs. Jerome Moskowitz

Mr. & Mrs. Abe Portnoy

Mr. & Mrs. Stanley S. Spielman

Mr. Howard Weingrow

Mrs. Muriel Weingrow

Cooperating Institutions:

Cultural Services of the French Embassy
New York City

German Information Center
New York City

Holiday Inn Convention Center
Hempstead, NY

Long Island Marriott Hotel
Garden City, NY

Nassau County Office of Cultural
    Development
Roslyn, NY

Nassau Library System
Uniondale, NY

L. F. O'Connell Associates
Garden City, NY

The Study, Inc.
Andover, NJ

Cover: Designed by Françoise Gilot

TWENTIETH-CENTURY WOMEN WRITERS' INTERNATIONAL CONFERENCE

November 4-7, 1982

CONFERENCE DIRECTORS: Alice Kessler-Harris
                                         William McBrien

CONFERENCE COORDINATORS: Natalie Datlof
                                         Alexej Ugrinsky

CONFERENCE COMMITTEE: Joseph G. Astman   Louis Kern
                                         Diana Ben-Merre   Myra Kogen
                                         Marie M. Collins   Joann Peck Krieg
                                         Peter D'Albert   Frank S. Lambasa
                                         Michael D'Innocenzo   Nora de Marval McNair
                                         Katherine C. Hill   Rhoda Nathan
                                         Robert N. Keane   Natalie Naylor
                                         Frederick M. Keener   Michael Steinman

                            CONFERENCE SECRETARY: Marilyn Seidman

COOPERATING UNITS OF HOFSTRA UNIVERSITY:

Black History Committee

David Filderman Gallery

Department of Comparative Literature and Languages

Department of Drama

Department of English and the Creative Writing Program

Department of Fine Arts

Department of French

Department of History

Department of Music

Department of Spanish

Emily Lowe Gallery

The Women's Center

Women's Studies Program    **UNIVERSITY CENTER FOR CULTURAL & INTERCULTURAL STUDIES**

HOFSTRA UNIVERSITY
HEMPSTEAD, NEW YORK 11550

Joseph G. Astman: Director

Wednesday, November 3, 1982

Pre-Conference Parallel Events   Film Festival

7:30 P.M.

Introductions: Joann Peck Krieg
                          Dept. of English, Hofstra University

"The Black Experience in the Creation of Drama" -
  Lorraine Hansberry

"Kate Chopin's 'The Story of an Hour'"

"When this You See Remember Me" - Gertrude Stein

"World of Light: A Portrait of May Sarton"

Student Center Theatre (North Campus)

8:00 P.M.

Special Address: Sawako Ariyoshi (Japan)

"The Author and Her Works: A Personal Update"

Great Neck Library, Community Room
Bayview Avenue at Grist Mill Lane
Great Neck, NY

Thursday, November 4, 1982

9:00 - 11:00 A.M.   Registration: Student Center Theatre Lobby (North Campus)

11:00 - 12:00   Greetings from the Hofstra University Community

                              Joseph G. Astman, Director
                              University Center for Cultural & Intercultural Studies
                              Hofstra Cultural Center

                              James M. Shuart
                              President

Introduction: Shirley Langer
                        New College, Hofstra University

Opening Address: Joyce Carol Oates

"The Faith of a (Woman) Writer"

12:00 - 1:30 P.M.   Lunch: Student Center Cafeterias (North Campus)
                                      (See p. 25 for schedule)

Thursday, November 4 (cont'd.) - Student Center Theatre (North Campus)

1:30 - 2:00 P.M.

> Introduction: Alice Kessler-Harris
>   Dept. of History, Hofstra University
>
> Special Address: Elaine Showalter
>
> "Joyce Carol Oates' The Dead and Feminist Criticism"

Dining Rooms ABC (North Campus)

2:00 - 3:30 P.M.   PANEL 1 - TONI MORRISON

(Parallel Panels)   Moderator: Vivian Wood
                                   Dept. of Acquisitions, Hofstra University Library

                       "Toni Morrison's Song of Solomon: The Creation of a New Typology"
                       A. Caroline Gebhard, University of Virginia

                       "A Dangerous Unity: Fair and Dark Women in Toni Morrison's
                          The Bluest Eye"
                       Vincente F. Gotera, Indiana University

                       "A Way of Ordering Experience: A Study of Toni Morrison's
                          The Bluest Eye and Sula"
                       Robert Sargent, Hofstra University

                       PANEL 2 - SCIENCE FICTION/WOMEN'S UTOPIA

                       Moderator: Barbara Bengels
                                   Dept. of English, Hofstra University

                       "Leigh Brackett: First Lady of Science Fiction"
                       Donna M. DeBlasio, Youngstown State University

                       "'To Weave Some Harmony': Communication as Goal in the
                          Works of Ursula K. LeGuin"
                       Twila Yates Papay, Hofstra University

                       "News from E. Nesbit: Socialism and the Story of the Amulet"
                       Suzanne Rahn, Pacific Lutheran University

                       PANEL 3 - CANADIAN WRITERS

                       Moderator: John Murphy
                                   Dept. of English, Merrimack College

                       "Margaret Atwood, Margaret Laurence, and Their Nineteenth-
                          Century Forerunners"
                       Ann Edwards Boutelle, Mount Holyoke College

Thursday, November 4 (cont'd.) - Dining Rooms ABC (North Campus)

2:00 - 3:30 P.M.   PANEL 3 - CANADIAN WRITERS (Cont'd.)

(Párallel Panels)   "Mothers and Daughters in Gabrielle Roy's The Tin Flute,
                             Street of Riches and The Road Past Altamont"
                         M. G. Hesse, University of Lethbridge (Canada)

                         "Beverley Simons, Canadian Playwright of the Pacific Rim"
                         Rota Herzberg Lister, University of Waterloo (Canada)

3:30 - 5:00   WRITERS ON THEIR CRAFT: THE NOVEL

                         Moderator: Kathrin Perutz

                         Marilyn French
                         Julia Markus
                         Nina Schneider

5:00 - 7:00   Opening of Gallery Exhibit and Reception

                         "Twentieth-Century Literary Women: A Selection"

                         David Filderman Gallery
                         Department of Special Collections
                         Hofstra University Library - 9th Floor

                         Dinner - Student Center Cafeterias (North Campus)
                                  (See p. 25 for schedule)

7:00 - 8:30   Dining Rooms ABC (North Campus)

(Parallel Panels)

                         PANEL 4 - AMERICAN WRITERS (a)

                         Moderator: Susan Lorsch
                                     Dept. of English, Hofstra University

                         "Anzia Yezierska and the Muddy Footprint of American
                             Female Ethnicity"
                         Mary Dearborne, Columbia University

                         "In Search of 'Ordinary Human Happiness': Male and Female
                             Value Systems in Mary Gordon's Novels"
                         Susan E. Ward, St. Lawrence University

                         "Defeating the False God: Janie's Self-Determination in
                             Zora Neale Hurston's Their Eyes Were Watching God"
                         Gay Wilentz, University of Texas/Austin

The Interart Theatre presents

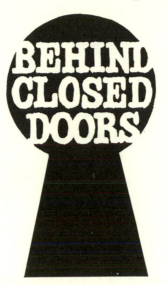

THE PRIVATE HOURS OF DR. DON AND DR. MAX

A Rehearsed Reading
by Clare Coss

Directed by Carol M. Tanzman

Discussion with the playwright and
director following the reading

Thursday, November 4   8:30 P.M.
Student Center Theatre, North Campus

The Interart Theatre, Women's Interart Center
549 West 53rd Street, New York, New York 10019
Margot Lewitin, artistic director

Thursday, November 4 (Cont'd.)   Dining Rooms ABC (North Campus)

7:00 - 8:30 P.M.   PANEL 5 - MARGARET DRABBLE

(Parallel Panels)   Moderator: Ellen Cronan Rose
                                          Dept. of English, Haverford College

                             "The Development of Narrative Form in Margaret Drabble's Novels"
                             Pamela S. Bromberg, Simmons College

                             "Acts of Self-Creation: Female Identity in the Novels of
                               Margaret Drabble"
                             Anne G. Hoffman, Fordham University

                             "Writing as Exploration: Drabble's Sense of the Middle Problem"
                             Jean Pickering, California State University

                             PANEL 6 - THE WRITER AS REVOLUTIONARY

                             Moderator: Anne Fremantle

                             "Women Writers up in Arms in Lebanon"
                             Miriam Cooke, Duke University
                             Durham, NC

                             "From Passivity to Passion: Woman as Revolutionary in
                               Joan Didion's A Book of Common Prayer"
                             Virginia Cox, University of Wisconsin

                             "Independence from India: From Delusion to Dust"
                             Charmazel Dudt, West Texas State University

8:30 P.M.   DRAMA PRESENTATION   Student Center Theatre (North Campus)

                             ┌───┐
                             │ "Behind Closed Doors (The Private Hours of Dr. Don   │
                             │   and Dr. Max)"   │
                             │   │
                             │ A Rehearsed Reading   │
                             │   │
                             │ Playwright: Clare Coss   │
                             │   │
                             │ Director: Carol M. Tanzman   │
                             │   │
                             │ Presented by: The Interart Theatre, New York, NY   │
                             │   │
                             │ Discussion with playwright and director following the performance │
                             │   │
                             │ Discussant: Linda Longmire   │
                             │   New College, Hofstra University   │
                             └───┘

                             Coffee

Friday, November 5 _____ Dining Rooms ABC (North Campus)

9:00 A.M. - 5:00 P.M.   Book Fair;   Student Center Mezzanine
                                           (See pp. 23-24 for Book Fair Directory)

                             Coffee: Student Center Mezzanine

9:00 - 10:30 A.M.   PANEL 7 - FRENCH WRITERS

(Parallel Panels)   Moderator: Avriel Goldberger
                                         Dept. of French, Hofstra University

                            "Effects of Urbanization in the Novels of Christiane Rochefort"
                            Anne D. Cordero, George Mason University

                            "Marguerite Yourcenar's Sexual Politics in Fiction, 1939"
                            Judith L. Johnston, New York City

                            "Resolution in Marguerite Duras' Novel Moderato Cantabile"
                            Jeanne K. Welcher, C.W. Post Center/LIU

                            PANEL 8 - GERMAN WRITERS

                            Moderator: Doris Starr Guilloton
                                         Dept. of German, New York University

                            "Clara Zetkin's Radical Cultural Policy and its Roots in the
                               Socialist Women's Movement of Wilhelmine Germany"
                            Joan Reutershan, New York University

                            "German Women Speak Out: Documentary Prose from the Sixties
                               to the Eighties"
                            Margaret Herzfeld Sander, New York University

                            "A German Deviation: Irmgard Keun"
                            Livia Z. Wittmann, University of Canterbury
                            Christchurch, New Zealand

                            PANEL 9 - PLAYWRIGHTS

                            Moderator: Andrew Kappel
                                         Dept. of English, Hofstra University

                            "Toward a New American Theater: Maryat Lee's Ecotheater"
                            William W. French, West Virginia University

                            "Rachel Crothers: A Twentieth-Century Phenomenon"
                            Zoe Coralnik Kaplan, John Jay College/CUNY

                            "'Sighted Eyes, Feeling Hearts': Lorraine Hansberry's
                               Quest for Community"
                            Maria K. Mootry, Southern Illinois University

10:45 A.M. - 12:15 P.M. (Parallel Panels)	**WRITERS ON THEIR CRAFT: PLAYWRITING** Moderator: Oleg Kerensky Clare Coss Elaine Jackson Maryat Lee **WRITERS ON THEIR CRAFT: POETRY** Moderator: Arthur Gregor Fay Chang Jane Cooper Carolyn Kizer Grace Schulman
12:30 - 2:00 P.M.	Lunch: Student Center Cafeterias (North Campus) (See p. 25 for schedule)

2:00 - 2:30

> **Dining Rooms ABC, Student Center (North Campus)**
>
> Introduction: James M. Shuart
>   President
>
>   Hugues de Kerret, Cultural Attaché
>   Cultural Services to the French Embassy
>   New York City
>
> Special Address: Françoise Gilot
>
> "Colette: From Perception to Language"

2:30 - 4:00	**PANEL 10 - SIMONE DE BEAUVOIR**
	
	Moderator/Discussant: Marie M. Collins, Acting Associate Dean
	                                     Rutgers University/Newark
	
	"Women and Choice - A New Look at Simone de Beauvoir and
	   The Second Sex"
	Carol Ascher, New York City
	
	"Simone de Beauvoir and the nouveau féminisme"
	Irène Pagès, University of Guelph (Canada)

Friday, November 5 (Cont'd.)   Dining Rooms ABC (North Campus)

2:30 - 4:00 P.M.   PANEL 11 - POETS IN PROTEST: CHILE, IRAN AND BULGARIA

(Parallel Panels)   Moderator: Mildred Jeffrey
                                          Dept. of English, Hofstra University

                              "From Watcher to the Militant" (A Bilingual Poetry Reading)
                              Marjorie Agosin, Wellesley College

                              "The Poetry of Snezhina Slavova"
                              Yuri V. Karageorge, East Carolina University

                              "'Only the Voice Remains': Forugh Farrokhzad, an Iranian
                                Poet in a Changing Society"
                              Julie Scott Meisami, University of California/Berkeley

                              PANEL 12 - WRITERS OF AUSTRALIA AND NEW ZEALAND

                              Moderator: Beate Josephi
                                          Adelaide, Australia

                              "A Woman on Her Own (Janet Frame)"
                              Elody Rathgen
                              Christchurch, New Zealand

                              "Miles Franklin: Chronicler of the Australian Bush and
                                Early Feminist"
                              Paulette Rose, New York City

                              "Things Fall Apart: The Political Novels of Christina Stead"
                              Louise Yelin, College at Purchase/SUNY

                              Student Center Theatre (North Campus)

4:00 - 4:30   Introduction: Alice Kessler-Harris
                                             Dept. of History, Hofstra University

                              Special Address: Paule Marshall

                              "A Long Apprenticeship"

4:30 - 6:00   WRITERS ON THEIR CRAFT: BIOGRAPHY

                              Moderator/Discussant: Maureen Howard

                              Carol Ascher
                              Blanche Cook
                              Eileen Simpson

INTERNATIONAL BANQUET

6:00 p.m.   Cash Bar -- Dining Room C (North Campus)

                   Banquet -- Main Dining Room (North Campus)

                   Concert -- Main Dining Room (North Campus)

PROGRAM

MUSIC BY WOMEN COMPOSERS

Judith Alstadter, guest pianist
*Ray Kunicki, violin
*Seymour Benstock, 'cello

Valse, Opus 9 (La Corbeille des Fleurs)................Teresa Carreño (1853-1917)
                   Ms. Alstadter

Andante cantabile..Kathryn E. Lucke

Pas d'Echarpes.......................................Cécile Chaminade (1857-1944)
                   Mr. Benstock
                   Ms. Alstadter

Trio in G Minor, Opus 17.............................Clara Schumann (1819-1896)
Allegro moderato

Allegretto
                   Ms. Alstadter
                   Messrs. Kunicki and Benstock

*Member of The Hofstra Quartet

Friday, November 5, 1982 (Cont'd.)   Evening Program - Main Dining Room

9:00 P.M.   WRITERS ON THEIR CRAFT: THE INTERNATIONAL NOVELIST

                             Introduction: Robert C. Vogt, Dean
                                            Hofstra College of Liberal Arts & Sciences

                             Moderator: Frank S. Lambasa
                                         Dept. of Comparative Literature & Languages
                                         Hofstra University

                             Sawako Ariyoshi - Japan

                             Dominique Desanti - France

                             Rachel Eytan - Israel

                             Gisela Elsner - Federal Republic of Germany

FOR THOSE NOT CHOOSING THE INTERNATIONAL BANQUET THERE WILL BE A FILM FESTIVAL

6:00 - 9:00 P.M.   Student Center Theatre (North Campus)

                             "The Black Experience in the Creation of Drama" -
                                Lorraine Hansberry

                             "Kate Chopin's 'The Story of an Hour'"

                             "When this You See Remember Me" - Gertrude Stein

                             "World of Light: A Portrait of May Sarton"

Saturday, November 6   Student Center Mezzanine (North Campus)

8:00 - 9:00 A.M.   <u>Continental Breakfast</u> -- Mezzanine

9:00 A.M. - 5:00 P.M.   <u>Book Fair</u> - (See pp. 23-24 for Book Fair Directory)

                          <u>Coffee</u>

David Filderman Gallery Exhibit, Library -- 9th floor
"Twentieth-Century Literary Women -- A Selection"

Saturday - 10:30 a.m. - 1:30 p.m.
Sunday   - 10:30 a.m. - 1:30 p.m.

9:00 - 10:30 P.M.   Dining Rooms ABC (North Campus)

(Parallel Panels)   PANEL 13 - EUDORA WELTY

                          Moderator: Carolyn Heilbrun
                                      Dept. of English and Comparative Literature
                                      Columbia University

                          "Eudora Welty: Listening to 'Powerhouse'"
                          Thomas H. Getz, Pennsylvania State University

                          "Invisible Woman: Eudora Welty and the Black Community"
                          Ruth Vande Kieft, Queens College/CUNY

                          "The Case of the Dangling Signifier: Phallic Imagery in
                            'Moon Lake'"
                          Patricia S. Yaeger, Williams College

                          PANEL 14 - BRITISH WRITERS

                          Moderator: Suzette Henke
                                      Dept. of English, SUNY at Binghamton

                          "Barbara Pym and the Africans"
                          Charles Burkhart, Temple University

                          "Communicating Differently: Doris Lessing's <u>The Marriages
                            between Zones Three, Four and Five</u>"
                          Ellen Peel, Yale University

                          "Cressida in the Twentieth Century: The Protagonist in the
                            Work of Jean Rhys"
                          Nikki Stiller, New Jersey Institute of Technology

9:00 - 10:30 A.M.   PANEL 15 - THE SEARCH FOR AUTHENTIC LANGUAGE

(Parallel Panels)   Moderator/Discussant: Hugues de Kerret, Cultural Attaché
                                                  Cultural Services of the French Embassy
                                                  New York City

                           "Lifting the Veil: Eleanor Clark's Linguistic Perceptions"
                           Alex Szogyi, Hunter College/CUNY & The Graduate Center/CUNY

                           "Use (and Abuse) of Language for Nathalie Sarraute"
                           Gretchen R. Besser, South Orange, NJ

10:30 - 12:00 Noon   WRITERS ON THEIR CRAFT: THE ESSAY

(Parallel Panels)   Moderator: Barbara Grizzuti Harrison

                           Susan Edmiston
                           Vivian Gornick
                           Nora Sayre

                           WRITERS ON THEIR CRAFT: PUBLISHING

                           Moderator: Nancy K. Bereano

                           Jo Baird
                           Vivian Cadden
                           Florence Howe

12:00 - 1:00 P.M.   <u>Lunch:</u> Student Center Cafeterias (North Campus)
                                          (See p. 23 for schedule)

(See p. 23 for schedule)

1:00 - 1:30

<u>Introduction:</u> Alexej Ugrinsky, University Center
                for Cultural and Intercultural Studies
 	
 <u>Special Address:</u> Gisela Elsner
 	
 "Women Writers in a Literary Ghetto:
   The Situation in Germany"

1:30 - 3:00 P.M.   PANEL 16 - VIRGINIA WOOLF

(Parallel Panels)   Moderator: Claire Sprague
                                              Dept. of English, Brooklyn College/CUNY

                                  "Characterization of Gender-Malaise: Gazing up at the
                                     Windows of Jacob's Room"
                                  Jane E. Archer, Birmingham-Southern College

                                  "Virginia, Virginius, Virginity"
                                  Louise A. DeSalvo, Hunter College/CUNY

                                  "'The London Scene': Gender and Class in Virginia Woolf's
                                     London"
                                  Susan Squier, SUNY at Stony Brook

                                  PANEL 17 - AUTOBIOGRAPHICAL WRITINGS

                                  Moderator: Friedrich Ulfers
                                              Dept. of German, New York University

                                  "Luise Rinser's Autobiographical Prose: Political Engagement
                                     and Feminist Awareness"
                                  Elke Frederiksen, University of Maryland

                                  "Records of Survival: The Autobiographical Writings of
                                     Marieluise Fleisser and Marie Luise Kaschnitz"
                                  Ruth-Ellen B. Joeres, University of Minnesota

                                  "The Twentieth Century Female Bildungsroman: A Late Arrival"
                                  Esther K. Labovitz, New York University

                                  PANEL 18 - AMERICAN WRITERS (b)

                                  Moderator: Joann Peck Krieg
                                              Dept. of English, Hofstra University

                                  "'Grave, Endearing Traditions': Edith Wharton and the
                                     Domestic Novel"
                                  Jeanne Boydston, Yale University

                                  "Edna St. Vincent Millay: Saint of the Modern Sonnet"
                                  Jean Gould, New York City

                                  "Pioneers in the Art of the American Theatre:
                                     Susan Glaspell"
                                  Dinah Pladott, Tel Aviv University (Israel)

Saturday, November (Cont'd.)   Dining Rooms ABC (North Campus)

3:00 - 4:30 P.M.   PANEL 19 - GERTRUDE STEIN

(Parallel Panels)   Moderator/Discussant: Edward Burns
                                                         Dept. of English, The Graduate Center/CUNY

                                  "The -Theatre of Gertrude Stein"
                                  Leon Katz, Yale School of Drama, Yale University

                                  "Stanzas in Meditation: The Other Autobiography"
                                  Ulla Dydo, Bronx Community College/CUNY

                                  WRITERS ON THEIR CRAFT: LITERARY CRITICISM

                                  Moderator/Discussant: ·Mary Ann Caws

                                  Edith Milton
                                  Catherine R. Stimpson

                                  PANEL 20 - WOMEN ON THE LEFT: WRITERS OF THE '30s

                                  Moderator/Discussant: Paul Lauter
                                                         The Feminist Press, Old Westbury, NY

                                  "Josephine Herbst"
                                  Elinor Langer, The Bunting Institute, Radcliffe College

                                  "Olive Tilford Dargan (Fielding Burke)"
                                  Anna Shannon, University of West Virginia

4:30 - 6:00   PANEL 21 - NEW DIRECTIONS IN VIRGINIA WOOLF CRITICISM:
                                     DISCUSSION
(Parallel Panels)
                                  Moderator: Carolyn Heilbrun
                                              Dept. of English and Comparative Literature
                                              Columbia University

                                  Rachel Blau DuPlessis
                                  Temple University

                                  Katherine C. Hill
                                  C.W. Post Center/LIU

                                  Brenda Silver
                                  Dartmouth College

Saturday, November 6 (Cont'd.)   Dining Rooms ABC (North Campus)

4:30 - 6:00 P.M.   PANEL 22 - AMERICAN WRITERS (c)

(Parallel Panels)   Moderator: Diana Ben-Merre
                                              New College, Hofstra University

                                   "A Distant Mirror: The Biographer's Relationship with
                                     Her Subject (Katherine Anne Porter)"
                                   Joan Givner, University of Regina (Canada)

                                   "The View of Nebraska in Willa Cather's Work"
                                   Doris Grumbach

                                   "Flannery O'Connor: A Question of Context"
                                   Sally Fitzgerald

                                   PANEL 23 - CHINESE WRITERS

                                   Moderator: Marilyn Young
                                              Dept. of History, New York University

                                   "The Woman Warrior: Claiming Narrative Power,
                                     Recreating Female Selfhood"
                                   J. S. Frye, The College of Wooster

                                   "The Doubly Bound Foot in The Woman Warrior"
                                   Margaret Miller, Southeastern Massachusetts University

                                   "Agnes Smedley's 'Cell Mates': A Writer's Discovery of
                                     Voice, Form, and Subject in Prison"
                                   Judith A. Scheffler, Drexel University

6:00   Dinner: Student Center Cafeterias (North Campus)
                                            (See p. 25 for schedule)

7:45 | Introduction: William McBrien
                                                   Dept. of English, Hofstra University

                                     DRAMA PRESENTATION: "Me Again: A Theatre Collage Based
                                                         on the Poetry of Stevie Smith"

                                     Director: Miriam Tulin
                                                Drama Department, Hofstra University

                                     Choreographer: Carl Morris
                                                    Drama Department, Hofstra University

                                     The Little Theatre, South Campus |

Saturday, November 6 (Cont'd.)   Dining Rooms ABC (North Campus)

8:45 P.M.

> SPECIAL EVENT: Remembering Jean Garrigue
>
> Arthur Gregor
> Stanley Kunitz
> Jane Mayhall
> Marjorie Garrigue Smith
> Nancy Sullivan
> Aileen Ward
> Robert Wilson
>
> Program Coordinator: Mary Anne Shea
>   New York University

Sunday, November 7   Dining Rooms ABC (North Campus)

8:00 - 9:00 A.M.   Continental Breakfast: Dining Rooms ABC

> David Filderman Gallery Exhibit, Library -- 9th floor
> "Twentieth-Century Literary Women -- A Selection"
>
> Sunday -- 10:30 a.m. - 1:30 p.m.

9:00 - 10:30   PANEL 24 - THE WRITER AS FEMINIST (a)

(Parallel Panels)   Moderator: Natalie Naylor, Teaching Fellow
                                   New College, Hofstra University

                       "Rebecca West: A Voice of Authority"
                       Jane Marcus, University of Texas/Austin

                       "Adrienne Rich Goes to the Advanced Placement Examination:
                          Women's Literature and Feminist Criticism in an Institu-
                          tional Context"
                       John Schilb, Denison University

                       "Kay Boyle's Feminism"
                       Sandra Whipple Spanier, SUNY at Stony Brook

                       PANEL 25 - H. D.

                       Moderator: Marylin Arthur
                                   Dept. of Classics, Wesleyan University

                       "H. D.'s Sea Garden: Myth of the Inner Life"
                       Eileen Gregory, University of Dallas

9:00 - 10:30 A.M.   "Gifts and Tributes: H. D.'s Autobiographical Writings"
                        Adalaide Morris, University of Iowa

                        "An End to Torment: H. D.'s Metonymic Course"
                        Paul Smith, Wesleyan University

                        PANEL 26 - SPANISH WRITERS

                        Moderator: Nora de Marval McNair
                                    Dept. of Spanish, Hofstra University

                        "The Dual Journey: Elena Poniatowska's Literary Trajectory"
                        Belle Gale Chevigny, State University of New York/Purchase

                        "Descent into the Self: A Study of Elena Quiroga's La Careta"
                        Carol Marshall, North Texas State University

                        "Women Poets from Puerto Rico: Affirmation and Resistance"
                        Gloria F. Waldman, York College/CUNY

10:45 - 12:15   WRITERS ON THEIR CRAFT: THE SHORT STORY

                        Moderator: Nancy Sullivan

                        Glenda Adams
                        Elizabeth Cullinan
                        Grace Paley

                        WRITERS ON THEIR CRAFT: EDITING

                        Moderator: Molly McKaughan

                        Elizabeth Bartelme
                        Elizabeth Pochoda
                        Nan Talese

12:15 - 1:15 P.M.   Brunch: Student Center Cafeteria (North Campus)
                                 (See p. 25 for schedule)

1:15 - 1:45   ┌──┐
                        │ SPECIAL EVENT: A Bilingual Poetry Reading   │
                        │   │
                        │ A Sampling of Spanish Poetry   │
                        │   │
                        │ Introduction: Nora de Marval McNair   │
                        │   │
                        │ Readings: Nora de Marval McNair   │
                        │   Mercedes M. de Rodríguez   │
                        │   │
                        │   Dept. of Spanish, Hofstra University   │
                        └──┘

1:45 - 3:15 P.M.   PANEL 27 - THE WRITER AS FEMINIST (b)

(Parallel Panels)   Moderator: Janet Wagner
                                     Reference Dept., Hofstra University Library

                         "Exorcising the House of Fiction: The Mysterious Case of
                            Shirley Jackson"
                         Lynette Carpenter, University of Cincinnati

                         "A Swiss-French Woman Writer: Anne Cunéo"
                         Monique Moser-Verrey, University of Montreal (Canada)

                         "Dacia Maraini, From Alienation to Feminism"
                         Augustus Pallotta, Syracuse University

                         PANEL 28 - THE HOLOCAUST

                         Moderator/Discussant: Ellen Fine
                                                Dept. of French, Kingsborough Community
                                                   College/CUNY

                         "Gertrud Kolmar: J(udith)' accuse"
                         Michael C. Eben, York University (Canada)

                         "Charlotte Delbo: The Woman/Book of Birkenau"
                         Rosette Lamont, The Graduate Center/CUNY

                         PANEL 29 - SEXUALITY

                         Moderator: Ann Snitow
                                     Dept. of English, Rutgers University/New Brunswick

                         "Culture-Making: Lesbian Classics in the Year 2000?"
                         Melanie Kaye, Vermont College

                         "Two Women: The Transformations from Hawthorne, to James,
                            to Djuna Barnes's Nightwood"
                         Alison R. Rieke, University of Kentucky

                         "Jocelyne François: An Introduction"
                         Nanette Shaw, University of North Florida

Sunday, November 7

3:00 P.M.   SPECIAL EVENT: Music Room, Emily Lowe Hall (South Campus)

                                          "Androgyny In Art"

                             Eleanor Antin -- Conceptual and Performance Artist

                                  Ms. Antin's performances are written and staged by
                                  her and employ a variety of art forms including
                                  drama, dance, video, photography, writing and
                                  painting.

2:00 - 5:00 P.M.   Reception: Emily Lowe Gallery (South Campus)

                                          "Androgyny In Art"

SPECIAL EXHIBITS: Book Fair -- Student Centre Mezzanine (North Campus)
                             Friday, November 5 - 9:00-5:00 P.M.
                             Saturday, November 6 - 9:00-5:00 P.M.

                             David Filderman Gallery
                             Hofstra University Library -- 9th floor (South Campus)

                             "Twentieth-Century Literary Women: A Selection"

                             November 4, 1982 - January 31, 1983

                             Gallery Hours: Monday - Friday -- 9:00 A.M. - 5:00 P.M.
                                            Saturday -- 10:30 - 1:30 (November 6)
                                            Sunday -- 10:30 - 1:30 (November 7)

                             Emily Lowe Gallery

                             "Androgyny In Art"

                             November 6 - December 19, 1982

                             Gallery Hours: Monday - Closed
                                            Tuesday - 10:00 A.M. - 9:00 P.M.
                                            Wednesday-Friday -- 10:00 A.M. - 4:45 P.M.
                                            Saturday & Sunday -- 1:00 - 5:00 P.M.

Twentieth-Century Women Writers' Conference
Book Exhibition

Participants

AMS Press, Inc.
New York, NY

Angus & Robertson Publishers
London, England

Bantam Books
New York, NY

Beacon Press
Boston, MA

R. R. Bowker Company
New York, NY

The Crossing Press
Trumansburg, NY

Dial Press
New York, NY

Farrar, Straus & Giroux
New York, NY

The Feminist Press
Old Westbury, NY

George Sand Books
Los Angeles, CA

Granite Books East
Penobscot, ME

Greenwood Press
Westport, CT

Harvard University Press
Cambridge, MA

Hofstra University Publications
Twentieth Century Literature
George Sand Newsletter

Houghton Mifflin, Co.
New York, NY

IKON Magazine
New York, NY

Indiana University Press
Bloomington, IN

The Iowa Review
Iowa City, IA

Kodansha International U.S.A.,Ltd.
New York, NY

Doris Lessing Newsletter

MacMillan Publishing Co.
New York, NY

Modern Language Association of America
New York, NY

New American Library
New York, NY

W.W. Norton & Company, Inc.
New York, NY

Oxford University Press
New York, NY

Paideia Books
Rochester, NY

Paulette Rose, Ltd.
Fine and Rare Books
New York, NY

Pergamon Press
Elmsford, NY

Persea Books
New York, NY

G. P. Putnam's Sons
New York, NY

Schoenhof's Foreign Books
Cambridge, MA

Summit Books
New York, NY

Sunbury Press
New York, NY

SUNY Press
Albany, NY

Taplinger Publishing Company
New York, NY

University of Chicago Press
Chicago, IL

Twentieth-Century Women Writers' Conference
Book Exhibition

Participants

(Cont'd.)

University of Lethbridge
Alberta, Canada

Viking Penguin, Inc.
New York, NY

Vintage Books
New York, NY

Twayne Publishers
Boston, MA

Womankind Books
Huntington, NY

Women's Studies Program
Hofstra University

Virginia Woolf Society
Virginia Woolf Miscellany

New York City Commission on the
   Status of Women
New York, NY

Nel Panzeca
Director, Book Exhibition

General Conference Information

Dining Schedule

Main Cafeteria:

Breakfast:

Mon. - Fri.	7:30 a.m. -- 10:00 a.m.
Sat. - Sun.	11:00 a.m. -- 2:00 p.m. (Brunch)

Lunch:

Mon. - Fri.	10:45 a.m. -- 2:00 p.m.
	11:00 a.m. -- 2:00 p.m. (Brunch)

Dinner:

Mon. - Fri.	4:30 p.m. -- 7:00 p.m.
Sat. - Sun.	4:30 p.m. -- 6:15 p.m.

The Netherlands:

Breakfast:

Mon. - Fri.	same as above
Sat. - Sun.	closed

Lunch:

Mon. - Fri.	10:45 a.m. -- 2:00 p.m.
Sat. - Sun.	closed

Dinner:

Mon. - Thurs.	4:30 p.m. -- 7:00 p.m.
Closed Fri., Sat., Sun.	

Rathskeller:

Mon. - Fri.	Open 11:00 a.m. -- 7:00 p.m.
	Bar -- 3:00 p.m. -- 7:00 p.m.

BOOK STORE HOURS

Mon. - Thurs.	9:00 a.m. -- 7:00 p.m.
Friday	9:00 a.m. -- 5:00 p.m.
Saturday	10:00 a.m. -- 2:00 p.m.
Sunday	CLOSED

POST OFFICE HOURS

Mon. - Friday	9:00 a.m. -- 1:00 p.m.
	2:00 p.m. -- 3:30 p.m.
Saturday & Sunday	CLOSED

CONFERENCE STAFF:

UNIVERSITY CENTER FOR CULTURAL & INTERCULTURAL STUDIES:

Barbara Bachenheimer
Karin Barnaby
Nel Panzeca
Stuart Weber

Paul Hefner
Doris Keane
Barbara Lekatsas
Marjorie Veneck
Sara Zug

FINE ARTS CLUB:

Troy Giorgio, President

GERMAN CLUB:

Janet Zale, President
Tricia Beck
Stephanie Dana
Michael Jakob
Robert Kirsch
Nancy Longe
Susan Mast
Pamela Salomon
Tina Tersigni

INTERNATIONAL HOUSE:

Mohamed Omar, Resident Assistant

WOMEN'S CENTER

Linda Neglia, President
Linda Remsen

CREDIT for the success of the Conference goes to more people than can be named on
    this program, but those below deserve a special vote of thanks:

HOFSTRA UNIVERSITY OFFICERS: James M. Shuart, President
                               Sanford S. Hammer, Acting Provost
                               Robert C. Vogt, Dean, HCLAS

ARA SLATER: Tony Internicola, Director, Dining Services
              Maureen Vining, Banquet Manager

DAVID FILDERMAN GALLERY: Department of Special Collections
                           Marguerite Regan, Assistant to the Dean of Library Services
                           Nancy Herb
                           Anne Rubino

DEPARTMENT OF ENGLISH: Barbara Stroh, Senior Executive Secretary
                         Susan Ciaccio, Secretary to the Faculty

DEPARTMENT OF HISTORY: Mildred Baker, Senior Executive Secretary

DEVELOPMENT OFFICE: Rochelle Lowenfeld, Director
                      Corey V. Geske, Assistant to Director

EMILY LOWE GALLERY: Gail Gelburd, Director
                      Mary Wakeford, Administrative Assistant

HOFSTRA LIBRARY ASSOCIATES: Walter Fillin, President

HOFSTRA UNIVERSITY. LIBRARY: Charles R. Andrews, Dean

OFFICE OF THE SECRETARY: Robert D. Noble, Secretary
                           Frances B. Jacobsen, Assistant to the Secretary
                           Marge Mirabella
                           Stella Sinicki, Supervisor, Special Secretarial Services
                           Jack Ruegamer, Graphic Artist
                           Ronnie Fitzwilliam
                           Doris Brown & Staff

OPERATIONAL SERVICES: James Fellman, Director

PUBLIC SAFETY AND TELECOMMUNICATIONS: Robert Crowley, Director
                                        John Fitzgerald, Deputy Director

SCHEDULING OFFICE: Charles L. Churchill, Assistant Facilities Manager
                     Dorothy Fetherston, Director

TECHNICAL AND MEDIA SERVICES: Robert J. Kleinhans, Director
                                Albert Nowicki and Staff

UNIVERSITY RELATIONS: Harold A. Klein, Director
                        James Merritt, Assistant Director
                        Eve Glasser, Editor/Writer
                        M.F. Klerk, Administrative Assistant

CONFERENCES AT HOFSTRA UNIVERSITY

George Sand Centennial - November 1976

Heinrich von Kleist Bicentennial - November 1977

The Chinese Woman - December 1977

George Sand: Her Life, Her Works, Her Influence - April 1978

William Cullen Bryant and His America - October 1978

The Trotsky-Stalin Conflict in the 1920's - March 1979

Albert Einstein Centennial - November 1979

Renaissance Venice Symposium - March 1980

Sean O'Casey - March 1980

Walt Whitman - April 1980

Nineteenth Century Women Writers - November 1980

Fedor Dostoevski - April 1981

Gotthold Ephraim Lessing - November 1981

Franklin Delano Roosevelt - March 4-6, 1982

Johann Wolfgang von Goethe - April 1-3, 1982

James Joyce - October 21-23, 1982

Twentieth Century Women Writers - November 4-7, 1982

Harry S. Truman: The Man from Independence - April 14-16, 1983

Romanticism in the Old and the New World - Washington Irving,
     Stendhal, and Zhukovskii - October 13-16, 1983

Espectador Universal: Jose Ortega y Gasset - November 10-12, 1983

Dwight D. Eisenhower - March 29-31, 1984

George Orwell - October 11-13, 1984

Friedrich von Schiller - November 8-10, 1984

Harlem Renaissance - February 28-March 2, 1985

John F. Kennedy - March 28-30, 1985

Eighteenth Century Women Writers - October 10-12, 1985

Avant Garde Art and Literature - November 14-16, 1985

"Calls for Papers" available

Index

Aichinger, Ilse, 165

Ainsley's (magazine), 132, 133

Albee, Edward, "Who's Afraid of Virginia Woolf?," 7

Alcott, Louisa May, 18, 38, 145; *Little Women*, 36, 37; *Work: A Story of Experience*, 34

Alexander, Shana, 14, 15

Allender, Nina Evans, 67

Ammons, Elizabeth, *Edith Wharton's Argument*, 31, 33–34

Anthony, Susan B., 67

Ascher, Carol, 3; *Simone de Beavoir; A Life of Freedom*, 173

Atwood, Margaret, 46; *The Journals of Susanna Moodie*, 41–45; *Lady Oracle*, 42; "Speeches for Dr. Frankenstein," 42; *Surfacing*, 42

Augustine, St., 242, 243

Austen, Jane, 185, 243, 285

Bachmann, Ingeborg, 165

Baez, Joan, Sr., 67

Baker, Carlos, 223

Balfour, Arthur James, 180

Balzac, Honoré de, *Seraphita*, 274

Bamberger, Charles, 205

Barker, Granville, 239

Barnes, Djuna, *Nightwood*, 71–79

Barth, Karl, 169

Beauvoir, Simone de, 3, 173–78; *America Day by Day*, 175; *The Ethics of Ambiguity*, 175–77; *Pyrrhus et Cinéas*, 175; *The Second Sex*, 175–78

Beckett, Samuel, 59

Beethoven, Ludwig von, 129

Bell, Clive, 283

Bell, Julian, 283

Bell, Quentin, 245

Bell, Vanessa, 280

Benet, Stephen, 136

Benet, William Rose, 136

Berryman, John, *The Dream Songs*, 10

Bibliothèque Nationale, 177

Bishop, Elizabeth, 10

Bishop, John Peale, 133, 134

Blunt, Evelyn, 130

Boissevain, Eugen, 137

Bombeck, Erma, 14, 15, 144, 147

Bone, Robert, *The Negro Novel in America*, 290

Boyle, Katherine Evans. *See* Kay Boyle

Boyle, Kay, 59–68; *Babylon*, (translation of Rene Crevel's work), 60; *Being Geniuses Together*, 60; "The Bridegroom's Body," 63, 64; "Episode in the Life of an Ancestor," 60; *Fifty Stories*, 60; *Generation without Farewell*, 62, 63; *His Human Majesty*, 62; *My Next Bride*, 65; *The Noblest Wit-*

nesses, 63; *Plagued by the Nightin-
gale*, 65; *This Is Not a Letter and
Other Poems*, 60; *Three Short Novels*,
60; *The Underground Woman*, 60, 62;
Wedding Day, 60; *Words that Must
Somehow Be Said: Selected Essays of
Kay Boyle 1927–1984*, 60
Brecht, Bertolt, 151, 167
Brenan, Gerald, 244
Bronte, Charlotte, 25, 243, 244; *Jane
Eyre*, 41, 42, 105–107, 111; *Shirley*,
15, 18
Bronte, Emily, 18; *Wuthering Heights*,
42, 106, 113
Brown, Gladys, 137
Browne, Sir Thomas, *Religio Medici*,
180
Buck, Pearl, 14, 15
The Bulletin, 119
Burke, Kenneth, 194
Bynner, Witter, 130, 131, 133

Carlyle, Thomas, 117
Carpenter, Lynette, 3
Céline, Louis-Ferdinand, *Journey to the
End of the Night*, 223
Charpentier, Jean, 222
Chekov, Anton, 17
Chicago, Judy, 114
Cixous, Helen, 116, 117
The Clarion, 238, 240
Clarke, James Freeman, 77
Cliburn, Van, 274
Cocteau, Jean, 224, 240
Cohn, Ruby, 67
Coleridge, Samuel Taylor, 281
Conrad, Joseph, *Heart of Darkness*, 111
Courbet, Gustav, 152
Crane, Hart, 59
Crosby, Caresse, 59, 67
Crosby, Harry, 59
Crowinshield, Frank, 133, 136
Cunard, Nancy, 67

Dante, 245, 248
Davies, Margaret Llewelyn, 241, 242
Davis, Cynthia, 27

Debs, Eugene, 203
Delbo, Charlotte, 3, 247–52; *None of Us
Will Return*, 248; "Phantoms, My
Companions," 249, 250; "Qui rap-
porters ces paroles?," 252; *La Sen-
tence*, 252
Dell, Floyd, 131–33, 137
The Dial, 132
Diaz, Selma Vaz, 106
Dickinson, Emily, 10, 16, 18, 115, 145
Dillon, George, 138
Dolittle, Hilda, 273–77; *End to Torment*,
273, 275; *Palimpsest*, 277; *Tribute to
Freud*, 276
Domin, Hilde, 165
Donne, John, 138
Dostoyevsky, Fedor, *Crime and Punish-
ment*, 224
Douglas, Ann, 31, 33
Drabble, Margaret, 23, 245; *The Garrick
Year*, 26; *The Ice Age*, 22, 25; *Jerusa-
lem the Golden*, 23; *The Middle
Ground*, 21–24, 26–28; *The Millstone*,
25, 26; *Realms of Gold*, 23, 26–27;
The Waterfall, 23, 26
Draws-Tychsen, Helmut, 151
DuBois, W. E. B., 230
Dudach, Georges, 247
Dworkin, Andrea, *Woman Hunting*, 181

Eakin, John Paul, *The New England Girl*,
77
Eastman, Max, 133, 141
Echevarria, Luis, 210, 217
Egerton, Lady Alice, 182
Eliot, George, 237; *Middlemarch*, 25
Eliot, T. S., 137, 224, 240, 277
Emerson, Ralph Waldo, 5, 18, 77, 78
Emma (magazine), 169
Euclid, 129
Euripides, 194

Fallada, Hans, "Little Man—What
Now?," 95–97, 100, 102
Feuchtwanger, Lion, 151
Ficke, Arthur Davison, 130–38
Flanner, Janet, 67, 68

Flaubert, Gustave, 17; *Madame Bovary*, 222

Fleisser, Marieluise, 149–56; "Aus der Augustenstrasse," 151

Ford, Ford Madox, 113; *Some Do Not*, 244

Forum, (magazine), 65

Foucault, Michel, 193

Franklin, Stella Maria Miles, 4; *All That Swagger*, 123–25; *Back to Bool Bool*, 123; *Cockatoos*, 122, 123; *My Brilliant Career*, 119–21, 123, 125; *My Career Goes Bung*, 121, 122; *Ten Creeks Run*, 122, 123; *Up the Country*, 121, 122

The Freewoman (magazine), 238–40

Freud, Sigmund, 276, 277, 280

Friedan, Betty, 147

Friedman, Lenemaja, 147

Frost, Robert, 130

Fuller, Margaret, 77

Furphy, Joseph, 123

Gardiner, Judith Kegan, 24

George, Lloyd, 180

Gide, André, 240; *The Immoralist*, 223

Gilbert, Sandra, *The Mad Woman in the Attic*, 16, 41, 185

Giraudoux, 251; *Electre*, 250

Glasgow, Ellen, 145

Goethe, Johann Wolfgang von, 243

Goldman, Emma, 203

Good Housekeeping (magazine), 143, 144

Gordon, Mary, 303–08; *The Company of Women*, 303–07; *Final Payments*, 303–06

Gould, Evelyn, "The Enigma of Woman and the Enigmas She Creates: On Sarah Kofman's *L'éEnigme de la femme*," 268

Gould, Louis, *Sea-Change*, 268

Grass, Gunter, *The Tin Drum*, 223

Graves, Robert, 10

Green, H. M., 119

The Guardian (newspaper), 216

Gubar, Susan, *The Mad Woman in the Attic*, 16, 22, 41, 185

Guggenheim, Peggy, 67

Haft, Cynthia, 247

Harvard Guide to Contemporary American Writing, 10, 14

Hawthorne, Nathaniel, *The Blithdale Romance*, 18, 71–74, 76–79

Heilbrun, Carolyn, 4

Heinemann, Marlene E., *Women Prose Writers of the Nazi Holocaust*, 248

Hemenway, Robert, 286

Hemingway, Ernest, 59

Herrick, Robert, 135

Hesse, Hermann, 166

Heydt, Erich, 273, 275

Hillyer, Robert, 141

Hitler, Adolph, 15, 166, 222, 223, 225

Holyroyd, Michael, 239

Homer, *The Iliad*, 184, 186; *The Odyssey*, 185, 186

Howells, William Dean, 71

Hudson Review, 144

Hughes, Richard, *High Wind in Jamaica*, 240

Hurston, Zora Neale, 4, 285–91; *Mules and Men*, 285; *Their Eyes Were Watching God*, 285–91

Hyman, Stanley Edgar, 144

Ibsen, Henrik, *A Doll's House*, 240; *Hedda Gabler*, 226, 241; *Rosmersholm*, 240

Jackson, Shirley, 3; *The Bird's Nest*, 145; *Come Along with Me*, 145, 147, 148; *Hangsaman*, 145; *The Haunting of Hill House*, 144–46; *Life among the Savages*, 144; "The Lottery," 143, 147; *Raising Demons*, 144; *The Road Through the Wall*, 144–47; *The Sundial*, 145; *We Have Always Lived in the Castle*, 145–47; *The Witchcraft of Salem Village*, 147

Jaloux, Edmond, 222

James, Henry, 17, 18; *The Bostonians*, 71–79

Jehlen, Myra, 3

Jhabvala, Ruth Prawer, 159–64; *Amrita*,

164; *Esmond in India*, 160, 161; *Heat and Dust*, 162–64; *Travelers*, 161, 162
Johnson, Diane, 19
Jolas, Eugene, 59
Jouvet, Louis, 248–51
Joyce, James, 17; *Dubliners*, 59, 67, 242, 243
Juhasz, Suzanne, 293

Kafka, Franz, 17
Kaschnitz, Marie Luise, 149–56, 165; *Orte*, 150, 152, 154; *Wohindennich*, 151
Keats, John, *Endymion*, 139
Kerr, Jean, 144
Keun, Irmagard, 3; *Gilgi—One of Us*, 95–97, 100–102
King, Michael, 275
Kingston, Maxine Hong, *The Woman Warrior*, 293–300
Kinnerly, Mitchell, 131, 135
Kollontai, Alexandra, *The Aims and Worth of My Life*, 102; *Pathways of Love*, 100, 101
Kramberg, Karl Heinz, 168

Lacan, 253, 277; *Écrits*, 253, 267; *The Four Fundamental Concepts of Psycho-Analysis*, 264
Ladies' Annuals (journal), 18
Ladies' Home Journal, 60
Lamont, Rosette, 3
Langgasser,Elisabeth, 165
Langtry, Lily, 282
Laurence, Margaret, *The Diviners*, 41, 42, 45, 46
Lawrence, D. H., 243, 244
Lawson, Henry, 123
Lessing, Doris, 10, 245; *The Golden Notebook*, 27, 28
Lewes, George Henry, 15
Literarische welt, Die, 95, 96
Livy, *History of Rome*, 182, 183, 186
Longfellow, Henry Wadsworth, 18
Lowell, Amy, *An American Misccellany of Poetry*, 137

Mabille, Elizabeth, 174
McAlmon, Robert, 59
Macauley, Rose, 241; *Towers of Trebizond*, 239
Macauley, Thomas Babington, *Lays of Ancient Rome*, 182, 184, 186, 188
MacLeish, Archibald, 59
Mailer, Norman, 245
Maitland, F. W., 279
Marshall, Paule, 2
Marvell, Andrew, 135
Marxism, 176
Marx, Karl, 191
The Masses (magazine), 133
Masters, Edgar Lee, 136
Melville, Herman, 5, 255; *Moby Dick*, 253, 254
Menschik, Jutta, *Equal Rights or Emancipation*, 168
Milholland, Inez, 129, 137
Millay, Edna St. Vincent, 14, 15, 129; "Aria da Capo," 129; "The Ballad of the Harp-Weaver," 137; *The Buck in the Snow*, 137; "Epitaph for the Race of Man," 129, 134, 140, 141; "Fatal Interview," 129, 137–40; *A Few Figs from Thistles*, 135, 137; "I'll Slap Your Face," 131; *The Lyric Year*, 130; "Renascence," 130, 131, 133; *Second April*, 135, 137; *Wine From These Grapes*, 140
Miller, Nancy, 15
Millett, Kate, 293
Milton, John, 117; *Comus*, 181–83; *Paradise Lost*, 61
Mitford, Jessica, 67
Moers, Ellen, 106; *Literary Women*, 41, 238
Molière, *Misanthrope*, 250
Monroe, Harriet, *Poetry*, 138
Moodie, Susanna, 41–46; *Life in the Clearings*, 42; *Roughing It in the Bush*, 42
Moore, Harry T., 65
Moore, Marianne, 10
Morrison, Toni, *The Bluest Eye*, 231–34, 236; *Song of Solomon*, 230, 233, 235; *Sula*, 229, 231, 234, 235
Murdoch, Iris, 245

Nabokov, Vladimir, *Speak, Memory: An Autobiography Revisited*, 6
Napoleon, 223, 226
National Woman's Party, 67
Nebeker, Helen, 105
The New Freewoman (magazine), 238
New Republic, 59
New York Call (magazine), 199, 201
The New Yorker, 60, 143, 144
New York Times, 14, 19, 65, 238
New York Times Book Review, 15
New York Times Sunday Magazine, 238
Nietzsche, Freidrich, 8, 117
Norton, Caroline, 241
Les Nouvelles Littéraires, 222
Novedades (newspaper), 213

Oates, Joyce Carol, 3, 14, 15; *The Bloodsmoor Romance*, 16, 18, 19; "The Dead," 16–18; "Luxury of Being Despised," 8, 9; *Marriages and Infidelities*, 17

O'Connor, Matthew, 79
O'Keefe, Georgia, 114
Olsen, Tillie, *Silences*, 65–67
Oswald, Pierre Jean, 252
Ovid, 196

Parsons, Trekkie, 279
Paul, Alice, 67
Paz, Octavio, *The Other Mexico: A Critique of the Pyramid*, 216
Pearson, Norman Holmes, 273
Plath, Sylvia, 10, 67; *Fever 106*, 114
Poe, Edgar Allan, 144
Poetry, 132
Poniatowska, Elena, 209; "Cradle Song," 211; *Dear Diego, with hugs from Quiela*, 212; *Massacre in Mexico*, 209, 210, 215, 216, 217; *Silence is strong*, 217; *Until I see you, my Jesus*, 209, 210, 213–15, 218, 219; *You come at night*, 211
Porter, Katherine Anne, 59, 107, 109; "The Grave," 111
Pound, Ezra, 139, 273, 275–77; *Cantos*, 274

Pratt, Annis, "The New Feminist Criticism," 68
Proust, Marcel, 251
Provincetown Players, 131
Puritanism, 77, 78

Quick (magazine), 170

Racine, 226, 250; *Bajazet*, 221
Ray, Gordon, *H. G. Wells and Rebecca West*, 238
Reed, John, 203
Reedy's Mirror, 130, 132, 133
Register, Cheri, 166
Rembrandt, 224
Robins, Elizabeth, *The Convert*, 243
Rhys, Jean, 105–14; *Voyage into the Dark*, 110; *Wide Sargasso Sea*, 41, 107
Ridge, Lola, 67
Rinser, Luise, *The Black Donkey*, 169; *Border Crossing*, 170; *Complete Joy*, 165; *Construction Site*, 170; *Diary from Prison*, 166, 167, 169; *Glass Rings*, 166; *Nina*, 165, 168, 169; *To Embrace the Wolf*, 165, 169, 170; *Toy of War*, 170; *Underdeveloped Country Woman*, 168; *Winter-spring*, 170
Roberts, W. A., 132
Rochefort, Christiane, *Les Petits Enfants du siècle*, 83–91; *Printemps au parking*, 83, 84, 96–91; *Le Repos du Guerrier*, 85; *Les Stances á Sophie*, 83, 85, 86, 88, 91, 92
Rose, Paulette, 4
Rosowski, Susan J., 201
Rubin, Gayle, "The Traffic in Women," 254, 268
Rukeyser, Muriel, 67

Sachs, Nelly, 165
Sacco and Vanzetti, 137
Sade, Marquis de, 196
Salomon, Ernst von, *The Outlaws*, 223
Sand, George, 237
Sanger, Margaret, 205; *Family Limitation*, 200, 201

Sartre, Jean-Paul, 174; *Being and Nothingness*, 176; *Situation II*, 57
Saturday Evening Post, 60
Schlack, Beverly Ann, 184
Schnell, Horst-Gunther, 170
Schreiner, Olive, 237
Schulkind, Jeanne, *Moments of Being*, 279
Schwarzer, Alice, *Women against 218*, 168
Sedgwick, Catherine, 31, 32, 38
Seghers, Anna, 165
Sexton, Anne, *Consorting with Angels*, 14
Shakespeare, William, 115, 135, 243; *Othello*, 105; *Romeo and Juliet*, 265
Sharp, Evelyn, *Rebel Women*, 243
Shaw, Charlotte, 239
Shaw, George Bernard, 239, 240; *Press Cuttings*, 239
Shay, Frank, 135, 137
Shelley, Mary, *Frankenstein*, 42
Showalter, Elaine, 117; "Woman and the Literary Curriculum" 66
Sinclair, May, *The Divine Fire*, 274; *The Tree of Heaven*, 244
Siniavsky, Andrey, 248
Slovova, Snezhina, Dujdovete moite priateli, 49–57
Smedley, Agnes, 4, 199; "Cell Mates," 199–206; *Daughter of Earth*, 200, 201, 204; "Some Women of Mukden," 202
Smyth, Ethel, 242, 243; *A Three-Legged Tour of Greece*, 239
Sontag, Susan, 14
Sophocles, *Antigone*, 170, 186
Spacks, Patricia Meyer, 151; *The Female Imagination*, 25
Stael, Madame de, 237
Stead, Christina, 4, 191; *Cotter's England*, 191; *For Love Alone*, 191, 192, 195, 196; *House of All Nations*, 191, 194; *Letty Fox: Her Luck*, 192, 195–97; *The Little Hotel*, 191; *The Man Who Loved Children*, 191–96; *Miss Herbert*, 191; *Seven Poor Men of Sydney*, 191
Steinem, Gloria, 14, 15

Stein, Gertrude, 59, 67, 117
Stendhal (Henri Beyle), *The Charterhouse of Parma*, 250
Stephen, Leslie, 279–83
Stephens, A. G., 119
Stern (magazine), 169
Stimpson, Catharine R. (Kate), 3, 115–18
St. Nicholas (magazine), 130
Stowe, Harriet Beecher, 31, 38, 71, 237; *Uncle Tom's Cabin*, 32, 33
The Strange Necessity, 242
Suffragette, 239

Taylor, Deems, 136
Thatcher, Margaret, 238
Thoreau, Henry David, 17, 18
Time and Tide (magazine), 240
Tolstoy, Leo, 243, 251
Traill, Catharine Parr, 41, 45, 46; *Backwoods of Canada*, 45; *Canadian Settler's Guide*, 45
Trombley, Stephen, 185
Tucholsky, Kurt, 95, 96, 100, 101
Turkle, Sherry, *Psychoanalytic Politics: Freud's French Revolution*, 267
Twain, Mark, 18

Untermeyer, Louis, *An American Miscellany of Poetry*, 137
Updike, John, *Picked-Up Pieces*, 10

Vail, Laurence, 67
Vanity Fair (magazine), 133–36
Virgil, *The Aenead*, 226

Walsh, Ernest, 59
Warner, Susan, *The Wide, Wide, World*, 18, 34, 37
Washington, Booker T., 230
Weltbuhne, Die, 95, 96
Wells, H. G., 238, 241, 244; *Ann Veronica*, 243; *The New Machiavelli*, 243
Welty, Eudora, *Delta Wedding*, 114; "Moon Lake," 253–69
West, Anthony, 238
West, Rebecca, 237–46; *Black Lamb and Grey Falcon*, 239, 242; *The Fountain*

Overflows, 239; *The Judge*, 243, 244;
    St. Augustine, 242
Wharton, Edith, 145; *The Age of Inno-
    cence*, 31, 32, 37, 38; *The Children*,
    32; *The Custom of the Country*, 31,
    32, 35–38; *Ethan Frome*, 31
The Glimpses of the Moon, 31, 32, 37;
    The Gods Arrive, 31; *The House of
    Mirth*, 32–35, 37, 38; *The Mother's
    Recompense*, 31
Wiesel, Elie, 248
Wilde, Oscar, 135, 240
Williams, William Carlos, 59, 67
Wilson, Edmund, 132–36, 138, 141
Wilt, Judith, 145
Wolf, Christa, 165
Wolfe, Thomas, 203
Wollstonecraft, Mary, 237, 241
Woman's Day (magazine), 144
Woolf, Virginia, 7, 9, 15, 241, 244; *Me-
    lymbrosia*, 180–84, 186; Mrs. Dallo-
    way, 23, 28, 41, 46, 114; *Night and

Day*, 243; *Orlando*, 181; "Professions
    for Women," 242; "Reminiscences,"
    280; *A Room of One's Own*, 23, 245;
    "A Sketch of the Past," 279–83;
    Three Guineas, 237; *To the Light-
    house*, 279; *The Voyage Out*, 111,
    112, 179–88; *The Waves*, 111, 221; *A
    Writer's Diary*, 6
Wordsworth, William, 258; *The Prelude*,
    257
World Woman's Party, 62
Wright, Richard, 286
The Writer's Digest, 14
Wylie, Eleanor, 139, 140

Yale Review, 144
Yeats, William Butler, 244
Yelin, Louise, 4
Yourcenar, Marguerite, 221; *Coup de
    Grace*, 221–28; *Memoirs of Hadrian*,
    221; *The Waves*, 221

About the Editors and Contributors

CAROL ASCHER divides her time between writing fiction and essays and acting as Research Associate for the ERIC Clearinghouse on Urban Eduction at Teachers College, Columbia University. She is the author of *Simone de Beauvoir: A Life of Freedom*, and an editor of *Between Women: Biographers, Novelists, Critics, Teachers and Artists Write About Their Work on Women*. Her short stories and essays have been published widely, including in *Ms.*, *Feminist Studies, Confrontation, Heresies*, and numerous anthologies; and several of her short stories have won national prizes.

ANN EDWARDS BOUTELLE teaches in the Department of English Language and Literature at Smith College. She is author of *Thistle and Rose: a Study of Hugh MacDiarmid's Poetry*, as well as numerous scholarly and journalistic articles.

JEANNE BOYDSTON is Assistant Professor of History at Rutgers University, Camden Campus. Her principal research is in the economic history of women's unpaid labor in the antebellum United States. She is co-editor of a forthcoming anthology of the writings of Catharine Beecher, Harriet Beecher Stowe, and Isabella Beecher Hooker.

LYNETTE CARPENTER is Acting Director of Women's Studies and Assistant Professor of English at the University of Cincinnati, where she teaches women's studies courses in American literature and film. She is currently co-editing with Wendy Kolmar of Drew University a critical collection, *Haunting the House of Fiction: Feminist Perspectives on Women's Ghost Stories*.

BELL GALE CHEVIGNY is Professor of Literature at the State University of New York, College at Purchase. Her principal research efforts have been directed at feminist studies and comparative literature of the Americas; her publications include *The Woman and the Myth: Margaret Fuller's Life and Writings* and *Reinventing the Americas: Comparative Studies of Literature of the United States and Spanish America.*

ANNE D. CORDERO is Associate Professor of French at George Mason University. Her principal research interests are in twentieth century French literature and translation. She has published articles in both disciplines and recently translated *Matière de rêves* by the French novelist Michel Butor.

LOUISE A. DeSALVO is Associate Professor of English at Hunter College of the City University of New York. She is author of *Virginia Woolf's First Voyage: A Novel in the Making*, editor of Virginia Woolf's *Melymbrosia, An Early Version of the Voyage Out*, co-editor of *Between Women*, and co-editor of *The Letters of Vita Sackvillle West to Virginia Woolf*. She has just finished *Nathaniel Hawthorne: A Feminist Reading* and has begun a study of Virginia Woolf's childhood and adolescence.

CHARMAZEL DUDT is Professor of English at West Texas State University, where she teaches Shakespeare. She is interested in contemporary Indian fiction, and the influences of classical and current ideologies upon it. She has been published in *The Journal of Indian Writing in English, Victorian Periodicals Review*, and *Christianity and Literature*, among others.

ELKE FREDERIKSEN is Associate Professor of German Literature at the University of Maryland, College Park. She has published extensively on women and literature in the nineteenth and twentieth centuries, including the anthology *Die Frauenfrage in Deutschland 1865–1914*. Her monograph on Luise Rinser is in press.

JOANNE S. FRYE is Associate Professor of English and Chair of the Women's Studies Program at the College of Wooster. She is the author of *Living Stories, Telling Lives: Women and the Novel in Contemporary Experience*, winner of the 1984 Alice and Edith Hamilton Prize. She has published articles on Gail Godwin, Tillie Olsen, and Virginia Woolf and is currently working on the relationship between Woolf's narrative strategies and those of contemporary women novelists.

JOAN GIVNER is Professor of English at the University of Regina, Saskatchewan. She is the editor of *Wascana Review*. Her biography of Katherine Anne Porter was published in 1982, and her collection of short stories, *Tentacles of*

Unreason, was published in 1985. She is currently at work on a biography of the Canadian novelist Mazo de la Roche.

JEAN GOULD is known principally as a biographer. Her first published book, *Miss Emily*, a biography of Emily Dickinson for young adults, appeared in 1944. Since then, she has published 18 books, including six full-length biographies of American poets, including, besides Dickinson, Amy Lowell and Edna St. Vincent Millay. Her latest work, *Modern American Women Poets*, is a sequel to *American Women Poets: Pioneers of Modern Poetry*.

KATHERINE C. HILL-MILLER is Associate Professor of English at the C. W. Post Campus of Long Island University. Her principal research has examined the influence of literary fathers on literary daughters and has appeared in *Publications of the Modern Language Association*. She has also published essays on Hardy, Joyce, and other twentieth-century writers.

ANNE GOLOMB HOFFMAN is Associate Professor of Comparative Literature in the Excel Division, College at Lincoln Center of Fordham University. She is the author of articles on Franz Kafka, Samuel Beckett, S. Y. Agnon, and Virginia Woolf. She is currently working on a critical and biographical study of Agnon.

RUTH-ELLEN B. JOERES is Professor of German and Director of the Center for Advanced Feminist Studies at the University of Minnesota. Her primary scholarly concerns involve the social and literary history of women in Germany in the eighteenth to twentieth centuries, and the development and application of feminist theory. She has published extensively on Louise Otto and other writers and is currently at work on a study of feminism and femininity in nineteenth-century Germany.

JUDITH L. JOHNSTON teaches English and Women's Studies at Rider College. Her research and publications focus on the interrelations between twentieth-century history and literature. She is President of the Women's Caucus for the Modern Languages and Project Coordinator for the state-wide and state-funded initiative to revise college curricula, The New Jersey Project: Integrating the Scholarship on Gender.

YURI VIDOV KARAGEORGE is Professor of French and Comparative Literatures at East Carolina University. His books include *Sadness in Ardor* (a collection of poems in French and in English) and *Voices of Sibyls: Three Bulgarian Poets*. He has also published film and literary criticism and fiction.

ALICE KESSLER-HARRIS is Professor of History at Hofstra University where she co-directs the Center for the Study of Work and Leisure. She is the author of *Women Have Always Worked: A Historical Overview*, and *Out to Work: A*

History of Wage-Earning in the U.S.; and has selected and introduced the fiction of Anzia Yezierska in *The Open Cage* and *Bread Givers*.

ROSETTE LAMONT, educator, writer, and translator, is the author of several books, among them: *The Life and Works of Boris Pasternak, De Vive Voix*, and *The Two Faces of Ionesco*. She has held fellowships from the Guggenheim and Rockefeller Foundations. A professor in the department of Romance Languages at Queens College and the Graduate Center of the City University of New York, she served as a visiting Professor at the Sorbonne in 1985–86.

JANE MARCUS, Associate Professor of English at the City University of New York Graduate Center is the editor of *The Young Rebecca West* and three volumes of essays on Virginia Woolf. Her *Virginia Woolf and the Languages of Patriarchy* is in press.

WILLIAM MCBRIEN is Professor of English at Hofstra University, New York, and editor of the scholarly journal, *Twentieth Century Literature*. He is the author of *Me Again: Uncollected Writings of Stevie Smith, Stevie: A Biography of Stevie Smith*, and numerous articles and reviews in *The Critic, Commonweal*, and *Times Literary Supplement*.

JOYCE CAROL OATES is the author of seventeen novels and many volumes of short stories, poems, and essays, as well as plays. She is the Roger S. Berlind Distinguished Lecturer in Creative Writing at Princeton University. Her book, *On Boxing*, was recently published, as was a new novel, *You Must Remember This*.

ALISON RIEKE teaches in the Department of English and Comparative Literature at The University of Cincinnati. Her research interests are focused upon theories of the boundaries of meaning in Modernist experimental writing. She is currently writing a book on stylistic non-sense in James Joyce, Gertrude Stein, Wallace Stevens, and Louis Zukofsky.

PAULETTE ROSE has taught French language and literature courses in the SUNY system and at Yeshiva University, and is currently President of Paulette Rose, Ltd., a member of the Antiquarian Booksellers Association of America. The firm specializes in material by and about women.

ROBERT SARGENT is Associate Professor of English and Chairman of the English Department at Hofstra University. He has published articles on the novels of Charles Dickens.

JUDITH A. SCHEFFLER is Assistant Professor of English at West Chester University in Pennsylvania. Her research interests include indentification and analysis of texts written by women prisoners. She is editor of *Wall Tappings: An Anthology of Writings by Women Prisoners* (in press).

ELAINE SHOWALTER is Professor of English at Princeton University. She is the author of *A Literature of Their Own: Women Writers from Bronte to Lessing*; and *The Female Malady: Women, Madness, and English Culture*. Her current project is a literary history of American women writers.

PAUL SMITH teaches film and critical theory at Miami University, Ohio. He is the author of *Pound Revised* and many articles on modern poetry, literary theory and feminism. His *The Abstraction of the Subject*, a book about theories of subjectivity in the humanities, is forthcoming.

SANDRA WHIPPLE SPANIER is Assistant Professor of English at Oregon State University. She is the author of *Kay Boyle: Artist and Activist*, a critical and biographical study and the first book-length treatment of Kay Boyle, who lent her cooperation and support to the project. In addition to her work on Boyle, she has published articles on Poe, Roethke, Hawthorne, Lawrence, Salinger, and Hemingway and currently is working on a project on Katherine Anne Porter.

CATHARINE R. STIMPSON is Professor of English and Dean of the Graduate School at Rutgers University. Currently the editor of a book series for the University of Chicago Press, from 1974–80 she was the founding editor of *Signs: Journal of Women in Culture and Society*. The author of a novel, *Class Notes*, and the editor of six books, she has also published over 80 monographs, short stories, essays, and reviews in such places as *Aphra, Transatlantic Review, Narion, New York Times Book Review, Critical Inquiry, boundary 2*, and *Women in Sexist Society*, edited by Vivian Gornick and B. K. Moran.

SUSAN WARD is Associate Professor of English at St. Lawrence University, where she teaches American Literature and Women's Literature. She is the author of numerous articles on Jack London and has also written on Elizabeth Stuart Phelps, Antonia White, and Helen Hunt Jackson. She is currently at work on a book about diaries written by nineteenth-century women in northern New York.

GAY WILENTZ is Professor of English at East Carolina University in North Carolina. Her research has been in the field of African, Afro-American and Caribbean literatures, specifically a comparison of African and Afro-American women writers. Presently, she is working on the relationship of writers Zora Neale Hurston and Fannie Hurst, and the most recent article on this topic is "White Patron and Black Artist: The Correspondence of Fannie Hurst and Zora Neale Hurston."

LIVIA Z. WITTMANN is Associate Professor of German at the University of Canterbury, New Zealand. He main research interests include comparative literary studies and feminist literary criticism. She is the author of *Alfred Andersch* and several articles on German Expressionism and the theory of poetry.

PATRICIA S. YAEGER is Assistant Professor of English and Head Tutor of the History and Literature Concentration at Harvard. She has published essays on Eudora Welty and Mikhail Bakhtin in *PMLA* and is the author of *Honey-Mad Women: Emancipatory Strategies in Women's Writing*, forthcoming from Columbia University Press. Her next project, "The Poetics of Birth," concerns images of pregnancy and parturition in nineteenth- and twentieth-century Anglo-American literature.

LOUISE YELIN teaches English and Women's Studies at the State University of New York, College at Purchase. She has written on Charles Dickens and on the uses of literary theory in the teaching of basic writing and is currently working on a study of women writers of the British colonies.

Hofstra University's
Cultural and Intercultural Studies
Coordinating Editor, Alexej Ugrinsky

Walt Whitman: Here and Now
(*Editor: Joann P. Krieg*)

Harry S. Truman: The Man from Independence
(*Editor: William F. Levantrosser*)

Nineteenth-Century Women Writers of the English-Speaking World
(*Editor: Rhoda B. Nathan*)

Lessing and the Enlightenment
(*Editor: Alexej Ugrinsky*)

Dostoevski and the Human Condition After a Century
(*Editors: Alexej Ugrinsky, Frank S. Lambasa, and Valija K. Ozolins*)

The Old and the New World Romanticism of Washington Irving
(*Editor: Stanley Brodwin*)

Women as Mediatrix
(*Editor: Avriel Goldberger*)

Einstein and the Humanities
(*Editor: Dennis P. Ryan*)

Dwight D. Eisenhower: Soldier, President, Statesman
(*Editor: Joann P. Krieg*)

Goethe in the Twentieth Century
(*Editor: Alexej Ugrinsky*)

Franklin D. Roosevelt: The Man, the Myth, the Era, 1882–1945
(*Editors: Herbert D. Rosenbaum and Elizabeth Bartelme*)

The Stendhal Bicentennial Papers
(*Editor: Avriel Goldberger*)